Theories of
Human Development

EXOGENOUS PARADIGM		CONSTRUCTIVIST PARADIGM	
Skinner	*Bandura*	*Piaget*	*Kohlberg*
innate reflexes	innate reflexes	innate reflexes	cognitive development
tabula rasa mind	symbolic capacity	proactivity	rational construction
proactivity	forethought	(p. 165)	differentiation
(pp.118–119)	vicarious learning		(pp. 199–200)
	self-reflection		
	(pp. 141–142)		
prediction and control of behavior (p. 119)	observational learning (pp. 142–143)	scientific and mathematical knowledge (p. 165)	moral reasoning (p. 200)
experiments (pp. 119–121)	observations experiments (pp. 143–144)	observations clinical interviews (p. 166)	clinical interviews (pp. 200-201)
differential reinforcement discriminative stimulus shaping (pp. 122–123)	triadic reciprocality (behavior, cognition, environment) (pp. 144–145)	assimilation, accommodation equilibration organization and adaptation (pp. 166–168)	cognitive conflict cognitive development role-taking (pp. 201–202)
schedules of reinforcement generalization chaining (pp. 123–126)	differential contributions temporal dynamics fortuitous determinants (p. 145)	schemes operations cognitive structures (pp. 168–184)	moral stages types A and B (pp. 202–206)
reinforcement (pp. 126–127)	production processes motivation processes (pp. 146–149)	equilibration (of maturation, experience, social transmission) (pp. 184–185)	cognitive conflict (p. 206)

Theories of
Human Development

A Comparative Approach

Michael Green
University of North Carolina at Charlotte

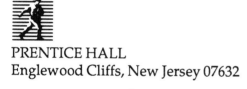

PRENTICE HALL
Englewood Cliffs, New Jersey 07632

Library of Congress Cataloging-in-Publication Data

Green, Michael
  Theories of human development.

  Bibliography: p.
  Includes index.
  1. Developmental psychology—Philosophy.   2. Child
psychology—Philosophy.   I. Title.
BF713.G7 1989   155   88–25444
ISBN 0–13–914607–5

Cover design: George Cornell
Manufacturing buyer: Raymond Keating

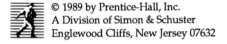
Printed in the United States of America
10 9 8 7 6 5 4 3 2 1   *70034760*

ISBN 0-13-914607-5

Prentice-Hall International (UK) Limited, *London*
Prentice-Hall of Australia Pty. Limited, *Sydney*
Prentice-Hall Canada Inc., *Toronto*
Prentice-Hall Hispanoamericana, S.A., *Mexico*
Prentice-Hall of India Private Limited, *New Delhi*
Prentice-Hall of Japan, Inc., *Tokyo*
Simon & Schuster Asia Pte. Ltd., *Singapore*
Editora Prentice-Hall do Brasil, Ltda., *Rio de Janeiro*

To Emily
for her loving dedication and support,
and to Megan and Matthew,
who confirm for me daily the
importance of developmental theories

Contents

Part IV
The Constructivist Perspective

Part V
Theoretical Applications

Preface

This book is intended for beginning graduate and upper division undergraduate courses dealing with child or human development. It would be appropriate as the core text, but it may also be used to supplement more age-descriptive, issue-oriented, or research-focused readings. It is organized so that in certain situations either Chapter 11 or 12 (or both) may be omitted.

The primary aim of the book is to describe what developmental theories are, what they do, where they come from, how they work, and how they are used to explain human nature. To manage the task, I have grouped the theories into three "families" or paradigms that differ in their world views about the essence of human nature. I have tried to show consistently how specific theories are really examples of larger organizers called paradigms. The theories chosen to represent the three paradigms were selected because they met several criteria: importance, as judged by teaching psychologists; fertility, as judged by the amount of research the theory has generated; and family resemblance, as judged by how pure an example each theory is of its paradigm. Quite aside from these considerations, five of the seven theories have generated significant controversy in the psychological community. Controversy is often a healthy sign that the theory is taken seriously by psychologists because it challenges widespread assumptions and commonly held beliefs about human nature.

The book reflects several of my beliefs. I believe it is important to understand what a theory is and what it is not, how theories represent specific examples of larger perspectives, and how theories reflect philosophical considerations. I also believe it is important to understand how developmental theories can be systematically evaluated in terms of their scientific worthiness and their ability to address characteristics of development. These beliefs are enacted in Part I, which introduces preliminary considerations that are used throughout the book. I describe why theories are both useful and necessary if one wants to know about how people develop. In addition, theories are defined, and their philosophical antecedents are described. Two different sets of criteria—scientific worthiness and developmental adequacy—are established for use throughout the book in evaluating the theories. It is not my intention to seduce readers into thinking they will become theory experts upon reading the book or to trick them into believing that one can tell how good a theory is simply by mimicking my ratings. However, it is important for readers to understand that even major developmental theories vary in how well they incorporate the values of science (scientific worthiness) and how well they explain general qualities of development (developmental adequacy). Toward that end and for purposes of comparison, chapters on each theory conclude with a summary of ratings on these two dimensions. Throughout the book, the relationship between theory and paradigm is stressed.

Parts II, III, and IV of the book contain descriptions of seven developmental theories. Part II is about the endogenous paradigm, and it contains the theories of Freud and Erikson. Also included is Wilson's sociobiology as an example of a developmental theory that explains population rather than individual development and that emphasizes the biological bases of human nature. Part III describes the work of Skinner and Bandura as examples of the exogenous perspective. I attempt to show how Skinner's radical behaviorism assumes a proactive rather than reactive individual, a point often missed in other texts. The latest version of Bandura's social cognitive theory, the impetus behind the cognitive-behaviorist movement, is described. In Part IV, the constructivist paradigm is played out through the familiar theories of Piaget and Kohlberg.

The theory chapters are organized in parallel fashion to facilitate comparisons within and between paradigms. For each theory, I describe its historical context by providing a brief sketch about the theorist and about the salient problems that motivated work on the theory. More important, the same organizing themes are presented for every theory (assumptions, problems for study, internal and bridge principles, and change mechanisms).

I believe that the case for studying and understanding a theory is strongest when it is presented in the best possible light. My belief in this position manifests itself in three ways. First, I have attempted to be an advocate for each theory as it is presented. In that vein, it was important to clearly identify a theory's "turf" so that its study could be appropriately framed. Second, the treatment of each theory is accompanied by a brief summary of supportive research. It would have been ideal to evaluate all the research on each theory, but the constraints imposed by my own life span and the publisher precluded comprehensive research reviews. Consequently, I have opted to concentrate on research studies that support each particular theory to maximize readers' appreciation of a theory's strengths. Third, I have described only criticisms of each theory which exist within its self-identified domain. However, I have not been uncritical. Evaluations of a theory's scientific worthiness and developmental adequacy, together with suggested readings of critical reviews, provide theoretically independent appraisals.

The theme of paradigms is carried through the last three chapters. Part V contains one chapter each on educational and counseling applications organized according to paradigmatic frameworks. These chapters are intended primarily for professional school students and may be omitted under certain circumstances.

Part VI contains an explicit treatment of the eclectic versus purist controversy seldom acknowledged in textbooks, even though its issues have tremendous impact on the work of both researchers and practitioners. The basic positions of each side are outlined, certain implications of each position are analyzed, and a systematic scheme is provided for readers to work out their own position.

The publication of any book requires the combination of both subtle and explicit efforts. The subtle influence of my own teachers—including Courtney Cazden, Carol Feldman, Jerome Kagan, Lawrence Kohlberg, Elliot Turiel, and Sheldon White—has been so sublime that I can no longer distinguish their views from my own. My students at the University of North Carolina at Charlotte have been an underlying influence on this work. Over the years, I have been challenged and renewed by their curiosity, questions, experiences, and frustrations. Finally, I owe a very special thanks to the two most important yet subtle characters in this book, Megan and Matthew. Without ever intending it, they have shown me the value of theories for understanding their marvelous antics, bewilderments, and insights.

I am grateful to the following scholars whose meticulous care in reading the manuscript led to suggestions for improving its precision: David Forbes, Forbes Associates; Gian Sud and Ignatius Toner, the University of North Carolina at Charlotte; Michael D. Berzonsky, State University of New York at Cortland; Belinda Blevins-Knabe, University of Arkansas at Little Rock; and Ruth L. Ault, Davidson College.

Finally, my appreciation goes to a very capable editorial and production staff: John Isley and Susan Finnemore at Prentice Hall and Roseann McGrath Brooks of P. M. Gordon Associates.

Theories of
Human Development

Chapter 1

Theories as Windows for Looking to See

Preview Questions

Why is it important to understand theories?
What is a theory?
How is a theory different from a model?
What are the structural components of a developmental theory?
Why do theories contain jargon?

REASONS FOR STUDYING THEORIES

Charles S. Peirce, one of the architects of American pragmatic philosophy, is credited with the saying that there is nothing more practical than a good theory (Lincourt, 1986). Theories are useful because they attempt to explain things that cannot explain themselves. Many important questions about human nature ultimately require theories rather than facts for answers (e.g., How do children learn new concepts? Why do infants form attachments with their primary caretakers? How do child-rearing practices affect personality development?). Theories are one of the hallmarks of science, and their importance is so fundamental that theories themselves are often a primary focus of the scientific enterprise.

Why should people want to study developmental theories? In my opinion, five principles provide the answer to this question and thereby help us understand why developmental psychologists spend so much time creating and testing them. Collectively, these principles imply that any systematic explanation of human nature must be preceded by an examination of its theories.

Principle 1. Theories tell us how to organize facts and interpret their meaning. Facts cannot explain themselves. They do not organize themselves for our review,

1

and they have no automatic force that indelibly stamps our minds with their meaning. Royce (1976) makes this point directly when he notes that theories are crucial to the conduct of science because facts can mean different things in different theoretical contexts. Theories organize and interpret facts differently, each according to its own principles.

It is a well-known fact, for example, that children around the world acquire the rudimentary grammar of their native tongue between approximately two and four years of age. While that fact is indisputable, its interpretation is not. Some theorists contend that biological maturation controls language acquisition. Others argue that language acquisition is a product of learning. While the facts of language acquisition are seldom debated, decisions about which body of facts and its theoretical interpretation are hotly contested. Facts cannot identify their own causes: that is the role of interpretation and theory.

Theories shape the collection, interpretation, and meaning of facts, but theories and facts are interdependent. Scientific advancement requires both information and theory. While bad theories are sometimes doomed through a failure to explain data, others are doomed simply because they explain facts later held to be irrelevant for new scientific interests. Moreover, the entire history of scientific ideas marks a trend away from concrete, physical concepts toward more abstract theories. This is in large part because concrete concepts explain only specific phenomena, whereas more abstract theories explain diverse and general phenomena. As researchers have collected more and more facts about human development, theories have become increasingly indispensable in organizing and interpreting them. As a general rule, theories make facts important, not the other way around.

Principle 2. Theories represent public knowledge. Virtually everyone attempts to explain human nature by inferring causes and motives for other people's behavior. But when we do that, we invariably rely on either public or private sources of knowledge. Public knowledge is available to everyone and is often found in books and journal articles. This knowledge is easily accessed, readily transferred from one location to another or from one person to another, and openly discussed, examined, researched, criticized, and amended. Theories represent public knowledge and are thus submitted to public scrutiny and debate.

Private knowledge, on the other hand, is only available to individuals: it is inaccessible, difficult to communicate to others, and, worst of all, not subjected to public scrutiny. This type of knowledge consists of our personal experiences, ideas, habits, beliefs, and opinions. We often explain others' motivations and actions in terms of our own experiences, attitudes, and memories, and these explanations often have a self-satisfying though unexamined quality about them. While some people still prefer the ease of conjuring up explanations about "Why Johnny can't read" (e.g., "he comes from a poor home environment"), such explanations are generally less reliable and less valid than those that arise through theory testing, careful scrutiny, and informed debate. The absence of reliability can be found in the inconsistency of personal explanations (e.g., "Johnny can't read because his parents don't care, but he doesn't know math because he hasn't applied himself").

Personal explanations are often invalid because they are simply untrue. I once helped a teacher conduct some simple observations on his students after hearing frequent and ardent complaints about how handicapped students were disruptive in his classroom. After several weeks of data collection, the embarrassed teacher reported back some insightful news. It turned out that nearly all the class disruptions were produced by his normal students. Because theories represent public rather than private knowledge, they tend to explain human nature in a more defensible way.

Principle 3. Theories are in principle testable. Theories contain various claims about human nature that can, in principle, be tested separately or in combination. Testability provides an element of self-correction for theories not found in private knowledge. A single experiment may at any time disprove one or more claims, but even when a theory is disproven, something about human nature can be learned. Sir Francis Galton put it succinctly: truth arises more readily from error than from confusion. At the same time, however, a theory cannot be proven true: it is virtually impossible to design and carry out all the experiments with all the individuals under all the circumstances needed to exhaustively establish proof. Yet, testability ensures that we can approximate truth by eliminating theoretical claims shown to be false.

What is at issue here is the testability of a theory's claims. Testability refers to the extent to which a theory's claims can be objectively verified. A separate issue concerns the accuracy of those claims. To be sure, the issues are related in that the second depends on the first. One cannot determine a theory's accuracy unless it is first testable.

Principle 4. Theories are less complex than people. Since the mind cannot produce ideas that are as complex as itself, theories must logically be less complex than the human mind that produced them. Bickard (1978) makes this point directly, noting that any system can itself be known and understood only by a higher level system. Any level of organization, including the human mind, cannot be perfectly self-reflective: it cannot know its own properties. A higher level organization is needed to do that. For example, people cognize only the results of their mental processes, not the mental processes themselves. Accordingly, humans are destined never to realize fully their own true nature. However, because theories of human nature are less complex than actual humans, they can be known and understood. Readers who would skip the study of theories to move directly to the "facts" about real children and real people miss this crucial point. Theories are understandable because they are simpler than the phenomena they attempt to explain.

Principle 5. Theories are generalizable. Theories are powerful because they explain characteristics of human nature that are generalizable across individuals. Consider an example. A perfect theory would be one that explained everything about a particular person with complete accuracy. We could even imagine ten perfect theories that explain ten individuals, or a thousand perfect theories that perfectly explain everything about a thousand individuals. Eventually, we might imagine a theory for each living person. But there is an inherent problem with this kind of reasoning. When a theory sacrifices generalizability (applicability to large numbers of individuals) for specificity and detail, it soon ceases to be a theory at all. Theories attempt to explain features of human nature that are common to all individuals. They are powerful and efficient because a single principle can explain a common characteristic of many individuals. In doing that, it also explains the same characteristic in each individual.

Taken together, these five principles provide strong motivation for understanding theories of human development. If psychologists shunned theories altogether and tried to fashion their images of human nature only from the nearly infinite wealth of factual details, their task would rapidly become unmanageable. In fact, some developmentalists devote more time to studying theories than they do to studying the facts of human nature.

THEORETICAL PARADIGMS: WINDOWS FOR LOOKING TO SEE

A theory is a linguistic abstraction. It is not a thing like a house or a rabbit. It is a complex set of statements with certain properties. But in order to understand what a theory is and is not, it is first necessary to introduce the notion of *paradigm*. *Paradigm* is one of those jargonlike terms that have caught on in recent years. Kuhn (1970) identifies two key features of a paradigm: a collection of beliefs shared by scientists and a set of agreements about how problems are to be investigated. Basically, a paradigm is a body of shared assumptions, beliefs, methods, and interpretations that constitute a particular vision of reality (Royce, 1976).

White (1976) provides some insight into how paradigms operate in developmental psychology, noting that different paradigms offer: (1) an orientation for viewing the world of human nature, (2) a set of "reals" observable from the orientation, (3) a club of scientists, and (4) mutual agreements among club members about what is and is not considered worthwhile research about the "reals." If one were to walk from one paradigm to another, dramatic changes in methods, jargon, concepts, and theories about the world would be encountered. In this manner, paradigms provide the implicit rules of the game by which scientists tacitly agree to conduct the business of science. A paradigm, then, is a general orientation that may entail several theories, like members of a family.

Few other disciplines put forth as many competing theories as does psychology. These multiple psychologies function like windows opening out onto the world of human nature. Some windows are close together providing similar but not identical views (shared paradigm). Other windows face different directions and provide virtually no overlap with the view from another perspective (different paradigms). Theories are like *windows for looking to see*, like conceptual lenses for observing, recording, and assessing human events. Windows and theories are also alike in that they both open up certain kinds of events for observation while constraining the view of other kinds of events. They give clear vision to certain phenomena of interest while occluding others that are out of sight and theoretically irrelevant.

A good example of the window metaphor can be found in von Uexkull's (1957) idea of *Umwelt*. Noting that animals possess different receptor systems for perceiving their environment, von Uexkull concluded that they actually have different world views—*Umwelts*. Receptor systems enable an organism to view the world of relevant information while selectively screening out information with no survival value. Ticks, snakes, toads, robins, and deer perceive different kinds of worldly events because they are perceptually tuned to obtaining different types of information about the world, all this in spite of the fact that they may inhabit the same ecological habitat. Like the *Umwelts* of von Uexkull's creatures, theories also function as windows to the world, but these windows do have limitations. Some selectivity always occurs; no theory, receptor system, or window is capable of collecting all the information that is available. Until scientists come to agreement among themselves about which window to peek through, windows will continue to be used to study and explain human nature.

THEORIES AND MODELS

Some people use the terms *theory* and *model* synonymously, and in doing so they tend to confuse the properties of one with those of the other. Because theories and models have unique and distinctly different properties, the terms will not be used interchangeably in this text. To understand how theories and models are different, we need to examine what each one is, how it works, what it can do, and what it cannot do.

Models

Models are useful in science because they are analogies drawn from something that is known and extended to the unknown (O'Connor, 1957, p. 90). Models come in several forms, depending on the nature and complexity of the entity they are built to represent. One of their primary functions is to aid in but not to replace theory building.

Zais (1976) identifies four kinds of models that range from concrete to abstract. *Physical models* have concrete substance: they exist in a tangible sense. They are often miniatures of the real thing, and to that extent they are usually designed to look or act like the thing they mimic. This type of model is generally considered to be the simplest form of model. For example, auto and airplane engineers construct scale models to test aerodynamic qualities of new products. From careful study of their models, the engineers can estimate how the actual auto or airplane will perform.

Graphic or *pictorial representations* are models designed to depict relationships. Graphs, like other models, often clarify and improve our understanding of theories, but their meaning is always determined by the theory they are intended to represent. In this vein, van Geert (1988) has developed a systematic approach to graphical displays of several developmental theories in terms of their developmental features. He shows how different kinds of graphs can be used to display (1) temporal and logical theoretical relationships between developmental stages, (2) hierarchical relationships in the development of individual abilities, and (3) different kinds of developmental processes. Van Geert's graphs are intended to be representations of theoretical claims and positions, but they do not attempt to explain the whys or hows of development. Rather, they depict, clarify, and exemplify how various features within a theory are related to each other. Other kinds of graphical and pictorial models include grammar diagrams of English sentences, the figures in this book, and topographical maps that condense three-dimensional elevations onto two-dimensional paper.

Linguistic models employ conceptual metaphors to assist our comprehension. Sociologists, for example, often use "games" metaphors to help them understand social interactions of large groups. Freud was heavily influenced by physical sciences and employed Newton's laws of energy conservation as a model for the human mind. Piaget used the model of scientist/philosopher as a metaphor for children's natural inclination to make sense of their experiences. Many of the tables used in this text exemplify this type of model. Such tables are not the theory: they are useful representations of theory concepts and their interrelations.

Logical models consist of expressions that reduce complex phenomena to the logic of equations. Examples abound in mathematics ($a^2 + b^2 = c^2$) and physics ($e = mc^2$), which describe the quantitative relationship between several variables. Work flow diagrams that represent the logical steps of computer decision making are another application of logical models. Statistical formulas used by psychologists are also logical models.

Models can't solve all our problems. Their primary function is to mimic, to represent, to simplify. They function by example rather than by explanation, a distinction that cleaves sharply the difference between a model and a theory. When our problems require explanations, such as figuring out why motivation influences human behavior or how children learn figurative meaning when they hear only literal uses of language, theories rather than models are needed.

Theories

In contrast to models, theories have one overriding purpose—to explain phenomena. The phenomena may be either real, like human nature, or entirely conceptual, like philosophy and mathematics. To explain phenomena, three minimal elements are required: phenomena, explanatory concepts, and principles that relate the concepts to their respective phenomena. Following Hempel (1966), I define a theory as *a coherent, integrated set of statements containing: (1) internal principles, (2) bridge principles, and (3) an identifiable body of phenomena to be explained. Internal principles* are primary concepts; they are the most important explanatory concepts employed by a theory. They are the basic abstractions, constructs, and processes invoked by a theory. These abstract entities exist as irreducible principles rather than as substances. Internal principles often consist of general laws or functions to which human nature is believed to conform. *Bridge principles* are secondary concepts used to describe the relationship between a theory's internal principles and human phenomena. *The phenomena to be explained* constitute the essential problems of the theory. These phenomena may be relatively small and specific (e.g., infant perceptual acuity) or relatively large and general (e.g., personality development). All three elements may spawn a unique theoretical terminology called *jargon*.

STRUCTURAL COMPONENTS OF DEVELOPMENTAL THEORIES

All developmental theories have in common certain structural components. Just as certain components make a car a car (steering wheel, engine, doors, tires) so, too, do developmental theories have certain shared attributes. These attributes are a theory's *structural components,* and they consist of (1) assumptions about the newborn's inherent capabilities, (2) problems of study (including phenomena to be explained and the methods of collecting data), (3) internal principles, (4) bridge principles, and (5) change mechanisms believed to produce development. These components may not be clearly identified in a theorist's work; they are often implied and sometimes embedded in a number of different publications. While developmental theories differ from one another in specific content, each theory can be analyzed in terms of these common structural components.

Assumptions

Theorists seldom make their own assumptions explicit. This situation arises in part because they have grown so accustomed to looking at human development through their own theoretical window that they may be unaware of prior beliefs upon which their work is based. Moreover, they are generally motivated to place their theory in the best possible light and may not wish to unduly jeopardize its acceptance by dwelling on its assumptions. Nevertheless, all developmental theories are based on unproven beliefs about the nature of the human neonate, the nature of the environment, and the nature of organismic-environmental interactions. One often has to "read between the lines" to identify a theory's assumptions.

Developmental theories typically explain human development beginning with birth rather than conception. The assumptions a theory makes about the infant's naturally endowed capacities and characteristics are its "starting blocks." They equip a theorist with presumed material from which an explanation of development can be launched. While the exact nature and number of assumptions vary from one theory to another, theorists attempt to make reasonable assumptions given the kind of phenomena they wish to explain. An important goal of this book is to identify the underlying assumptions each theory makes with regard to the neonate's capabilities.

Problems for Study

No theory can explain everything about human development. Consequently, each theory limits itself to identifying a cohesive set of problems that will occupy its attention, although these may be expanded from time to time with new discoveries or theoretical advances. These problems generally entail at least two considerations: a specific body of phenomena that needs explaining and an appropriate methodology for systematically collecting information.

The phenomena to be explained pose problems for the theory because their explanation is not given in the phenomena themselves, nor does information spontaneously organize itself for the theorist's purposes. Theories define problems differently, in part due to the influence of the paradigm they operate within and in part due to the nature of the phenomena they address. *Methods* used to collect information are matched to the kind of phenomena a theory attempts to explain. Metaphorically, a theory's methods are its "eyes": they restrict and organize the information to be collected. Sometimes different theories will utilize the same methods. Other times, as in the case of Freud's psychoanalysis, highly specialized methods are developed to tap highly specific phenomena that are unique to the theory's purpose. Often the most important information contained in a research article will be the research methodology, which describes how researchers can replicate each other's work. The most pervasive methods employed within each theory are described in the theory chapters. Conscientious readers will take special note of how well a theory's research methods actually match the phenomena the theory attempts to explain.

Internal Principles

Each developmental theory entails a number of internal principles that comprise the theoretical architecture; these are the *fundmental core concepts* of the theory. Core concepts are usually described in three ways: constitutive definitions (dictionary-like statements of meaning), operational definitions (how a concept is actually measured), and examples or analogies of how the concept works. Internal principles are conceptual abstractions and are not directly visible. They are the most basic, irreducible explanatory constructs to which qualities of human nature can be reduced. Internal principles are so important that a theorist cannot afford to have them misunderstood, as often occurs when we encounter concepts already familiar and loaded with prior meanings. Consequently, these principles tend to be given unique names and definitions. This is the origin of theoretical jargon.

Bridge Principles

The concepts that connect a theory's internal principles to the phenomena it attempts to explain are called bridge principles. Put differently, bridge principles are "show" rules. They show how the theoretical architecture (internal principles) is extended, mapped, and projected onto the phenomena. In this way, bridge principles show how a theory's core concepts operate in specific situations to explain specific data. Theorists generally give their bridge principles specialized names to improve clarity and precision about their theory's meaning.

Readers sometimes have difficulty learning theory jargon. They consider it nothing more than a required nuisance, just a bizarre list of new terms and phrases to be memorized and regurgitated on a quiz. I suspect that such an attitude may exist in part because there is so much jargon and in part because jargon requires much more effort and precision than everyday language. The difficulty is understandable, but it can be partially avoided if readers understand the role jargon plays in theories of development. Jargon is not just important for a theory; *it is essential*. Specialized vocabularies serve specific purposes. They prevent misconceptions or common biases associated with less specialized language by providing clear, explicit, unambiguous, and efficient communication between specialists. Without theoretical jargon communication would be needlessly vague, cumbersome, and subject to personal meanings habitually associated with everyday usage.

The power and importance of jargon can be placed in a more personal context. Imagine, for example, that you visit two physicians and report symptoms that include swollen glands, fatigue, and prolonged sleepiness. Each physician orders the same blood tests, for which you are charged $40. The office visit is an additional $30. Each physician asks you to return in three days to learn the results of the lab tests (another $30 office visit). On the follow-up visit, the first physician tells you that you are "sick" and that you should go home and rest for six weeks. The second physician reports that you have infectious mononucleosis and that six weeks' rest is the only cure. What is your reaction to the two physicians, each of whom charged the same, did the same blood tests, and suggested the same remedy? Which would you be more likely to visit again? Why? The difference between being told that you are "sick" and being given the name of your disease is in the technical language used, the jargon. This book has an implicit foreign language requirement—readers are expected to become at least moderately fluent in "jargon."

Change Mechanism

A unique feature of developmental theories is that they must specify some process or mechanism responsible for producing the changes that constitute development. The change mechanism constitutes a "motor" that powers development. This element is crucial. How can one explain development without identifying something that brings it about? More often than not, it sparks more discussion, debate, and criticism than any other aspect of a theory, primarily for two reasons. First, it is one of the most critical features of developmental theories, and second, it is often one of the weakest components.

Competing paradigms appeal to different mechanisms of change. For example, several theories in one paradigm posit biological maturation as the cause of development, thereby implying that individual growth is relatively fixed and mostly immune to environmental stimuli. Accordingly, maturational theories hold that the development of such domains as personality, thinking, temperament, language, and morality is the result of an innate plan that governs their timing and form and that cannot be altered very much by environmental events. In contrast, theories in a competing paradigm may argue that individuals are inherently malleable and flexible. Consequently, while these theories view maturation as setting broad limits on learning, they contend that it is specific environmental events that govern development.

LIMITATIONS OF DEVELOPMENTAL THEORIES

As noted earlier, paradigms constrain theories in certain important ways by admitting some but not other assumptions, problems, methods, and data. Since theories operate within a paradigmatic framework, they have inherent limitations. *These shortcomings do not invalidate the theory;* they merely require that one understand what theories cannot do.

First, a theoretical window precludes certain kinds of information. In any study of human nature, only a fraction of what actually takes place can be recorded. For example, if we are studying children's social learning, we are likely to ignore a great deal of irrelevant behavior—yawning, trips to the lavatory, scratching, and other kinds of fidgeting. A theory defines the kinds of events that are to be recorded and studied. It is necessarily accompanied by conscious, deliberate choices that certain kinds of events are deemed noteworthy and that others are not (White, 1976).

Second, human events that do get recorded will always be distorted to some extent. This distortion is a direct consequence of the methods used by the investigator. Research requires the measurement of bridge principles with certain tools (the researcher's methods) applied under replicable conditions. These methods act like filters to screen in and screen out certain kinds of information. The information obtained in research studies is always incomplete in terms of the total data available in a given situation. However, incompleteness may be relatively minor, as in the use of a sensitive scale to chart the daily growth of an infant's weight (the distortion occurs in condensing a day's worth of weight gain into a single measure). On the other hand, distortion may be extensive, as occurs when a child's weight is measured annually by a pediatrician: an entire year's growth is condensed into a single moment. Whatever the case, instruments must be used to collect information, but they always provide fractional assessments of the entire event under study. This type of distortion varies from one method to another, but the important point is that it always occurs not as the fault of a particular method but by the very fact of having to use a method at all to collect data.

Third, theories are necessarily *incomplete explanations* of human nature. Once again, because theories reflect limitations of the paradigm that frames them, they are constrained from encompassing the totality of human nature and experience. A new problem arises when one realizes that *humans* write theories and conduct research. The "facts" collected by researchers are only facts because they reflect a researcher's own interests and attention. After all, researchers could have been interested in other things and in actuality could have collected different facts. Personal choices like these influence the larger body of theory and information about human nature (Mischel, 1976). Moreover, issues about which facts are to be collected ultimately lead to different research programs and to different kinds of theories (Hanson, 1958; Toulmin, 1961). This incompleteness in the large sense is *not* the same as saying that they cannot provide a complete and adequate explanation of the limited problems they address.

Theories will probably never provide us with the ultimate truth about human nature (neither can our personal experiences, memories, anecdotes, and the like), though they do provide a systematic means for approaching it. While the inherent limitations of theories may imply to some that we should despair of ever fully understanding or appreciating the entirety of human nature, such a conclusion would be unwarranted. If theories are genuinely testable, then they provide a means for eliminating the mistaken ideas we hold about human nature. By removing the inaccuracies in our collective knowledge, we can gradually approximate truth. Judicious research gradually chips away at erroneous concepts, thereby leaving a portrait of humanity less tainted with errors than before.

SUMMARY POINTS

1. Five principles support the contention that there is nothing more useful than a good theory. Theories (1) give meaning to facts, not vice versa, (2) represent public rather than private knowledge, (3) are testable, (4) are less complex than people, and (5) are generalizable.

2. Paradigms contain multiple theories, a set of observable "reals," a club of scientists, and mutual agreements about reality. Paradigms are the framework within which a theory operates.

3. Theories, like von Uexkull's *Umwelts*, are windows for looking to see.

4. Theories are not models. Models are physical, linguistic, logical, or graphic/pictorial representations. Models exemplify rather than explain. Theories propose explanations rather than representations.

5. A theory is a coherent, integrated set of statements containing internal principles, bridge principles, and an identifiable body of phenomena to be explained. This definition implies that developmental theories have common structural components (assumptions, problems of study [phenomena and methods], internal principles, bridge principles, and change mechanisms) although the content of these components differs from theory to theory.

6. Developmental theories have inherent limitations: incompleteness of information, distortion of information, and subjective and personal choices by scientists about what information to collect.

SUGGESTED READINGS

Hanson, N. R. (1958). *Patterns of discovery.* Cambridge, England: Cambridge University Press.

Kuhn, T. S. (1970). *The structure of scientific revolutions.* (2nd ed.). Chicago: University of Chicago Press.

Wartofsky, N. W. (1968). *Conceptual foundations of scientific thought.* London: Macmillan.

Chapter 2

Evaluating Theories: Developmental Adequacy and Scientific Worthiness

Preview Questions

What characteristics are implied by the concept of development?
How can a theory's developmental adequacy be assessed?
What criteria are used to determine a theory's scientific worthiness?

THE CONCEPT OF DEVELOPMENT

The term *development* is used in many different fields, and its usage is accompanied by many different connotations. This state of affairs makes it difficult to derive a formal definition for the concept. In fact to do so would probably deprive the term of a certain openness and flexibility that has contributed to its appeal. Nevertheless, in a book about theories of development, some attention must be given to defining the concept. As a starting point, we can begin by noting that development is fundamentally a biological concept linked to the idea that certain relatively permanent changes occur over time in the organization of living structures and life processes (Harris, 1957, p. 3). Differing conceptions of development presuppose one of several more basic doctrines: *vitalism, mechanism,* and *organicism.*

    Vitalism is a metaphysical position that holds that living organisms contain some entity that is not reducible to inanimate components (e.g., chemical substances) and that the activities of this entity produce the qualities characteristic of living beings (Beckner, 1972b, p. 254). The proposed entity is said to be the "vital essence" of life, hence vitalism. In this view "life" is seen as an autonomous, irreducible process that occupies no space and that somehow controls the course of organic processes (Driesch, 1914). Developmentally, vitalism holds that differences in ontogenesis (individual development) from identical origins must be explained in terms of this "vital essence" (Nagel, 1957, p. 19). Vitalism is today not a popular position among developmentalists. Historically, though, the idea that such a vital essence differentiated living from nonliving entities was a common notion. In fact, it was sufficiently powerful to suggest that one might be able to capture this essence and channel its life-giving power into a corpse and bring it back to life, a theme recognizable to those familiar with Mary Shelley's *Frankenstein.*

Mechanism (Pepper, 1942) is a doctrine antithetical to vitalism. It denies the presence of any "vital essence" that alone constitutes life. It holds that individuals can best be understood in terms of the mechanical operations of lower-level physical and chemical substances that, in combination and interaction, produce a living being (Beckner, 1972a, p. 252). A mechanistic approach to development implies a reductionist orientation: that is, properties that describe the individual are believed to be decomposable into more primitive, functionally prior laws. The mechanistic orientation utilizes a machine metaphor, but this does not imply that a scientist views living organisms and all their parts as simple "machines." Rather, the doctrine of mechanism holds that biological phenomena are simply patterns, sometimes very complex patterns, of lower-order nonbiological events that follow the law of additive composition: the whole is the sum of its parts (Nagel, 1957, p. 19).

Behavioral psychology adopts a mechanistic orientation in attempting to find causal laws to explain how behavior is changed in relation to environmental stimuli (Kendler, 1986). Ultimately, mechanism would lead researchers to investigate how human nature is produced by physiological and biochemical processes.

Organicism is a doctrine that rejects the tenets of both vitalism and mechanism. According to organicism, the individual is composed of different levels or systems that are hierarchically arranged and tightly integrated, and one of its primary goals is to explain the relationships between the systems and the whole individual. In this way, individuals are as important to the understanding of their parts as the parts are to the whole individual, but neither the whole nor parts are reducible to each other. This view stems from two beliefs about the nature of living creatures. First, organisms are composed hierarchically; that is, various systems that comprise the individual (e.g., cognitive, pulmonary, digestive, nervous) are developed and arranged in such a way that some play superordinate and others subordinate roles. In adult humans, for example, the muscular system is subordinate to the behavioral system, which is itself subordinate to the intellectual system. Second, organicism is a variant on the principle of *emergence,* which holds that traits displayed by a hierarchically organized system cannot be explained in terms of properties that occur on a lower rung of the hierarchy (Nagel, 1957, p. 19). This means that the various components of intellectual functioning, for example, cannot be decomposed into or explained in terms of more primitive biochemical or biophysical processes.

Each of these three doctrines amounts to a stance taken with respect to how one should conceive of the developing individual. Concerning human development, the variation among assumptions taken up in these positions indicates that development is a complex concept whose definition will not be simple or straightforward.

Characteristics of Development

Not only do developmental theories have to explain something about human nature, as do other psychological theories, but also they must explain how it gets that way. To accomplish the task, most (but not all) developmental theories attempt to explain *ontogenesis,* the relatively permanent changes individuals undergo during their life span. But what do we mean when we claim that a person *develops?* An adequate answer requires that we distinguish between the concept of change and the concept of development. While the concept of development necessarily implies that some kind of change has taken place, the fact that some kind of change has occurred does not necessarily imply that something has developed. For example, filing one's fingernails, brushing one's hair, and waking up in the morning are all manifest changes in the individual's state, but no developmental psychologist would contend that they represent developmental changes.

Development connotes the presence of one or more complex changes. The following characteristics are usually implicated when the term *development* is used. An advantage of defining development in terms of these characteristics is that they can serve as a set of criteria against which theories can be evaluated for their *developmental adequacy.* That is, theories may represent weak, moderate, or strong developmental explanations, depending on how well they account for these characteristics.

Temporality. All development presumes an element of temporality, which means that changes tend to occur over time (Harris, 1957, p. 3). The duration of time is generally presumed to involve an extended rather than a short interval (Harris, 1957, p. 10), such as the several years needed to acquire secondary sex characteristics during adolescence. The process of "growing up" and "growing old" is another way of expressing the relationship between time and development, which is not to say that older necessarily means more developed. For example, when we say that interpersonal relationships take time to develop, we don't mean that time alone develops a relationship, only that time provides the opportunity for events, decisions, and experiences that contribute to development.

Cumulativity. Cumulativity means that developmental changes result in the addition of some new feature(s) to the organism: first one thing, then another, is acquired. Developmental acquisitions imply a degree of permanence;

they in turn modify later acquisitions, thereby altering the shape of the individual's entire being (Anderson, 1957, p. 39). Cumulative changes may be dramatic (acquiring language) or incremental (extending grasping behavior from a spoon to a fork). Some achievements may ultimately be diminished after having served a transitional function for later achievements, as when, for example, crawling gives way to walking.

An important element of cumulativity is that of causal recession (Anderson, 1957, p. 40), wherein developing individuals will tend to retain some of the effects of past changes. For example, it may be difficult to explain certain behaviors in a given situation (e.g., bad habits) without appealing to some earlier origins in the individual's life history.

Cumulativity is necessary but not sufficient to claim that a developmental change has occurred. After all, hair growth, piling up hours watching television, and learning who is buried in Grant's tomb are all cumulative processes, but they are not particularly developmental in nature.

Directionality. Russell (1945) has argued that organic development must on logical grounds implicate a sense of "directedness." The direction may be from the general to the specific (Hamburger, 1957), toward increased maturity (Gesell & Ilg, 1949), toward greater differentiation and hierarchic integration (Werner, 1957), toward increased efficiency and specificity (Anderson, 1957), or toward increased distance from some initial state (Chapman, 1988).

Directionality implies that developmental changes are progressive, relatively durable, and irreversible. The progressive element means that individuals change in ways that are in some respect better or more advanced than previous states. We do not necessarily have to know what the developmental terminus is, nor do we have to specify the precise point of origin (although theories in developmental psychology use birth as their starting point, there is no necessary reason that requires them to do so). What we do have to account for is the direction of development in terms that imply progressive accumulations between two points in time.

The element of durability implies that development results in improvements that facilitate relatively long-lasting, though not necessarily permanent, change. Most developmentalists would argue, for example, that crawling represents a progressive developmental change for infants (though not for adults), even though it eventually gives way to walking. In cases like that, the durability element is preserved in the sense that crawling facilitates the acquisition of balance and coordination needed to walk.

Directionality also implies that developmental changes are relatively irreversible in that they cannot easily be undone. While individuals change in many ways over their lifetimes, only a portion of these changes are irreversible and thus constitute development. Growing bald, learning to read, and forming a personality all reflect directional changes (progress, durability, irreversibility). In contrast, joining a political party (reversible), memorizing the definition of *vitalism* for an exam (probably nondurable), and acquiring more and more credit cards (non-progressive) do not.

New Mode of Organization. Strong claims of development describe changes that result in new modes of organization (Anderson, 1957, p. 40; Meredith, 1957, p. 115; Nagel, 1957, p. 1). This characteristic is different from cumulativity and directionality; it implies the emergence of new phenomena and new properties not manifest in previous states (Harris, 1957, p. 5).

It takes more than the addition of a new behavior or other element (these are included in the cumulativity characteristic) to comprise a new mode of organization. This characteristic requires a radical alteration or reorganization in the arrangement, constitution, or structure of the individual. In short, the *rules of the system* change. Caterpillars that change into butterflies, maggots that become flies, and children who learn to walk and talk all represent examples of new modes of organization. Theories that explain the development of new modes of organization are more adequate developmental theories than those that do not, because they account for these kinds of developmental changes.

Several issues are related to this characteristic. One concerns whether or not development should be conceptualized in terms of stages. Without prejudging material presented later, it must suffice here to note that not all developmentalists see human nature in terms of stages. Even those who do propose a set of stages to describe human development may have in mind quite different kinds of properties. For example, Gesell and Ilg (1949, p. 60) define developmental stages as a "level of maturity," simply a "passing moment" in the life cycle. This notion implies temporality, cumulativity, and directionality, but it does not imply that later stages represent new modes of organization vis-à-vis earlier stages. Rather, stages of this sort reflect incremental, bit-by-bit improvements continuously linked together along a relatively linear developmental path. In contrast, other theorists may view development in terms of radical transformations and reorganizations of earlier stages into qualitatively different later stages. This latter conception clearly implies that later stages are new modes of organization.

A related issue concerns whether or not development is best construed as a continuous or discontinuous process. This is the *continuity-discontinuity* debate, a controversy that has occupied some attention in the annals of developmental psychology. The two poles of the continuity-discontinuity debate can be described as follows. On the continuity side are those theorists like B. F. Skinner (Chapter 7) and Albert Bandura (Chapter 8) who maintain that development is fundamentally quantitative. In their view, development is viewed as a uniform, *linear progression* from relatively few behaviors to quantitatively more behaviors that comprise an individual's repertoire. At the other extreme are theorists like Jean Piaget (Chapter 9) and Lawrence Kohlberg (Chapter 10) who cast development primarily in terms of a sequence of qualitatively distinct stages. Others (e.g., Pinard & Laurendeau, 1969; Wohlwill, 1966) believe that the issue is essentially a false dichotomy, a conceptual artifact determined by a theorist's level of analysis. As

Werner (1957) has noted, the issue is theoretical (a matter of interpretation) rather than empirical (a matter of fact).

Increased Capacity for Self-Control.   The concept of development implies that as people develop, they become more proactive and less reactive, thereby increasing their capacity for self-control (Harris, 1957, p. 5). Self-control entails the use of feedback so that one's activities can be continuously monitored and adjusted. While a person does not have to be completely self-controlling at any time, some aspect or function must display an increase in this property.

Biologists refer to self-control as *autoregulation,* an organism's ability to regulate itself within its ecology. But self-control as autoregulation is more than just conscious control, willpower, and deliberate action. It implies some mechanism that anticipates the consequences of a particular activity, adjusts the activity to the expected outcome, initiates the activity, monitors the consequences as they unfold, and continuously readjusts the activity to achieve planned consequences. Moreover, higher forms of self-regulation may also involve an ability to anticipate environmental events before they occur (e.g., weather prediction, flood control). The increased capacity to think out solutions to problems and to experiment mentally with ideas before tackling them on a concrete level are examples of increased capacity for self-control in comparison to, for example, the directed gropings of an infant.

Along with an increased capacity for self-control comes a simultaneous increase in independence from environmental fluctuations. The two achievements go hand in hand. Increasing independence from environmental changes occurs with the ability to foresee, plan, forecast, and anticipate events in the proximal (nearby) and distal (far away) ecology that may have important consequences. Through anticipation, individuals can better adjust themselves to avoid any foreseeable adversities and to take advantage of fortuitous events. For example, as children develop they gradually acquire the capacity to predict the path of a baseball and to spot and avoid hazardous traffic or other situations.

In this book, the five characteristics just described are used as a set of criteria for judging how "developmental" a developmental theory is. Not every developmental theory accounts for each characteristic. To that extent, the number of characteristics a theory accounts for is an important measure of its *developmental adequacy.*

The use of these characteristics as criteria of developmental adequacy presumes a certain degree of fairness and neutrality to the theories presented in this book. In this regard, Kendler (1986, p. 87) has argued that these characteristics, exemplified in Nagel's (1957) conception of development, are a good example of the doctrine of mechanism. Two important points should be made here. First, there is nothing that requires a theory to ignore or to include one or another of these characteristics in its account of development. Neither vitalistic nor organismic theories are precluded from accounting *in their own way* and *through their own analysis* for these characteristics. Second, if there is a systematic bias implicit in the use of this set of developmental characteristics, it should result in higher ratings for the developmental adequacy of mechanistic theories. Whether such a bias manifests itself will be left up to the reader to judge.

SCIENTIFIC WORTHINESS

Most scientists and philosophers hold certain beliefs about the relationship between theory and data. Collectively, these beliefs help define the enterprise of science and guide expectations about what constitutes an adequate scientific explanation of reality. According to Hempel (1966, p. 1), science attempts to explore, describe, explain, and predict worldly events. Science depends on empirical evidence to verify its claims, but theories are also necessary because they propose themes for organizing and explaining evidence.

In the following section, several of the most important values of science are described. These values are in one sense arbitrary and in another sense pragmatic. They are arbitrary in the sense that they represent tacit agreements about how to pursue science; in a different time and place these principles could have been (and historically have been) different. However, the same values are also pragmatic, since they define the goals of scientific theorizing and the rationale for its pursuit.

Evaluations of a theory's scientific worthiness throughout the book provide a second basis (in addition to developmental adequacy) of comparison among the developmental theories. The following discussion derives in part from treatments of logic and scientific explanation given by Hempel (1966), Hurley (1982), and Quine and Ullian (1978). This material, like the characteristics of development, should be learned because it will be used throughout the book. A synopsis of evaluative criteria is shown in Table 2-1.

Testability. A theory should in principle be testable in order to verify the claims it makes about developmental phenomena. To be testable, a theory must provide a degree of clarity for its concepts, because only then can its proposals be checked against the actuality of human nature. Testability is probably the most important measure of a theory's scientific worthiness. A theory that is testable can be objectively verified. We may learn in testing a theory that one or more of its claims are wrong. But if a theory is untestable, we have no way of finding out if it

Table 2-1 Evaluative Criteria

SCIENTIFIC WORTHINESS	DEVELOPMENTAL ADEQUACY
Testability	Temporality
External validity	Cumulativity
Predictive validity	Directionality
Internal consistency	New mode of organization
Theoretical economy	Increased capacity for self-control

is wrong. In this sense, a theory that is testable but false makes a greater scientific contribution than a theory that is untestable (even though it may be right, no one would ever know).

Two requirements must be met for a theory to be testable. First, its constructs and claims must be measurable. The measurement need not be quantitative, but it must derive from observable events. Science relies on measurement for precision and accuracy. Second, a theory's claims must be specific enough to allow us to make predictions. "If I do *A,* then *B* will happen." A theory may be testable but wrong, but its testability must be established before its accuracy can be determined. Testability and accuracy are separate issues. Accuracy is taken up later under the criteria of *external validity* and *predictive validity.*

It is important to recognize that sometimes theoretical claims are not testable simply because they are definitions. Definitions are accepted by any scientist who uses the theory. So long as a theorist is consistent in the employment of a definition, it need not be testable. One may agree or disagree with theorists' definitions, but they are usually granted flexibility in defining concepts in almost any way that is reasonable. Other theoretical claims may not be testable because they are circular. For example, a theory might define an angry person as one who fights rather than talks through conflict. Such a claim cannot be tested because an angry person could not, by definition, choose to talk through a conflict. There would be no way to find angry negotiators since they have been defined out of existence.

External Validity. External validity refers to a theory's accuracy; it means that a theory provides accurate descriptions of *what we already know* about human nature. Because a theory is limited, it need only account for the phenomena it attempts to explain. Two or more theories may rate high on this criteria because they may explain with equal accuracy different kinds of human phenomena. Most research with human subjects (infants, children, adolescents, or adults) attempts to test the external validity of a theory—does the theory explain the facts of human development?

A second definition of external validity is sometimes used. Hurley (1982, p. 416), for example, notes that a theory reflects external validity when it agrees with other well-established hypotheses. Hultsch and Hickey (1978) extend this point in noting that external validity implies more than just a correspondence between a theory and the real world. They argue that because different theories and paradigms actually view different worlds, external validity can only be assessed within the context of a particular framework. That is, different paradigms will require different kinds of information and hence different methods to establish external validity. For example, two theories may correspond with a specific set of facts (first kind of external validity). However, they may propose entirely different explanations for the same phenomena because they emphasize different facts. Hultsch and Hickey's point is that external validity requires more than fact matching. It requires an attention to the paradigm in which a theory operates. Newton may well explain falling bodies as a function of mass, distance, and force, but Einstein does the same thing in terms of space, time, energy, and frames of reference. Each explanation, while different, has external validity in terms of its paradigmatic world view.

Predictive Validity. Predictive validity reflects a second kind of accuracy, the accuracy of *foretelling new phenomena* that are not already known. Where external validity refers to how well a theory explains what we already know, predictive validity is a measure of a theory's capacity to generate new facts and new knowledge. According to Baldwin (1967) this kind of foretelling is really just an accurate empirical statement about a future event. Scientific predictions consist of "if...then" statements: *if* certain conditions are established, *then* some predicted phenomenon will occur. The more specific the prediction, the greater the predictive validity (all other things being equal) of a theory. Moreover, Baldwin notes that it is not the human scientist, but the theory that makes the prediction—any scientist can make an accurate prediction, but if the prediction cannot be clearly derived from the theory in question, its predictive validity has not been strengthened.

Another element of predictive validity is sometimes referred to as fruitfulness. Fruitfulness is not explicitly an index of a theory's accuracy; rather, it denotes the amount of research a theory generates. A theory is said to be fruitful if it suggests new ideas for future research and if it leads to the discovery of new facts (Hurley, 1982, p. 416).

Internal Consistency. Internal consistency is sometimes referred to as the *principle of noncontradiction*. It holds that a theory should not be self-contradictory. In other words, various parts of a theory (assumptions, internal principles, bridge principles, change mechanism) should be rationally interconnected in such a way that they are logically compatible (Hurley, 1982, p. 415). The purpose of a theory is to unify and thereby explain a body of data. Consequently, if theoretical concepts are not rationally interconnected, there would be no way to interconnect the data to which they apply. This quality of interconnectedness is sometimes called integration (Quine & Ullian, 1978, p. 11), which implies that each part of a theory should be related to all other parts.

There are at least three general indicators that flag a theory's internal consistency: (1) the number of exceptions acknowledged, (2) relative simplicity (more complex theories increase the probability of inconsistency), and (3) adherence to a central theme or line of reasoning (the more identifiable this central theme, the more likely it is that deviations from it will not tend to contradict one another). In other words, internal consistency requires that the theoretical "rules of the game" do not change without good reason. Inconsistency would result if a theory proposes one kind of change mechanism for a certain type of human conduct and an entirely different mechanism for a very similar type of behavior. For example, a hypothetical theory that proposes that all personality traits are formed by the same underlying mechanism, say maturation, would rate high on internal consistency. In contrast, one that proposed that introversion is caused by maturation, while claiming extroversion is learned, would probably rate low.

Theoretical Economy. Theoretical economy is a measure of efficiency as determined by the relationship *between* the phenomena explained by a theory and its underlying assumptions. Theoretical economy can be figured in two ways. First, two theories may explain exactly the same phenomena but make different assumptions. In that case, the one with fewer assumptions or with less complex assumptions would have greater theoretical economy (as an analogy, imagine that two cars travel the same distance, but one began with less gas). Second, two theories may make exactly the same assumptions, but one may explain more phenomena than the other. In that case, the one that explains more phenomena reflects greater theoretical economy (analogously, of two cars beginning with the same amount of gas, one travels farther than the other). *Morgan's Canon* expresses the idea differently: if two explanations of phenomena fit all the facts equally well, then the more economical explanation is to be preferred. In other words, science constitutes the most complete explanation of facts with the least expenditure of effort. Sometimes the term *simplicity* or *parsimony* is used to express the idea.

Theoretical economy is relative, not absolute. It requires a certain degree of balance between theoretical assumptions and principles and the number, kind, and complexity of phenomena explained. Moreover, assessments of theoretical economy are probably more subjective, reflecting elements of aesthetic and personal impression, than the other criteria of scientific worthiness. Nevertheless, this criterion is widely used under one rubric or another in science.

The five criteria just described provide one means for answering the question "How good is this theory?" The reader is encouraged to form an independent opinion about how well each theory meets these criteria. In addition, readers should also identify a set of personally meaningful criteria for evaluating theories. For example, I have found a personal interest in evaluating important theories in terms of their *aesthetic* appeal. I look for qualities of texture (richness, depth), novelty (imagination, creativity), interest (attention holding), and revolutionary impact (breaks new frontiers, shows a new way of viewing something). I don't expect others to judge theories on the basis of their aesthetic appeal, nor do I necessarily expect them to understand what I mean when I do it.

Professionals who plan to use theories in their work might formulate their own set of criteria. These could include, for example, relevance to one's needs, translatability of theory concepts into personally meaningful situations, ease of using a theory's principles, availability of literature about applications of the theory, and adequacy of practical applications (how well the theory works). However, one should expect that whatever criteria are used to evaluate theories, they will be used consistently.

SUMMARY POINTS

1. Development always implies some kind of complex change, whereas change does not necessarily imply development.
2. Development connotes five characteristics: temporality, cumulativity, directionality, new mode of organization, and increased capacity for self-control.
3. A theory's scientific worthiness is determined by its testability, external validity, predictive validity, internal consistency, and theoretical economy.

SUGGESTED READINGS

Harris, D. B. (Ed.). (1957). *The concept of development.* Minneapolis: University of Minnesota Press.

Hultsch, D. F., & Hickey, T. (1978). External validity in the study of human development: Theoretical and methodological issues. *Human Development, 21,* 76–91.

Pepper, S. C. (1942). *World hypotheses.* Berkeley: University of California Press.

Reese, H. W., & Overton, W. F. (1970). Models of development and theories of development. In L. R. Goulet & P. B. Baltes (Eds.), *Life-span developmental psychology.* New York: Academic Press.

Chapter 3

Families of Developmental Theories

Preview Questions

What types of causal explanation are employed by developmental theories?
What are the philosophical origins of developmental theories?
What are the three paradigms or families of developmental theories?

CAUSES AND EXPLANATIONS

With few exceptions, modern theories view development in terms of the *interaction* between the organism and its environment. In that context, the theories described in this book are interactional at least in a weak sense; they all ascribe some importance to both organismic and environmental influences in producing development. However, substantial variation across theories exists in the degree of influence they attribute to the organism or the environment. One theory may locate the causes of development within the individual, another outside the individual, and yet another within the process of individual-environmental interaction. Since locating the causes of development is inextricably linked to explaining it, theories can be classified according to the type of explanation and the locus of causes they espouse.

According to Cassirer (1960, pp. 159–181), the problem of explanation requires answering questions about *why* and questions about *what*. The why and the what of human development refer to the problem of cause and the problem of structure or form, respectively. Causal explanations and formal explanations are complementary though opposing approaches to the task of telling what data mean. Moreover, each kind of explanation is indispensable; each has a limited claim; and neither can replace the function of the other. As will be shown in later chapters, theories of human development have tended to incorporate either causal or formal explanations, not both.

Causal explanations consist of formulations about *cause and effect* relationships. Aristotle believed that people do not think they know a thing until they have grasped the "why" of it, so to answer the "why of it," he proposed four kinds of causal explanations still recognized today: *final, material, efficient,* and *formal. Final causality* is the end or goal for which a change has been produced. The principle use of final causality in modern thinking is primarily associated with religious doctrines that often claim some ultimate purpose that motivates human activity and existence. *Material causality* refers to the substance of or that in which a change is wrought. For example, the human body is composed of a variety of elements—teeth, hair, muscle, bone. Material causality holds that bone tissue, by virtue of its substance, cannot be turned into muscle tissue. Similarly, a pubescent male will predictably find hairs growing on his chin instead of fingernails. This type of causal explanation is seldom invoked in contemporary thought. Both *efficient causality* and *formal causality* are often employed in modern science, and because they have utility in our discussion of developmental theories, each is described a bit more fully.

Explanations of *efficient causality* entail three subordinate properties. First, *necessary connection* implies that two states are so related that neither can occur in the absence of the other. For example, if a person lets go of an object, then it is not merely true that the object will drop—rather, it must drop due to the necessary connection produced by the mutual attraction of unrestrained bodies (gravity). Second, *priority of causes to their effects* implies that a cause must occur before its effect. Third, *the direction of necessity* simply means that an effect cannot necessitate its own cause (e.g., the freezing of water cannot cause a reduction in its temperature, and being raised as a boy cannot cause a youngster to grow a penis). Developmental theories that employ causal explanations imply that if scientists could manipulate certain variables, then this manipulative control would result in specific, predictable, and systematic variations in the course of development. Parts II and III of this book describe several theories that posit causal explanations of human development.

What Aristotle terms *formal causality* is what Cassirer (1960) refers to as *formal explanation.* It reflects the attempt to explain development by describing emergent properties of organismic processes, functions, states, and their interrelationships with each other and the environment. Such explanations do not appeal to cause-and-effect principles. For example, cosmology is a branch of philosophy concerned with the design and extent of the universe (including all its substances) and represents a search for formal explanations for "what is real" rather than causal explanations for why the real world got that way. Additionally, mathematics represents a highly abstract search for formal theorems that reflect logical rather than causal necessity. Developmental theories that use formal explanations attempt to identify principles of organization and relationship to show how certain properties get combined and differentiated to form new emergent properties. In Part IV two theories that attempt to use formal explanations of human development are described.

PHILOSOPHICAL ANTECEDENTS
OF DEVELOPMENTAL THEORIES

Three seminal movements in modern epistemology (a branch of philosophy concerned with explaining knowledge) established the conceptual framework from which psychological paradigms emerged. The following synopsis briefly describes the lines of argument that differentiate these three philosophical approaches and their corresponding paradigms.

Rationalism

Modern philosophy began with the insights of René Descartes, a seventeenth-century thinker whose ideas about the origin of knowledge became known as *rationalism*. In his *Discourse on the Method* (1637), Descartes set forth his "method of doubt" and the conclusions he drew from its results. Using this method, he simply suspended his belief in anything for which he could imagine the slightest possible doubt. What was left over, beliefs that resisted all doubt, could be considered certain and hence "true" knowledge.

Descartes recalled many occasions when his senses had been fooled into providing false information about the real world. From these lessons he concluded that true knowledge could not derive from error-prone sensations. To experience the kind of suspicion Descartes held toward sensations, imagine placing one hand in a pan of cold water and the other in a pan of hot water, each for several minutes. Next place both hands into a single pan of lukewarm water. Each hand will transmit different sensations, yet both hands are subject to the same experience. Which hand is transmitting false impressions? Perhaps both? How, reasoned Descartes, are we to tell when our senses do and do not deceive us if they provide the only information we have for making that judgment? Examining his memories and experiences, Descartes initially concluded that any beliefs about the physical world, God, and even about himself could no longer be justified. Since no knowledge was completely trustworthy, he found himself in a position where he could believe in nothing.

Such a preliminary conclusion was short-lived, for Descartes soon noticed that he was at least aware of his ever-present doubting. The brilliance of his discovery lies in the fact that if he was to have any doubt at all, then something must be doing the doubting—*cognito ergo sum* (I think, therefore I exist). Since his own thinking was the only substance that was beyond doubt, Descartes argued that *all external substances must be extensions of one's own reasoning*. Because true knowledge of the world could not be derived from the senses, any knowledge must, like reason itself, have an internal origin. His *rationalism* is a philosophical position that holds that all knowledge is an extension of internal, *innate reason*, and even knowledge of the physical world is merely an extension of inborn reasoning.

Endogenous Theories. Rationalism is the philosophical antecedent of the *endogenous* paradigm. The term *endogenous* derives from two roots: *endo*—from within, and *genesis*—development. Like rationalism, endogenous theories explain development as the result of predominantly internal influences. The family of endogenous theories places primary emphasis on the organism's internal nature, especially those inner workings believed to produce human development. Moreover, theories in this family employ causal explanations of development and locate the change mechanism within the internal components of the organism (usually in the form of a hereditary plan or blueprint for growth). Theories in the endogenous family typically conceive of development as an unfolding of relatively fixed patterns and being relatively impervious to environmental pressures.

Some endogenous theories, like those of Sigmund Freud and Erik Erikson, stress the view that developmental milestones and stages are maturationally predetermined. Endogenous theories that reflect a strong maturational orientation sometimes invoke a notion of developmental *critical periods*. Critical periods are maturationally timed changes that result in rapid, specialized learning. The timing of these periods and the objects of specialized learning are innately determined, as happens, for example, with imprinting. Endogenous theories sometimes describe environmental influences on development, but these influences are invariably subordinated to the natural plan operating within the organism. The endogenous theories of Freud and Erikson both stress biological maturation as a developmental change mechanism, whereas Edward Wilson emphasizes the effects of evolution through genetic mutation and recombination.

Empiricism

An important turn in modern philosophy resulted from the efforts of two seventeenth- and eighteenth-century British writers, John Locke and David Hume, who individually attempted to refute Descartes's notion of innate reason. Locke's *Essay Concerning Human Understanding* was a direct effort to demonstrate that knowledge derives from the external world, not from the mind.

The analytic spirit of science that prevailed at the time motivated Locke to think of the mind as composed of elements or units called *ideas*. Locke wondered how ideas in the mind become connected with each other to form the meanderings of conscious thought. He began by assuming that things, actions, events, substances, and processes have a "real" existence (otherwise one could not explain how our ideas are so well matched with an external reality). His key contribution was the notion of *idea*, which he defined as an object of thought. Ideas constitute the building blocks of knowledge, and they derive from experience, either directly through sensations or indirectly through reflection, in the following manner. The newborn comes into the world with a *tabula rasa* mind (an empty file cabinet or blank slate, available to receive information but possessing none at birth). Equipped with a *tabula rasa* mind, the infant also possesses a body that, with virtually no effort, rubs up against and comes in contact with a world replete with a great variety of real substances. These contacts constitute experience. When substances evoke sensations, they are conveyed to the mind, where ideas are formed. An infant first begins to think when the first sensation produces the first idea.

Ideas, however, are of two types: simple and complex. Simple ideas are produced by single, irreducible sensations (a color, a tone, an odor). The mind cannot invent new simple ideas; they can only be produced from sensations. Complex sensations (the smell of breakfast, playing with a parent, and listening to a story) are sorted into distinguishable single sensations, each of which gives rise to its arrangement of simple ideas. For simple ideas, the mind acts like a receptacle to be filled. Knowledge of the world is limited by the simple ideas supplied through sensations.

Once a sufficient quantity of simple ideas has been stored, the mind can repeat, compare, and unite them through reflection into virtually limitless combinations, thereby producing complex ideas. By habit, simple ideas become gradually integrated into the unified experience of complex ideas, and through reflection we come to anticipate that things that produce certain sensations will also produce other expected sensations (e.g., the sound of the dentist's drill is accompanied by painful sensations in our teeth).

Locke's *Essay* proposed a radical departure from the path to knowledge forged by Descartes and firmly established the philosophical orientation called *empiricism*, the belief that knowledge derives from experience. Locke failed, however, to explain why ideas occur in an organized rather than random fashion (since simple ideas could be combined with limitless variety). This problem was solved by Hume.

David Hume's *A Treatise of Human Nature* set forth two fundamental principles. First, all ideas derive from sense impressions of the external world or sense impressions of internal states. Consequently, we are incapable of imagining anything (much less understanding it) that we have not experienced. Second, to explain how we get abstract or complex ideas that are organized instead of random, Hume invoked the doctrine of *associationism*, a kind of "mental chemistry" wherein mental elements, in this case ideas, combine with one another into compounds or complex ideas.

The merit of Hume's associationism is that it explained how general ideas could be formulated in an organized manner. Simple ideas get associated with one another through the processes of *resemblance, contiguity,* and *cause-effect* (Lana, 1976). Through resemblance ideas call up one another when they have derived from similar sense impressions (e.g., girl-woman, car-truck). Contiguity leads to associations between two ideas whose sense impressions occur together in space and time; thus the presence of one conjures up the other (e.g., mother-father, mother-baby, baby-bottle). Cause and effect associations result when the sense impressions underlying one idea compel the sense impressions of a second idea (e.g., needle-pain, hit-hard, drop-fall). Individual associations, through resemblance, contiguity, and cause-effect, gradually interconnect into a network that evokes abstract relationships called concepts. Concepts for Hume were merely the family of associations that existed between individual ideas.

Locke and Hume shaped the modern empiricist movement in philosophy and science. They gave it a forcefulness, an elegant simplicity, and a direction that is clearly evident in the family of *exogenous* developmental theories.

Exogenous Theories. The term *exogenous* derives from two roots: *exo*—from outside, and *genesis*—development. Theories in the exogenous paradigm attempt causal explanations of development and seek to locate these causes in specific environmental factors external to the individual. While these theories recognize that infants are biologically endowed creatures, the genetic blueprint is viewed as a malleable plan of possibilities rather than necessities. The newborn is seen as innately flexible and predisposed to conform to pressures exerted by environmental forces. Exogenous theories tend to reflect a *mechanistic* approach to human development. B. F. Skinner's theory of operant conditioning and Albert Bandura's social cognitive theory are good examples of the exogenous perspective, and they propose reinforcement and observational learning, respectively, as mechanisms of development.

Constructivism

The third major influence on modern philosophy was Immanuel Kant, an eighteenth-century philosopher who proposed a critical approach to determining what knowledge the mind could and could not produce. Kant fashioned the most salvageable ideas from rationalism and empiricism into a synthesis that is not a simple adding together of the two positions. His *Critique of Pure Reason* provided the foundation for what is known today as *constructivism.*

By the late eighteenth century, sense experience was widely accepted by most thinkers as immutably linked to the origin of knowledge (Lana, 1976). Kant appeared to accept this limited proposition, though he extended it by asking how sense experience itself could lead to genuine knowledge. The challenge he set for himself was to explain how humans could understand such abstract ideas as logic and mathematics, neither of which derive from sense impressions and hence cannot derive from associations of simple ideas.

Kant began his *Critique* by showing that the senses and the intellect are not capable of the same type of knowledge; each produces different qualities and is constrained by different restrictions. Kant believed that to know and to act necessitate to sense and to think. This point is crucial. Where Descartes viewed sensation as an extension of the mind, and where Locke and Hume reduced thought to a derivative of the senses, Kant maintained that neither sensation nor thought could be derived from each other. He reasoned that knowledge derived from the conjoint application of two components—sensibility and understanding—to each other. Simply put, "the mind without sensation is empty; sensation without the mind is blind."

Kant argued that what is innate is not reason or knowledge but rather innate *categories* that act like filters to analyze information from sensory input. The categories are very different from the kinds of ideas described in rationalism and empiricism. They are processors for *constructing* knowledge from sensations much like rules for putting sensations together in ways that make sense rather than being the content or the sensations themselves.

Kant's innate categories are fundamentally different from sensations because they are concepts of a higher order than concepts derived from direct experience. Like intuitions of space and time, the innate categories have to do with the form of experience rather than its material substance. These categories supply no knowledge of particular things (a rejection of rationalism), and empirical sensations provide only the aliment or food for "digestion" and are not themselves knowledge of the external world (a rejection of empiricism). For Kant, knowledge must be a synthetic construction that derives from the application of innate analyzers that confer meaning on the content of sense impressions.

Constructivist Theories.   Constructivist theories attempt to *describe* the course and constitutive properties of development and thereby posit formal rather than causal explanations. They represent an *organismic* (see Chapter 2) approach to development in that they place primary emphasis on the synthetic, holistic qualities of individual-environmental interactions and locate the source of development within the dynamic commerce of that interactive engagement. Rather than being either innately or environmentally determined, development is viewed as a natural product of progressive organizations and reorganizations that are *constructed* in the process of adapting to and interacting with the external world. The theories of Jean Piaget and Lawrence Kohlberg represent relatively pure examples of constructivist theories, and both propose cognitive conflict as the mechanism of developmental change.

CLASSIFICATION OF THEORIES

Table 3-1 shows how some developmental theorists can be classified according to the two organizing principles described in this chapter: type of explanation (efficient causality versus formal causality) and psychological paradigm (endogenous, exogenous, constructivist). This classification scheme provides the plan for studying human development theories used in this book. Note that constructivist theories employ formal explanations, whereas endogenous and exogenous theories provide causal explanations.

While there are many developmental theories one might study, those selected for inclusion in this book meet several conditions that make them important. First, each one is a macrotheory in that it attempts to explain a relatively broad spectrum of human behavior rather than highly specific qualities. Second,

Table 3-1   Classification Scheme of Developmental Theorists

PARADIGM	TYPE OF EXPLANATION	
	Causal	*Formal*
Endogenous	Noam Chomsky Erik Erikson* Sigmund Freud* Arnold Gesell Carl Jung Edward O. Wilson*	
Exogenous	Albert Bandura* John Dollard *Mechanistic* Clark Hull Neal Miller B. F. Skinner* Edward Thorndike John B. Watson	
Constructivist		Lawrence Kohlberg* Jean Piaget* Klaus Reigel Robert Selman Elliot Turiel

*Theory covered in this book.

one represents a relatively pure example of the properties of its paradigm family. This is important because if one can learn the basic ingredients of theories central to each paradigm, it makes learning about other theories within the same paradigm much easier. Third, each theory in this book has generated a sufficient body of published work by its author to enable our identification of its structural components (see Chapter 1). Fourth, each theory has generated a sufficiently large body of interested researchers to warrant its study by new generations who would take their place.

The preliminary considerations of Part I have now been completed. Part II contains a description of endogenous theories: Freud's psychoanalysis (Chapter 4), Erikson's psychosocial theory (Chapter 5), and Wilson's sociobiology (Chapter 6). Part III contains examples of the exogenous perspective: Skinner's operant conditioning (Chapter 7) and Bandura's social cognitive theory (Chapter 8). Part IV, the constructivist perspective, presents Piaget's cognitive-developmental theory (Chapter 9) and Kohlberg's theory of moral development (Chapter 10). Part V contains example applications to educational settings (Chapter 11) and to clinical psychology and counseling (Chapter 12). Finally, Part VI completes our study of developmental theories by directly addressing one of the most widespread, least acknowledged issues faced by professionals—theoretical eclecticism versus theoretical purity (Chapter 13).

SUMMARY POINTS

1. Developmental theories typically employ one of two types of explanation—efficient causality or formal causality. The first type attempts to specify cause-and-effect relationships, whereas the second attempts to answer *what* or *how* questions by describing relationships of forms, structures, and functions that are progressively manifested in development.
2. Developmental theories reflect three major philosophical considerations about the source and nature of knowledge: rationalism, empiricism, and constructivism.
3. Psychological paradigms are matched to philosophical positions as follows: endogenous–rationalism; exogenous–empiricism; and constructivist–constructivism.
4. Theories of human development can be classified according to the kind of explanation employed (causal or formal) and family resemblance (endogenous, exogenous, and constructivist).
5. Endogenous and exogenous theories employ causal explanations of human development. Constructivist theories employ formal explanations.

SUGGESTED READINGS

Lana, R. E. (1976). *The foundations of psychological theory*. Hillsdale, NJ: Lawrence Erlbaum.

Looft, W. R. (1972). The evolution of developmental psychology. *Human Development, 15*, 187–201.

Reese, H. W., & Overton, W. F. (1970). Models of development and theories of development. In L. R. Goulet & P. B. Baltes (Eds.), *Life-span developmental psychology*. New York: Academic Press.

Chapter 4

Psychoanalysis

Preview Questions

What two historical trends are unified in psychoanalysis?
What assumptions underlie psychoanalytic theory?
What major problems does psychoanalysis study, and how are its methods matched to its problems?
What are the theory's internal and bridge principles?
What change mechanisms account for development?
What are the important contributions and criticisms of the theory?
How does psychoanalysis rate for scientific worthiness and developmental adequacy?

HISTORICAL SKETCH

Sigmund Freud, the oldest of eight children, was born in 1856 in Moravia (now part of Czechoslovakia). As a child he moved to Vienna, where he later entered medical school at the University of Vienna and specialized in neurology. His training stressed biological determinism—a view that attributes all human activity to biological/neurological causes—and inspired him to conduct research on brain neurology. When he discovered that his Jewish origins would retard his academic aspirations, he gave up his research to enter private practice in the treatment of mental disorders.

Until the turn of the century, Freud suffered quietly from anti-Semitism and deliberate exclusion from learned societies throughout Europe. In 1909 he visited America and delivered a series of lectures at Clark University that propelled him to international fame, which later prompted his appointment to full professor at the University of Vienna. Three decades later, the Nazis invaded Austria, but Freud refused to flee. Only when both American and German ambassadors intervened did he escape to London, where he died in 1939 apparently unaware that his sisters had been murdered in concentration camps.

Psychoanalysis developed out of Freud's synthesis of two historically independent lines of work: the search for neurological brain structures and the practice of psychic curing. This synthesis combined his deterministic training in neurology with his clinical treatment of mental disorders. Systematic attempts to isolate discrete brain functions marked the *zeitgeist* of Freud's medical training. About the same time, humanitarian movements in America, England, and France were underway to reform treatment of the mentally insane by invoking a new concept—*mental disease*—which assumed mental rather than physical causes of insanity. I think Freud's contribution to our understanding of human development cannot be fully appreciated without some attention to how these two historical trends were unified in his work.

The Search for Neurological Structures

In the early 1800s the study of brain anatomy occupied the attention of Franz Joseph Gall and his student G. Spurzheim, who together invented the "science" of *phrenology*. They developed a cranial map that located discrete mental faculties in specific areas of the brain (Boring, 1957, pp. 50–60). While phrenology had tremendous popular appeal, it provided scientists with testable hypotheses and was easy to disprove. In its wake came the legitimate, truly scientific study of brain anatomy found in the work of John Hughlings Jackson. Jackson, often called the father of neurology, was best known for his meticulous mapping of the nervous system. In the tradition of Jackson's pioneering work, Brucke and Meynert became two of the leading authorities in the field. Freud studied neurology and neuropathology under them, and they infused in him an unshakable belief that every behavior was strictly determined by inner forces and mechanisms. With their strongly deterministic orientation instilled in him, Freud became convinced that all human behavior (even slips of the tongue) was caused by some underlying mental agent. Under Brucke's direction, he attempted to determine how the anatomical structure of the nervous system produced psychological phenomena (Fancher, 1979). Meynert was responsible for perfecting Freud's ability to diagnose symptoms of brain damage. For his labors Freud won a fellowship to study in Paris with the celebrated psychic healer Jean Charcot. While working with Charcot, Freud's neurological training became intertwined with the art of psychic healing.

Psychic Healing

By the mid 1700s gravitational and magnetic forces had been well documented. About that time a Viennese physician, Friedrich Anton Mesmer, posited a force called "animal gravitation," a plausible notion coming in the wake of Newton's discoveries about physical gravitation. Mesmer's importance here lies in his attempts to cure mental illness by harnessing "animal gravitation." He believed that a misalignment of the body's magnetic force resulted in certain "mental" diseases and their accompanying symptoms. At first he tried to realign his patients by exposing them to magnetic ores, but he eventually discarded this therapy when he discovered that many of his patients could be cured without magnetic ores; all he had to do was pass his hands over the afflicted areas. Rather than conclude that magnetism was unrelated to healing, Mesmer decided that his own body possessed unusually large amounts of animal gravitation and that he had personally effected the cures. His personalized healing eventually became associated with his name—*Mesmerism*—though his method fell into disrepute when a scientific committee investigated and found no scientific basis for his psychic cures.

With Mesmerism properly debunked, James Braid, a respected physician and interested witness at many public mesmerizings, produced an unexpected discovery. He showed through carefully planned experiments that the mesmerist's trance could be induced through sensory fixation, a technique he termed *hypnosis*. Because it was based on physiological processes rather than animal gravitation, Braid's hypnotism gained an aura of scientific respectability. Eventually two French physicians, Joseph Breuer and Jean Charcot, attempted to use hypnosis with patients suffering from hysteria. Charcot had tremendous personal influence and attracted several very gifted students: Alfred Binet, William James, Pierre Janet, and Sigmund Freud.

Freud's Clinical Work

Freud's fellowship from the University of Vienna allowed him six months with Charcot to learn hypnosis. When he returned home in 1886, Freud gave up his faculty position and entered private practice with the hypnotist Joseph Breuer. Together they refined the hypnotic technique and published several papers concerning cures for hysteria before theoretical and clinical differences prompted the two men to sever their professional relationship.

Shortly after the break with Breuer, Freud abandoned hypnosis altogether when he discovered that its cures were most often only temporary. He developed a new technique he called *free association*, which uncovered his patients' memories of childhood and had prolonged healing effects. Frequently, such memories revealed sexual intimacies between his clients as children and their adult relatives. These revelations prompted him to suggest a theory of childhood sexuality, a formulation that met with considerable disdain. The severity of public ridicule itself convinced Freud that the strict sexual attitudes of the day were only a mask for deep-seated, disguised sexual passions. However, he suffered a deep personal crisis when he discovered that his patients' memories—the very ones on which his ideas had been based—were almost always *not true*. It turned out that his patients had been imagining sexual intimacies that had never really occurred. This discovery marked a turning point in his theorizing, because he concluded that "false memories" must serve some purpose (a reflection of his deterministic training) and that some unconscious mental force must be hidden beneath the memories themselves. There is some controversy today about Freud's reasons for abandoning his early views of infantile sexuality, but his discovery of unconscious motivations is one of his enduring contributions to our understanding of human nature.

STRUCTURAL COMPONENTS

The deterministic orientation inspired by his medical training, coupled with his clinical practice, prompted Freud to construct a theory of personality development. Because many of his early ideas were later modified, emphasis in this chapter is given to later formulations of the theory.

Assumptions

Scientific thinking in the late 1800s assumed the correctness of Newton's elegantly simple laws of energy conservation. This scientific *zeitgeist* influenced Freud by directing his attention to the dynamic, energetic qualities of human nature, in particular the psychic energy Freud called *libido.*

Freud assumed that infants are born with a fixed pool of instinctual energy, the libido, which energizes all human activity. While individuals may vary from one to another in amount, each person maintains the same amount of libido throughout life; thus, in the spirit of Newton, libido is conserved. Psychic energy may be transformed (changed in form), but its total value remains constant. An analogy can be drawn between libido and a reservoir of water. The water possesses potential energy, which may be transformed into thermal, kinetic, mechanical, and electrical energy without altering the amount of total energy. Similarly, the libido can be transformed into behavioral and psychic activities without diminishing its total value.

Instinctual energy is of two types. *Eros* is the positive energy of life, activity, hope, and sexual desire. *Thanatos* is a counterbalancing negative energy of death, destruction, despair, and aggression. Eros initiates motion and goal seeking; thanatos balances eros by curtailing, revising, or redirecting activity.

Problems for Study

Freud's medical training engendered in him a belief in *no causes without effects— no effects without causes.* This determinism guided his analysis of dreams and neurotic symptom formation. Most of his clinical work consisted of treating middle-class, Austrian women whose afflictions had been diagnosed as imaginary by local physicians because their own medical training had led them to seek only physical causes.

Phenomena to Be Explained

Given his clinical situation, Freud attempted to diagnose the psychic causes of psychic symptoms. As his treatments progressed, he gradually became convinced that the underlying causes could always be found in his patients' early traumatic experiences and parental relationships. More specifically, he believed that unfulfilled wishes, needs, and desires (ungratified libidinal instincts) had been repressed because of the pain caused by their unfulfillment. His immediate clinical problem was to recover an accurate representation of an individual's childhood to identify early events that later triggered particular kinds of symptoms. Thus, the primary phenomenon to be explained is the formation of adult personality traits in terms of social patterns and habits established in childhood. Ultimately, Freud envisioned the potential explanation of all behavior, including many previously inexplicable phenomena—tip-of-the-tongue forgetting, Freudian slips, erotic humor, memory distortion, dreams, and abnormal personalities.

Methods of Study

To gain access to childhood memories, three techniques are used. Freud developed *free association* and *dream interpretation* in his own clinical work; *projective tests* are a more recent addition to psychoanalytic methodology.

Free association is a technique used to obtain verbal memory traces of past experiences. Patients, when placed in a calm, quiet, nondistracting environment, are asked to report any ideas that come to mind. All associations are believed to be important, even though their meaning may not at first be recognized. The therapist records associations without interrupting the spontaneous flow of thoughts. Although patients initially censor their thoughts, they become more trusting and candid over time. The therapist looks for tendencies to dwell on certain associations more than others as well as opposing tendencies to delete normal associations. While unusual associations may represent unfulfilled fantasies, deleted ones may reflect unconsciously "forgotten" material. Either type of pattern signals telltale forces at work in the patient's unconscious mind. In this manner, free associations provide data about childhood events that continue to influence a person's behavior.

Dream interpretation consists of the analysis of dream content in terms of both symbolic and hidden meanings (Freud, 1900). The symbolic content Freud termed *manifest* meaning; it consists of the meanings associated with events, colors, shapes, sizes, relations, words, and people represented in the dream. For example, if a person dreams of falling off a cliff, the manifest meaning consists of the collective meanings of the separate symbols that denote time, place, activity, agents, actions, and feelings involved in the fall. The *latent* meaning of a dream is the meaning ascribed to the hidden motivations that prompted the dream. Latent meaning is initiated by libidinal energy; this meaning has been distorted to make it palatable to the semiconscious of the dreaming mind. Dreams are often illogical, precisely because their unconscious source—the fantasies, wishes, impulses, and repressed desires that motivate them—is not governed by rational control. Latent meaning is the real meaning of a dream, but it is difficult to interpret since its true meaning has been repressed and disguised. For example, falling off a cliff may unconsciously represent a wish to free oneself from family expectations or a fear of unconstrained freedom. Freud's *Interpretation of Dreams* is considered a classic in psychology because it set forth a framework for analyzing the previously unexplored and overlooked territory of dreams.

Contemporary psychoanalysts also use *projective tests,* which consist of pictures containing ambiguous stimuli—ink blots, random shapes, people engaging in ambiguous behavior. Subjects, in describing the stimuli, must supply their own meanings. Since the stimuli themselves are ambiguous, any meaning attributed by a patient is believed to reflect deep-seated libidinal forces. Today, normative data are used to facilitate diagnosis of responses.

Internal Principles

Each of the three internal principles that comprise the core explanatory concepts of psychoanalytic theory is like a "mini-theory" in itself. The *dynamic system* reflects Freud's concern with the antagonistic conflict between irrational desire and rational control. The *structural system* includes Freud's concepts of *id*, *ego*, and *superego*. Finally, the *sequential system* is a series of stages that ultimately determine the basic scope, shape, and content of adult personality. Figure 4-1 shows that these three systems reflect distinctive but partially overlapping components of personality development.

The Dynamic System

The *dynamic system* consists of the psychic energy that, even though hidden from our awareness, activates personality functioning. Psychic energy has been called various names: nervous energy, instinctual energy, drive energy, mental energy, libido, and tension. Freud thought psychic energy was as much a part of our phylogenetic evolution as the organic energy that empowers metabolic, respiratory, and other biological processes.

Instinctual energy has four key characteristics that reflect the dynamic and deterministic properties Freud imputed to human nature; these are the *source, aim, object*, and *impetus*. The *source* of instinctual energy derives from inborn biological needs. Such needs include nourishment, water, comfort, sleep, pleasure, and sex. The instinctual source of a need arises primarily from certain of the body's regions.

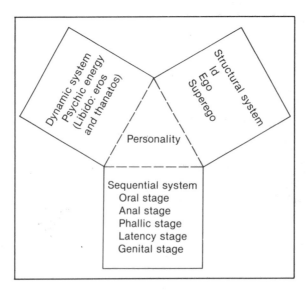

Figure 4-1. Internal principles of psychoanalysis.

When needs go unfulfilled, we experience tension, discomfort, and pain. The *aim* of instinctual energy is to satisfy the need through tension reduction or by energy discharge through pleasurable stimulation. The aim represents a general tendency; the instinctual *object* provides a specific goal for achieving the aim. The object may be a person, a part of a person, a part of the self, a physical object, or even a mental representation of an object, as long as it reduces tension. For an infant, such objects may be a pacifier, a blanket, a mother's breast, a bottle, or even a toy. When libidinal energy is repeatedly associated with particular objects that satisfy needs, the libido is said to be "cathected" or channeled toward those objects. Infants often cathect and form strong attachments to their mothers, pacifiers, and blankets. Finally, the *impetus* refers to the degree of force or pressure that underlies a need.

Figure 4-2 illustrates the cyclic manner in which the dynamic system components operate. An infant, for example, lives through numerous repetitions of the hunger–food-finding–ingestion–gratification cycle. Similarly, adults whose mature libido is well developed also experience throughout their lives a repetition in the sexual cycle, each involving the four basic elements of the dynamic system.

Freud believed that psychic energy motivated the widest variety of phenomena—from acts of war and aggression to acts of benevolent self-sacrifice, from book burnings to creations of artistic masterpieces, from the most intimate expression of love to aggression and torture. Through Freud's eyes the most mundane and the most perverse human activities were viewed as either direct or indirect attempts to satisfy instinctual drives.

Figure 4-2.   Operation of the dynamic system.

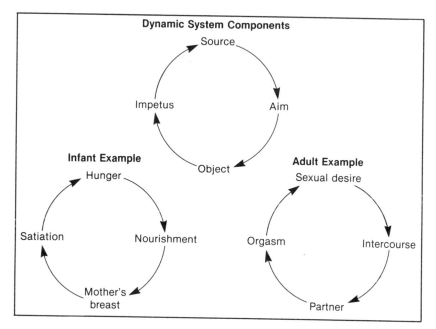

The Structural System

The theory's structural system complements the dynamic system. While Freud viewed human nature as driven by powerful forces, he also provided a portrait of mental structures that channel these forces. The *id, ego,* and *superego* constitute the architecture of the mind (Freud, 1923).

Id. Our innate psychic energy constitutes the primitive id. The id is irrational, pleasure driven, and unsocialized. In accordance with the *pleasure principle,* the id seeks immediate gratification and tension reduction for all its urges (Freud, 1963, p. 311). The primary aim of the pleasure principle is the achievement of tensionlessness (experienced as pleasure) through need gratification (Freud, 1920). Unconstrained by any rules (except the pleasure principle), the id makes no distinction between reality and fantasy. This fusion is the essential quality of *primary process* thought, a primitive form of cognition that directs the id's energy toward pleasure. Id energy is so facile and dynamic that it can be readily channeled from one object to another or from one image to another. Thus an infant whose drive impetus is just beginning to produce hunger may be satisfied momentarily with a pacifier, but as hunger increases, a new object—food itself—must ultimately be forthcoming to satisfy the drive. In a similar vein hallucinations and daydreams (which fuse together reality and fantasy) are examples of primary process thinking that use wish fulfillment to partially achieve tension reduction. The id is a seething cauldron of insatiable desires (Freud, 1933a) that continues its unconscious influence throughout our lives. Its influence is often disguised, such as when we "forget" certain experiences or suffer through a series of recurring dreams.

Because the id's desires are irrational, its needs often do not match what is available in the immediate social and physical environment. For example, a hungry infant, incapable of feeding itself, may not obtain immediate gratification for its hunger. The tension associated with the accompanying hunger pangs unconsciously motivates the infant to discharge energy through crying, sucking, and other activities that may coincidentally signal feeding time to a caregiver. When the infant eats, its hunger decreases, and the unconscious tension subsides. Over time, with repeated episodes like this, the infant gradually comes to associate certain external events (e.g., the mother's appearance) with the repeated discharge of psychic energy. However, the reality of the real world forces the id to adjust itself to external situations, and this is done by harnessing a portion of the id's energy and transforming it into a new personality structure—the ego. This transformation is depicted in Figure 4-3.

Ego. The ego is the organ of reason and sanity (Freud, 1923). Its energy derives from libidinal instincts that have been displaced from the id to create a pool of neutralized energy. This displacement turns a portion of the erotic libido into an ego libido, which is accomplished by a partial desexualization or an abandonment of sexual aims (Freud, 1923, p. 65). The process whereby instinctual ener-

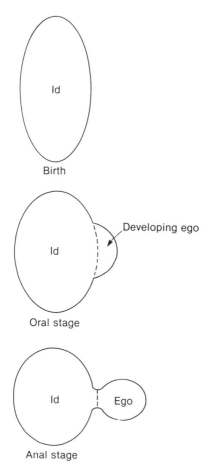

Figure 4-3. Developmental formation of ego from id.

gy becomes displaced, neutralized, and transformed into ego functioning is not well understood. In fact, the problem of generating rational thought from irrational desires has led some psychoanalysts to propose alternative hypotheses about the origin of the ego.

The ego also seeks pleasure for the id, but in a diminished and delayed capacity in accord with the *reality principle,* that is, within limitations set by surrounding circumstances. The psychic energy of the id gets channeled by the ego and directed at available objects that produce pleasure. Freud uses the analogy of a rider on horseback to characterize this important relationship between the ego and the id. The rider (ego) must control and direct the horse (id), but to avoid being thrown, the rider must sometimes guide the horse where it wants to go; analogously, the ego is obliged to follow the wishes of the id as if they were its own (Freud, 1923). However, circumstances sometimes arise where gratification must be delayed. The result is the arousal of *anxiety,* a psychic tension that acts as the ego's warning that executing certain plans could be either physically or psychological-ly threatening. The ego also mediates between the conflicting desires of the id and society's restrictive demands.

The ego acts as a remarkably flexible executive decision maker. It operates on the basis of *secondary process* thought, which is more organized, rational, and integrated than the id's primary process where irrational desires rule. Secondary process thinking is comprised of such intellectual abilities as dreams and dream censorship, language, hallucinations, sensory perception, problem solving, symbol recognition and use, defense mechanisms, recognition and recall memory, and reality testing. When the ego is unable to cope with particularly stressful events, it may channel psychic energy to an earlier, regressive developmental mode of coping that is more secure and less threatening. It does not replace the id's primary process thought, but rather adds a new level of organization to it.

In summary, the ego is a constellation of interrelated functions that control mental conflict by mediating the demands of the id and the limitations imposed by external reality. In time, some of the ego's own neutralized energy evolves into a new psychological structure, the *superego*.

Superego. Like the ego, which evolved from the id to adapt to the constraints of the situational "here and now," the superego evolves from the ego to adapt to society's conventions and morals. This evolution is depicted in Figure 4-4. The parents, as the primary agents of socialization, demand, teach, and encourage certain behaviors in their children while prohibiting and punishing others. To conform to these expectations, a portion of the child's ego gets transformed into what Freud called a superego because it is differentiated from, but superior to, the ego. The superego contains the *conscience* and the *ego ideal*. The conscience consists of society's moral prohibitions and values that have been learned from one's parents, whereas the ego ideal comprises the standards of perfection toward which we strive.

The superego constantly demands that we think and behave in accord with cultural expectations and will punish us with guilt if we give in to the id's irrational desires. Moreover, the superego makes no distinction between thought and behavior: thinking something is as bad or as good as actually doing it. Freud's recognition of the importance of society in controlling impulsive, aggressive urges is quite ironic, given the atmosphere of anti-semitism, rigid Victorian sexual attitudes, and Nazi terror that reigned during his lifetime.

The Sequential System

The third internal principle in psychoanalytic theory is the sequential system of five maturational stages. Before describing each stage, however, it is important to understand what Freud means when he uses the term *stage*.

First, the biological determinism ingrained in Freud's thinking is manifest in his belief that psychosexual stages are *critical periods* of development. Critical periods promote the development of crucial species—specific abilities that are believed to be acquired during biologically determined intervals. The kind of

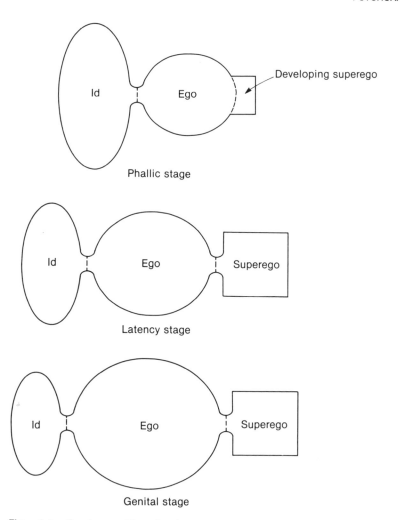

Figure 4-4.   Developmental formation of superego from ego.

change and its timing differ with each critical period, but all critical periods are marked by a biological onset, the rapid learning of some specialized function or ability, and a biologically timed closure. The acquisition of a special function or ability is seen as indispensable to development and often facilitates other changes that occur later. Failure to acquire the critical ability at the proper time also implies both that it cannot be acquired later on and that the individual will be developmentally impaired. For this reason, Freud placed tremendous importance on the early psychosexual stages.

Second, Freud was convinced that sexuality played such a dynamic and vital role in motivating human behavior that he sought to determine the origin of its development in infancy and childhood. While the concept of *infantile sexuality* shocked Freud's Victorian contemporaries, it is understood today not as a literal proposition about adult sexuality present in infants, but as Freud's attempt to emphasize the *nonbiological* sources of pleasure. To make his point, he defined "sexual" to mean a striving for pleasure independent of nourishment (Freud, 1940). In short, Freud believed that infantile sexuality evolves gradually from a state of global, undifferentiated oral pleasure toward the differentiated, mature state of adult sexuality. During each stage along this journey, an individual's sexuality (pursuit of pleasure) is reflected in prototypic patterns of adjustment.

Third, at each stage psychic energy is invested in a particular body region whose increased sensitivity produces an *erotogenic zone* (Freud, 1963, p. 275). This localized energy charges the zone with tension that must be discharged and thereby reduced. Tension reduction is experienced as pleasure. The erotic desire associated with a particular erotogenic zone is directly related to the psychodynamic needs required for each stage's critical period. Childhood forms of erotic pleasures associated with the erotogenic zones lay the psychological infrastructure for increasingly adultlike erotic pleasures.

Oral Stage (birth to approximately 1 year). The oral stage is a critical period for achieving the ability to "incorporate" external objects as part of oneself. Freud believed that incorporation was a developmental prerequisite for later being able to identify with the parents and psychologically incorporate their values as one's own. The infant's erotogenic zone is the mouth, so infantile sexuality is characterized by ingestion-related pleasures.

The infant's mouth, charged with psychic energy, seeks pleasure from stimulation, which may account for why infants suck instinctively even while sleeping. Such stimulation, however, is double edged; it introduces the infant to both pleasure and pain. Pleasure results from eating, biting, gumming, sucking, smiling, and noise making, all of which discharge sexual, pleasure-seeking tensions. While some activities result in satisfaction from hunger reduction, it should be noted that the activities themselves may also be experienced as pleasurable. The infant relates to objects in the world by *cathecting* them. At the same time, the mouth introduces the infant to pain when teething begins, or when certain objects are ingested (hot formula, medicine). Moreover, anxiety may be aroused when hunger pangs are not immediately satisfied, when weaning occurs, or when regular feeding rituals are interrupted, delayed, or altered.

While the mouth provides both pleasure and pain, the parents also come to represent a similar conflict. They are responsible for meeting the infant's biological needs, and in that capacity, they are cathected as pleasure-producing objects. However, with the infant's growing mobility, parents begin to exert increasing control over their child's insatiable desires. Consequently, they become associated with pain when they prevent satisfaction, as occurs when demand feeding is altered to a more regular schedule or when the nighttime bottle is withheld.

The emotion produced by delayed gratification and pain is *anxiety*, which occurs whenever the infant's pleasure is threatened. Throughout infancy, anxiety is experienced when sexual tensions mount and gratification is not forthcoming. Parents too, especially the mother, with her daily comings and goings, may provoke feelings of intense anxiety, a special area of infant psychodynamics extensively investigated by Bowlby (1958, 1969, 1973, 1980).

Important personality characteristics first appear during the oral stage. These may, under certain circumstances, lead to an *oral personality*. For example, the pain associated with teething can be unconsciously transformed into the pleasure-pain of early sadism associated with biting, and the psychodynamic precursors of rejection may be associated with the infant's spitting up of unpleasant foods. Psychoanalytic theory suggests that both active and passive babies may be establishing unconscious patterns of social interaction later associated with extraversion and introversion.

The conflicts between satisfaction and anxiety, pain and pleasure, incorporation and rejection all lead to the establishment of patterns for interacting with objects, termed *object relations* (Freud, 1963, p. 288). For example, too much oral satisfaction results in *fixation*, the cathexis of psychic energy to specific objects and a resulting inability to cathect new objects. Fixation may produce neurotic smoking, alcoholism, or obesity in adults. Too little oral satisfaction has its own consequences—a shy, overly dependent, jealous, anxious, or pessimistic personality preoccupied with obtaining oral pleasure. The pedagogical problem here is to ensure an "appropriate" balance between satisfaction and frustration—a mixture of both is needed for healthy mental development. Unfortunately, Freud provided little guidance for us about how to ensure such a balance.

Anal Stage (approximately 1 to 3 years). The critical period associated with the anal stage involves the acquisition of a sense of personal power and control. Psychic energy shifts from the mouth to the anus, making it the new center of erotogenic interest and making the bowels highly sensitive to stimulation. Sexual pleasure is associated with elimination of body wastes.

The urge to defecate creates tension. However, this tension produces a conflict when parents instigate toilet training because the infant must choose between (1) the pleasure of immediate elimination and pain of parental disappointment or (2) the pain of control and delayed elimination for the pleasure of parental pride and approval. The conflict is resolved by bringing involuntary urges under voluntary control and thereby forging a new psychic instrument, the ego.

To control elimination, the ego must channel the id's impulses and direct them toward ends that, on the one hand, are pleasurable, and on the other hand, accord well with the constraints of the external situation. If parents initiate toilet training in an easygoing, relaxed, and nonthreatening manner, the child should gradually master bowel control and experience the parental approval that follows the use of the socially desirable "potty." On the other hand, if toilet training is premature and demanding, the accompanying anxiety may create later symptoms such as fear of authority, paranoia, overdependence, and impulsive behavior.

In a larger sense, the conflict inherent in toilet training is prototypical of the many conflicts of power and control that occur between parents and child.

These conflicts center on children's growing independence and self-control and propel them to differentiate between self and external reality (Freud, 1908). Increased mastery over toilet habits, accompanied by enhanced self-control in manipulation, mobility, and delay of gratification, combine to establish a beginning sense of self-identity. By the end of the anal stage, the child knows that pure gratification must be controlled and that negative consequences occur when parental standards are violated.

A child may unconsciously adapt to parental authority by becoming irresponsible, sloppy, narcissistic, and overindulgent. Moreover, unusually frustrating experiences may produce an anal personality that tends to be excessively neat, clean, and stubborn and may distort reality by unconsciously making experience conform to neat, unambiguous categories.

Phallic Stage (approximately 3 to 6 years). The phallic stage is a critical period for the development of sexual identity and socially sanctioned sex roles. Sexual energy is invested in the genitals, making them the dominant erotogenic zone. Genital stimulation produces tension, along with the need for tension reduction and pleasure. Sexual energy, instinctively driven by unconscious, erotic desire, is channeled toward the opposite-sexed parent. At the same time social taboos prohibit such incestuous relations. The conflict between the unconscious desire to possess and social prohibitions that prevent it brings about profound changes in the child's personality.

By the beginning of the phallic stage, children generally have a good sense that their identity is different from others. This awareness sharpens and then exaggerates their feelings of love and hate for their parents. Moreover, the boy's emotions have differentiated from an initial global state into a complex of interrelated feelings termed the *Oedipal complex,* a name derived from the classic Greek tragedy *Oedipus Rex.*

Oedipus, son of the King of Thebes, spent his life unknowingly fulfilling a fateful prophesy. Upon his birth, an oracle predicted that Oedipus would murder his father and marry his mother. To thwart the oracle, his father abandoned him to die of exposure and starvation. However, Oedipus was found by strangers and raised unaware of his royal heritage. As a young man, he returned unwittingly to Thebes, slew the King (his father), freed the kingdom from a terrible mythical creature (the Theban Sphinx), and married the Queen (his mother). Only then did Oedipus learn of his fate; in remorse, he gouged out his eyes to wander blindly through the world. Thus, Freud's reference to the Oedipal theme again reflects the determinism of his thinking—a male is destined from birth to unconsciously want to kill his father and desire his mother.

In seeking the affection and warmth of their mothers, young males become increasingly aware of competition for this love from their fathers. In comparing his own power and size to that of the father, a boy is unconsciously compelled by feelings of frustration and inferiority to display aggression toward the father. In spite of cultural taboos, the child pursues his unconscious desires for the mother, thus forcing the Oedipal confrontation between son and father over who will receive the mother's affection.

A boy, in his love-hate relationship with his father, grows increasingly fearful of being punished for his erotic desire for the mother. This fear produces *castration anxiety*, a special unconscious fear that the father will cut off his penis, the primary zone of erotic pleasure. While the anxiety is unconscious, it is not without some foundation in the real world. Boys are often aware of the fact that they, but not females, have penises. It is the absence of a female penis that makes sense as a living example of castration.

Castration anxiety produces an important sequence of events in the child's personality development. Realizing the superior power of the father, the young male's ego designs a compromise strategy for usurping the power of the father through *identification* with his values, attitudes, behaviors, and habits, and thereby incorporating the father's traits into his own personality. Identification thus serves the purposes of both the ego and the id; the ego reduces anxiety by repressing desire for the mother, while the id obtains vicarious satisfaction as the child acquires his father's traits.

Identification with the father requires part of the ego to become transformed into a new psychic organ, the superego, capable of representing the cultural values and expectations incorporated from the father. By identifying with the father, the child becomes truly socialized, since for the first time the masculine sex role, with its accompanying prohibitions and prescriptions, is taken on as part of his own personality.

Freud described a comparable complex in young girls to which the term "Electra" has often been applied. He did not write extensively about it, but what he did set forth indicates that it is a time of considerable conflict in females. At the beginning of the phallic stage, girls have also begun to realize that there are anatomical differences between males and females. In short, they realize that their clitoris is not as large as the male penis, which they associate with power and strength, primarily because their fathers have one and are seen as possessing those attributes. The lack of a penis generates unconscious feelings of inferiority, which Freud termed *penis envy*. These feelings intensify desire for the father and rejection of the mother, who is unconsciously held responsible for depriving the young girl of a penis. When the girl eventually realizes that she will never obtain a penis, her erotic desire for the father is channeled into identification with her mother, who is the primary recipient of the father's attention. By identifying with the mother, the young girl transforms part of her ego into a superego, which in turn brings on genuine socialization and sex role learning.

While the Oedipal and Electra complexes are functionally similar, there is a fundamental difference between boys and girls. In boys, castration anxiety motivates identification with the father and thus the end of the Oedipus complex. With girls, the unconscious belief that castration has already occurred is an important factor in the cause of her conflict.

In recent decades serious objections have been raised about the underlying "sexist" implications of Freud's interpretation of the Oedipal and Electra complexes. Whereas the young male is depicted as fundamentally concerned with erotic pleasure obtained from penile manipulation, the young female is depicted as being preoccupied with the inferiority of her genitalia. Traditional Freudians, for example, believe that girls experience less fear than boys because their lack of a penis precludes castration anxiety and consequently generates less repression. Less repression results in a weaker identification with the mother than the boy experiences with the father. Ultimately this weaker identification in girls is believed to fashion a weaker superego and conscience in them than in boys. Other Freudians argue that the combination of a male dominant society, nurturant rather than aggressive female sex roles, and the absence of a penis makes the Electra complex much more complicated for girls than the Oedipal complex is for boys.

This brief account of the Oedipal and Electra complexes may lead the reader to the erroneous conclusion that young children have a fairly easy time sorting out the appropriate parent to identify with. Just the opposite is true. Freud believed that young children were to some degree biologically and psychologically bisexual:

> A boy has not merely an ambivalent attitude towards his father and an affectionate object-choice towards his mother, but at the same time he also behaves like a girl and displays an affectionate feminine attitude to his father and a corresponding jealousy and hostility towards his mother (Freud, 1923, p. 33).

These inherent bisexual urges mean that children always experience some degree of identification with both parents. The two identifications differ of course depending on such things as the personalities of the parents, the differential strength of masculine and feminine impulses in the child (due to both biological differences and differences in oral and anal experiences), the specific customs of one's culture, the severity of castration anxiety or penis envy, and the social patterns established in the first two stages.

The interplay between unconscious desires charged with psychic energy, the exaggerated dynamics of Oedipal and Electra complexes, and the beginning of genuine socialization with the onset of superego functioning makes the phallic stage an important critical period with lifelong consequences as the ultimate source of masculine and feminine personalities. Most children experience some degree of trauma and emotional difficulty during this stage. At best the resolution of unconscious conflicts represents successful compromises. The interactive patterns that originate in the love-hate relationship with parents influence all later relationships with others, which is why psychoanalysts often attempt to trace adult symptoms back to the conflicts and experiences of the phallic stage.

Latency Stage (approximately 5 or 6 years to puberty). The latency stage is a critical period for expanding relationships beyond the family but primarily with same-sexed peers. The sexual instincts, strongly repressed from the phallic stage conflicts, get channeled into learning a variety of social, athletic, and intellectual skills needed for healthy adult functioning. There is no specific erotogenic zone during this stage, hence its name "latency."

Freud identified but gave relatively little attention to this stage of development, largely because he believed this time was marked by sexual quiescence and dormancy (Freud, 1930). There is, however, some controversy over this claim. White (1960, p. 127), for example, believes that Freud ironically underestimates the importance of sex during the latency period. Moreover, he notes that anthropological research and child development research both show latency-aged children to be intensely interested in sexual matters. While minor disagreements among theorists are common, White's contention poses a major challenge to the Freudian interpretation of latency because it implies that sexual motives are developmentally continuous rather than temporarily interrupted as suggested by Freud.

Genital Stage (puberty to adulthood). The genital stage is a critical period for establishing patterns of mature heterosexual functioning. Sexuality is directed toward obtaining sexual pleasure with another person. Psychic energy is again invested in the genitals, making them the erotogenic zone for this stage.

The genital stage is characterized by intense psychic activity, a lust dynamism directed toward fulfilling mature sexual desires. The hormonal surge of puberty produces dramatic physical changes in the sex organs and equally dramatic modifications in psychic functioning. For example, the ego attempts to harness and channel these forces into heterosexual love, which Freud believed was the ultimate form of pleasure. At the same time, unconscious libidinal instincts also infuse romantic and sexual meaning into dreams, fantasies, and jokes. These meanings are also sought in an attractive partner, where "attractive" to Freudians implies someone who unconsciously reminds us of our parental love object. Partners may be unconsciously selected because they are dominant or shy, intellectual or weak minded, liberal or Puritan, all depending on the values, attitudes, identifications, and repressed memories acquired during childhood.

Bridge Principles

Levels of Consciousness

The realm of the id is the psychic *unconscious,* one of Freud's most important discoveries. Unconscious means much more than simple nonawareness. It means that we cannot know about or think about the id's contents or functioning under normal circumstances. Unconscious psychic energy motivates psychological and behavioral functioning throughout life. On the one hand, unconscious motives gain less influence over behavior because they are increasingly controlled by ego and superego. On the other hand, the unconscious continues to influence behavior throughout life because it gains more channels of expression through the ego's coping mechanisms.

The unconscious is "prelinguistic"; it contains no semantic associations, since it existed long before language was learned. The unconscious region also stores memories repressed by the ego.

The ego resides in the second level of consciousness, the *preconscious*, a region of the mind in direct contact with the immediate "here and now" of one's ongoing experiences. The preconscious stores images, memory traces, words, and symbols that represent both actual experience and unconscious desires. We are not normally aware of the contents of our preconscious, since these have been at least partly repressed, but preconscious content occasionally forces its way into our conscious life in the form of memories of the past, slips of the tongue, and dream symbols. The preconscious also contains the *dream censor*, a specific ego mechanism that channels unconscious sexual energy (the id) into socially acceptable but pleasurable dream processes, images, and symbols.

The functioning of the superego, building on the adaptive capacities of the ego, activates the third region of the mind, the *conscious*, which contains only a relatively small and ever-changing portion of an individual's mental life. It contains the immediate, constantly changing sensations, thoughts, and memories that occupy our awareness at any given moment. While id and ego influence the content of our consciousness, neither enters our conscious awareness. "Awareness" is an awareness of the mental conscious.

Consciousness is like that portion of an iceberg above the surface, with so much more material remaining below the surface of our awareness. Stafford-Clark (1965) suggests the analogy of a stage. If mental life is like a vast, dark arena, then consciousness is like the small area lit up by a spotlight. Preconscious material then would consist of the vague, hazy, diffuse images barely discernible at the edges of the spotlight. Portions of the arena, like the psychic unconscious, remain forever out of view beyond the reach of the spotlight. The unconscious, preconscious, and conscious regions of the mind interact with each other in a particular way. The preconscious contains words and symbols that are socialized representations of unconscious motives, wishes, and desires. In turn, the conscious contains moral imperatives and cultural prescriptions for behavior motivated by conscious material. The unconscious and preconscious are directly linked, as are the preconscious and conscious regions of the mind. However, the unconscious and conscious interact only through the mediational function of the preconscious. In short, we are always aware of conscious behavior—it is goal oriented and deliberate. We are seldom aware of preconscious behavior—it is unconsciously controlled but directed toward realizable goals. We cannot normally be aware of unconscious material.

Defense Mechanisms

Insatiable instinctual desires and constant threats from the external world arouse anxiety. The ego attempts to reduce anxiety by employing its problem-solving strategies. However, anxiety is sometimes so overpowering that the ego's strategies prove inadequate. In such cases, energy is channeled into automatic patterns that defend against the fear and threat of anxiety. These patterns are the *defense mechanisms*. The presense of defense mechanisms is associated with a weak ego, since a strong ego is able to adjust to external problems in spite of unconscious memories. Defense mechanisms can function intermittently, or they can become an ingrained part of the personality and operate virtually nonstop. Several of the most important defense mechanisms include the following.

Repression is the mental inhibition of memories and threatening thoughts that arouse frustration, guilt, or anxiety. By keeping such harmful thoughts buried in the unconscious, the ego protects us from experiencing anxiety. Thus, we may momentarily forget the name of a close acquaintance against whom we harbor resentment, or we might forget an appointment with someone we unconsciously fear may have bad news.

Regression is the re-emergence of early modes of mental functioning and is possible in psychoanalytic theory because primitive forms of mentation continue to exist side by side with more mature forms throughout our lives. If the anxiety of a current situation is too much for the ego, it may psychologically "return" to an earlier stage when problems were less complex and fewer controls were placed on problem-solving strategies. For example, some people may regress to telling childish nonsense jokes at a party, kicking the family dog for wetting the carpet, celebrating holidays by drinking too much, or attempting to re-create their own childhood experiences with their children.

Projection is the attribution to others of traits or motives that are unconsciously ingrained in the self. Thoughts and memories that evoke anxiety sometimes get attributed to others, in which case the self may see others as a threat. For example, a young woman may unconsciously desire her boyfriend's affectionate advances, but because her desire provokes fear, she projects the desire onto him, accusing him of being overly amorous. Projecting onto others one's own preoccupations may, in the extreme case, lead to paranoia—the belief that others are preoccupied with oneself.

Reaction formation occurs when the ego disguises an unacceptable impulse in the form of its psychological opposite, often in an exaggerated manner. An unconscious desire to engage in uninhibited sexual activities may lead to chaste or frigid sexual conduct. Jealousy at maternal attention paid to a newborn may prompt a husband to become overattentive and overprotective with the infant.

Displacement is the unconscious shifting of psychic energy from one object to another, particularly when it does not belong to the latter. It occurs most frequently in dreams and is the result of the ego's redirecting instinctual energy away from a threatening object toward one that is not threatening. For example, in Ted's dream (which appears as an exercise at the end of this chapter), his ego magically transforms him into a Mafia character to achieve revenge by shooting a co-worker who had cut off his fingers. Ted's ego felt too threatened to allow Ted to do the shooting himself, so it displaced Ted's aggression onto the Mafia figure.

Change Mechanism

Psychoanalysis posits two types of change mechanisms. First and foremost, the psychosexual stages are governed by maturation, which propels individuals through a series of prefabricated critical periods. Because maturation both produces and limits the development of the personality, it is the main developmental mechanism in Freud's theory and is the primary reason the theory is classified as an endogenous theory.

A second mechanism, psychosexual conflict, results from the conflicting demands between superego's rigidly conforming mandates and id's irrational impulses and erotic desires. Psychosexual conflict is *intra*psychic, and it results in the formation of defense mechanisms and patterns of adjustment found in one's personality—habits and other symptoms of psychopathology like compulsions, phobias, paranoia, schizophrenia, and Freudian slips.

EXPLAINING HUMAN DEVELOPMENT: THE RESEARCH

Psychoanalytic theory has yielded two distinct lines of research. The first consists of extremely rich single-subject case studies, some of which are included in Freud's original writings. Many other case studies can be found in the international journal *The Psychoanalytic Study of the Child*, which contains two recent examples. In one, Kennedy (1986) used psychoanalytic treatment to trace an adolescent's sadomasochistic masturbation fantasies back to a peculiar constellation of early childhood problems: unmet early needs, forced feeding, rigid toilet training, and penile infection followed by circumcision at age two. In another case study, Winestine (1985) found that inappropriate weeping in a pre-anorexic girl could be traced to a childhood event in which the girl accidently dropped and broke a glass in a fancy restaurant, an event that prompted the girl's discovery that she would never again be perfect. Since case studies function primarily to exemplify rather than test a theory, they will not be described here.

The second line of research consists of more direct tests of theoretical assertions on groups of individuals. Although psychoanalysis is one of the classical developmental theories, many more systematic studies could be found several decades ago than can be found today, so some of these may appear dated by today's standards. Attention is given here to studies that emphasize recurrent themes in the psychoanalytic literature.

Personality Types

The Oral Personality. The predominant mode of the oral stage is incorporation, a concept whose generality makes it difficult to verify empirically. However, Fisher and Greenberg (1985, p. 84) identify two characteristics of the oral stage that can be scientifically verified: onset (during the first year) and parenting style (resulting in either overgratifying or frustrating the child's oral needs). Additionally, Abraham (1927) extended Freud's analysis of the oral character and identified the following characteristics of the orally fixated individual: (1) unidimensional traits, such as ambivalence, openness, restlessness, and impatience, and (2) bipolar traits, such as concerns with giving-taking, dependence-independence, passivity-activity, optimism-pessimism, and being alone versus belonging to a group. The following clusters of personality traits have been found to exhibit the kinds of intercorrelations expected by psychoanalysis: passivity, dependence, pessimism, egocentricity, and rejection of others (Lazare, Klerman, & Armor, 1966); dependency, pessimism, avoidance of responsibility, demandingness, and envy (Gottheil & Stone, 1968); pessimism, rigidity, and biting (Barnes, 1952); pessimism, passivity, verbal aggression, and withdrawal (Goldman, 1948); pessimism, impatience, and aggression (Goldman-Eisler, 1951), pessimism, dependency, anxiety, passive hostility, exhibitionism, and impulsive acting out (Finney, 1961a, 1961b); and dependency, need for approval, deference, and conformity (Comrey, 1965, 1966). Because these researchers have employed diverse methodologies in their studies, the relative consistency of these findings indicates some level of support to the typology of an oral personality.

Evidence supporting the early experience determinants of the oral personality comes from studies by Goldman (1950–51) and Goldman-Eisler (1951), who interviewed 100 mothers to assess the effect of their breast-feeding and weaning patterns on their children. Those who had experienced early weaning tended to develop pessimistic traits, whereas those who breast fed until much later developed optimistic attitudes. In a study of 40 normal preschoolers, increasing levels of dependency were correlated with the severity of weaning (Sears, Whiting, Nowlis, & Sears, 1953). Finally, in a longitudinal study, Heinstein (1963) followed 94 individuals for 18 years and reported correlations between certain oral traits and type of feeding (breast versus bottle fed), warmth of mothering, and difficulty of weaning.

Other research addresses the question of whether or not oral characters tend to seek excessive oral gratifications. For example, some evidence suggests that obese individuals possess significantly more oral imagery (responses to Rorschach or Thematic Apperception tests) than normal individuals (Masling, Rabie, & Blondheim, 1967; McCully, Glucksman, & Hirsch, 1968; Weiss & Masling, 1970). Similarly, alcoholics possess more oral character traits than do nonalcoholics (Story, 1968), depressed individuals (Weiner, 1956), or psychiatric patients (Bertrand & Masling, 1969). Finally, some studies have identified intense oral motivations among smokers (Jacobs & Spilken, 1971; Jacobs, Knapp, Anderson, Karush, Meissner & Richman, 1965; Kimeldorf & Geiwitz, 1966; Veldman & Bown, 1969).

In summary, evidence suggests some support for the psychoanalytic construct of an oral personality: its association with early infancy, breast feeding, weaning and mothering styles, and later preoccupation with excessive forms of oral gratification. The diverse methodologies used to explore the oral personality are a source of both strength and weakness for the theory. They provide mutually corroborative external validation (see Chapter 2), but there is virtually no convincing evidence available about the validity of these measures or the extent to which they are correlated with one another (Fisher & Greenberg, 1985, p. 132).

The Anal Personality.   The evolution of an anal personality is similar to that of an oral personality, with two important differences. First, the anal personality is hypothesized to involve a different constellation of traits, and second, its evolution is to be traced to the anal rather than the oral stage. The following cluster of traits is believed to underlie the anal personality: neatness, orderly life style, excessive control, cleanliness, predictability, precision, trustworthiness, frugality, obstinacy, stubbornness, sadistic and masochistic tendencies, hostile and aggressive fantasies, and obsessive-compulsive habits (Freud, 1908, 1917). Anal character traits should originate in anal stage frustrations or disturbances (Freud, 1909).

Considerable research supports Freud's description of an anal typology. The following examples indicate even more pervasive patterns than those identified with the oral personality: perseverence, orderliness, and cleanliness (Brooks 1969); neatness, love of routine, meticulousness, and negative impulsivity (Comrey, 1965); orderliness, stinginess, stubbornness, and rigidity (Finney, 1961a); hypocrisy, attention to detail, hoarding, and anal sadism; and orderliness, obstinacy, rigidity, and rejection of others (Lazare, Klerman, & Armor, 1966).

The early determinants of the anal personality are claimed to lie in particularly frustrating experiences associated with toilet training. Although many studies have attempted to connect toilet training experiences with the later development of anal personality traits (see for example Beloff, 1957; Finney, 1963; Hetherington & Brackbill, 1963; Kline, 1969; Miller & Swanson, 1966; Sears, Rau, & Alpert, 1965), only modest support for a connection has been reported. At the same time, other evidence strongly suggests a connection between individuals' anal personalities and the existence of anal traits in their mothers (Beloff, 1957; Finney, 1963; Hetherington & Brackbill, 1963). While it is reasonable to suppose that anal-oriented mothers would tend to exercise rigid toilet training, it is also likely that these mothers provided a controlling environment throughout their children's youth and not only during the anal stage.

The Oedipal Complex

While Freud made a number of claims about the Oedipal complex, only two have been systematically investigated. First, prior to the Oedipal complex, both male and female children focus their energy primarily on the mother. Second, because girls have no penis to begin with, they should experience relatively greater penis envy and relatively lower castration anxiety than boys.

Focus on Mother.   Studies of pre-Oedipal development suggest that both male and female infants and toddlers prefer their mothers over fathers and others as objects of attachment, especially in situations that provoke anxiety, and this preference appears in American (Ainsworth, Bell, & Stayton, 1972; Bowlby, 1969, 1973), Scottish (Schaffer & Emerson, 1964), and Ugandan cultures (Ainsworth, 1967).

Castration Anxiety and Penis Envy.   One of the striking images in Freud's description of the Oedipal complex is that of the powerful, threatening father, who evokes penis envy in daughters and castration anxiety in sons. Fisher and Greenberg (1985, p. 193) have noted that castration anxiety is often equated with bodily injury and mutilation, and this manifestation has been the object of a number of investigations. For example, boys are more likely than girls to include themes of physical injury in their spontaneous speech (Gottschalk, Gleser, & Springer, 1963) and in stories they are requested to make up (Pitcher & Prelinger, 1963). College males are more likely than females to exhibit castration anxiety responses to projective tests (Blum, 1949; Schwartz, 1956). Finally, men more than women report dream content related to castration anxiety (Hall & Van de Castle, 1965).

Concerning penis envy, Freud theorized that unconscious disappointment accompanies young girls' discovery that they lack a penis. Consequently, he claimed that females live out their lives haunted by a negative body image that unconsciously motivates them to seek substitutes for the "loss" of this member. This controversial claim has not been supported by research. In an extensive research review, Fisher (1970, 1973) has concluded that women, if anything, are more comfortable with their own body images and experiences than are men. Moreover, women on the average exceed men in terms of self-awareness, personal security, and flexibility in adjusting to body sensations and appearance (Fisher & Greenberg, 1985).

Dreams

It is important to note that dream research has been handicapped by a particularly vexing problem: determining if the source of dream content is in fact unconscious (another of Freud's important claims). In spite of this problem, dreams are certainly one of the most intriguing of all psychological processes. In Freud's *Interpretation of Dreams*, two major theoretical claims are introduced. First, dream symbols represent both manifest and latent meaning; manifest meaning reflects a disguised "shell" of symbolic content that masks the true latent meaning. Second, dreams serve as a tension vent for the expression of repressed memories and unconscious desires.

Manifest and Latent Meaning. Because of the difficulty of measuring latent meaning, most investigations of dream content have been correlational. For example, when psychiatric interpretations are used, significant correlations between manifest and latent dream content have been reported for college students (McReynolds, Landes, & Acker, 1966) and psychiatric patients (Proctor & Briggs, 1964; Sheppard & Karon, 1964). Other correlations have been found between manifest dream content and projective test responses (Bolgar, 1954; Eiduson, 1959) and storytelling themes (Brender & Kramer, 1967; Cartwright, 1966; Foulkes, 1969). In a somewhat different vein, a number of research studies have reported correlations between manifest dream content and personality traits such as introversion (Rychlak & Brams, 1963), authoritarianism (Meer, 1955), hostility (Foulkes & Rechtschaffen, 1964), hypertension (Saul, Sheppard, Selby, Lhamon, Sachs, & Master, 1954), and dominance (Rychlak & Brams, 1963).

Tension Venting. Freud believed that dreams provide a venting outlet for unconscious impulses. As has been well documented, dreaming takes place at specific times in the sleep cycle and is accompanied by easily detectable rapid eye movements (REM). Psychoanalytic researchers have utilized the REM signal to interrupt sleep and thus deprive subjects of the opportunity to dream (Fisher & Greenberg, 1985, p. 47), which should preclude the venting of unconscious tensions and result in increased levels of disturbance, irritability, agitation, and anxiety. Not only have such predictions been confirmed (Dement, 1960; Dement & Fisher, 1963; Fisher, 1965a, 1965b), but some instances have been reported of subjects who responded with near psychotic, paranoid suspiciousness (Dement, 1960). Moreover, while sustained dream deprivation does not appear to affect simple cognitive functioning, it greatly increases the degree to which deprived feelings and wishes are produced in response to the Rorschach test (Greenberg, Pearlman, Fingar, Kantrowitz, & Kawliche, 1970). In a typical study of dream deprivation, Fiss, Klein, and Bokert (1966) awakened subjects from both REM and non-REM sleep and asked them to tell stories in response to thematic apperception pictures. Story analyses indicated that REM sleep deprivation resulted in more complex, bizarre, and emotionally vivid compositions than did non-REM sleep interruptions. The greater intensity of stories following dream interruption supports Freud's contention that dreams provide a special release function.

CONTRIBUTIONS AND CRITICISMS OF THE THEORY

Contributions

Focus on Infancy and Childhood. It is difficult to imagine that at the turn of the century there was virtually no interest in studying the development of infants and children. Freud's work focused attention on the importance of development during the early years. He attempted to show how an individual's personality had its roots in the maturation of psychosexual stages. By showing how the infant's primitive instincts gradually unfolded to produce socialization, Freud irreversibly altered the course of developmental psychology. He created widespread public interest in infancy and childhood and made psychology accountable for explaining the influence those years had on adult behavior.

Unconscious. One of Freud's most enduring contributions is his concept of the psychic *unconscious.* Today's widespread acceptance of the idea of an unconscious mind stands in stark contrast to its original frosty reception. Freud argued that unconscious drives and impulses underlie anthropological phenomena (1913), art (1914), religion (1927), literature (1928), sociology (1930), and interpersonal as well as international aggression (1933b). Over the past several decades, parents have become increasingly sensitive to their children's sibling rivalry, sexual curiosity, toilet training, and unrealistic fears in large part due to the powerful impact on child rearing Freud's concept of unconscious has had.

Defense Mechanisms. Freud's analysis of the ego's defense mechanisms represents another landmark discovery in our understanding of human nature. The role these mechanisms play in the psychopathologies of everyday life (e.g., sexual humor, Freudian slips, tip-of-the-tongue forgetting), as well as their etiology in the more extreme forms of pathological behavior, has gained widespread recognition. The conversational use of terms such as *repression, projection,* and *denial* reflects a recognition of these mechanisms at work in everyday social interactions.

Recovering an Individual's History. Like Freud, many educated people today believe that children's early experiences and family interactions establish lifelong habits and patterns of social interaction. Still, psychoanalysis is the only developmental theory whose methodology is specifically designed to recover the individual's memories of childhood experiences. Information garnered through free association and dream analysis is believed to reflect elements of early experiences that have been repressed by the ego. While questions can be raised about the validity of the technique and the accuracy of our memories, these methods represent original and important contributions for both theoretical and clinical applications.

Pedagogy. Freud denounced the overly harsh techniques utilized by his society in child rearing. In psychoanalysis, he painted a scene of childhood as one rife with conflicts and frustrations, emotional needs and desires, and wishes and fantasies. His insight fostered a new sensitivity to children's emotional needs. In large part because of Freud, contemporary parents and teachers are generally more sympathetic toward than critical of the frustrations children experience in such events as the birth of a sibling, toilet training, the Oedipal situation, parental divorce, sexual curiosity, and school learning.

Psychotherapy. The search for psychic cures to mental illness was one of the early influences on Freud's thinking. His solution to that problem was the development of a therapeutic technique he called psychoanalysis. Psychoanalytic therapy was the forerunner of contemporary psychotherapy, and it is the framework from which many variations have been spawned (see Chapter 12). In addition, Freud's approach to psychopathology established abnormal psychology as a legitimate subfield within psychology.

Criticisms

Freud (1933a) clearly believed that his theory was not subject to criticism unless the critic had first undergone psychoanalysis. Such a stance notwithstanding, the following problems with the theory have been identified.

Operationalizing Variables. Many of Freud's most significant theoretical constructs are extremely difficult to measure. For example, it is difficult to imagine how one might directly or even indirectly measure constructs such as unconscious, libido, id, or the various defense mechanisms. Most of the evidence described earlier in support of oral and anal personalities and the characteristics of the Oedipal conflict can be challenged on grounds that it is mostly circumstantial. Consider the problem of determining whether or not and to what extent repressed, unconscious memories motivate dream symbols and content. How does one meaningfully test such a cause-effect relationship? Moreover, how can one establish the prior case that memories have actually been repressed in the first place? The difficulty of establishing reliable and valid measures for psychoanalytic concepts is a major reason many judge Freud's theory to have little scientific merit (see, e. g., Schultz, 1975).

Phallocentrism. Some writers have criticized Freud's view of women, pointing to his ideas about their allegedly weak superego and penis envy. These views, argue the critics, reflect unexamined cultural stereotypes, social attitudes, and biases rather than a scientific appraisal of facts. Thompson (1950), for example, argues that while girls may envy boys, their envy reflects jealousy not of the penis, but of the male's privileged social status and relatively greater opportunity for freedom and success. Horney (1967) has further suggested that boys may suffer as much from womb envy as girls do from penis envy. *Phallocentrism* refers to Freud's emphasis on the male's penis and his belief in female "inferiority."

EVALUATION OF THE THEORY

Scientific Worthiness

Testability. Table 4-1 shows that psychoanalysis rates at the very bottom of the scale for its testability. Such a low rating derives almost exclusively from Freud's extreme mentalism and the techniques he uses to elicit data. Problems encountered in attempting to test some of Freud's most central concepts are pervasive, deep, and essentially unsolvable. One frequently encounters criticisms about the difficulty of trying to figure out what Freud means: he often resorted to analogies or metaphors to help communicate ideas that were fundamentally difficult and imprecise. What, for example, are the measurable properties of psychic energy?

Table 4-1   Ratings of Psychoanalysis for Scientific Worthiness

CRITERION	HIGH	MODERATE	LOW
Testability			X
External validity		X	
Predictive validity		X	
Internal consistency			X
Theoretical economy			X

A second difficulty arises in trying to formulate testable hypotheses; the theory sometimes predicts contradictory but equally likely phenomena. For example, frustrating events during the oral stage may lead to habits of conformity and pessimism *or* they may promote the opposite habits of exhibitionism and optimism. Since science presumes unique causes for specific effects, there seems to be something logically wrong in attempting to explain opposite effects in terms of the same underlying cause. Consider a second example. Freud explained natural sex play as one manifestation of libidinal energy, but the opposite behavior—Puritanical avoidance of sex—is also a manifestation of the same libidinal energy that this time has been channeled through the defense mechanism of reaction formation. The problem is that it is virtually impossible to test a theory that postulates the same underlying cause for diametrically opposed behaviors.

External Validity. I have judged psychoanalysis to have moderate external validity. On the one hand, Freud has captured the infant's oral predispositions (a phenomenon Piaget also noticed but explained differently), the ambivalent love-hate feelings toward parents, the importance of dreams, the form and function of defense mechanisms, and the role of the unconscious in motivating human activity. On the other hand, it is difficult to believe that latency-aged children suspend all curiosity about sexual matters (see White, 1960), that the complexities of human cognition can be accounted for solely by characteristics of primary process and secondary process thought, and that tensionlessness is the ideal state (since we often seem to seek certain degrees and forms of tension). Moreover, by emphasizing exaggerated forms of psychosexual adjustment, Freud may have greatly overestimated their importance during development.

Predictive Validity. The moderate rating theory for predictive validity derives from a balance of offsetting arguments. On the one hand, many psychologists have worked within the psychoanalytic framework to deduce important hypotheses and to construct new implications. For example, Carl Jung, an eminent student of Freud, derived extensive insight from psychoanalytic theory and extended it through his own analysis of symbolism (Jung, 1953), the psychic unconscious (Jung, 1921), and the psychic complexes (Jung, 1923). Anna Freud (1946) extended her father's work with her detailed analysis of defense mechanisms. René Spitz (1965) made extensive use of the theory in understanding the importance of mothering to the neonate's development. At the same time, many of these psychoanalytic "who's whos" have found it necessary to revise, improve on, or divorce themselves from some of Freud's specific contentions. In some cases, the severity of the schism called into serious question the predictive validity of Freud's ideas. One prominent example of just such a challenge can be found among the ego psychologists who broke from Freud over disagreements about the properties and development of the ego.

Internal Consistency. The theory's moderately low rating for internal consistency derives from concerns described earlier in the section on criticisms of the theory. It may be recalled that a major difficulty of psychoanalysis is its use of a single cause to produce logically incompatible effects. Such inconsistencies are not unusual in psychoanalytic theory; in fact they occur far too frequently to be occasional exceptions. The theory was not rated at the very bottom of the scale on this criterion because Freud is consistent in other important ways, as, for example, when he maintains that the role of the unconscious and the motivating energy of the libido underlie all behaviors.

Theoretical Economy.   I have given the theory a moderately low rating for theoretical economy. The rating reflects the extensive coverage Freud gives to explaining emotions, personality, character disorders, dreams, and the psychopathology of everyday life. However, the scope of his theory is tempered by the relatively large number of assumptions required to support its internal and bridge principles. Not only does Freud begin with more predisposing assumptions about the nature of the infant, but also these assumptions are considerably less orthodox than those made by many other theorists. The ratio of assumptions to explanatory power in the case of psychoanalysis is not impressive; hence the moderately low rating on this criterion.

Developmental Adequacy

The ratings summary for developmental adequacy is shown in Table 4-2. Psychoanalysis actually consists of two types of developmental explanations: the sequential system (maturation) and the structural system (psychosexual conflict). Consequently, separate evaluations are shown.

Temporality.   Psychoanalysis clearly posits a sequence of maturational stages that occur between birth and adulthood. Moreover, the ontogenesis of the personality structures are viewed as time- and experience-dependent. Thus, each of the two systems posits a temporal component to development.

Table 4-2   Ratings of Psychoanalysis for Characteristics of Development

CHARACTERISTIC	RATING	
	Sequential System	*Structural System*
Temporality	Pass	Pass
Cumulativity	Pass	Pass
Directionality	Pass	Pass
New mode of organization	Fail	Pass
Increased capacity for self-control	Fail	Pass

Cumulativity. "The child is psychologically the father of the man," wrote Freud in describing how adult personality is determined by maturation and early social encounters. Socialization entails increasingly adaptive habits as children encounter other youngsters, adults, and social expectations outside the family. Simultaneously, the ego evolves from the biologically prior id and the superego from the ego. Thus, both the stages and the personality structures represent new adaptations built on earlier ones.

Directionality. There is inherent directionality contained in the psychosexual stages—from id-centered autoeroticism toward mature, heterosexual adult functioning. Simultaneously, the evolution of the ego and superego promote increased socialization. In each case, *progress* is related to increasing psychological maturity and social adjustment.

New Mode of Organization. Freud's psychosexual stages are organized solely in terms of the predominant erotogenic zone, the libidinal energy that sensitizes it, the objects that provide pleasure, and the instinctual tensions that are the source of psychosexual conflict. While the contents of these organizational properties change from stage to stage, the overall organizational pattern does not. For example, development from the anal to the phallic stage is accompanied by the following changes in organizational content: the erotogenic zone shifts from the anus to the penis; the libido energizes a new erotogenic zone; the object of desire shifts from one's feces to one's opposite-sexed parent; and the instinctual tensions shift from conflict over expulsion-retention to the love-hate conflict over one's parents. While these content changes have occurred, the triune organizational *pattern* of instinctual desire, pursuit of pleasure and avoidance of pain, and psychosexual conflict *remain the same throughout each stage.* Because the stages are associated with changes in psychic content without corresponding changes in psychic organization, the theory fails this criterion.

At the same time, the development of the ego and superego each represents the addition of a fundamentally different type of personality organ. The id is organized according to the pleasure principle, the ego according to the reality principle, and the superego according to a conscience principle. These different organizing principles reflect the type of characteristic addressed by this criterion, so the structural system is judged as passing.

Increased Capacity for Self-control. The sequential system reflects a biological/maturational blueprint of changes over which the individual has no control. Furthermore, the instinctual desires that become prepotent with each successive stage exert powerful, hidden pressures that can only be controlled by the ego and superego, each elements of the structural system. For this criterion, the failing and passing marks in the respective columns reflect the discrepancy between the sequential and the structural systems' ability to account for increased capacity for self-control.

SUMMARY POINTS

1. Psychoanalytic theory represents an integration of two historically separate lines of inquiry: the search for brain structures and the search for psychic cures.

2. Freud defined sexuality as the pursuit of pleasure independent of biological needs. Psychosexual stages are biological critical periods for the development of personality. The stagewise development of personality occurs through the sequential localization of libido, which energizes bodily zones, thereby sensitizing them to stimulation.

3. The theory assumes that psychic energy is a biological instinct consisting of a fixed pool of energy that is irrational in nature, functions as the primary, efficient cause of mental and behavioral activity, and directs these activities in the pursuit of pleasure and tension reduction.

4. The clinical problem of psychoanalytic theory is to recover and understand important childhood experiences. The primary methods of investigation include free association, dream interpretation, and projective tests.

5. Psychoanalysis posits three internal principles: the dynamic system (consisting of nonperishable but transformable psychic energy), the sequential system (psychosexual stages), and the structural system (id, ego, and superego).

6. The bridge principles include levels of consciousness and defense mechanisms.

7. Psychoanalysis posits two mechanisms of change. Maturation produces changes in developmental stages, and psychosexual conflict produces changes in personality structures (id, ego, superego).

8. Enduring contributions of the theory include its concept of the psychic unconscious, delineation of the defense mechanisms, development of methods uniquely suited to recovering childhood memories, and pedagogical implications. Recurrent criticisms of psychoanalysis include the difficulty of measuring crucial variables and cultural biases reflected in Freud's "phallocentrism."

9. Overall, psychoanalysis was rated moderately low for its scientific worthiness. Freud's structural system does a more adequate job accounting for developmental adequacy than does his sequential system.

PROBLEMS AND EXERCISES

Class Exercises

1. Ted is 22 years old, the product of a large family (three brothers and two sisters). He describes his childhood as peaceful, fun, and very normal. His father "brought home the bacon," and his mother raised the kids. She also "wore the pants in the family" and was the major disciplinarian. Ted is living with Sue, a woman he describes as "warm, loving, giving, alive, and the *finest* woman I've ever known, and I've known quite a few." (Ted implies that Sue is especially good in bed.) One day Sue goes grocery shopping, leaving Ted only the chore of changing a faulty light switch. She returns nearly two hours later and discovers him just beginning to change the switch. In anger, she grabs the screwdriver from his hand, changes the switch in a matter of moments, then hands the screwdriver back to Ted saying sarcastically, "There, now at least that's finished!" That evening when Ted attempts to engage in sex, he is unable to achieve an erection. He's never experienced anything like that before and finally falls asleep a little concerned about his per-

formance. For ten days in a row Ted is impotent, in spite of a great deal of help from Sue. On the tenth night Ted has the following dream, which exerts therapeutic effects on his love life. The next morning, he is able to perform sexually as if his impotence had never occurred. Here is Ted's description of his dream.

At the end of work one day, this old woman and I started just talking. It was the first time we ever talked to each other. Anyway, it was time to go, and we walked out together and went over to her car. We were just talking, nothing serious. Well, she went and opened her car door, got in, and rolled down the window, so we could continue talking to each other. Anyway, I put my hands on the top of the car door to lean against it sort of. Next thing I knew, and it all happened in slow motion, she reached out and slammed the door shut. It was like I was watching the whole thing and not really a part of it. Somehow, I changed from my normal self into a classical Mafia type—the hat, the gun, the suit, the sneer, the whole bit. Well, I looked down and all my fingers had been cut off by the car door. They were just spurting blood. I've never, ever dreamt about even hurting anyone before, but I watched from outside myself as I reached in my vest, pulled out a gun, aimed it through the window, and emptied it into her, shot after shot after shot. I don't remember her moving or anything. Then I woke up pretty scared about the dream; it was a real shocker.

Given Ted's dream, his upbringing, and the precipitating event, analyze his dream for its manifest content and latent meaning.

2. Alan is a 29-year-old whose background is about as normal and all-American as one could find. He was very proud of his father, who was a decorated hero in World War II. Alan viewed his father as an extremely moral man, one who would stand up for his beliefs. He remembers always wanting his father to be proud of him. When the Vietnam war came along, Alan applied for and was granted Conscientious Objector status, thus exempting him from military service. His father was devastated, disowned Alan, and refused to see, write, or talk to him for nearly six years.

   Alan and his best friend, Wesley, have over the past few years become very good friends (nothing homosexual here, each is going steady with a longstanding girlfriend). Lately, however, both men seem to be becoming increasingly macho in their friendly competitions with each other. Each is engaged in trying to "one-up" or "outdo" the other, and these antics are becoming increasingly antagonistic. Alan and Wesley recognize that their friendship is reaching a crisis, and they discuss their motives. That night, following this discussion, Alan has the following dream.

A powerful group of whites were coming to take over the island. They knew they'd have to deal with Wesley; he was chief of the native black tribe. That's really weird, why I'd make him black in my dream; he's really white. Well, anyway, Wesley made a bargain with them that he'd lead the tribe in putting all the tourist whites on the island to a test of personal goodness. As part of the bargain, any tourist white who passed the test was to be released and allowed to stay on the island. The powerful whites agreed because they didn't think anyone would pass the test. Well, I remember all the tourist whites had been rounded up and thrown, one by one, into a pit of poisonous snakes. If the person were really a good, moral person, the snakes weren't supposed to bite. Well, Wesley knew I was the only remaining white on the island, but he had made a bargain, so he continued to hunt me anyway. The tribe finally caught me and took me to the pit. I remember Wesley telling me to just project my personal goodness and nothing would happen. I was really scared and let out a huge scream when they threw me into the pit. When I landed, I looked up and was surrounded by snakes. But they didn't seem to mind me; they weren't biting. After a while, I got to my feet and looked up at Wesley, who was standing on the edge of the pit smiling down at me. Anyway, then it was over, and Wesley reached down to pull me out of the pit. Just as our hands met, all the snakes leaped out at him, biting his arm and pulling him down into the pit to kill him.

Considering Alan's background and the precipitating events, analyze his dream for manifest content and latent meaning.

Individual Exercises

1. Most people (both children and adults) are unable to remember any events that occurred before their second or third birthday. This widely recognized phenomenon is called *infantile amnesia*. How would Freud explain this phenomenon?
2. Keep a note pad and pencil next to your bed. Each night for two weeks, keep a record of your dreams, and the following morning record any important events that happened the previous day that could have precipitated the dream. Write as much detail as you can. If pencil and paper is too slow for you, talk into a tape recorder. Analyze several of your own dreams for manifest content and latent meaning. Several weeks later return and reanalyze the same dreams.
3. Keep notes for two weeks of the occasions when you experience a Freudian slip or tip-of-the-tongue forgetting. Try to analyze each of these in terms of unconscious motivations.

SUGGESTED READINGS

More about the Theory

Freud, S. (1900). *The interpretation of dreams.* Vols. 4 and 5. In J. Strachey (Ed. and Trans.), *The standard edition of the complete psychological works of Sigmund Freud.* 24 vols. London: Hogarth Press, 1953–66.
——— (1935). *A general introduction to psychoanalysis.* New York: Simon & Schuster.
——— (1962). *The ego and the id.* New York: Norton.
Hall, C. S. (1954). *A primer of Freudian psychology.* New York: World.
Rappaport, D. *The structure of psychoanalytic theory: A systematizing attempt. Psychological Issues,* Monograph 6. New York: International Universities Press.

Reviews of Research

Fisher, S., & Greenberg, R. P. (1985). *The scientific credibility of Freud's theories and therapy.* New York: Columbia University Press.
Kline, P. (1972). *Fiction and fantasy in Freudian theory.* London: Methuen.

Critical Reviews

Eysenck, H. J. (1952). The effects of psychotherapy: An evaluation. *Journal of Consulting Pscyhiatry, 16*, 319–324.

Hook, S. (Ed.). (1959). *Psychoanalysis, scientific method, and philosophy.* New York: New York University Press.

Chapter 5

Erikson's Psychosocial Theory

Preview Questions

What is the most basic disagreement between Erikson and Freud? What implications arise from this disagreement for Erikson's analysis of ego development?

What assumptions underly Erikson's theory of psychosocial development?

What major problem(s) does the theory address?

What is the method of *psychohistory*?

What is the *epigenetic principle*, and how does it work?

What stages does Erikson propose to explain development, and what important conflicts are associated with each stage?

How does Erikson's view of the social environment differ from Freud's?

What change mechanism accounts for development?

What are the important contributions and criticisms of Erikson's theory?

How does psychosocial theory rate on criteria of scientific worthiness and developmental adequacy?

HISTORICAL SKETCH

Erik Homburger Erikson was born in Frankfurt, Germany, in 1902. Following Erikson's birth, his mother married Dr. Homburger, a Frankfurt physician, and together the Hombergers kept from Erikson throughout all of his childhood the secret that his real father had abandoned him (Erikson, 1972, p. 15). Ironically, Erikson, like Freud, suffered from his Jewish ancestry. While his mother and stepfather were both Jewish, young Erik was typically Danish in appearance—tall, blond, and blue-eyed—which led to his being called "the goy" (non-Jew) by his Jewish classmates and "the Jew" by his Gentile classmates (Erikson, 1972, p. 16).

After high school Erikson skipped college and began to wander about Europe in search of purpose and meaning for his art (Coles, 1970, p. 15). Dissatisfied with vagabonding but possessing a wealth of travel experience, Erikson found a job teaching children in an American school in Vienna. While there, he met Anna Freud; under her influence, he began to study psychoanalytic theory and even underwent psychoanalysis by her. That experience added meaning and understanding to his childhood experiences and adolescent wanderlust. Consequently, Erikson enrolled in the Vienna Psychoanalytic Institute where he was taught firsthand by Sigmund Freud. He graduated in 1933, the year Hitler rose to power in Germany.

Erikson makes a particular point about this time in his life. He was profoundly struck by the fact that psychoanalytic theory (1) had turned *inward* to open up the unconscious world to systematic study, (2) had searched *backward* to find the origin of mental disease, and (3) had pushed *downward* into the instinctual energies humans thought they had overcome. However, he believed that what was needed was a vision of humanity that led *outward* from the self to mutuality, love, and communality; that moved *forward* from the enslaving elements of the past toward the liberating anticipation of new potentialities; and that looked *upward* from the unconscious impulses to contemplation of the mystery of consciousness (Erikson, 1972, p. 13). This thread of reasoning is one of the guiding principles that undergirds Erikson's later work.

Fearing the Nazi Anschluss, Erikson moved to Boston in 1933. He became that city's first child analyst and enrolled in Harvard's graduate psychology program, which he failed to complete (Brenman-Gibson, 1984, p. 60). He became a U.S. citizen in 1939, the year Hitler invaded Poland.

After three years in Boston, Erikson took up a prestigious position at Yale for two years before moving to an Indian reservation in South Dakota, where he experienced the Sioux culture firsthand. He later joined the faculty at the University of California at Berkeley, where he resumed his psychoanalytic practice and participated in a longitudinal study of normal children in the San Francisco Bay area. He also collaborated with such eminent anthropologists as Gregory Bateson, Alfred Kroeber, and Margaret Mead, who influenced Erikson to view children's socialization in the context of the dominant values and interpersonal practices of their culture.

During the McCarthy era, Erikson's own moral principles brought him into direct conflict with his employer, the University of California, when it suddenly demanded a loyalty oath of its faculty. Erikson refused to sign, was fired before his first year was up, but was eventually reinstated because he was deemed politically dependable. However, he resigned from the position because other politically suspect faculty who had not signed the loyalty oath were not similarly reinstated (Erikson, 1972, p. 20). Upon returning to Massachusetts, Erikson set up a clinical practice that afforded him the opportunity to write. His most important works were published in the next two decades. These writings made Erikson increasingly popular among psychologists, and in 1960 he was offered a professorship at Harvard University, where today he is Professor Emeritus. In 1984, *Harvard*

Magazine published an interview with Erikson in which, at the age of 82, he provided an important retrospective on his life, his work, and the importance of the nonviolent ethics of survival preached by Gandhi (Brenman-Gibson, 1984).

Erikson has never attempted to separate himself or his work from Freud. While some of Freud's students later split over profound theoretical disagreements, Erikson clearly locates his work in the mainstream of Freudian psychology. His theory, like Freud's, was born in clinical practice. Like Freud, he posits a series of maturational stages. However, where Freud's stages emphasized the sequential localization of psychic energy, Erikson's capture development in terms of a sequence of unique crises that occur between the individual and society.

Erikson's psychosocial theory is an example of an attempt to extend psychoanalytic theory rather than modify it, but it does differ from Freud's in several important respects. First, the ego's struggle for identity is emphasized over the id's influence on personality. Second, the healthy, adaptive mechanisms of ego functioning are given priority over the formation of psychopathological symptoms. Third, his theory casts development across the entire life span rather than concentrating on childhood and adolescence. Erikson's theory has gained widespread attention in recent years, in part due to a surge of interest in life-span developmental psychology.

STRUCTURAL COMPONENTS

Erikson embraces important Freudian concepts: the structural and sequential systems, maturational stages, and unconscious motivation. Still, there are important differences between the two.

Assumptions

Erikson's most important assumption concerns the autonomous source of the ego. Where Freud posited only the id's existence at birth, with the ego deriving from the id's structure and energy, Erikson assumes that the ego already exists as a functioning organ at birth. This assumption has several important implications. First, since the ego exists independently, there is no need to assume it derives its energy from the id. Second, since the ego does not depend on the id's energy, there is no need to posit intrapsychic conflict. Third, and most important, because there is no antagonism between id and ego, Erikson believes the ego is "conflict-free." This is not to say that individuals experience no conflict. Rather, conflict arises between the individual and society, not, as Freud had maintained, between the antagonistic internal forces of id and superego. In this respect, Erikson's theory postulates an ego free of internal conflict, but susceptible in its development to psycho*social* rather than psycho*sexual* conflict.

As mentioned earlier, Freud viewed the ego as an organ of the personality that becomes differentiated through experience from the original id. In contrast, Erikson believes that the ego is the primary organizer of personality and that it functions independently and autonomously at birth. For this reason, Erikson views infancy as far more complex than Freud had. Where Freud's infant is unconsciously driven toward pleasure, Erikson's is driven to establish interpersonal, and therefore adaptive, relationships. Unlike Freud, Erikson emphasizes the interpersonal nature of early development because these more directly reflect the cultural context of social interactions than do Freud's psychosexual drives.

Problems for Study

The overarching problem Erikson sets for himself is to explain how one's ego identity functions within the totality of the personality and how it evolves throughout the life span.

Phenomena to Be Explained

Erikson (1980, p. 17) argues that psychoanalysis has not provided a sufficiently specific theory of the development of the ego. In addition, he believed that Freud had underestimated the role of an individual's social environment. To correct these serious errors, Erikson offers a far more extensive and specific version of ego development within the context of culture and history. In short, the focus of psychosocial theory is to understand the relationship between ego and society (Erikson, 1963, p. 16).

Both the ego and the cultural environment are in constant flux. Erikson views the dynamic nature of this flux as a series of crises that individuals must resolve as their advancing life cycle propels them from one kind of social role to another. In this context, psychosocial theory attempts to explain how individuals resolve basic tensions between themselves and society. Implied here is the need to understand (1) the relationship between psychosocial crises and the formation of personal identity, (2) how resolution of earlier psychosocial crises prepares individuals for later crises, and (3) how a sense of personal identity maintains an enduring stability while changing and evolving throughout the life span.

Methods of Study

In the study of identity formation, it is difficult to separate personal growth from social change (a point Erikson tried to make in *Young Man Luther*). It is equally difficult to separate an individual's identity crises from social crises that occur in a historical moment (Erkison, 1968, p. 23).

In addition to his psychoanalytic training, Erikson has been strongly influenced by anthropology. To study the dynamic processes of ego development, he employs naturalistic observations of infants, children, adolescents, and adults in different cultures. The observational method is particularly important as a means of gathering data about cultural child-rearing practices.

A second method called *psychohistory* is a novel analytical technique that involves a synthetic application of psychology, anthropology, history, and sociology. Psychohistory consists of analyzing people's psychological development in terms of their writings, public statements, and their activities. Psychohistory is an alternative to methods used by classical psychoanalysis for analyzing a person's history. Erikson uses psychohistory to show the ego's resilience to hardship and crisis. To demonstrate that point, Erikson has written several psychohistories of important figures who experienced and overcame great adversity. Among his published works are psychohistories of Martin Luther, Maxim Gorky, George Bernard Shaw, and William James. His most famous psychohistory, Mohandas Gandhi, resulted in a Pulitzer Prize and a National Book Award.

Internal Principles

The Ego

Erikson's concept of ego derives from Freud with some important differences. One difference is that Erikson posits a conflict-free ego, which functions autonomously from the id at birth. A second difference is that he sees ego as more differentiated and more influential in its intrapsychic functions than Freud had. Third, Erikson believes ego evolves continuously throughout the life cycle.

For Erikson, ego is the capacity to unify one's experience in an adaptive manner (1963, p. 15); like Freud, he positions ego between the id and superego (1963, p. 193). Its function is to balance the extreme demands of id and superego and thereby direct the individual's action by constantly testing reality, selecting memories, and orienting attention to the historical zeitgeist. To achieve its purposes, ego may employ defense mechanisms.

The ego encounters the reality of physical objects, other individuals, and a historical moment. Such encounters are extremely complex in a threefold sense. First, everything is new; the same situation is never encountered a second time. Second, the individual is never the same individual, since earlier encounters bring about ego adaptations to circumstances that can never be undone. Third, different capacities are sensitive to different opportunities (Erikson, 1980).

The Epigenetic Principle

Erikson explains ego development in terms of the *epigenetic principle,* a belief that holds that development unfolds according to a genetically programmed plan of increasing differentiation and specialization. Accordingly, ego development is predetermined in the individual's programmed readiness "to be driven toward, to be aware of, and to interact with a widening radius of significant individuals and institutions" (Erikson, 1968, p. 93). Erikson's version of the epigenetic principle implies that the development of each person is the product of innate laws that determine a fixed sequence of psychosocial stages comprised of predictable crises between the individual and significant social figures. Like Freud's stages, Erikson's crises represent critical periods in the ego's development. However, individuals interact with other people and social institutions, and these interactions produce superficial differences in patterns of adjustment from one culture to another. Nevertheless, Erikson contends that superficial cultural differences do not mask far more important biological laws, which fix a sequence of crises between the individual and significant others within the culture to which the ego must adapt.

Psychosocial Conflict

Erikson (1980) places far more emphasis on the role of society and cultural organization than Freud. He also believes that Freud tended to define the ego too much in terms of its "better-known opposites," the biological id and the societal superego, whose opposition produced the *intra*personal conflict Freud termed psychosexual. While Freud understood the role of parental and societal contacts as immediate sources of superego, he failed to understand the pervasive role culture plays in the larger sense of personality development.

Psychosocial conflict is the mitigating but not the originating factor in each of Erikson's developmental stages. This kind of conflict occurs when the individual's ego interests and society's interests oppose each other, as, for example, when (1) a young girl tries to help set the table only to be scolded by her mother for breaking a glass, (2) a married father cleans the entire house but is scolded because he forgot to scour the sinks and clean under the sofa, or (3) grandparents take their grandchildren on an outing and are chastized for forgetting to provide suitable snacks and nap times. The two essential ingredients in psychosocial conflict are an individual and an external source of opposition.

Psychosocial conflict is endemic to living and the developmental process. It manifests itself in various ways, including in the predominant crises that define Erikson's eight stages. Psychosocial conflict together with the epigenetic principle and Erikson's notion of ego identity make up the set of core theoretical concepts used to explain development across the life cycle.

Bridge Principles

As noted earlier, Erikson accepts many of the tenets of psychoanalysis, including the basic outline of psychosexual stages, levels of consciousness, and defense mechanisms, which together comprise the bridge principles of that theory. However, the bridge principle unique to his own theory consists of a sequence of eight psychosocial stages.

The Psychosocial Stages

Erikson accepted Freud's account of psychosexual stages as accounts of personality development between infancy and adulthood, but he also believed that Freud had been insensitive to historical and cultural variations in children's socialization experiences. Consequently, his extension of psychoanalytic theory concentrates on the social and historical context of development across the life span. To do this, Erikson reconceptualized developmental stages as a series of psychosocial crises or tensions between the individual and society.

Erikson characterizes each crisis in terms of interactions with significant other persons and the predominant psychosocial activities that occupy the individual's attention. He often presented a summary of his insights in the form of worksheets. Table 5-1 shows a summary of important elements in psychosocial stages.

Trust versus Mistrust. Erikson's first stage parallels Freud's oral stage. Erikson, however, concentrates on the need for continuous care, attention, and protection for infants to achieve the peaceful satisfaction and security that their basic needs will be met. Herein lies the crisis between a sense of basic trust, being able to predict that one's needs will be satisfied, and basic mistrust, the fear that one cannot count on others for care or affection. The infant's rudimentary sense of self derives most readily from the mother's consistency in responding predictably to her infant (Erikson, 1963, p. 247). Consequently, mother is the most important social agent at this time, since she is seen as the source of comfort, nurturance, and security. The amount of food, attention, or mothering is not crucial; what counts is the quality of the infant-mother relationship, which ideally should combine reliability and trustworthiness with loving attention to the baby's needs within the framework of their culture's life style (Erikson, 1963, p. 249).

The infant-mother relationship provides the child with its fundamental orientation toward the consistency and dependability of the world; Erikson

Table 5-1   Worksheet of Psychosocial Development

STAGE	CRISIS	RADIUS OF SIGNIFICANT OTHERS	PSYCHOSOCIAL MODALITIES	VIRTUES	APPROXIMATE AGES
I	Trust versus mistrust	Maternal person	To get To give	Hope	0–1
II	Autonomy versus shame and doubt	Parental persons	To hold on To let go	Will	2–3
III	Initiative versus guilt	Basic family	To make To "make like"	Purpose	3–6
IV	Industry versus inferiority	Neighborhood and school	To make things To make together	Competence	7–12
V	Identity versus identity diffusion	Peer groups and outgroups; leadership models	To be oneself To share being oneself	Fidelity	12–18
VI	Intimacy versus isolation	Partners in friendship, sex, cooperation	To lose and find oneself in another	Love	the 20s
VII	Generativity versus stagnation	Divided labor; shared household	To make be To take care of	Care	20s–50s
VIII	Integrity versus despair	Humanity; belonging	To be, through having been To face not being	Wisdom	50s and beyond

Source: Adapted from *Identity and the Life Cycle* by Erik H. Erikson, by permission of W. W. Norton & Company, Inc. Copyright © 1980 by W. W. Norton & Company, Inc. Copyright © 1959 by International Universities Press, Inc.

believes healthy development is a product of a balance between trust and mistrust that emanates from social relationships that are neither too indulgent nor too harsh. The world and its people often act in a predictable fashion, but one may acquire a sense of misgiving if events are not consistently predictable. Some mothers, for example, may unconsciously frustrate their infants' needs (e.g., tardy with feedings, cries for comfort, emotional longings) and inadvertently produce adults who are largely skeptical about interpersonal relationships and mistrustful others. Overindulging an infant, however, may produce a gullible individual. Children who are unable to resolve the crisis between trust and mistrust may forfeit some progress in later personality development because the foundation for later resolutions is predicated on successful resolutions of earlier crises. At the same time, even if a child has achieved a good sense of trust, it may be somewhat undermined later by consistent experiences with people who are untrustworthy.

Autonomy versus Shame and Doubt. Erikson's second stage parallels Freud's anal stage, and both men stress the consequences of the infant's developing digestive system, the growing control over muscles, and, in particular, the increase of self-awareness over expelling bodily wastes. Children experience a sense of power and pride with growing control over bowel and bladder elimination. Erikson views this experience as a double-edged struggle between achieving a sense of autonomy or ending up feeling shame and doubt about oneself. Children who successfully cope with potty training will experience a sense of power that fuels their maturing autonomy and sense of self-esteem; they learn they are able to do certain things for themselves. On the other hand, children who are continually frustrated in their potty training experiences, who receive scoldings or ridicule for their failures, may end up feeling shameful and doubting their own abilities. Some balance between cooperation and competition, and between self-expression and self-control, is necessary for a lasting sense of goodwill and pride (Erikson, 1963, p. 254).

The child in Erikson's second stage faces the possibility of failure on two fronts if potty training is too rigid or initiated too early. In such a case, the unfortunate child is maturationally unable to control his own bowels and by implication is also unable to control his parents. Children require a sensitive blend of parental consistency that firmly establishes the limits of acceptable behavior and parental flexibility that sets limits commensurate with children's own abilities.

In addition to toilet training, other important forces are at work. Children become aware that they can affect other people in their social world, and they discover how much control they have over their own and others' behavior. They can control their parents' delivery of approval and praise by performing well. They lose that control and risk shame when their performance is not up to parental expectations. Children who are given many opportunities to test the limits of their power and opportunities to succeed as well as fail without retribution will develop a strong sense of personal autonomy. However, children who are overprotected or given inadequate opportunities to test their own limits of competence will end up with a sense of doubt about their ability to cope with their world.

Initiative versus Guilt. Erikson's third stage depicts the crises that arise as children encounter an expanding world of maturing abilities and social agents. Children in this stage struggle to achieve independence from their parents and thereby attain competence in the commerce of adultlike social transactions. Their interpersonal skills take shape as they try to master various adult behaviors, and their physical skills mushroom in ways determined appropriate by the culture. These changes are similar to those Freud describes as outcomes of the Oedipal conflict, when superego development prompts children into learning society's sex roles and propels them to master a variety of adultlike social crises.

Children's guilt arises from the *difference between* the level of competence needed to perform certain tasks and their self-perceived abilities. Preserving children's initiative is important at this time because it motivates them to participate actively in the social world around them. A sense of initiative prompts children to try new things, engage social companions, and master new skills. Given support for such efforts, they will develop a sense of personal prowess and initiative. At the other end of the continuum, children whose efforts have been frustrated or whose initiative has been punished for transgressing established limits will experience guilt. While Erikson (1963) believes that the timing of this crisis is maturationally fixed by the epigenetic plan, he also believes that a successful resolution is more a matter of social forces than internal determinants.

Industry versus Inferiority. Erikson's fourth stage parallels Freud's latency period. During this time children learn to pursue social and intellectual activities favored by society—establishing peer groups, attending school, exercising independence in play and learning. Make-believe and use of imagination constitute important milestones of childhood, but excessive use of these channels may be frustrating for the child who wants to accomplish something worthwhile and thereby gain satisfaction and earn adult recognition.

Because the crisis at this age requires the child to learn cooperation, it is socially the most decisive stage. It marks the origin of the work ethic, wherein a sense of what is valued by society is inculcated in children.

Parents, teachers, and other adults who offer tasks deemed worthwhile foster a sense of industry. However, earlier failures or assignment of tasks that impose greater requirements than the child has mastered tend to produce a sense of failure and inferiority. Children's feelings of inferiority due to their social heritage (e.g., racial, class, or sexual differences) may be spawned if consistently linked to differential performance on tasks deemed desirable by them.

Identity versus Identity Diffusion. One of Erikson's most important discoveries was the adolescent *identity crisis,* which has been the focus of considerable research attention. With the onset of puberty, the body undergoes complex biological/hormonal changes, which produce in the adolescent a new sense of self-awareness. Adolescents gain a fresh awareness of themselves as individuals, as sexual mates, as potential workers and parents, and as new persons occupying what used to be a child's body. New attractions toward the opposite sex awaken, and a search for ideas and people who are trustworthy begins. New expectations for the self are adopted, and these self-images tend at first to be very flexible, often changing with the time, place, and situation. The cognitive confusion that accompanies these changes Erikson termed the *identity crisis.*

Ego development has up to this point prepared the adolescent for the burden of self-identity. That is, earlier resolutions of psychosocial crises prepare and refine the child's psychological architecture for the heavy burden of establishing a sense of personal identity. The adolescent's identity will ultimately reflect the earlier achievements (or nonachievements) of trust, autonomy, initiative, and industry. The earlier resolutions promote an appreciation of continuity and the ability to develop *into the future.*

The adolescent psychosocial crisis reflects the opposition between the need to determine a self-identity and the profusion of possible social identities supported by the culture (Erikson, 1963). Youth in industrialized cultures perceive a multiplicity of role models; youth in other cultures experience relatively fewer adult models. As a possible defense against identity diffusion, Thomas (1985, p. 242) suggests that adolescents may be overly ardent in their identification with superheroes, cliques, crowds, and causes, each of which can be a focus of personal devotion that requires commitment without conviction. Consolidation of personal commitment may also be reflected in identification with fashions, fads, and fancies of the adolescent zeitgeist. Parents of adolescents know well the sublime irony of that age; teenagers often plead that adults are intolerant and rigid while they themselves proclaim intolerance for those who do not countenance their own stereotyped ideals, rock idols, and ideological proclivities.

Adolescents often attempt to resolve their identity crisis by experimenting with different roles, values, and relationships. Those who achieve a sense of personal identity come through the crisis with a sense of self-worth that reflects their self-determined value to society. Those who fail this crisis may continue throughout adulthood to be intolerant and immature in their treatment of and attitudes toward others who are different.

Intimacy and Solidarity versus Isolation. Unlike Freud, Erikson viewed adulthood as a time of change and transition that gives rise to new opportunities for close interpersonal relationships. The adult with a secure sense of personal identity faces the new task of establishing a close, loving, sexually satisfying, give-and-take relationship with another of the opposite sex. Erikson views the ideal relationship as a satisfying marriage, although he acknowledges that intimacy can also be established outside of marriage. Intimate relationships require one to make a meaningful commitment to another, to invest one's beliefs, feelings, and values in a trustworthy recipient. Such a commitment is possible only for identity achievers, since a secure sense of "self" is prerequisite to being able to commit oneself to another self. Only through commitment is genuine intimacy possible.

Conversely, the lack of a secure sense of self often leads to superficial, selfish, or exploitive relationships with others. The failure to establish intimacy results in feelings of loneliness, low self-esteem, and a sense of social, psychological, and emotional isolation.

Generativity versus Stagnation.   During the adult years the psychosocial crisis is between the need to be productive both in work and family and a tendency to become self-absorbed with one's personal achievements and life-style. Generative individuals seek productive work, involved child rearing, new adventures and challenges, and important goals. Those who become self-absorbed or who fail to incorporate the needs of others in their personal lives tend to become stagnated.

Integrity versus Despair.   Postretirement and the later years often lead to certain spiritual concerns. Erikson believes that a successful resolution to the crisis of integrity versus despair requires a lifetime of earlier conflict resolutions as well as a sense of peaceful satisfaction with one's past. The successful aging individual gains a broader vision of life and gains ego strength from this awareness. Ego integrity also helps one adjust to the frailties of aging and one's eventual death. In contrast, despair results when one fears the inevitability of old age and death. Sometimes attempts to compensate for lost time by "trying to catch up" or by "making amends" may prompt feelings of futility, dread, regret, and emptiness.

Change Mechanism

The change mechanisms in psychosocial theory are also among its important internal principles. Erikson describes a primary change mechanism, *epigenesis,* and a secondary change mechanism, *psychosocial conflict.* Each functions differently and results in a different kind or quality of change.

Epigenesis, or the epigenetic principle, is Erikson's primary mechanism of development across the life cycle. Epigenesis has its origins in the genetic design containing all the biological information needed to initiate a sequence of critical periods that traverse a lifetime. In short, one's age determines when particular crises will begin and when they end.

Psychosocial conflict is a secondary change mechanism in Erikson's theory. It consists of the day-to-day exchanges between individuals and others that provide an abundance of interpersonal challenges and frustrations. Social experience from infancy to old age consists of many culturally sanctioned events that confront one with higher expectations, challenge one to do better than one's peers, and motivate one to achieve increasingly complex goals. Psychosocial conflict is experienced as competition between one's personal and one's social ego. For example, one's personal ego strives for identity and self-worth while the social ego battles for conformity in the cultural context of expectations, stereotypes, habits, customs, and skills taught by parents and significant others during one's lifetime.

It is important to note here exactly what Erikson posits as due to epigenesis and what he posits as due to cultural influence. First, his stages are endogenous in origin; each psychosocial crisis is one manifestation of the fixed, epigenetic plan. Individuals can do nothing to prevent a crisis from occurring or to speed up the sequence of crises. Second, the sequence of crises is universal, not because of necessity or chance, but because of history. Although each culture has evolved methods of child rearing that differ in specifics, although individuals engage in the same social spheres. For example, infants are nursed by mothers, are raised by families, work in societies, raise new generations during adulthood, and pass on to new generations the cultural traditions. Third, while the general structure of psychosocial crises is universal, there are specific cultural and individual variations. For example, infants in all cultures experience a natural conflict between themselves and their mothers, but how this conflict manifests itself may vary. In some cultures mothers may lavish attention on their infants; in other cultures such attention may be relatively short-lived. Within a culture some infants may experience prolonged nursing, while others may be weaned within months of their birth. In each instance, a crisis of interpersonal trust and dependency is experienced by infants. At the same time, the circumstantial ingredients of this crisis may differ from one infant to another even within the same culture.

An analogy may be helpful in understanding the differential contributions of primary and secondary determinants. The life span is like an extended vacation in which our basic plan (the epigenetic blueprint) is the primary determinant of where we go and when. In comparison, psychosocial conflict is analogous to the events that comprise the actual vacation experience. Sometimes events go as planned; often they do not because unforeseen events intervene (e.g., bad weather, missed transportation) to upset and frustrate the plans. The day-to-day experiences and hour-to-hour pressures are like psychosocial conflict in that they influence how well our vacation actually works out. In this way psychosocial conflict is a secondary determinant of development whose effects are subordinated to the primary limitations imposed by epigenesis. Psychosocial stages ultimately result in favorable or unfavorable resolutions, depending on the particular events one experiences.

EXPLAINING HUMAN DEVELOPMENT: THE RESEARCH

Aside from some indirect research on infant attachment, there has been very little research that directly tests Erikson's claims about early and middle childhood, adulthood, or old age. In fact, researchers generally have not investigated the predictive validity of the theory in terms of how well it explains successful aging (Ryff, 1982), and while Erikson is often cited in research studies, his theory is seldom studied directly in adults or the aged (Tesch, 1985). In sharp contrast, research on the adolescent identity crisis has appeared in a number of publications in the past two decades. Because of this situation, research that bears on Erikson's claims about adolescent identity formation will be emphasized in this section.

Indirect Research on Infancy

According to Erikson, infancy entails a crisis of trust versus mistrust. It is reasonable to expect that infants whose basic physical and emotional needs are met, who are nurtured with tender care, and whose caretakers are consistent in their interactions, would respond by establishing a basic sense of trust in others.

In the past decade, research on infant attachment to mothers has uncovered a number of patterns that indirectly bear on Erikson's thesis about the infant's crisis of trust versus mistrust. For example, mothers who are highly affectionate, respond quickly to infant distress, and exhibit emotional and verbal responsiveness to their infants tend to have infants who display more secure attachments than mothers without these qualities (Bates, Maslin, & Frankel, 1985). In fact, the correlation between positive maternal characteristics and quality of infant attachment has proven quite robust. A number of cross-cultural studies have found essentially the same relationship in Germany (Grossmann, Grossmann, Spangler, Suess, & Unzner, 1985) and Japan (Miyake, Chen, & Campos, 1985), and among kibbutz-reared children in Israel (Sagi, Lamb, Lewkowicz, Shoham, Dvir, & Estes, 1985).

Resolutions to the trust versus mistrust and autonomy versus shame and doubt crises may have long-term impact when mothers who had experienced severe family disruptions or childhood separation from their own parents later attempt to raise a family of their own. For example, mothers who have their children taken into custody by local agencies tend to have suffered severe discord or rejection as children (Rutter, Quinton, & Liddle, 1983). Mothers from disrupted families of origin are also less likely than other mothers to talk to, look at, or touch their infants, and they also respond less to their infants' vocalizations, whether fretful or positive (Hall & Pawlby, 1981; Pawlby & Hall, 1980). There is also evidence that the quality of early attachment experience is correlated with the quality of later marital relations. For example, women who experienced separation or disruption of primary attachments during infancy later tend to experience marital disharmony (Frommer & O'Shea, 1973; Wolkind, Hall, & Pawlby, 1977).

Research like this does not directly assess Erikson's contentions about infancy and childhood, but it is suggestive. It indicates that secure attachments are most likely to occur in situations where parents are consistently warm, sensitive, and responsive in meeting their infants' needs, qualities that could reasonably be expected to foster a sense of basic trust.

Adolescent Identity

An important element of adolescent identity formation is what Erikson (1968) calls a *psychosocial moratorium*. All societies provide a scheduled time for the completion of a personal identity. While considerable cultural variation exists in the timing, duration, intensity, and ritualization of adolescence, societies afford their youth a "time out" during which the adolescent is expected to begin to make certain lifelong commitments and establish a fixed self-definition (Adams & Montemayor, 1983, p. 194). This "time out" is the psychosocial moratorium.

The moratorium can be described as commitment without conviction. Adolescents suspend their beliefs in ideas and people to search out individuals and points of view that are genuinely trustworthy, that are objectively true rather than subjectively valued. The moratorium may involve a prolonged state of psychological confusion about the many varied roles one might take on in adult society, and it may involve active experimentation with different roles, values, and beliefs to "see if the shoe fits."

Moreover, the psychosocial moratorium is accompanied by a sense of *crisis.* Erikson (1968, p. 16) defines crisis as an unavoidable turning point or a crucial moment when development has to move in one direction or another. The timing, nature, and density of irreversible adolescent decisions—moving away from home, relocating for a job or college, getting married, choosing a career—all pose important dilemmas, because once a decision has been made it is difficult if not impossible to undo it. A number of studies directly assess the psychosocial characteristics of adolescent functioning.

Marcia's (1966) analysis of the identity crisis led him to identify four modes of resolution: *identity diffusion, foreclosure, moratorium,* and *identity achievement.* Many investigators have chosen to assess Marcia's identity statuses as indirect tests of Erikson's concept of the identity crisis. For example, Archer (1982) examined adolescents in the sixth, eighth, tenth, and twelfth grades to determine the age at which identity achievement was reached. Her results indicated that identity achievement was correlated with age; that is, the older adolescents were more likely to have attained identity achievement than younger ones. She found similar patterns for boys and girls and noted specifically that identity diffusion and identity foreclosure were more common at each grade level than any other status. In a similar study of twelve- to twenty-four-year-old males, Meilman (1979) found that most of his subjects, including young adults, were in either identity diffusion or identity foreclosure. These findings do not, of course, preclude many adolescents from attaining identity achievement later in adolescence or early adulthood. For example, Meilman (1979) also reported that the years between eighteen and twenty-one produced the most significant development in identity formation, with the most prominent shifts being from identity diffusion and foreclosure to identity achievement. Additional support for Marcia's four identity statuses can be found in studies by Toder and Marcia (1973); Adams, Shea, and Fitch (1979); and Waterman and Goldman (1976).

Age alone, however, may not be the only functional variable in determining one's identity status. Adams and Fitch (1982), in a two-year study of college students, found that approximately half remained stable in their identity status, while the other half either regressed or advanced. Both identity-diffused and moratorium students tended to advance. Students who were identity achieved, however, either remained that way or regressed to a moratorium status. An interesting point here has been made by Waterman and Waterman (1971), who have argued that the very nature of college, which stimulates students to reevaluate their beliefs and values, may exert a powerful influence to move toward a moratorium status, whether that status is an advance or a regression. Between the first and last year of college, however, one generally finds an increase in the frequency of adolescents who have made identity commitments and successfully resolved their identity crisis (Constantinople, 1969).

Cultural Context

The cultural heritage and historical zeitgeist an adolescent encounters in the transition from childhood to adulthood have been examined by Paranjpe (1976), who presents several case studies in the form of psychohistories. He shows how several individuals developed a sense of identity in spite of dramatically different personal experiences. Paranjpe's case studies are intriguing because they took place in India, a culture undergoing rapid progress from traditional to contemporary male-female sex roles. Vinu, for example, was a young man who between the ages of 17 and 29 kept a diary. During that period Vinu attended college, attempted to enter a monastery, became celibate, tried a number of religious sects, tried being a teacher, and finally found a sense of occupational achievement as a journalist. This sense of achievement changed Vinu's life. He renounced his celibacy, married a traditional Indian woman his parents had selected for him (according to Indian custom), and finally stopped writing in his diary. In other case studies, two young Indian women, Meera and Sheela, each made personal sacrifices, experienced considerable doubt about their future as women, underwent personal hardship, and ended up choosing diametrically opposed paths to identity resolution. The other psychohistories reported by Paranjpe (1976) also reveal considerable adolescent turmoil, in some cases ending in identity achievement and in others ending in identity confusion. In a different cultural context, Josselson (1973) has reported several case studies of the identity crisis in American female college students, giving careful attention to the ways they examined identity commitments related to vocational choice, religion, political ideologies, and sex-role preferences.

Because societies so strongly differentiate adult roles on the basis of sex, Erikson's theory would suggest that adolescent girls and boys would have different identity experiences. Limited evidence suggests that such a pattern does occur. For example, the identity profiles of late adolescents indicate that males are more focused on career identity issues and that females are more firmly established in their sense of interpersonal competence and identity (Josselson, 1973; Josselson, Greenberger, & McConochie, 1977). In addition, several researchers have suggested that females resolve relationship and career issues simultaneously while males deal with them sequentially (Hodgson & Fischer, 1979; Thorbecke & Grotevant, 1982).

Child Rearing

Many researchers have tried to assess the impact parents have on the behavior and personality of their adolescent children. A portion of that work has attempted to examine the relationship between parental characteristics and adolescent identity. La Voie (1976) reports, for example, that male adolescents high in ego identity were less controlled by their parents and received more frequent paternal praise than low-identity peers. Similarly, high-identity adolescent females experienced less maternal restrictiveness and closer parental relations than low-identity females. Other research (Mattheson, 1974; Waterman & Waterman, 1971) supports La Voie's findings and seems to indicate that high-identity adolescents experience more open parental communication and less restrictive control over their activities than low-identity adolescents.

Young adolescents, motivated to change from subordinate to more peer-like relationships, typically initiate changes in their relationships with parents (Hill, 1980; Younniss, 1980). One indication of this change is reflected in the increase in assertiveness displayed in family interactions by young adolescents (Alexander, 1973; Jacob, 1974; Steinberg, 1981). This growth of autonomy is believed to indicate a desired transformation in the emotional bond with parents rather than a desire for detachment or total freedom from parental influence. Psychosocial theory would suggest that parents who are able to adapt to their children's challenge for autonomy create a different family context for development than do those parents who are unable to change. Adams and Fitch (1982), for example, studied longitudinally a sample of university students and reported that the parents who tended to inhibit adolescent role exploration had children who experienced early identity foreclosures. Other evidence suggests that identity formation is positively related to supportive, cohesive, and accepting family contexts and to adolescent autonomy (Grotevant, 1983).

Sequence and Preparation

Some research has examined the sequential character of psychosocial stages. Erikson (1968) argues that the successful resolution of one crisis is a developmental prerequisite that prepares the individual for successful resolution of the next. There is no guarantee, however, that successful resolution of one crisis automatically produces successful resolution of the following crisis. A small body of research addresses this general question by examining the relationship between identity achievement and the following crisis of intimacy. According to Erikson, genuine intimacy is only possible if there is a self (identity achieved) to share with another self. Identity-confused individuals may be able to relate to others, but they cannot form a truly intimate relationship with another.

Similar to his taxonomy of identity statuses, Marcia and his colleagues (Orlofsky, Marcia, & Lesser, 1973) have characterized the achievement of intimacy in the following manner. *Intimate* individuals are capable of forming one or more committed, long-lasting love relationships marked by close, interpersonal caring and sharing. *Preintimate* individuals are ambivalent about making a commitment to another and may offer love but without any sense of enduring obligation. *Stereotyped* persons tend to find friendship more meaningful than love. Consequently, these people tend to have superficial relationships often dominated by multiple friendships with same-sex rather than opposite-sex others. *Pseudointimate* individuals maintain an enduring heterosexual relationship, but it has relatively little emotional strength or depth. Finally, *isolated* people shy away from social relationships because they tend to be anxiety provoking.

In other research both intimate and preintimate individuals have been found to be more sensitive and empathic to their partner's needs and more open in their friendships than people characterized by other intimacy statuses (Orlofsky, 1976). Similarly, college students who had attained an identity-achieved status were found to be more likely than members of other identity statuses to be involved in intimate relationships (Kacerguis & Adams, 1980).

Concerning the actual sequence of identity crises, the data are mixed. Constantinople (1969), for example, has reported that the primary pattern in both cross-sectional and longitudinal studies is that most individuals move toward identity-achieved status and away from identity-diffused status. Moreover, Whitbourne and Waterman (1979), in a reanalysis of Constantinople's (1969) data, found some support for the sequence of industry versus inferiority, identity versus identity diffusion, and intimacy versus isolation crises, especially for males. However, other evidence suggests that some women may experience the intimacy crisis before identity, while males are more likely to experience identity before intimacy (Douvan & Adelson, 1966; Fischer, 1981). These studies suggest some support for the sequence of crises between childhood and adulthood, but they also reveal that the progression of stages may be less universal and more flexible than Erikson thought.

Adulthood and Aging

The adult stage of *generativity versus stagnation* involves a conflict between becoming so involved in one's own career and personal preoccupations that normal activities like fostering, nurturing, and guiding the next generation go unattended. Although child rearing is typical of this stage, generativity can occur in the absence of children (Erikson, 1959) when an adult generates something of lasting significance (e.g., art, literature, ideas, customs). Several studies involving a variety of methodologies have attempted to validate the ascendancy of this stage over *identity versus identity diffusion*. The findings have been generally supportive of Erikson's descriptions (Boyd & Koskela, 1970; Ciaccio, 1971; Gruen, 1964).

In order to assess the relationship between generativity and later ego development, McAdams, Ruetzel, and Foley (1986) examined the identity status of fifty midlife adults and their personal plans for the future. Future plans were assessed in four categories: occupational, interpersonal, recreational, and material.

The researchers found that individuals high in ego development also tended to specify a variety of personal goals for the future, whereas those low in ego development described significantly fewer personal goals. Individuals with high ego development also had more complex personalities than did subjects rated low in ego development.

In a different kind of study, Nehrke, Bellucci, and Gabriel (1977–78) found that three independent measures of ego integrity—life satisfaction, locus of control, and the absence of death fear—were positively correlated in a group of forty elderly adults. More recently Walaskay, Whitbourne, and Nehrke (1983–84) examined ego integrity in forty elderly adults who ranged in age from sixty-five to ninety. The researchers reported that integrity-achieving individuals displayed consistently higher late-life adaptation in terms of ego intimacy, ego generativity, preparation for and acceptance of death, and emotional balance than did despairing individuals, thus suggesting that elderly persons who have achieved ego integrity tend to be better adjusted emotionally than despairing individuals.

CONTRIBUTIONS AND CRITICISMS OF THE THEORY

Contributions

Healthy Personality. Where Freud emphasized the ego's function as mediator between the competing demands of id and superego, Erikson concentrates his attention on the ego's role in healthy personality development. His theory views the ego as basically healthy and conflict-free. This means that individuals are not doomed to a life of anxiety and impulse-ridden compulsions. People may, depending on their resolutions to the various psychosocial crises, lead lives that are relatively satisfying and happy. Erikson has given the entire field of psychoanalytic theory a choice—a choice that on the one hand leads *inward, backward,* and *downward* or on the other hand leads *outward, forward,* and *upward* (Erikson, 1972, p. 13). Such an optimistic view of human nature is fundamentally different from Freud's.

Stages that Span the Life Cycle. Until the late 1950s and early 1960s, developmental psychologists primarily concerned themselves with infant, childhood, and adolescent development. The explosive surge of interest in life-span human development that has occurred in the past two decades has created an important need. Theories that concentrate only on development up to the adolescent years have the same drawbacks as theories of adult development that ignore the early years: both leave important segments of the life span unexplained. Against the predominance of such theories, Erikson's stands in sharp contrast. The importance of having a single unifying lifelong theme (ego identity) and set of theoretical constructs allows the developmental psychologist to link elements of adult or old-age functioning with earlier patterns of psychosocial adjustment.

Identity Crisis. One cannot outline Erikson's contributions to human development without acknowledging the concept of identity crisis. The relevance of his ideas on adolescent identity formation is reflected in the previous section, where it was noted that this concept has occupied more research interest than all other elements of his theory combined. Much of the literature on adolescence acknowledges the importance of Erikson's contribution here. Identity functioning is generally considered to be a vital element of the adolescent experience, and many believe that the ego identity statuses associated with Marcia's work reflect meaningful patterns of identity formation. These in turn have contributed to our understanding of the impact that adolescence has on an individual's functioning later in life.

Psychohistory. It is unfortunate that Erikson's psychohistorical method has been ignored by many developmentalists. The method provides a triune synthesis of personal ego identity, one's cultural context, and the historical zeitgeist. In this respect, Erikson overcame two of the criticisms leveled against Freud, namely that the latter relied too heavily on neurotic personalities and failed to account adequately for the role of society in personality development. Erikson not only sampled more widely than Freud, but also many of his observations were drawn from different cultures. In that light, the psychohistory method served his purpose well. No other psychological method produces quite the richness and variety of data for analysis. The method is inappropriate, however, for individuals who have not left written documentation of their thoughts while undergoing psychosocial crises.

Criticisms

Measurability. Erikson's theoretical constructs, like Freud's, have been criticized because they are extremely difficult to measure. Marcia's (1966) and Constantinople's (1969) particular innovations notwithstanding, only limited empirical studies have been done on infant, childhood, and adulthood psychosocial crises. In large part this shortcoming is due to the difficulty of measuring psychosocial crises. How does one, for example, actually measure whether the infant is experiencing trust, distrust, or a conflict between the two? One can observe an infant's and a child's behavior, note their interests and protests, but aside from direct self-reports, no method has been developed for measuring psychosocial trauma. The problem with being unable to measure theoretical constructs is that researchers cannot establish either the external validity or predictive validity of the theory.

Stage Sequence. Only limited research supports Erikson's contention that ego identity is prerequisite to being able to form genuinely intimate adult relationships. Moreover, relatively few cross-cultural or longitudinal studies have been conducted to support the claim that psychosocial crises occur in a universal sequence. Given the importance of this claim for psychosocial theory, the absence of appropriate empirical support cannot easily be overlooked.

EVALUATION OF THE THEORY

Scientific Worthiness

Testability. Given the foregoing discussion about the difficulty of measuring Erikson's constructs, it is difficult to imagine how one could test his theory. Various methods have been used to tap ego identity: semistructured interviews, clinical discussions, projective tests, and observations. These methods simply cannot, for example, test the veracity of Erikson's claim that epigenesis governs the unfolding of psychosexual stages. In addition, indirect measures are sometimes used to tap attitudinal or personality variables believed to correlate with ego identity at a particular stage. But such measurements provide only indirect information about an individual's ego status, and they rely heavily on interpretations of the meaning of particular data. Even Erikson's belief that ego identity reflects an individual's cultural and historical context is difficult to test, case studies notwithstanding. For these reasons and others mentioned in consideration of Freud's theory, Table 5-2 shows a low rating for psychosocial theory.

External Validity. Many of Erikson's psychosocial crises seem intuitively correct: the infant's crisis of trust versus mistrust, the crisis of industry or inferiority of middle childhood, the adolescent's identity crisis. Yet, with the exception of the identity crisis, there is relatively little research on childhood and adult psychosocial crises. Moreover, studies employing cross-cultural and longitudinal designs are virtually absent in the literature. The identity crisis does, however, appear to be a relatively accurate portrayal of self-searching examination and self-doubt experienced by many adolescents. Given the relative absence of research on the other stages but the relatively good research support for Erikson's portrayal of adolescence, I have judged his theory moderately low on this criterion.

Predictive Validity. Because relatively little work has been done to derive empirical predictions of Erikson's concepts, it would rate low on this basis

Table 5-2   Ratings of Psychosocial Theory for Scientific Worthiness

CRITERION	HIGH	MODERATE	LOW
Testability			X
External validity		X	
Predictive validity		X	
Internal consistency		X	
Theoretical economy		X	

alone. However, Marcia's (1966) derivation of four identity statuses from Erikson's description of the identity crisis is precisely what predictive validity is all about. Given the relatively good empirical support for Marcia's work but the absence of validation in other areas, Erikson's theory is rated as moderately low rather than low on this criterion.

Internal Consistency.   Erikson adheres to the majority of psychoanalytic theses. However, important differences between Freud and him do warrant consideration. Erikson, for example, has consistently posited a conflict-free ego that undergoes a sequence of epigenetically determined crises and whose resolutions to those crises are influenced by the individual's cultural and historical context. The ego is conflict-free in the sense that it is not, like Freud's depiction, constrained to feeding off the id's psychic energy, nor is its sole function to mitigate against the conflicting demands of id and superego. Rather, ego identity uses its own energy to resolve psychosocial crises that occur between the individual and society. Erikson has also been consistent in his description of the kinds of social forces that impact on the various identity crises. On balance, given Erikson's own relative consistency about psychosocial development together with his reliance on the basic tenets of psychoanalysis (which rated low on this criterion), I have given the theory a moderate rating for its internal consistency.

Theoretical Economy.   Erikson's adherence to basic Freudian principles ensnares him in the problems endemic to the parent theory, including the rather major problems of theoretical economy described in the chapter on Freud. His assumptions are more restrained than Freud's. His focus on ego development is narrower than Freud's, but his theory covers the entire life span. On balance, the ratio of assumptions to phenomena explained is marginally better than Freud's for theoretical economy, so a moderate rating for this criterion is given.

Developmental Adequacy

Temporality.   Table 5-3 shows Erikson's theory as passing this criterion. Development, in Erikson's view is a lifelong, time-dependent process.

Cumulativity.   The theory describes ego development as a sequence of crisis resolutions in which earlier crises have important implications on resolu-

Table 5-3   Ratings of Psychosocial Theory for Characteristics of Development

CHARACTERISTIC	RATING
Temporality	Pass
Cumulativity	Pass
Directionality	Pass
New mode of organization	Fail
Increased capacity for self-control	?

tions of later crises. According to Erikson, successful resolutions at later stages are built upon previous crisis resolutions. Moreover, later crises gradually add to and enlarge one's sociohistorical identity. For example, research indicates some support for the claim that establishment of interpersonal intimacy is predicated on successful identity achievement. Consequently, the theory passes this criterion.

Directionality.   Erikson claims that the development of ego-identity occurs through the resolution of crises that increasingly expand the individual's sense of self in both cultural and historical contexts. Beginning with infancy, the individual is involved in a crisis of trust versus mistrust, a crisis that requires it to form its original interpersonal relationship with its mother. By the time the infant has reached old age, many interpersonal crises have been faced, each expanding its sociocultural sense of self and responsibility to include ever-widening spheres of personal identification. Thus, Erikson's theory does imply a direction to development—a move from self-centered concerns to humanity-centered concerns, and so it passes this criterion.

New Mode of Organization.   Erikson's theory stresses the continuity of ego formation throughout the life span. However, one does not leave behind a well-adapted identity to forge a new one; rather, the new one is forged within the limits established by previous identity successes. At successive stages ego functioning continues adjusting to new social influences (cumulativity), but new organizational schemes are not imposed on old ones. New elements of identity functioning incorporate rather than replace old ego adaptations. Epigenesis is a continuous unfolding of ego crises that incorporate earlier achievements rather than reorganize previous resolutions. Consequently, Erikson's theory fails this criterion.

Increased Capacity for Self-Control.   It is helpful to review what is meant by this criterion. Increased capacity for self-control means that as individuals develop, they acquire certain skills or abilities that improve the regulation of person-environment interactions. Because of competing concerns, I cannot decide if Erikson's theory should pass or fail this criterion, so I have left a question mark for future research to decide. The competing concerns are these. Although individuals enlarge their psychosocial spheres, they do not necessarily exert an increased capacity to control their own destinies. For example, individuals whose resolutions to earlier crises were unsuccessful tend toward unsuccessful later resolutions, no matter how much will power they might exert. In a similar manner, later stages do not necessarily imply an increase in self-control, since ego functioning occurs below the level of awareness. Finally, individuals are influenced indirectly by their cultural and historical zeitgeist, each of which is beyond personal control. To the extent that individuals are capable of free choice, their choices are always constrained largely by previous crisis resolutions, culture, and historical context. One cannot, for example, simply decide to choose generativity over self-absorption (seventh-stage crisis) or integrity over despair (eighth-stage crisis) as a way of ego functioning. These arguments notwithstanding, it is also the case that the development of ego identity, especially when crises are resolved favorably, results in adaptive patterns of social adjustment in which people learn to choose the kinds of activities they engage in and the types of people they come in contact with. Because Erikson places more emphasis on the former concerns than the latter, and because it is the latter that are related to increased capacity for self-control, I remain undecided on his rating for this criterion.

SUMMARY POINTS

1. Erikson's major differences with Freud include his focus on ego identity, healthy personality functioning, culture and history, and life-span stages.

2. The overarching problem of study for Erikson is to understand how the ego adapts itself to a sequence of psychosocial crises. The phenomena to be explained include the status of the ego at any point in the life span, the sequence of crises individuals must resolve, and the historical-cultural context of a person's development. Erikson utilizes naturalistic observations and a method he termed psychohistory.

3. The internal principles of psychosocial theory include ego identity, the epigenetic principle, and psychosocial conflict.

4. The eight psychosocial stages are the theory's bridge principle.

5. Epigenesis and psychosocial conflict are the change mechanisms that govern the development of ego identity. Epigenesis is the innate plan of stages that unfold in sequence according to a maturational timetable and are immune to environmental input. Psychosocial conflict, in turn, influences whether or not the crises are successfully resolved.

6. Erikson has made four enduring contributions to our understanding of human nature. He has described how a healthy personality functions and how it evolves through the entire life span. He has also given psychology the method of psychohistory and an explanation of the adolescent identity crisis.

7. The two primary criticisms of Erikson's theory are its vague, imprecise concepts, which have been difficult to measure, and the universal sequence of his stages, which have not been adequately verified.

8. Overall, the theory was rated moderately low for its scientific worthiness but moderately high for its developmental adequacy.

PROBLEMS AND EXERCISES

1. Many students keep diaries during their adolescent years. If you kept one, reread it now. Evaluate your thoughts and feelings in terms of Erikson's description of the identity crisis. If you didn't keep a diary, try to find several old high school essays you wrote. Evaluate them in terms of Erikson's description of the identity crisis.

2. Spend several hours this week jotting down notes about your parents. Consider the prevailing social climate of their upbringing, the important historical events that accompanied their adolescence (interview them about this), their aspirations about you, and the importance of family or social traditions they wanted you to learn. From your data, see if you can evaluate each of their ego identities in terms

of Erikson's last two stages (whichever is appropriate). Be careful not to categorize either one according to any one specific statement or belief; psychosocial identity reflects a complex integration of influences.

3. Compare and contrast Freud's and Erikson's theories of childhood stages. What are their similarities and differences?

4. Analyze the possible consequences on ego development of any of the following childhood conditions: poverty, wealth, child abuse, absence of siblings, youth groups, or urban versus rural environment.

SUGGESTED READINGS

More about the Theory

Coles, R. (1970). *Erik H. Erikson: The growth of his work.* Boston: Little, Brown.

Erikson, E. (1958). *Young man Luther: A study in psychoanalysis and history.* New York: Norton.

Erikson, E. (1963). *Childhood and society* (2nd ed.). New York: Norton.

Reviews of Research

Bourne, E. (1978). The state of research on ego identity: A review and appraisal. Part I. *Journal of Youth and Adolescence, 7,* 223–251.

Bourne, E. (1978). The state of research on ego identity: A review and appraisal. Part II. *Journal of Youth and Adolescence, 7,* 371–392.

Waterman, A. S. (1982). Identity development from adolescence to adulthood: An extension of theory and a review of research. *Developmental Psychology, 18,* 341–358.

Critical Reviews

Roazen, P. (1976). *Erik H. Erikson: The power and limits of a vision.* New York: The Free Press.

Chapter 6

Sociobiology

Preview Questions

What are the basic principles of evolution? What is phylogenesis?
How are genotypes and phenotypes related to natural selection?
What four assumptions about human nature are made by sociobiology?
What problems constitute the purpose of sociobiology? What methods does it
   use?
What are the theory's internal and bridge principles?
What are the theory's change mechanisms?
What are the major contributions and criticisms of sociobiology?
How does the theory rate for its scientific worthiness and developmental ade-
   quacy?

HISTORICAL SKETCH

Sociobiology is a theory about the cultural evolution of social behaviors. The
theory concentrates on *phylogeny*—the developmental history of a species from its
origin to its present form—rather than on *ontogeny* (development of the individual). This is an important point to remember throughout the entire chapter,
since the theory views change as something that occurs between generations of
individuals instead of something that happens during one's lifetime. A short
review of Darwin's theory provides vital background.

The Legacy of Darwin

When Charles Darwin returned to England in 1836 from his five-year voyage on
the *Beagle,* he was convinced about the fact of evolution. In his notebook on the
"transmutation of species," he noted his belief that new species had been created
from gradual changes in older species, but he had no idea how the changes had
been rendered (Gould, 1977). In the following year, Darwin read Malthus's essay

on populations and discovered that under natural conditions, certain individuals in a species tended to survive while others tended to perish in the struggle for survival. Darwin concluded that this *natural selection* must be the mechanism of evolution, but for political and religious reasons he delayed publication of his work for nearly twenty years. The publication of the *Origin of Species* in 1859 contained his carefully reasoned description of evolution and the principle of natural selection.

Darwin's theory of evolution is elegantly simple in its three components. First, individuals naturally vary from one another (due to differences in genetic makeup), and these variations are passed along to their offspring. Second, individuals collectively produce more offspring than can survive with the limited food resources available. Third, offspring that possess variations favored by the environment will tend to survive, while less favored offspring will tend to perish. In other words, some variations tend to be naturally selected.

Modern evolutionary theory, given the discovery of genes after Darwin, contains the following essential elements. Evolution works on three levels: the genetic level, the individual level, and the species level. Genes are the building blocks of individuals; individuals are the building blocks of species. Evolution requires variations between individuals, because natural selection cannot differentially select for individual differences if everyone is identical. Genes mutate and are the original source and basic unit of variation. Individuals are the units that get naturally selected. But individuals grow, reproduce, and die; they do not evolve. Species evolve and are the unit of evolution. This is shown schematically in Figure 6-1.

Mutations are random changes in genetic information that occur in either the ova or sperm (or both) and are passed along to offspring through sexual reproduction. Most mutations are nonadaptive because they alter a highly complex organization that has already undergone a long period of prior selection for a particular geographical niche. Genetic mutations seldom produce monsters, since mutations are nearly always small, incremental differences. A second mechanism for introducing variation, *sexual recombination,* occurs when genetic information on the chromosomes is shuffled and reshuffled through the the union of ova and sperm.

Natural selection accepts or rejects entire individuals, not specific parts or traits. Only in the very rare case where a cluster of mutations orchestrates an advantageous change in one individual will that person experience more favorable selection than the average individual. To understand how individuals get naturally selected, biologists draw a distinction between *phenotypes* and *genotypes.* *Phenotypes* are anatomical traits and features. They are observable physical characteristics that either manifest themselves directly (e.g., body size, hair color, eye color, nose shape) or remain latent and observable only under special conditions (e.g., maximum power, speed, visual acuity). *Genotypes* consist of the individual's genetic makeup; they comprise the patterns of DNA codes that produce phenotypes. Genotypes are the internal, theoretical causes of phenotypes, a relationship clearly reflective of Descartes's rationalism. No genotype has ever been directly observed nor has its actual connection to a phenotype. It is this link,

Level 1: Genes mutate and sexually recombine.

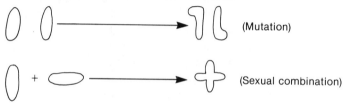

Level 2: Individuals are naturally selected.

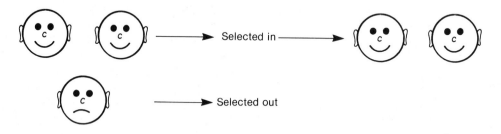

Level 3: Species evolve over many generations.

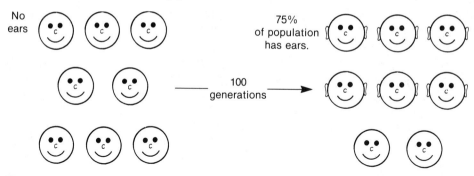

Figure 6-1.   Three levels of evolutionary theory.

however, that provides evolution a means for indirectly selecting genotypes by way of natural selection acting on phenotypes.

An individual is favorably selected when a new genotype, through mutation or recombination, creates a phenotype that is better adapted to a geographical niche. When a genotype is closely related to a phenotype, the selection is direct. However, since the entire individual is selected, any particular phenotype gets selected only as part of the total arrangement of phenotypes and the entire package of underlying genotypes.

Edward O. Wilson and the Roots of Sociobiology

For over a century after Darwin published the *Origin*, evolutionary theory had undergone only minor revisions. The publication of Edward O. Wilson's *Sociobiology:*

The New Synthesis in 1975, however, is considered a radical departure from traditional evolutionary theory (Caplan, 1978, p. 8) because it claims that social behaviors, in addition to physical traits, have evolved as phenotypes. In short, the *New Synthesis* extends Butler's aphorism—a chicken is merely the egg's way of making another egg—all the way to human culture: society is the gene's way of ensuring more genes.

Born in Alabama just before the Great Depression, Wilson had no siblings. After his family moved to Washington, D.C., he frequented the National Zoo and Smithsonian Institution to satisfy his curiosity about plants and animals. The adolescent Wilson spent considerable time collecting and studying insects, eventually deciding to become an entomologist (insect scientist). He attended the University of Alabama then Harvard University, where he received his doctorate in entomology in 1955 and joined that prestigious faculty in 1958. Fifteen years later he was appointed curator of entomology at the Harvard Museum of Comparative Zoology, where he remains today.

One of Wilson's important discoveries in the 1950s was that ants communicate with one another by means of chemical substances. In 1971 he published *The Insect Societies*, a comprehensive treatment endorsed in the *Library Journal* as the finest synthesis of knowledge about the social insects to be published in the preceding half-century. His analysis of insect societies was extended in the *New Synthesis*, where he catapulted biological evolution all the way from the genes to culture itself.

The central thrust of Wilson's argument is as follows. Over many hundreds of generations cultures have gradually established certain customs because they express powerful genetic forces. Many cultures have, for example, evolved such common practices as personal names, games, superstitions, hospitality rituals, and styles of decorative art. Other customs and rituals exist that represent implicit prohibitions—rites of passage, sex-role differentiation, funeral rites, and incest taboos. In the extreme, societies may erect formal institutions that ensure conformity with strong genetic predispositions, a phenomena Wilson (1975, 1978b) calls *hypertrophy*. Wilson believes that just as the elephant's tusk represents an extreme development of a preexisting tooth, so too do certain institutions reflect extreme social adaptations. Schools, families, law enforcement agencies, judicial hierarchies, religious organizations, and management and military chains of command all function to ensure conformity in individual behavior. These are hypertrophic adaptations. According to Wilson (1978b), hypertrophy is the key to the emergence of civilization—relatively simple adaptations of hunter-gatherer tribes have over thousands of generations evolved into the complex social institutions of modern societies.

STRUCTURAL COMPONENTS

Assumptions

The assumptions of sociobiology derive from classical evolutionary theory. First, infants are born with a species-specific set of genetic instructions for programming and setting constraints on general modes of behavior. Second, genetic instructions determine the infant's inborn reflexes. This assumption does not mean that a genetic signal is behind every reflex, merely that strong, phenotypic predispositions to react in certain species-specific ways are present in the genotype. Third, random mutations of genetic information are assumed to be the source of individual variation. This element must be considered an assumption at this point since it is the imputed *effects* of genes, rather than the genes themselves or their mutations, that are directly observed. Fourth, sociobiology assumes that the *potential* for rapid, specialized social learning *is programmed* by the genotype. Unlike Freud or Erikson, Wilson assumes no stages in development, in part because he directs his attention to the species level rather than to individuals.

Problems for Study

The overriding problem of sociobiology is to classify social behaviors according to genetic categories and to explain the evolution of those behaviors. The identification of genetic categories requires one to isolate qualities of social behavior that have survival value from those that do not. To achieve this task, Wilson (1975) posits ten *qualities of sociality*. In addition, explaining how these qualities evolved requires evidence of their *universality, continuity,* and *adaptation* (Gould, 1977).

Phenomena to be Explained

According to Wilson, there are ten *qualities of sociality* that, rather than being specific behaviors, are the necessary conditions that underlie the concept of what it means to be "social." In addition, the theory attempts to address three *kinds of evidence.*

Qualities of Sociality

Group size is a vital quality of a population, since a true society requires a minimum number of demographically diverse individuals who interact with one another with sufficient frequency for social behaviors to occur. The larger the group size and the greater the demographic diversity, the more likely it is that adaptive social behaviors will be favorably selected.

Demographic distribution constitutes the variables of a differentiated population where individuals vary according to age, sex, caste, size, marital status, and so forth. A heterogeneous population can only occur if individuals differ from one another along important, socially relevant dimensions.

Cohesiveness refers to the spatial closeness of group members to one another. It is not the same as psychological closeness or kinship; rather, it is the degree to which individuals occupy the same geographical locale at the same time. A platoon of GIs and a group of sorority sisters exhibit relatively high cohesiveness; farmers and hermits do not. On the whole, human cultures tend to be far less cohesive than, say, a school of fish (Wilson, 1975).

Amount and pattern of connectedness refers to nonrandom interactions between individuals. Social groups that display hierarchies, chains of command, or castes reflect a high degree of patterned connectedness—the flow of communication is directed primarily toward and from certain individuals more than others. Patterns of connectedness are a relatively direct measure of the degree of organization underlying common social behaviors (contrast, for example, patterns of connectedness between military ranks and Saturday shoppers). Wilson believes that advanced societies display a high degree of connected patterning though not necessarily a large amount of it.

Permeability is the degree to which a society is open or closed to communication with and immigration by members of other cultures. A society with high permeability is relatively open to such commerce. Permeability is optimized when the rate of inbreeding within a culture is balanced by the rate of outbreeding between it and other cultures.

Compartmentalization is the extent to which small groups of individuals tend to operate as discrete, self-contained units within the culture. Families, businesses, athletic teams, cities, counties, states, and classrooms are examples of independently operating but partially overlapping social compartments. Compartments make up the larger whole of a culture, and they maintain a social context through exchange of individuals, products, and information governed by either formal or informal expectations.

Differentiation of roles refers to the kinds of specialized functions individuals perform within a social framework. Societies that are well organized tend to display highly specialized roles for their members. For example, most societies practice *sex polyethism* (dividing labor according to sex) as well as *age polyethism* (dividing labor by age), but roles may also be differentiated according to many other kinds of criteria, such as job title, social status, kin relationships, education, wealth, or health status.

Integration of behavior is the tendency of cultures to expect certain roles to fulfill multiple social functions. Parents may function as caregivers for their children, home managers, employees of some business firm, volunteers in local civic or religious groups, political activists, and innumerable other roles.

Information flow refers to the extent to which societal members communicate with one another. Wilson views communication flow in terms of the total number of signals, the amount of information per signal, and the rate of signal transmission. Signals can function to warn of danger, differentiate roles, pass greetings, and increase or decrease permeability. Ants communicate with chemicals called pheromones, but such signals are rigid and convey highly specific information between members. The information contained in human signals is flexible in both form and content—music, nonverbal gestures, graffiti, and language.

Fraction of time devoted to social behavior is viewed by sociobiologists as a separate index reflecting the common attributes of cohesiveness, compartmentalization, role specialization, and rate of information flow (Wilson, 1975). Few individuals spend all their time engaging in social behaviors. The more time one spends engaging in nonsocial behavior, the less time one has for social interaction. Some cultures are highly socialized precisely because many activities are sanctioned for socializing. In other cultures opportunities for socializing may revolve around a somewhat limited number of activities—food gathering, cooking, defending, eating, storytelling, and child rearing.

Kinds of Evidence

To establish a convincing argument that the ten qualities of sociality have evolved requires the sociobiologist to demonstrate *universality, continuity,* and *adaptation.*

Universality requires the identification and cataloging of social behaviors common to all social species, and hence an argument that certain qualities are universal. Wilson's *New Synthesis* contains his own classification of social behaviors into the ten qualities of sociality just described. Wilson contends that social qualities found in both human and primate cultures are a necessary but not sufficient condition for proposing a common genetic evolution.

Continuity requires demonstrating that the factors at work in the evolution of human social behavior are identical to those that operate on primate social behavior and those that controlled early homo sapiens cultural practices. For example, Hamilton's (1964) notion of *kin selection* holds that by benefiting close relatives, altruistic behaviors in primates actually help preserve the altruist's shared genes with those relatives even if the altruist does not itself produce any offspring. Consequently, an argument for continuity in kin selection can be mounted by showing that altruistic acts in human societies (as with primates) occur more often between relatives than nonrelatives.

Adaptation requires sociobiologists to distinguish between adaptive and nonadaptive phenotypes to formulate hypotheses about natural selection and evolutionary change. Nonadaptive social practices should eventually decrease and disappear; adaptive practices should eventually disperse throughout the culture. The sociobiologist's chore is to show how particular qualities of an individual's phenotype provide a differentially better, more advantageous fit with the specific environmental niche of the culture, thereby affording that individual a greater adaptive advantage vis-à-vis other individuals.

Methods of Study

Sociobiology utilizes a plethora of research methods. The primary requirement here, due to the theory's phylogenetic approach, is that data collected during one generation be comparable to available data about other generations. Observational methods are often used to gather information about animal, insect, and human social behaviors in different ecological niches. Self-reports and tests may be used to examine how individuals look or behave in certain situations. Experiments are seldom done with humans because of ethical problems and the inordinately long time spans necessary to examine evolutionary change, but they are most often likely done with social insects and rapidly reproducing animals. In addition, sociobiologists derive considerable evidence for their theory from the disciplines of biology, economics, psychology, and sociology.

Internal Principles

Sociobiology explains human cultural evolution by introducing two basic principles: *genetic fitness* and *ultimate causes*. The elements of Wilson's theory are summarized in Table 6-1.

Genetic Fitness

The most radical part of Wilson's theory is his extension of the traditional definition of phenotype (anatomical traits) to include qualities of social behavior. Wilson believes that individuals initially displaying an adaptive social phenotype tended to produce more offspring than individuals not displaying the phenotype. This reproductive advantage between individuals is called *genetic fitness.*

In order for natural selection to work on individuals, those possessing an adaptive phenotype must survive at relatively greater rates and experience relatively greater reproductive success than others. By producing relatively more viable offspring than others, those possessing an adaptive phenotype pass it on to an ever-increasing proportion of each succeeding generation. In this way, any in-

Table 6-1   Causes and Qualities of Sociality

BRIDGE PRINCIPLES	INTERNAL PRINCIPLES		SOCIAL QUALITY (TO BE EXPLAINED)
	1. Genetic Fitness		
	2. Ultimate Causes		
	Phylogenetic Inertia	Ecological Pressure	
Demographic variables (reproduction rates, fertility rates, life span, death rates, optimum population size, actual population size)	Genetic variability Antisocial factors Complexity of social behavior Effect of evolution on other traits Kind of food eaten	Changing food sources Predation Climactic changes Reinforcing and counteracting selection Catastrophies Intrusions by other populations Natural terrain	Group size Demographic distributions Connectedness Cohesiveness Permeability Compartmentalization Role differentiation Integration of behavior Information flow Fraction of time devoted to social behavior
Rates of gene flow (degree of inbreeding, degree of outbreeding)			
Coefficients of relationship (degree to which individuals share identical genes)			

crease in the adaptive advantage of a phenotype or a combination of phenotypes increases an individual's genetic fitness vis-à-vis other individuals. Finally, individuals need not themselves produce offspring, as long as their close relatives (those sharing common genes) do. One's genes can thus be reproductively successful and display genetic fitness simply by having siblings who are reproductively successful.

Ultimate Causes

The ultimate causes of social behavior are the "prime movers" of evolution that render some phenotypes adaptive and others nonadaptive. The two types of ultimate causes—*phylogenetic inertia* and *ecological pressure*—operate over very long periods of time on entire cultures.

Phylogenetic Inertia. *Phylogenetic inertia* represents all the inherited properties of a culture that determine its *resistance to change.* The concept is not the same as more common notions of "genetic endowment" or "genetic heritage," which imply a fixed collection of innate capacities. High inertia reflects a species' tendency toward stability with little change; low inertia reflects relatively rapid evolutionary change. There are many sources of phylogenetic inertia, though Wilson mentions four major ones: *genetic variability, antisocial factors, complexity of social behavior,* and *the effect of evolution on other behaviors.*

Genetic variability reflects the extent to which individuals possess different genes. This variability results in phenotypic differences where members of a population display different social behaviors, some of which are more favorably selected through reproductive success than others. Genotypes linked to reproductively successful phenotypes are passed on to increasing numbers of individuals in succeeding generations. Genetic variability and phylogenetic inertia go hand in hand. When evolution works on gene pools with low variability (few differences between individuals), a given number of random mutations affects a larger ratio of genotypes than the same number of mutations occurring in a gene pool with high variability. Figure 6-2 shows that low variability is associated with low inertia and rapid evolution.

Antisocial factors affect the social equilibrium of a population by detracting from the amount of time engaged in social interaction, thereby gradually moving it in the direction of decreased socialization and concomitantly decreasing the genetic fitness of the society as a whole. Conversely, prosocial forces tend

Figure 6-2   Factors affecting the speed of social evolution.

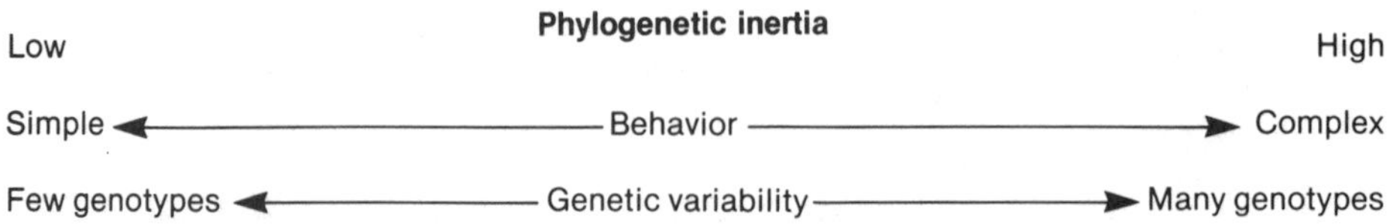

to move a population toward a more socialized state by providing opportunities for social interaction and thereby increasing its overall fitness as a society.

Complexity of social behavior refers to the amount of interconnectedness between social behaviors. As shown in Figure 6-2, the more complex a behavior, the more interconnected it is with other behaviors and the higher its phylogenetic inertia or resistance to evolutionary change. In this manner, behaviors that exist in isolation from other behaviors can be easily selected, either favorably or unfavorably, if their link to an underlying genotype is direct. However, behaviors that are highly integrated with others tend to be displayed as an interwoven package. Complex behaviors evolve more slowly because genotypes cannot be easily isolated for selection.

The *effect of evolution on other traits* reflects the degree to which genotypes produce phenotypes that work at cross purposes. Such a situation could arise, for example, if a population spent a disproportionate amount of time engaging in status displays that tend to cut into feeding and mating time, which, in turn, would select against individuals who display status signals. Over many generations, the time spent signalling status displays would tend to be diminished because of its inverse relationship to feeding and mating behavior, which are directly subject to natural selection.

Ecological Pressure. *Ecological pressure* is Wilson's term for Darwin's concept of natural selection. It is the set of all environmental forces that enhance or detract from individuals' reproductive success.

A well-known example of phenotypic selection through ecological pressure is described by Barash (1977). Among certain West African populations, up to 40 percent of individuals suffer from a genetic disease called sickle-cell anemia. Because the disease is fatal, one might expect that individuals who carry its genes would have failed to reproduce, thus eventually eliminating the disease and leaving only healthy individuals to reproduce. Ironically, however, carriers are much less susceptible to malaria than others. Malaria, in turn, kills many children who thus fail to reproduce, but not those with the sickle-cell gene. Sickle-cell children tend to mature and to produce offspring who also carry the fatal gene with its malarial immunity. Consequently, sickle-cell anemia has been retained in the population for many generations. The absence of malaria in North America provides a different ecological pressure that selects against carriers of sickle-cell anemia. Among U.S. blacks of West African descent, a much smaller ratio suffer from the disease because, according to sociobiology, the selective advantage of the disease in a malaria-free environment has been eliminated. In addition, the nutritional advantage of North American blacks over Africans represents another difference in ecological pressure.

Of the four types of ecological pressure discussed by Wilson, three are outlined here. *Change in food supply* is an example of an environmental change that makes previously efficient social behaviors and traits either more or less adaptive in the new context. During times of famine, for example, behaviors that lead some individuals to exploit new food sources will tend to be selected. Moreover, *preda-*

tion exerts a very effective selection pressure against some forms of social behavior related to combatting predators, signalling their presence, or occupying their hunting territory. Individuals especially adept at utilizing shelter, weapons, or escape strategies would tend to improve their reproductive success in relation to others less well equipped for counteracting the presence of predators. *Competition* between individual members of a population also acts as a natural selector when it bestows reproductive advantage on certain members. In polygamous societies, for example, where one male weds several females, competition for women determines which males will and will not produce offspring. Competition may also occur within cultures for jobs, money, grades, status, and mates.

Bridge Principles

Wilson invokes the term *proximate causes* to refer to the immediate influences on individuals, environmental conditions, and phenotypes that trigger social behaviors. Whereas ultimate causes operate over long time spans and across many generations, proximate causes always operate within an individual's lifetime. The proximate causes are comprised of *demographic variables, rates of gene flow,* and *coefficients of relationship.*

    Demographic variables exert direct impact on cultures through the interplay of reproduction rates, fertility rates, individual life spans, death rates, and the actual population size. Cultures influence individuals by establishing patterns that are beneficial to bearing and raising offspring to reproductive viability. In this vein sociobiology contends that genotypes related to mating rituals and child-rearing practices should be selected for reproductive success, whereas genes of individuals who fail to reproduce or to utilize natural resources efficiently would gradually be eliminated from a population through natural selection.

    Rate of gene flow refers to the degree of inbreeding and outbreeding between individuals within a culture. Inbreeding occurs when members of a culture mate with one another; outbreeding occurs when individuals from different cultures mate. The rate of gene flow is a direct reflection of the amount of variation introduced into a population (recall that natural selection operates only when sufficient variation among individuals exists to produce differential adaptive advantage for their corresponding phenotypes). If members of a culture inbreed, their offspring tend to decrease genetic variability in the population; conversely, outbreeding increases genetic variation by introducing genes not present in the culture's gene pool. Over many generations, rates of gene flow may either increase or decrease genetic fitness of the culture. Taking a family as a social unit, if the rate of gene flow is low, the family practices a high degree of inbreeding, which would ultimately reduce the genetic fitness of successive offspring.

    Coefficient of relationship is a measure of kinship. The coefficient of relationship can have a profound evolutionary effect on a society if at either extreme all members share identical genes (no variation) or if no members share genes (no common ancestors, so no altruism or phenotypic continuity).

Change Mechanism

Wilson posits two change mechanisms to account for evolution: (1) genetic mutations and sexual recombinations and (2) reproductive success through natural selection. Evolution requires that each phenotype display a range of variation so that natural selection has the raw materials upon which it can operate. Genetic mutations and sexual recombinations are the origins of this genetic diversity.

Although the production of genetic variation is highly random, natural selection is not; it produces the very complex, nonrandom systems we call individuals. But there are two kinds of selection. First, *counteracting selection* occurs when ecological pressures on two or more levels of organization (e.g., individual, family, relatives, tribe, population) operate in favor of genes at one level but in disfavor of genes at another level. For example, children who steal food from the family storehouse during times of famine may enhance their own survival at the expense of other family members. If the tendency to steal is genetically encoded, then stealing may have a later payoff only if it results in greater reproductive success than that experienced by other family members. Second, *reinforcing selection* occurs when ecological pressures on two or more levels of organization favor genes at all levels, resulting in an acceleration of gene spread throughout the entire population. For example, reinforcing selection may occur when a genotype produces a tendency to communicate between individuals cooperating on a group project. If their cooperation results in greater status for both the individuals and the class as a whole, then members of the whole class would share a reproductive advantage over classrooms with noncooperative individuals.

In summary, sociobiology posits two basic types of mechanisms that oppose each other. First, random mutations and novel genetic recombinations occur between individuals and their offspring that together produce a never-ending supply of genetic variation. The growth and development of any individual (and hence all individuals) unfolds according to the biological information encoded in their genes. This is an important aspect of sociobiology that marks it as a clear example of endogenous theories. Second, evolution operates on species through the natural selection of individuals who experience differential reproductive success.

EXPLAINING HUMAN DEVELOPMENT: THE RESEARCH

Four considerations should be kept in mind when examining the research support for sociobiology. First, the theory attempts to explain phylogenesis rather than ontogenesis. Second, Wilson's *New Synthesis* was published barely a decade ago, which means that research specific to human social evolution is less prevalent at this point than that for social insects and animals. Third, sociobiology attempts to explain general qualities of social behavior rather than any particular behavioral event. A sociobiologist, for example, would be more interested in a general tendency of cultures to establish status hierarchies than with the fact that in some cultures ownership of a Mercedes-Benz accords one more status than does a Ford.

Fourth, sociobiologists borrow extensively from research in biology, psychology, sociology, and anthropology. While the studies reported here draw from those disciplines, their results are interpreted from the sociobiologist's point of view.

Aggression and Dominance Hierarchies

Sociobiology contends that status signals are highly adaptive for both dominant and subordinate individuals regardless of what forms they take in different cultures (Barash, 1977). Dominants are better off because they gain important resources without having to compete for them each time access is desired, and subordinates, who lose contests most of the time anyway, are better off avoiding the futile costs of unsuccessful challenges to dominant individuals. Accordingly, evolution is assumed to favor societies that utilize status signals that convey both aggression and dominance.

Lorenz (1963) describes displays of aggression that vary widely in form, from actual fighting at one extreme to strutting or verbal assault at the other as a show of strength. Barash (1977) distinguishes between the extremes of social aggression. *Contest competition* occurs when individuals compete for freely available resources by displaying status in socially recognized formal or informal games (sports, wealth, dress style, language inflection, domicile furnishings, one-upmanship).

Scramble competition occurs when individuals compete for vital but limited resources, and it involves attempts to use as much of a critical resource as possible with almost complete disregard for the tacit elements of social gamesmanship (Barash, 1977). Compared to contest competition, scramble competition occurs infrequently in human cultures. Examples include sibling fights, cheating, gang fights, and riots.

Kinship Systems and Nomenclature

Sociobiology contends that cooperation among individuals should be displayed in direct proportion to their coefficients of relationship. By cooperating with one another, relatives are believed to increase the collective fitness of related kin, thereby promoting *kin selection* when any relative behaves so as to enhance the reproductive success of other relatives. Virtually all cultures recognize kinship relationships by endowing them with special titles—aunt, mother, cousin, brother-in-law. This kinship nomenclature has clear adaptive advantages in bonding alliances between tribes and provides a means for immigration of tribal members. It also supports the bartering system by which some males achieve dominance and leadership over others. Finally, it helps groups through hard times because it tells individuals whom to call on for altruistic assistance (close relatives) during hard times. In short, kinship customs reflect a genetic pattern of connectedness between families, increase cohesiveness between individuals, frame settings and occasions that promote integration of behavior, and provide opportunities for increasing the amount of time devoted to social behavior.

Youngsters who are adopted and raised in close proximity to genetically unrelated individuals provide an interesting test of sociobiological theory. For example, stepparents in general are more likely than biological parents to abuse children (Daly & Wilson, 1981; Lenington, 1981; Lightcap, Kurland, & Burgess, 1982), and biological mothers are less likely than stepmothers to abuse children (Lenington, 1981; Lightcap et al., 1982). Because natural selection favors those who are socially and physically fit, it should not be surprising that the risk of child abuse is inversely related to family income (Daly & Wilson, 1981; Lenington, 1981), and children with health problems or physical abnormalities are more likely than normal children to experience abuse (Daly & Wilson, 1981; Lenington, 1981; Lightcap et al., 1982). Frequency of adoption is also more likely among related than unrelated kin, and biological children tend to be recipients of more frequent and more favorable parental interactions than stepchildren throughout the world (Ainsworth, 1967; Silk, 1980). Interestingly, nonindustrial cultures tend to restrict adoptions to closely related kin (Freedman, 1979). Moreover, adopted children, even when well cared for, often experience an urge to locate their biological parents (Triseliotis, 1973). Ironically, transracial adoptions in the United States were practiced for a brief time, but blacks and Indians (whose cultures were most directly threatened) raised such strong objections about the absence of racial matching that such adoptions are rather rare today (Simon & Alstein, 1977).

Sociobiological theory also contends that genetically related individuals should exhibit greater degrees of cohesiveness and proximity than unrelated individuals, a pattern that would be expected to increase sociality while decreasing antisocial behavior. A number of direct and indirect tests of such a hypothesis have been undertaken in several diverse cultures. For example, Chagnon (1979, 1981, 1982) studied villages of Yanomamo Indians on the border of Brazil and Venezuela both before and after they broke into smaller villages. He found that villages with higher coefficients of relatedness between individuals tended to grow larger before fissioning into smaller villages than those with smaller coefficients. He also found that more closely related kin tended to remain together after a village fission. More specifically, Chagnon found that after fissioning of the original village, individuals in each of two smaller villages tended to remain with close relatives of their own and descending generations. Concerning potential for reproductive success, Chagnon also found that the more support a male had from kin in his own generation and his ascending generations, the greater his success in finding a mate.

Other studies support the claim that genetically related individuals exhibit social patterns not characteristically found among unrelated people. For example, Barkow (1982) found that among the Migili in Nigeria, donations were more likely among relatives, whereas exchanges were more likely among unrelated individuals. Essock-Vitale and McGuire (1980) also found that amount and frequency of unreciprocated aid was higher and that aid was withdrawn more slowly among relatives than nonrelatives. Finally, social interactions among Ye'kwana Indians varies in direct proportion to their coefficients of relatedness (Hames, 1979).

Altruism

Sociobiologists typically define altruism solely in terms of its consequences—being helpful or caring toward others; no assumptions are made about the altruist's motives. In more technical terms, altruism is any act that decreases the individual reproductive success of the actor while increasing the reproductive success of the recipient. Sociobiologists have concentrated much attention on explaining altruism because it is an apparently self-destructive activity—one that presumably cannot be to the reproductive advantage of the altruist. However, sociobiology argues that if two individuals share the same genes by common descent, and if an altruistic action of one increases the joint contribution of both individuals' genes in succeeding generations, then the tendency toward altruism should gradually be spread through the population (Wilson, 1975).

Trivers (1971) has explained the evolution of altruism in the following manner. The chances of evolution selecting for altruistic genes would be greatest when (1) there are many potential altruistic situations, (2) altruists interact repeatedly with the same individuals, and (3) pairs of potential altruists can render approximately equal benefits to one another with similar costs. Under these circumstances, reciprocity in altruistic acts would be likely to evolve among intelligent, cohesive species whose members spend a relatively large proportion of time engaging in social activities. Humans, with their particularly long life span (much of which is spent in neighborhoods where individuals repeatedly interact with one another) and long-term memory, can have a reasonable expectation that a recipient will later remember to reciprocate, especially if the two individuals interact on a regular basis. Reciprocal altruism occurs when the benefiting individual also bestows some favor back on the original altruist. The fact that city dwellers are consistently less helpful to strangers in distress than are their rural counterparts (Piliavin, Rodin, & Piliavin, 1969) may be due to the difference in how often the same individuals come into contact with one another as well as the difference in coefficients of relationship normally found in city versus rural residents.

Reciprocal altruism has been empirically studied in the United States and other cultures. For example, Thompson (1980) found that reciprocity between individuals in a large New York City apartment complex mirrored the probability of situation reversal. The more likely it was that others could experience a need for assistance, the more likely they were to help strangers. Moreover, Thompson found, as predicted by Trivers, that reciprocal altruism increased as benefits to the recipient increased, but it declined as cost to the donor increased. In another study of six cultures in Africa, Oceania, North America, and South America, Essock-Vitale and McGuire (1980) found that the degree of interpersonal friendship tended to be symmetrically reciprocal.

Sociobiology views reciprocal altruism as the biological basis for the cultural tendency to establish economic mediums of exchange. Exchange mediums make barter and trade possible, and coupled with human memory and written records, allow reciprocal interchanges to be stretched out over time as well as generations. Money, for example, has virtually no intrinsic value, yet it represents a hypertrophic adaptation—a simple but effective quantification of reciprocal altruism (Wilson, 1975).

Differential Selection

Males typically suffer a greater mortality rate at an earlier age and for a longer period of time than females. Among humans, 130 males are conceived for every 100 females, but through spontaneous abortions, only 104 males are born for every 100 females. Males experience a higher mortality rate than females, so by the peak of reproductivity parity is reached. Thereafter and with increasing age, females increasingly outnumber males (Freedman, 1979, p. 59). The point is that males are both born and obliterated at a greater rate than females because selection operates differentially on each sex. Nature treats males as relatively expendable, since only a few are biologically necessary for insuring cultural continuity.

Since sociobiology contends that males' and females' reproductive success is subject to different selective pressures, it is reasonable to predict that their sexual selection would respond to different partner characteristics. At least in part, this prediction seems to hold up. Lockard and Adams (1981) sampled 4,048 couples in two Seattle shopping malls. Although the ages of the sample were estimated and their marital status was not directly obtained, Lockard and Adams observed that males were much more likely to be coupled with younger-aged females than with same-aged or older-aged females. Moreover, more children were observed accompanying this selection strategy than with couples exhibiting other age-paired strategies. This conclusion was circumstantially validated by an independent examination of Seattle area divorce records, which showed that divorce rates among women tend to rise as they approach menopause. Similar findings have been reported by Paterson and Pettijohn (1982), who found that of the 250 marriage licenses issued in one Ohio county between 1928 and 1978, most went to males who were marrying younger females.

Other indirect tests of differential selection between the sexes comes from several cross-cultural studies. For example, among the people of Cameroun (Clignet & Sween, 1974) and the Bedouin (Musham, 1956), monogamous wives tend to average more children than their polygamous counterparts. Just the reverse is true for men in Cameroun (Clignet & Sween, 1974) and Sierra Leone (Dorjahn, 1958), who have greater reproductive success in polygamous than monogamous marriages. Among Sierra Leone's polygamous women, senior wives tended to be hyperfertile and junior wives tended to be hypofertile, as compared to women of the same ages in monogamous marriages (Isaac & Feinberg, 1982).

Concerning the role of jewelry in sexual differentiation between males and females, Low (1979) has tested the hypothesis that ornamentation should differ along sexual lines. She found that the prevalence of ornamentation was highly likely in a sample of 138 societies, with differences in form associated with sex differences. Moreover, she reported that ornamentation reflects ecological pressure in that women tend to display jewelry mirroring their marital status, while males tend to exhibit their wealth, power, or sexual potency.

According to sociobiology, ecological pressure has evolved a number of adaptations found in human infants. For example, newborns react positively to sweet tastes and negatively to salty or bitter tastes (Nowlis & Kessen, 1976); turn away from strong odors (Rieser, Yonas & Wikner, 1976); turn toward loud voices and sounds (Butterworth & Castillo, 1976; Wertheimer, 1961); and even flinch at onrushing objects (Bower, 1977). All these reactions prime newborns for survival and rapid learning about the physical and social qualities of the world that surrounds them. With such reflexes in mind, sociobiologists marshall a prima facie case for the genetic control of infant behavior and learning strategies.

Striking cultural differences in newborn capabilities are also believed to be the result of evolution acting on specific cultural phenotypes. Cultural differences in neonate postures, muscle tone, and emotional responses are interpreted by sociobiologists as evidence of cultural evolution of phenotypes (Freedman, 1979). For example, neonates among the Navajo and Hopi Indians, who confine infants to cradleboards, are capable of holding their heads erect from birth—an adaptation that serves both mother and infant well since the cradleboard requires erect head posture from the outset. Aboriginal infants also display the erect head posture, but Caucasian and Japanese infants do not (Freedman, 1979). Finally, cultural differences in temperament have also been found between Caucasian and Asian infants (Freedman, 1979).

Language

Human speech is believed to represent a dramatic leap in the evolution of communication flow (Wilson, 1975). The human ability to produce differentiated vocal signals accompanies the ability to position signals in relation to one another. This signal pattern is called *grammar*; it is the system of rules that specifies word arrangements that constitute meaningful communication. A number of psycholinguists (e.g., Chomsky, 1957, 1965, 1976; Lennenberg, 1967; McNeill, 1970) have argued that the unfolding of language, particularly into elements of grammar and syntax, is innately determined, and although Wilson relies extensively on psycholinguistic evidence to support his theory, psycholinguists do not necessarily endorse sociobiology.

Four groups of facts lend themselves to Wilson's contention that language is a genetically determined capacity. First, even deaf infants go through the same initial stages of babbling found in normal-hearing infants, as if the spontaneous tendency to produce speech was initially dependent on innate instructions rather than imitation of adult speech (Lennenberg, 1967). Second, infants throughout the world develop through the same sequence of stages in sound production, regardless of specific grammatical differences in language content (Lennenberg, 1967). Third, during the first stages infants from all cultures babble in sounds of their own native tongue as well as the sounds of nonnative tongues that they could not have heard or learned (Lennenberg, 1967). Fourth, children acquire the basic grammatical rules of their native language even without specific instruction (Chomsky, 1959). Taken together, these biologically determined capacities and programmed activities provide sociobiology with strong support for the notion that language acquisition is genetically programmed. However, some linguists may agree that language acquisition and grammar is under genetic control without explicitly accepting sociobiological theory. On the one hand, they may not as yet have read about sociobiology, which is entirely compatible with their position. On the other hand, they may believe that language is under genetic control without attributing such control to other types of social behavior. In that case, their disagreement with Wilson would be rather extensive.

The kinds of social behavior patterns just described represent only a fragment of those actually described by Wilson and his colleagues. Sociobiology is extremely comprehensive in its explanation of many forms of human, animal, and insect social evolution. The theory contends that most social behavior is the product of ecological pressures acting on behavioral phenotypes. At the same time, the theory is in its relative infancy, and research is only beginning to test out its many possible implications.

CONTRIBUTIONS AND CRITICISMS OF THE THEORY

Seldom has a new scientific field produced such a sharp dichotomy between enthusiasm and dread as has accompanied sociobiology (Barlow, 1980; Wilson, 1978a). In fact, the initial treatment accorded Wilson is reminiscent of the public ostracism experienced by Darwin and Freud. Still, two contributions will probably have an enduring impact on developmental psychology.

Contributions

The Debate.   Two sociobiology debates followed Wilson's *New Synthesis.* The first consisted of a wave of charges concerning potential abuse, prejudice, politics, and sex biases perceived to be inherent in the theory (Allen et al., 1978; Alper et al., 1978). The essential argument of those attacks maintained that the theory tended to belittle humans by ignoring their free will and that right-wing political and social stances would find ideological support for maintaining a biological basis for a social status quo (Caplan, 1978).

The awarding of the Pulitzer Prize in nonfiction to Wilson for *On Human Nature* (1978) may have been something of a vindication for him. Moreover, the prize probably affirmed for Wilson the importance of a critical examination of the relation between biology and culture in projecting the future of humanity. In this context, the initial charges against sociobiology seem to have been overblown and exaggerated by many accounts.

The second debate has focused more directly on the theory's claims by challenging its basic principles and evidence. The sociobiology debate (Caplan, 1978) has resulted in (1) improved clarity about what the theory is and is not claiming about human social behavior, (2) increased emphasis on the need for empirical validation of the theory's assertions, and (3) better understanding about what does and does not constitute sufficient evidence for a theoretical claim. In the past few years, for example, speculative essays seem to have given way to more empirical tests of sociobiological claims. Thus, the debate itself represents an important contribution to the scientific understanding of the relationship between culture and evolution.

Unity. A second contribution is the theory's attention to certain principles that tend to unify the continuity between humans and their ancestors. First, it implicitly holds that all humans are of one basic kind—homo sapiens. Whatever differences may be superficially apparent in cultural, geographical, or ethnic variations, they are relatively insignificant in comparison to the much more important and pervasive ways in which members of the species are alike. Second, the theory proposes a unifying approach to the biological and behavioral sciences by synthesizing widely diverse phenomena and their respective disciplines under the umbrella of sociobiology. According to Ruse (1979), no other theory rivals sociobiology in explaining such a wide scope of human characteristics. Third, sociobiology recognizes that modern homo sapiens had ancestors; they are immutably linked with the animal kingdom. In this vein, the theory holds that there is a unifying continuity between humans and their ancestors of earlier generations. This continuity is made understandable in terms of evolutionary principles— phylogenetic inertia and ecological pressure. Fourth, Wilson has constructed a unifying set of principles to explain both the physical and social elements of human adaptation, which he contends are subject to the same, immutable, all-pervasive forces of evolution.

Criticisms

Two broad categories of criticisms have been mounted against the theory. The first addresses conceptual and philosophical problems; the second concerns the theory's empirical evidence.

Conceptual Problems

Determinism. Caplan (1980) notes that many scientists have difficulty accepting the endogenous determinism inherent in sociobiology. This extreme form of determinism, while somewhat reminiscent of Freud, is unusual at a time when most human scientists tend to agree that social behavior is a function of both biology and experience.

Genotype-Phenotype Distinction. The theoretical link between genes and their phenotypic manifestations is crucial to the theory. But according to Gould (1980), no matter how adequate a job is done in identifying which behaviors are actually adaptive and which are not, no one can tell if they are genetically programmed. There is nothing given in the behavior that necessarily ties it in with genetic information in the same way as eye color can be tied to genes; behaviors and bodily features are categorically different. The distinction is vital, since the link between social behavior and genes (phenotypes and genotypes) is entirely theoretical rather than empirical. The onus is on the theory to be able to demonstrate this invisible linkage when it asserts genetic control over behavior. Such a linkage has not been convincingly demonstrated.

Adaptation. Sociobiology provides no clear conceptual basis for distinguishing between behaviors that are adaptive and those that are not. The distinction always relies on post hoc (after the fact) explanation. If a behavior leads to reproductive success, it is adaptive; if not, it is nonadaptive. Such an explanation is really no explanation at all, since a behavior that produces differentially more viable offspring is presumed to be adaptive while any behavior that is adaptive by definition produces more offspring. Since the theory defines adaptation solely in terms of its consequences rather than any constitutive qualities, it is difficult to see how one could establish the predictive validity for the concept of adaptation.

Empirical Problems

Universality. Leacock (1980) and Livingstone (1980) have identified a number of instances in which sociobiological claims of "universality" appear to be false. For example, women are not always saddled with domestic chores while men busy themselves with the commerce of business and politics. In most sub-Saharan West African cultures, women retain important and publicly recognized social, political, and economic roles (Mullings, 1976; Sudarska, 1976). Moreover, a number of West African societies have dual political systems for men and women, and on the women's side, their interests are represented at all levels (Onkjo, 1976). Women of the Mbuti of Zaire are not housebound; they participate with men in hunting wild animals (Leacock, 1980). In still other cases the biological double standard simply does not hold up. For example, in over half of the 93 cultures examined by Whyte (1978), no evidence was found for a double standard in sexual restrictions. Moreover, in 54 percent of these cultures, women were allowed to have or commonly engaged in extramarital affairs. Such data indicate that the supposed universal practice of male-female stereotyping is not quite so universal after all.

The universality of the incest taboo has not been established. Incest occurs more frequently than is generally thought (Sarles, 1975) and is apparently increasing in modern societies (Livingstone, 1980). Some societies include relatively high levels of inbreeding and even prescribe some degree of it. For example, some viable populations in South India have a high frequency of uncle-niece marriage (Sanghvi, 1966) with apparently minimal effects (Rao & Inharaj, 1977).

Continuity. It is unclear how the problem of evolutionary continuity from ancestral origins to current social practices can be adequately addressed. Gould (1980), for example, refers to the practice among sociobiologists of "story-telling," wherein possible events, links, and situations that "might have been" are related to the current status of cultures. This appraisal of the theory's demonstrations of continuity seems accurate, but it is not clear how any other means of addressing the continuity issue could be more adequate. After all, fossil remains provide physical evidence, but one cannot recover bygone behaviors or social practices from prerecorded history. While cross-cultural studies provide correlational verification for many of sociobiology's claims, there seems to be no means other than reasonable "storytelling" for connecting current data to ancient generations.

EVALUATION OF THE THEORY

Scientific Worthiness

Testability.   The moderate rating of the theory for testability (see Table 6-2) reflects a trade-off between empirical studies and some of the theoretical criticisms already raised. The tendency of sociobiologists to, in Gould's (1980) terms, "tell stories" about hunter-gatherer societies is probably necessary because the fossil record contains no direct evidence of ancient cultural behaviors. Equally important, the conceptual problems inherent in differentiating between genotypes and phenotypes seem to be insurmountable. This distinction is crucial to the theory, yet no scientific procedure has been established for testing the connection between a genotype and a social phenotype. However, sociobiology does make testable predictions about the relationship between adaptation and reproductive success (e.g., reproductive success will occur at different rates for different kinds of phenotypes). In addition, other theoretical hypotheses have been empirically tested (see Gray, 1984, for a review of research on altruism).

External Validity.   Sociobiology rates moderately high for external validity. The comprehensiveness of the theory has been extensively documented by Wilson in several works, of which the *New Synthesis* will probably be the leading reference for decades to come. While some of the claims made by the theory about cultural universals appear to be unfounded, the theory does a remarkable job of accounting for an extremely broad range of social behaviors and qualities.

Predictive Validity.   The theory rates moderate for its predictive validity. Concerning anatomical phenotypes, the predictive validity of evolutionary theory has been consistently demonstrated by plant and animal breeders. On the other

Table 6-2   Ratings of Sociobiology for Scientific Worthiness

CRITERION	HIGH	MODERATE	LOW
Testability		X	
External validity	X		
Predictive validity		X	
Internal consistency	X		
Theoretical economy	X		

hand, the difficulty of predicting adaptive social phenotypes cannot easily be overcome because adaptation is a post hoc concept. For example, phenotypes that are adaptive in one environment may not be adaptive in another (recall the case of sickle-cell anemia). If a phenotype has evolved, we can look backward and say that it is adaptive, but it is far more difficult to tell if it will be adaptive at some future time. The complexity of interacting ecological pressures contributes to this problem. In terms of potential, sociobiologists are really just getting started on testing the theory's predictive validity, so ratings on this criteria may change in the future.

Internal Consistency.   The theory is rated high on internal consistency. Throughout the chapter, a broad array of specific social behaviors have been explained using the same internal and bridge principles. Few, if any, exceptions need be made by the theory. While sociobiology has been criticized for explaining opposite tendencies of aggression and altruism with the same mechanism of natural selection, there is no necessary contradiction between the two as there was for some of Freud's concepts. It is possible and likely that both aggression and altruism have been selected as complementary (rather than conradictory) behaviors because they have been adaptive in solving different kinds of interpersonal problems in different situations. While Wilson's genetic "determinism" reflects a recurrent criticism of the theory, it also heralds the consistency of his interpretation of social behaviors.

Theoretical Economy.   Sociobiology rates high for its theoretical economy. No other theory of human nature approaches it for the breadth of scope in explaining a plethora of human, animal, and insect phenomena. Of course the theory doesn't explain everything. It does not tell us why Henry is always grumpy on Mondays or why workers call in sick more often on Fridays than any other day of the week. Nevertheless, Wilson's assumptions are minimal in terms of what he tries to explain. Moreover, relatively few core concepts are needed. The various facets of phylogenetic inertia that determine any individual's fitness in a social-environmental context are clearly important, and the variety of selection pressures set forth by the theory are not burdensome. In short, Wilson's preliminary assumptions deliver superb theoretical mileage—he explains much with relatively few principles and a small list of reasonable assumptions.

Developmental Adequacy

Temporality.   The theory passes this criterion (see Table 6-3) because it is an extension of evolutionary biology to human social behavior, thereby relying on the notion of gradual change over many generations. Such changes certainly take place over time.

Cumulativity.   Changes from one generation to the next in human social behavior result from mutations and genetic recombinations. These changes

Table 6-3   Ratings of Sociobiology for Characteristics of Development

CHARACTERISTIC	RATING
Temporality	Pass
Cumulativity	Pass
Directionality	Pass
New mode of organization	Pass
Increased capacity for self-control	Pass

produce small phenotypic modifications that gradually accumulate over time until a new social behavior is formed. For example, the evolution of status hierarchies has taken thousands of generations to change from scramble competition over food, goods, and mates into the contest competition of clothing, etiquette, and cars. In addition, language has gradually evolved from simple signals into what we know as grammar and syntax in modern speech. In these cases and many others, incremental evolutionary changes are added to preceding adaptations, so the theory passes this criterion.

Directionality. Sociobiology contends that natural selection moves evolution in the direction of increasing adaptation. This is not to say that less adaptive forms do not occasionally evolve, but as with dinosaurs, when such forms are no longer adaptive within an ecological context either new adaptations get selected or else extinction occurs. Even a social behavior that is highly adaptive in one context may become nonadaptive if the social context changes dramatically. Consequently, there is no absolute position from which to view the direction adaptation may take. Nevertheless, evolutionary adaptation is one measure of progress, and progress is one of the concepts used to define development, so the theory passes.

New Mode of Organization. Wilson believes that evolution has produced forms of social regulation that are more differentiated and more integrated patterns of social interaction than was displayed by cultures even a few thousand years ago. He argues, for example, that new modes of social government mark each of the progressive phases of civilization—from band to tribe, from tribe to chiefdom, from chiefdom to state, and from state to nation. While not every evolutionary change is regarded as a new mode of social behavior, those that do occur are regarded as expressions of the same underlying principles as other adaptations. In my judgment, the theory does an adequate job of addressing this characteristic.

Increased Capacity for Self-Control. Humans may well be unique in their capacity to predict and control their environment in many respects. The capacity of humans to erect institutions to control their social interactions (e.g., schools, police departments, courts, social service agencies, churches) means that some environmental pressures can actually be systematically altered to favor rather than oppose human survival. Moreover, the evolution of the human brain has made possible self-reflection, the capacity for rapid specialized learning, and self-control over aggressive emotions. Recall that Wilson does not argue that every behavior is controlled by a gene, only that certain qualities in a population have undergone cultural evolution. Human behavior is far less automatic and involves more flexibility and conscious choices than with any other animal. These considerations lead me to judge sociobiology as passing this criterion.

SUMMARY POINTS

1. Sociobiology explains phylogenesis rather than ontogenesis.
2. Social behavior is a pnenotypic expression of genotypes that have evolved over many generations.
3. Evolution involves three levels of organization: the genetic, the individual, and the species or cultural level. At the genetic level, random mutations and genetic recombinations occur to produce genetic variation between individuals. At the individual level, natural selection operates to accept or reject whole individuals. Favorable selection occurs through differentially higher reproductive success. At the species level, evolution operates to produce gradual changes in social behavior over many generations.
4. Sociobiology attempts to explain ten qualities of sociality by demonstrating universality, continuity, and adaptation.
5. The theory's internal principles include genetic fitness and what Wilson calls the "prime movers" of evolution—phylogenetic inertia and ecological pressure. Its bridge principles include the proximate causes of evolution that operate within the lifetime of individuals: demographic variables, rates of gene flow, and coefficients of relationship.
6. The ultimate mechanism of evolutionary change is genetic mutation and recombination.
7. The theory has contributed certain unifying concepts and a clarifying debate about the relationship between evolution and culture. Criticisms of the theory include the theory's determinism, its distinction between genotype and phenotype, the concept of adaptation, and problems with verifying universality and continuity.
8. The theory rates moderate for its scientific worthiness and high for its developmental adequacy.

PROBLEMS AND EXERCISES

Class Exercise

1. Have the class develop a measure of "family tradition" to test the claim that more cohesive families tend to engage in more reciprocal altruism. Also assess the extent to which kin selection leads to reproductive success by comparing the following two groups: (1) average size of students' uncles' and aunts' families that are highly cohesive versus (2) average size of students' uncles' and aunts' families that are low in cohesiveness. Do the results support the theory's predictions?

Individual Exercises

1. Harry and Beth are killed in a plane crash, leaving behind their three young children. Suppose that a thousand Harry and Beths have the same experience. On the basis of sociobiology, which specific relatives should volunteer most often to raise the three orphans? Justify your answer using internal and bridge principles derived from the theory.

2. Using sociobiology, describe why small children throw temper tantrums. (Hint: consider the self-competing interests between children and their parents.)

3. Many religions rely on some version of the Golden Rule to regulate interpersonal conduct. Outline a sociobiological "story" to describe the evolution of the Golden Rule. (Hint: you'll need to explain why some phenotypes are more adaptive than others and how the Golden Rule is related to phenotypes.)

SUGGESTED READINGS

More about the Theory

Barash, D. P. (1977). *Sociobiology and behavior.* New York: Elsevier.

Caplan, A. L. (Ed.). (1978). *The sociobiology debate: Readings on the ethical and scientific issues concerning sociobiology.* New York: Harper and Row.

Freedman, D. G. (1979). *Human sociobiology: A holistic approach.* New York: The Free Press.

Wilson, E. O. (1978). *On human nature.* Cambridge, MA: Harvard University Press.

Reviews of Research

Gray, J. P. (1984). *A guide to primate sociobiological theory and research.* New Haven, CT: HRAF Press.

Wilson, E. O. (1975). *Sociobiology: The new synthesis.* Cambridge, MA: The Belknap Press of Harvard University Press.

Critical Reviews

Gould, S. J. (1978). Biological potential vs. biological determinism. In A. L. Caplan (Ed.), *The sociobiology debate.* New York: Harper and Row.

Kings College Sociobiology Group (Eds.). (1982). *Current problems in sociobiology.* Cambridge, UK: Cambridge University Press.

Ruse, M. (1979). *Sociobiology: Sense or nonsense?* Boston: D. Reidel.

Sahlins, M. (1976). *The use and abuse of biology: An anthropological critique of sociobiology.* Ann Arbor, MI: University of Michigan Press.

Chapter 7

Operant Conditioning

Preview Questions

What is the difference between operant and respondent conditioning?
What assumptions underlie operant conditioning?
What types of phenomena does operant conditioning attempt to explain?
What methods are used to study operant conditioning and why?
What are the theory's internal and bridge principles?
What is the difference between negative reinforcement and punishment?
What is involved in an effective behavior modification plan?
What change mechanism accounts for learning?
What are the most important contributions and criticisms of the theory?
How does the theory rate on scientific worthiness and developmental adequacy?

HISTORICAL SKETCH

Burrhus Frederick (B. F.) Skinner was born in 1904 in Susquehanna, Pennsylvania, and attended Hamilton College in upstate New York, where he graduated Phi Beta Kappa in English literature. After college he turned his talents to writing, including serious attempts at fiction and poetry. Two years spent trying to write with "nothing to say" turned Skinner's thoughts toward graduate school (Skinner, 1976, p. 264), and in 1928 he enrolled at Harvard for graduate work in psychology. Several important influences in the history of psychology provided a context for his work.

Behaviorism

The central tenet of behaviorism is that individuals should be studied only in terms of observable characteristics. This attitude is displayed in two identifiable forms: *methodological behaviorism* and *radical behaviorism*. *Methodological behaviorism* assumes that inner exneriences (thoughts, ideas, feelings) do not exist because they are unobservable. *Radical behaviorism* takes the position that mental entities may exist and may be studied with techniques like introspection, but such techniques cannot lead to objective verification and thus cannot produce scientific knowledge. Skinner considers himself a radical behaviorist.

The Legacy of Ivan Pavlov

The experiments of Ivan Pavlov comprise one of psychology's founding landmarks. Pavlov distinguished between innate (unconditioned) and learned (conditioned) reflexes. Through a technique he called *conditioning,* he demonstrated a remarkable feat: that a dog's salivation response to food could be trained to occur in the presence of previously neutral stimuli—a bell, a light, and a whistle. He reasoned that unconditioned reflexes occur naturally as part of an organism's constitution; that is, a dog salivates when food is placed near the mouth. The food acts as an unconditioned stimulus (*US*), since it automatically elicits salivation as an unconditioned response (*UCR* or *UR*). When a neutral stimulus, say a bell, is paired a number of times with the introduction of food, then the bell itself will come to elicit the salivation response. Thus, what was initially a neutral stimulus becomes a conditioned stimulus (*CS*) that produces a conditioned response (*CR*). The key components of Pavlovian conditioning, termed *classical conditioning* today, are diagrammed in Figure 7-1.

Pavlov advanced the scientific analysis of behavior through carefully documented experiments, and he demonstrated that some kinds of responses could be systematically trained to new stimuli. However, classical conditioning has an inherent shortcoming: it cannot explain how new behaviors are learned. Note that with classical conditioning all conditioned responses originate from unconditioned responses. That means that the *UR* and the *CR* are always very similar, differing primarily in the stimuli that elicit them. Potential *CRs* would have to already exist as *URs*; new *CRs* do not emerge out of thin air. While classical con-

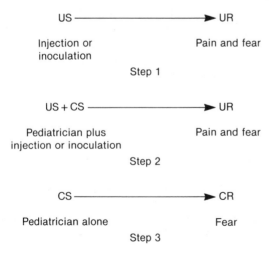

Figure 7-1   Elements of classical conditioning.

ditioning accounts for the fact that already existing responses can be conditioned to novel stimuli, it does not tell us how novel responses are acquired.

John B. Watson and the Science of Behaviorism

John B. Watson, the founder of American behaviorism, took Pavlov's basic ideas about conditioning, systematized them, and showed how psychology could be applied to problems of child development. He argued that psychology could become truly scientific only by studying behavior that is objectively measurable and by demonstrating the precise prediction and control of behavior (Watson, 1919, 1924). Watson, a methodological behaviorist, specifically rejected such mentalistic concepts as motivation, intention, thought, idea, and will because these states could never be objectively verified.

Watson initially took an extreme exogenous position in maintaining that he could, irrespective of talent, tendency, and ability, train healthy infants to become whatever he might select—doctor or lawyer, beggar or thief (Watson, 1924, p. 104). In later years he softened this position somewhat, but still maintained a strident behaviorist orientation. His interest in emotional behavior led him to study the conditioning and control of fear, and he embarked on the famous experiment with Albert, an eleven-month-old infant he trained to fear a white rat (Watson & Raynor, 1920). Watson used a classical conditioning technique, pairing a loud noise with the presentation of a white rat. After a number of trials, Albert became afraid, and whenever he saw the rat, he cried and tried to crawl away. Watson later tested for *stimulus generalization* (the tendency for a response to occur in the presence of similar stimuli) and found that Albert also feared a rabbit, a dog, cotton, and a Santa Claus mask—all furry objects that had not been previously feared. Watson's original and influential writings firmly established classical conditioning as a central theme of American psychology.

Edward Thorndike and the Law of Effect

Edward Thorndike observed that a cat placed in a cage with a simple latch would learn how to undo the latch to retrieve a piece of fish placed outside its cage. The observation is remarkable only in its implications. Thorndike argued that no conditioned response was involved in the cat's learning to escape, since there was no conditioned stimulus for that behavior. Rather, the cat appeared to "want" to get at the fish, and its goal-oriented behavior led it to learn an efficient method for procuring its escape for the fish meal. To explain this type of behavior, Thorndike (1933) proposed the *law of effect*, which emphasized goal-oriented behavior. All organisms emit responses that produce certain effects. The *law of effect* holds that responses increase or decrease in likelihood as a function of the effects they produce. Sometimes the effects make the previous response more likely to occur in the future; sometimes they make responses less likely.

Thorndike had discovered a new type of learning principle not accounted for by classical conditioning. The law of effect provided an explanation for how the *likelihood* of a response is systematically altered as a function of response consequences. However, Thorndike failed to account for the acquisition of new behaviors that had not already been acquired. That breakthrough came in the work of B. F. Skinner.

Operant Conditioning

Skinner skillfully employed Thorndike's law of effect and showed how it could explain the acquisition of new behaviors. Skinner's approach is called *operant conditioning* because organisms operate on their environment, thereby producing consequences. Operant conditioning is a dramatically different view of human nature from that found in classical conditioning.

Skinner (1950) claims that he has not written a "theory" at all, primarily because he is philosophically opposed to most kinds of theory building. However, the inclusion of his work in this book is justified on at least three counts. First, Skinner is opposed to theories of an axiomatic nature that place their hypotheses and propositions in logical priority over the empirical facts needed to support them. He is not opposed to theories constituted of descriptions and generalizations of empirical facts. In fact, it is this latter type of "theory" that he proposes. Second, operant conditioning contains all the necessary elements I use to define a theory. Third, behavioral researchers have used principles of operant conditioning to design and carry out experiments in a manner identical to what would be expected if one were basing research and development work on a "theory."

The controversies surrounding some of Skinner's books (*Beyond Freedom and Dignity, Walden Two*) have been due more to misconceptions than to careful analyses of his beliefs. In Skinner's view, behavior is shaped by its effects. Human nature is *not* puppetlike in responding to stimuli (that would be classical, not operant, conditioning). Skinner sees the organism as essentially acting on the environment and thereby producing certain consequences. These consequences come, over time, to control behavior. Simply put, people behave in certain ways because those ways tend more often than not to produce certain consequences. Because the environmental consequences of behavior are seen as the ultimate determinants of learning, Skinner's operant conditioning represents an empiricist view of human nature, a view that falls squarely within the exogenous paradigm.

STRUCTURAL COMPONENTS

Assumptions

Operant conditioning makes three fundamental assumptions about the infant's constitution at birth. First, the neonate is born with a set of species-specific reflexes. Second, the infant is born with a *tabula rasa*, "blank slate" mind. The blank mind does not remain empty for long, because the neonate immediately comes into contact with worldly sensations. These function to begin storing associations. Third, and most important from Skinner's point of view, the infant is essentially active; that is, its nature is to emit or give out with responses *not* to simply react to specific stimuli. According to Skinner, "Operant conditioning may be described without mentioning any stimulus which acts before the response is made....Operant behavior, in short, is *emitted,* rather than *elicited*" (1953, p. 107).

Problems for Study

Phenomena to Be Explained

Skinner believes that the primary task of psychology is to discover the laws that relate the behavior of organisms to the environmental forces acting on them. Additionally, behavioral theory specifically attempts to explain how behaviors are learned and how one's past experiences are related to future actions (Schwartz & Lacey, 1982, p. 13). Such an understanding requires establishing in quantitative terms the laws and principles whereby prediction and control of behavior change can be achieved. The theory does not attempt to account for mental phenomena.

The theory acknowledges only three factors that are important in deriving the "laws of operant conditioning": past learning (the habits and inhibitions already acquired), the present conditions (the array of consequences and possible consequences that control behavior), and behavior. While past learning, termed *intervening variables,* cannot be directly observed or measured, it can be controlled for in several ways: raising laboratory animals in identical environments from birth, keeping careful records of past behavioral acquisitions and their associated stimulus events, and conducting experiments that control situational elements to test predictions about causes and their effects on behavior change.

It is helpful to examine the behaviorists' agenda in more detail to highlight the scientific values underlying their structuring of the research problems. Operant conditioning attempts to describe, in precise quantitative terms, the relationship between independent (stimulus) variables and dependent (response) variables. In operant conditioning terms, *a stimulus is a consequence,* and stimulus variables are defined as *measurable* characteristics of physical consequences. A response, in turn, is measured in terms of its effect on the organism's environment. In Skinner's terminology, an *operant* is a general class or typology of responses. Thus, bar pressing is considered an operant, while any single behavior that results in the pressing of the bar is a response. By manipulating consequences (stimuli) in specific ways, measurable effects on learning can be recorded and evaluated. When measurable changes in stimulus variables produce regular, predictable, and measurable effects on response variables, a quantitative relationship or law will have been discovered. Table 7-1 shows some of the possible contents of the three categories of variables.

Methods of Study

The theory is strongly oriented to the use of experimental methodology, and animals more often than humans are used to study its concepts. Toward this end

Table 7-1   Categories of Variables in Operant Conditioning

STIMULUS VARIABLES	ORGANISMIC VARIABLES	RESPONSE VARIABLES
Reinforcement schedule	Habits	Response rate
Number of reinforced trials	Drives	Amplitude
Type of reinforcement	Inhibitions	Latency
Length of deprivation	Motivation	Resistance to extinction
Kind of deprivation		
Reinforcement delay		
Reinforcement amount		

Skinner designed a small, self-contained conditioning chamber (today known as a "Skinner box") that made the scientific study of behavior possible. The chamber allows an animal ample space for limited movement, but is not so large that the animal spends much time exploring it. The sides of the chamber are opaque and contain few distracting stimuli. Each chamber contains a control panel with feed box, lever (for rats) or response key (for pigeons), and lights for signalling when a response will produce a reward. The lights do not "elicit" the response; they signal that a lever press will result in a food reward. Initially, animals don't know what the light means, but because they are rewarded for responding only when the light is turned on, they learn to match their responding to the presence of the signal light. The lever or response key is connected to electronic switches that record each response on a *cumulative record*. The cumulative record is a graphic display of some measurable element of responses (amplitude, frequency) that has been emitted over time. Figure 7-2 shows two examples of a cumulative record. The first displays a rat's lever pressing as a function of the number of reinforced trials. The second shows a first-grader's hand raising as a function of the number of days this behavior has been reinforced each time it occurs.

The electrical switch in the Skinner box provides an objective recording of behavior; personal judgment and opinion are held strictly in check. Moreover, the resulting cumulative record shows in quantitative terms the precise degree of behavior change in a given unit of time. As a matter of definition, it makes little difference to a behaviorist what specific response actually presses the lever; all that matters is that the lever is pressed and that this fact has been recorded on the cumulative record. To perform experiments efficiently, responses should ideally be relatively quick and should require little energy. All behaviors that succeed in lever pressing are equivalent; in this way they constitute an *operant* or general class of responses. Finally, researchers systematically control variables. They determine

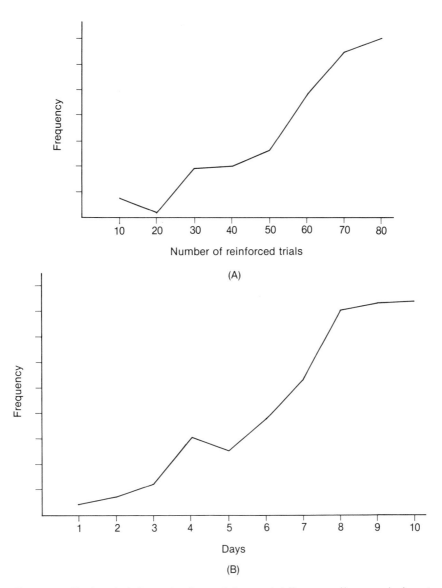

Figure 7-2   Two hypothetical examples of a cumulative record. *A*, Frequency of lever pressing in a rat as a function of the number of reinforced trials. *B*, Frequency of hand raising in a first-grader with reinforcement of each operant over a ten-day period.

which operants will be reinforced, when to deliver reinforcement, and what type and amount of reinforcement to administer. These qualities—objectivity, quantitative measurement, and controlled experiments—are the hallmarks of modern science.

Internal Principles

Differential Reinforcement

Infants, children, and adults emit behaviors. Some behaviors produce favorable consequences and thus tend to occur with increasing frequency in similar situations. Such a pattern can be explained by the principle of *differential reinforcement,* which holds that some behaviors more than others produce consequences, and by association those behaviors increase in frequency. For example, imagine the first day of school when a class of elementary students is confronted with a new teacher. The students at first emit a variety of behaviors: whispering, pointing, throwing spitballs, raising hands, reading comics. Suppose also that the new teacher studiously ignores all behaviors except hand raising, which is systematically followed by praise and attention. The principle of differential reinforcement accounts for the subsequent increase in hand raising among the students.

A differential reinforcer occurs after a behavior has been emitted. The consequence or stimulus differentiates between behaviors, hence its name. Differential reinforcers account for a wide variety of behaviors—how we walk down the street, shopping and study habits, manners, and smiling at someone on the street. We do these things because of the consequences generated by past behaviors, not because specific stimuli elicit them. The mere sight of a telephone does not, for example, automatically elicit phone-calling behavior. Rather, whether we decide to call someone is based on the present circumstances and the past consequences of our phone-calling experience.

Some events, like the presentation of food when we are hungry or drink when we are thirsty, are reinforcing on their first presentation. These are called *primary reinforcers* because their effect is direct and need not be conditioned. However, primary reinforcers are not necessarily limited to food and water; they also include brain stimulation, the opportunity to exercise, and tactile stimulation.

A different order of stimulus, such as mother's face, money, kissing, and watching television may initially be neutral, but with certain kinds of experiences they may acquire their own reinforcing effects (Kling & Schrier, 1971, p. 660). Events of this type, termed *secondary reinforcers,* are far more prevalent consequences of everyday behavior than are primary reinforcers. For example, the reinforcing effects associated with talking on the phone, reading a letter, achieving a goal, and receiving meritorious recognition are all acquired secondary reinforcers. Because secondary reinforcers acquired their effect during the individual's past experiences, their effects may be more limited than with primary reinforcers. For example, while approval and praise are often secondary reinforcers for middle class students, they may not have the same effect on other students.

The Discriminative Stimulus

A *discriminative stimulus* signals the conditions under which some behaviors will be reinforced and others will not, but it is *not* the reinforcing effect and thus cannot bring about changes in behavior. However, when reinforcement occurs in the presence of or following its presentation, the discriminative stimulus will come to be associated with the behavior that produces the reinforcing effect (Skinner, 1953). The relationship between a discriminative stimulus, an operant behavior, and a reinforcing stimulus is shown schematically in Figure 7-3.

My daughter Megan has learned that soliciting parents for play when they are in the den is reinforced, but not when they are in the kitchen cooking dinner. Thus, the sight of parents sitting in the den has become a discriminative stimulus for her because it signals a condition under which her request for play will be reinforced. Similarly, children learn to pick flowers according to their discriminative stimuli—blossoms. The blossoms are not themselves reinforcing, but they signal the availability of reinforcement for certain behaviors, like presenting them to a parent and receiving a kiss.

Shaping

Even with differential reinforcement and discriminative stimuli, new operant behaviors do not suddenly appear from nowhere. They must be learned through *shaping*, sometimes called the *principle of successive approximation* because behaviors already present (operants) are reinforced for their gradual, incremental approximation of a new behavior. For example, children do not automatically put their toys away after playing with them. In fact, if we were to wait for that to happen in order to reinforce it, we'd have a very long wait. Fortunately, such a behavior can be shaped. First, a discriminative stimulus needs to be established. This can be done by announcing, "Its time to put the toys away." Given that situation, reinforcement could be administered whenever the child approaches a toy. That increases the frequency of approaching toys after the verbal signal. Then reinforcement can be withheld until the child approaches and picks up a toy, after which reinforcement is administered. When picking up toys has been established, reinforcement may again be withheld until the child picks up a toy and turns toward the shelf where it goes. This routine may be repeated until the child learns successively to pick up a toy, turn toward its shelf, walk there, and place the toy in its place. Similarly, I am shaping my daughter Megan's bicycle riding behavior by raising the training wheels one notch every few weeks. By next summer her coordination and balance should be sufficient for me to take them off her bike.

Bridge Principles

Schedules of Reinforcement

Consequences can be administered according to different timetables called *schedules* or *contingencies of reinforcement. Continuous* reinforcement is the ad-

Figure 7-3   Relationship between discriminative stimulus, operant behavior, and reinforcing stimulus.

ministration of a stimulus after each operant, such as when a toddler is praised each time he uses the potty. Continuous reinforcement produces faster learning than any of the other schedules, but behaviors that are continuously reinforced are also the easiest to forget.

Intermittent reinforcement occurs when stimuli are administered either on the basis of a ratio (reinforcing only a certain percentage of behaviors) or on the basis of a time interval (reinforcing only after a certain duration has elapsed). A *fixed ratio* schedule administers reinforcement every *nth* behavior, as when a fourth-grader receives one star on each seventh correct answer. Fixed ratio schedules produce high response rates. With *variable ratio* reinforcement, the stimulus is administered *on the average* of every *nth* behavior. For example, such a schedule would describe a young child trying to hit a nail with a hammer. While missing most of the time, the child makes irregular contact with the nail (number of swings varies between reinforcements) *an average* of once every seventh swing.

Interval reinforcement parallels ratio schedules, except that it applies to time rather than number of behaviors. Interval schedules reinforce the first response that follows a predetermined interval of time (Kling, 1971, p. 605). With a *fixed interval* schedule, reinforcing stimuli are administered following a specified period of time during which some ongoing behavior is performed. For example, a teacher could reinforce his students once every five minutes that they spend "on task." With a *variable interval* schedule, time intervals vary from one reinforcement to the next according to *an average* of one reinforcer per time period. For example, parents sometimes unwittingly use such a schedule to encourage their children to clean up their toys. In that situation, variable reinforcement might average once every five minutes over a half hour's time, although the time interval between reinforcing stimuli would vary.

Ratio schedules tend to produce relatively high response rates when the ratio is small, lower response rates when the ratio of rewards to behaviors becomes large (Ferster & Skinner, 1957). Exactly what constitutes "small" and "large" ratios is a function of both the organism and the situation. For example, a ratio of 100 lever presses for one dollar in reinforcement would produce many responses from a teenager hankering for video machine change. The same reinforcement and response ratio would produce virtually no responses from either a migrating pigeon on its way south or from a corporate executive fighting a takeover bid for her company. Additionally, fixed ratio schedules tend to produce postreinforcement pauses as well as some complete interruptions in responding (Ferster & Skinner, 1957). This pattern can be avoided by using variable schedules, which produce consistently high responding. Interval schedules produce a very steady, stable response rate with relatively few pauses or bursts of responses (Schwartz & Lacey, 1982) and are useful in maintaining continuous behaviors like doing homework and raking leaves.

Random schedules administer reinforcement in a completely haphazard manner. It is relatively easy to get computers to generate completely random reinforcement schedules in today's modern experimental laboratory. Because there is no systematic pattern to administering reinforcement, the individual never knows when a particular behavior will be reinforced. Consequently, behavior that has received random reinforcement is extremely difficult to extinguish. This may account for why teachers sometimes find it so difficult to extinguish certain undesirable behaviors that were learned under or continue to be randomly reinforced.

When it is desirable that an individual acquire a new behavior, the schedules of reinforcement can be used to shape and maintain the desired behavior. One usually begins by shaping the desired behavior using continuous reinforcement to produce the fastest learning. When the behavior has been learned, it can be maintained with the least effort using intermittent reinforcement. Complex routines can be established in which two or more schedules operate simultaneously and independently, each tied to a different operant. Such procedures are called *concurrent schedules*. Children, for example, may receive a kiss each night from their mothers (fixed interval) and occasional gifts when they have been especially good (variable ratio). The schedule to be preferred is determined by one's particular circumstances.

Extinction, the elimination of a behavior, occurs when behaviors produce no effective consequences. Ironically, the fact that an undesirable behavior continues to be emitted when a parent steadfastly provides no reinforcing consequences may indicate that other reinforcing effects (whether by teachers, peers, or unknown others) may still be occurring.

Generalization

Behavior that occurs in a given situation will often generalize or transfer to new but similar situations. Children who have begun to talk may talk to strange people who resemble parents but not to squirrels, fire hydrants, or sofas. Responding to different situational cues with the same behavior is called *stimulus generalization* because the similarity of situational cues to an original discriminative stimulus is generalized. Stimulus generalization accounts for many behaviors ranging from children's use of "Daddy" in greeting other adult males, to test and math anxieties, to my son Matthew's brandishing the family yardstick and fallen tree branches as his "sword."

In contrast, *response generalization* occurs when different responses occur in the presence of the same discriminative stimulus. This might be displayed, for example, when children learn to balance, then brake, then steer, then pedal, then turn corners on a new bicycle. While the discriminative stimulus (bicycle) remains constant, these responses are learned generalizations of balancing posture.

Chaining

Individual behaviors can be combined into complex strings called *behavior chains*. Animal performances seen in circuses are probably the most visible examples of behavioral chaining. People also display behavior chains when they take a walk in the neighborhood, change an infant's diaper, get dressed, cook a meal, or flip the television dial for the most interesting (reinforcing) program. Each of these acts can be performed in a relatively smooth, integrated series of steps. However, it is the effect *produced by the last behavior in the sequence* that produces reinforcement for the chain. For example, the odor of a smelly diaper provides a discriminative stimulus for a father to pick up his son, take him to the changing table, remove his garments, take off his diaper, throw it in the wastebasket, clean his son's bottom, reach for a new diaper, put it on, reclothe the infant, and set him down off the changing table thereby gaining negative reinforcement by removing a noxious odor.

Change Mechanism

Skinner's work has focused on consequences that both increase the likelihood of behavior and that, through shaping, lead to new behaviors. To account for behavior learning, Skinner distinguishes between positive and negative reinforcers. The distinction is relatively simple: *positive reinforcement* consists of the *administration of a stimulus* that increases behavior, as when children are rewarded with praise, candy, or attention. Similarly, *negative reinforcement* also increases behavior but in a different manner. It denotes the *release from* a noxious or aversive stimulus (Skinner, 1953, p. 73). In both cases the effect is similar—strengthening of antecedent operant behaviors. For example, a child sitting in "time out" may apologize for hitting another and then be sent off to play. The cessation of "time out" acts as a negative reinforcer whose effect is to increase the likelihood that the child will apologize in the future when placed in "time out" for hitting. Note that with negative reinforcement the child is already experiencing a noxious stimulus. Consequently, release from "time out" provides a favorable consequence—no more sitting alone.

Punishment is not the same as negative reinforcement. It decreases the probability of a behavior. Consequently, it may be utilized to eliminate rather than instigate certain operant behaviors. Punishment can consist of either the *administration* of an aversive stimulus or the *elimination* of a positive reinforcer (Skinner, 1953, p. 73). For example, administration of an aversive stimulus could be used to punish misbehavior with a spanking, tardiness with a scolding, or interrupting with a frown. Similarly, removal of a positive reinforcer, such as taking away dating privileges, could be used to punish a teenager for breaking curfew.

Skinner (1971) has personally argued against the use of punitive coercion, although he also concedes that it is the most widespread controlling technique. He believes that while punishment may temporarily remove undesirable behaviors, in the long run it does not actually eliminate them (Skinner, 1953, p. 190). Moreover, he contends that it may produce unintended side effects like fear, anxiety, awkwardness, timidity, and stuttering.

It is important to note that reinforcement and punishment are defined by their effects on antecedent behaviors. Prime rib, for example, may be a positive reinforcer for some people, but a vegetarian (for whom the sight of red meat is noxious) might view the same entree as punishment. Alcoholic beverages produce reinforcing effects for some, punitive effects in others. My daughter treats raw coffee beans as a rare delicacy (ugh!). The point here is that a stimulus is defined solely in terms of its effect on behavior.

EXPLAINING HUMAN DEVELOPMENT: THE RESEARCH

An extensive research literature on operant conditioning exists. Even a fairly limited list of citations would exhaust the limits of this chapter. What follows then is only a brief outline of different types of research that demonstrate applications of operant conditioning.

Discrimination Learning

Discrimination learning is the general term given to most types of behavior change involving responses in the presence of a discriminative stimulus. For example, learning the names of shapes requires one to discriminate between stimuli on the basis of their geometrical properties, and learning when it is safe to cross a street or drive through an intersection requires discriminating between the consequences implied by red and green traffic lights. Discrimination learning is one of the most pervasive types of learning, as evidenced by the following areas of research.

Concept Learning. Concept learning is a specific kind of discrimination learning. Concepts, like those taught in school, can be viewed as requiring complex learning of a myriad of associations between discriminative stimuli and appropriate behaviors. Cast in this light, considerable research has been undertaken to demonstrate the viability of using behavioral principles to teach academic content. Concept learning requires programming both the stimulus material and the contingencies of reinforcement (Bijou, 1970). In turn, programming the stimulus materials may also include such necessary preparatory steps as: (1) discrimination training on a sequence of progressively more difficult tasks (e.g., Hively, 1962); (2) the use of response errors to signal incomplete learning and the necessary return to earlier, less difficult tasks (Holland, 1961); and (3) *fading* or gradual changes in stimulus salience. Fading procedures require the gradual introduction or *fading in* of incorrect alternatives in discrimination tasks (Terrace, 1963), as when students must choose between alternative answers on multiple-choice tests. One may also *fade across* stimulus dimensions by transferring control from one stimulus to another. The gradual progression that takes many years to shift the toddler from "reading" picture books to reading word books is an example of fading across stimulus dimensions (Reese, Howard, & Rosenberger, 1977, p. 280). A variety of studies have demonstrated the effectiveness of fading procedures in concept and skill acquisitions. For example, it has been used to teach handwriting (Skinner & Krakower, 1968), basic reading skills (Corey & Shamow, 1972), number concepts (Suppes & Ginsberg, 1962), right-left concepts (Jeffrey, 1958; Tochette, 1968), and form discrimination (Macht, 1971; Sidman & Stoddard, 1967).

Prosocial Behavior. Another area of children's discrimination learning is their acquisition of *prosocial* behaviors, defined generically as any cooperative social behavior. Operant conditioning would predict that the frequency of children's helping and sharing would increase following reinforcement. The prediction tends to hold up. For example, if preschoolers are reinforced for donating something (marbles given to them by an experimenter) to a classmate, they are likely to make future donations when the experimenter is in their room (Fischer, 1963). Moreover, behavior modification programs typically produce dramatic improvements in children's cooperative behavior (Mithaug & Burgess, 1968; Vogler, Masters, & Merrill, 1970; Vogler, Masters, & Merrill, 1971). In a typical study, children between seven and twelve years of age were required to work together to solve a problem. They cooperated with each other much more readily when they were individually reinforced for synchronous work, but their cooperation waned when the reinforcers were withdrawn (Azrin & Lindsley, 1956). While praise is often an effective reinforcer that increases sharing behavior in preschool children (Gelfand, Hartmann, Cromer, Smith, & Page, 1975), it seems to be more effective with middle-class preschoolers than with those from lower classes (Doland & Adelberg, 1967).

Deviant Behaviors. Deviant behaviors may be categorized as another type of discrimination learning, since the behaviors are assumed to have been acquired under some type of reinforcement contingency. Three techniques are typically employed to get rid of deviant behaviors: differential reinforcement of incompatible behaviors, extinction, and punishment. The first two techniques are often used in tandem when undesirable behaviors are ignored (extinguished) and desirable behaviors are reinforced. For example, disruptive classroom behaviors have been eliminated and replaced by more desirable ones using differential teacher attention as a reinforcer (Becker, Madsen, Arnold, & Thomas, 1967; Hall, Lund, & Jackson, 1968; Ward & Baker, 1968). Increasing the frequency of behaviors incompatible with disruption, like in-class studying, both reduces disruptive behavior and improves classroom productivity (Broden, Bruce, Mitchell, Carter, & Hall, 1970; Cossairt, Hall, & Hopkins, 1973; Madsen, Becker, & Thomas, 1968).

Differential social praise and attention are also useful in modifying behavior problems. For example, differential attention has been used to decrease inappropriate crying exhibited by two preschool children (Hart, Allen, Buell, Harris, & Wolf, 1964); to eliminate a nursery school girl's crawling around the nursery school floor (Harris, Johnston, Kelley, & Wolf, 1964); to reduce excessive crying in infants (Etzel & Gewirtz, 1967); and to shape sitting still in a hyperactive preschooler (Twardosz & Sajwaj, 1972).

Learned Helplessness. Some people act as if they have the world on a string; others act as if the world, in all its whimsical calamities, deliberately conspires to render them helpless. Psychologists believe such people have learned how to be helpless, a behavior pattern that can also be unlearned. *Learned helpless-*

ness can be clarified by a simple example. Suppose that parents irregularly administer love and affection mixed with abuse and punishment to their children, but neither type of consequence is consistently tied to their children's behavior. Sometimes the children will be reinforced and sometimes punished for the same behavior (e.g., asking permission to do something, requesting a snack). Such interactions may in fact be fairly typical for children of alcoholic parents. These children learn that parental behavior, in terms of consequences, cannot be controlled. Couple this specific learning with stimulus generalization, and they may also learn that the larger environment is unresponsive to their efforts; consequences that they cannot control continue to befall them. Over time and with enough experiences like these, such children will learn a special kind of behavior called *helplessness*. Learned helplessness (Maier, 1970; Maier & Seligman, 1976; Seligman, 1975) has been demonstrated in both the laboratory and natural environments, with both humans and other species.

CONTRIBUTIONS AND CRITICISMS OF THE THEORY

Contributions

Scientific Methodology. Operant conditioning has greatly advanced our understanding of the behavior of organisms, largely through the use of experimental procedures. The laboratory environment provides the scientist with (1) a means for systematically controlling animal experiences and (2) a situation for precisely measuring the quantitative relationship between independent (causes) and dependent (effects) variables. By concentrating their attention on the measurement of directly observable behaviors, these scientists have avoided many of the problems inherent in mentalistic and introspective approaches to human nature.

Laws of Operant Conditioning. Skinner's approach to science represents the *inductive* method. Rather than postulate a theory and then proceed to test it (deductive method), he starts with his empirical observations and only gradually proceeds toward tentative generalizations or laws (Wolman, 1981, p. 124). He has described five *static* laws, seven *dynamic* laws, and eleven *interaction* laws that account for the behavior of organisms (Skinner, 1938). For example, the *law of compatibility* holds that two or more responses may occur simultaneously only if they do not overlap or interfere with one another. Accordingly, one could exhibit singing and bicycle riding at the same time, whereas studying and watching television cannot occur simultaneously because they are incompatible. The *law of conditioning of type R* holds that an operant is strengthened by the presentation of a reinforcing stimulus. Such laws represent an elegantly simple account of the behavior of organisms within a single encompassing theory.

Practical Applications. Because predictable effects are consistently produced by manipulating reinforcing/punishing stimuli, behavioral research has had widespread practical impact in a variety of arenas. Educators use behavioral principles to manage student learning and conduct; psychologists implement behavior modification programs in institutional settings; parents use reinforcers to shape children's toilet habits and manners. It is probably reasonable to claim that operant conditioning has had greater practical impact (in both number and variety of uses) than any other psychological theory. Several examples are described more fully in Chapters 11 and 12.

Behavior Modification. A systematic plan for altering behavior is called *behavior modification* and is one of the most useful contributions of operant conditioning. The following steps give a brief outline of how one might establish a behavior modification plan.

STEP 1—IDENTIFY A REINFORCER. It is important to establish rather than assume that a consequence has reinforcing effects. To do this, one must first establish a baseline or *operant level* of responding for some commonly occurring behavior (e.g., eye contact, smiling, uttering the word "I"). Next, one administers continuous reinforcement whenever one of those behaviors occurs. Keep a cumulative record covering a specific period of time. If the response rate of the behavior for this time period does not increase significantly, then the "reinforcement" is not producing reinforcing effects and cannot be counted on to produce learning under the behavior modification plan. Try several other possible reinforcers and record their effect on response rates. Only when responding significantly increases during your selected time period can you have confidence that the consequence produces the necessary reinforcement. It is often advisable to establish several reinforcers; if the subject becomes satiated on one, another can be substituted.

STEP 2—ESTABLISH THE FINAL FORM. The second step requires one to establish a specific description of the behavior to be learned, being sure to observe at least two rules. *First,* the final form must be observable and measurable. Thus, specifying "a positive attitude toward school" would not constitute an observable behavior. However, "smiles when entering the classroom" is observable and might be taken as evidence of a positive attitude. *Second,* always specify the *presence* of a specific operant. The subject must act to receive reinforcement. Getting rid of a behavior can be accomplished through extinction; no behavior modification plan is needed, provided one has control over the reinforcers. Specifying that "Judy has to stop shouting in the hallway" would be inappropriate since it describes the absence of behavior. The final form may be an entirely new behavior, or it may be a change in an already existing behavior (e.g., change in frequency or amplitude).

STEP 3—ESTABLISH A REINFORCEMENT SCHEDULE. It is important to plan and follow an established reinforcement schedule. It may be best to begin with continuous reinforcement, since that schedule produces the fastest learning. Once a behavior has been established, one might switch to one of the intermittent schedules to maintain the behavior.

STEP 4—DESIGN A LEARNING ENVIRONMENT. Set up a total environmental situation designed to maximize learning the final form specified in step 2. Designing an effective environment may require a bit of creative behavior, or it may be as simple as telling the subject what will be required to obtain reinforcement (e.g., "Each time you smile, I'll smile back"). In setting up an environment, it is sometimes helpful to arrange conditions so that behaviors incompatible with the final form are eliminated.

STEP 5—SHAPE THE FINAL FORM. If the final form of behavior is not already part of the subject's repertoire, it will be necessary to shape it. To do that, first reinforce gross approximations to the final form. On successive occasions, reinforce only increasingly closer approximations to the final form. Using this "law of successive approximations" should enable one to proceed with the behavior modification once the final form is emitted often enough to be reinforced. *If the final form is already a part of the subject's behavioral repertoire, step 5 may be skipped.*

STEP 6—IMPLEMENT THE PLAN. Only when the first five steps have been carefully planned (including establishing rather than guessing at a reinforcer) is one in position to implement the behavior modification plan. It is important to keep cumulative records of responding and reinforcement, because revision of the plan may be necessary. Revisions should be made in the reinforcement, the reinforcement schedule, or the learning environment when data indicate that progress toward the final form of behavior is not being accomplished.

Criticisms

Reductionism. One of the most frequent criticisms made against operant conditioning is its inherent *reductionism.* In the classic sense, reductionism represents efforts to reduce higher order processes to physiological/biochemical processes. In this sense, Skinner is manifestly anti-reductionistic. However, there is a much broader sense in which operant conditioning is reductionistic—namely in its assumption that complex behaviors can best be understood when they are broken down, differentiated, and separated into smaller units. By studying and testing the properties of each unit, a more thorough and detailed understanding of the complex behavior may be gained.

The problem with reductionism is that complex behaviors may not be adequately explained by adding together the properties of its discrete elements. There is considerable debate, for example, about whether such complex behavior as talking, teaching, and programming a computer can be adequately explained in terms of their discrete elements.

Definition of Behavior. Skinner shrewdly defines a behavior in terms of its effect on the environment. The advantage of such a definition is twofold. On the one hand, behavior can be objectively quantified—frequency, response laten-cy, resistance to extinction, and so forth. On the other hand, behavior can be, within a laboratory situation, conveniently segmented into discrete units. However, naturally occurring behavior tends to be like William James's consciousness: it seems to unfold as one long continuous stream of motion and activity. How one goes about segmenting a continuous behavioral stream into separable units that can then be measured as repeatable events is a serious issue. If, for example, be-havioral events occur in different time spans (e.g., pressing a lever, turning off an irritating alarm clock, completing a triple gainer off a diving board), then a mean-ingful explanation of behavior must necessarily admit to different types of divisions of the behavioral stream (Zeiler, 1979, p. 79). Skinner is quite aware of this problem, and he hopes that in the future behavior analysis will be able to ac-count for the fluidity of behavior (Evans, 1968, pp. 20–21).

The search for meaningful units of behavior reflects, in part, the extreme-ly vital role "units" have played in the development of the sciences (Marr, 1979). Units allow measurement, and objective measurement is a vital element to scien-tific activity. The fact that natural behavior is artificially segmented in the laboratory reflects both a decision of convenience and an assumption about the orderliness of science. The gain for the psychologist is that such segmentation makes it simpler and hence easier to study behavior. The important question is, however, whether laws about conveniently segmented units of behavior can ade-quately account for even a part of the range of time spans (ranging from small to very large) over which natural behaviors occur.

Biased Relations and Belongingness.   The goal of behaviorism is to es-tablish a set of exhaustive, general laws that, in quantitative terms, accounts for behavioral learning. In this effort, it is vital to differentiate between a unique law that accounts for only a single operant emitted from a single organism in only one situation from a more general law that accounts for many operants in many or-ganisms in many situations. The behaviorist is not, for example, interested in general laws of lever pressing, but lever presses are studied because they are "ob-jective" operants that can be easily counted to measure changes produced by stimulus variation (Schwartz & Lacey, 1982, pp. 174–191). The difficult problem here is to separate individual and species-specific characteristics from more general behavioral laws. This overarching goal has prompted behaviorists to seek out "unbiased" tests of behavioral principles.

While the behaviorist's laboratory was believed to promote the study of unbiased relations between operants and reinforcers, certain problems have arisen. Imagine, for example, that a rat has been conditioned to press a lever to ob-tain a drink of water containing a mild saccharin solution. Twenty minutes after its last drink, the rat is injected with a mild poison that produces nearly instant nausea. The nausea is not caused by anything the rat has done, yet in the future the rat steadfastly avoids drinking the water. Similarly, imagine that precisely one hour after returning from a marvelous meal at a local French restaurant, you suddenly become violently sick. It is almost certain that you would place the cause of your illness in something you had just eaten. You would certainly not blame the location of the table where you ate, nor would you likely blame either the decor, the lighting, or the music in spite of the fact that each of these stimuli bears exactly the same temporal relation to your nausea (Schwartz & Lacey, 1982, p. 182).

These two examples reflect an organismic tendency to associate certain types of events with certain types of causes, a phenomenon called *belongingness*. Eating and nausea just seem to be naturally connected in a way that audio tones and nausea are not. The problem of belongingness is that it undermines the behaviorist assumption that artificial laboratory settings measure unbiased relationships between operants and conditioned stimuli. Consequently, it may be far more difficult to separate general laws from species-specific responses than was ever contemplated.

Of Mice and Men.   Behaviorists believe that general laws of learning apply to humans as well as animals. The implication of this belief is that the study of animal learning in no way prejudices the explanation of human learning. In light of the previous discussion on belongingness and biased relations, one can at least question whether it is possible to learn about humans by studying animals (Schwartz & Lacey, 1982, p. 184).

Behavioral theory has, over the years, concentrated its efforts on examining learning effects that reveal the adaptability and flexibility of organisms, because these are precisely the phenomena that support the position that environmental events control behavior. In contrast, relatively little attention has been directed at those types of behaviors that reflect biased relations. The problem here is that the presence of biased relations in organisms *prevents* certain types of learning from occurring. These organismic *constraints on learning* imply that there are distinct, qualitative differences between species in terms of what they can learn as well as in the facility with which different types of learning can occur. Such a claim undermines the behaviorist's search for general laws because it implies that there can be nothing more than species-specific laws of learning.

Reinforcement Reconsidered.   Probably one of the most vexing problems behaviorists face is explaining what makes a reinforcer reinforcing. Put differently, why do some stimuli have reinforcing effects (Kling & Schrier, 1971, p. 660)? The behaviorist attempts (possibly unintentionally) to circumvent this problem by defining reinforcement solely in terms of its effects, but that solution does little to further our understanding of the intrinsic qualities of reinforcers. Moreover, the solution is a tautology: a stimulus is reinforcing if it increases behavior; increases in behavior are caused by a reinforcing stimulus. There is a clear need for some thoughtful analyses of the concept of reinforcement, especially since it plays such an important role in the explanation of operant behavior.

EVALUATION OF THE THEORY

Scientific Worthiness

Operant conditioning, with its strong empiricist tradition and its emphasis on control and prediction of observable, measurable behavior, garners very high ratings for its scientific worthiness (see Table 7-2).

Testability.   Many aspects of the theory contribute to its high ranking for testability. The researcher can control and manipulate a wide variety of independent variables. Modern equipment also makes possible the objective measurement and recording of learning. The effects of different reinforcement schedules can be assessed with great accuracy across many individuals. The failure to provide conceptual definitions for behavior and for reinforcement undermines the theory's conceptual soundness, but it does not detract from laboratory tests of the quantitative relations between stimulus and response variables.

External Validity.   There is little doubt that at least some portion of children's behavior is acquired as the direct result of the administration of reinforcement. In actual life, reinforcement may be as much a matter of "hit and miss" inconsistency as of fully intentional planning. Nevertheless, it is probably true that the circumstances under which children receive reinforcement closely approximate several of the schedules of reinforcement described earlier. The examples described here of discrimination and concept learning, learned helplessness, and control of deviant behaviors represent only a portion of the many published demonstrations of how behavior can be predicted and controlled by operant conditioning. Thus, the theory is given a high ranking for external validity.

Predictive Validity.   Two kinds of concerns must be taken into account in judging the theory's predictive validity. On the one hand there is adequate demonstration that in laboratory studies the laws of operant conditioning hold up quite well as predictors of animal performance. Predictions derived from the theory are also upheld with adequate frequency when applied to humans in naturalistic settings. On the other hand, however, the problems described above

Table 7-2   Ratings of Operant Conditioning for Scientific Worthiness

CRITERION	HIGH	MODERATE	LOW
Testability	X		
External validity	X		
Predictive validity		X	
Internal consistency	X		
Theoretical economy	X		

with biased relations and with extrapolating from laboratory studies to humans, reflect serious concerns about the theory's predictive validity. Moreover, the fact that human behavior exists in the context of multiple stimuli that may be reinforcing or punishing, may occur according to different schedules, and may exert diverse efficiencies indicates that the complexity of the human situation cannot easily be reduced to simple quantitative laws. The relative merits of these considerations have lead me to judge the theory as moderate in terms of its predictive validity.

Internal Consistency. The high ranking for internal consistency owes its explanation to the simplicity of operant conditioning principles. To explain behavior change, the theory relies on limited but simple internal and bridge principles with no need for recourse to other *ad hoc* concepts. Moreover, the small number and magnitude of exceptional findings (those unexplainable by the theory) has not been occasioned by many attempts to shore up the theory with revisions (there are, of course, some exceptions to this point, like those found in social cognitive theory in the next chapter). Overall, the simple mechanisms of operant conditioning provide clear, straightforward, and internally consistent explanatory principles.

Theoretical Economy. From the foregoing discussion, it should be clear that the high rank of operant conditioning for theoretical economy also rests on the elegant simplicity of the theory. Relatively few and modest assumptions are made about the nature of the infant. With these the theory proceeds to explain an incredible diversity of behavioral learning that spans both humans and animal species.

Developmental Adequacy

Temporality. Shaping through reinforcement is the means by which new behaviors are acquired, and it necessarily implies a period of time during which a behavior is gradually learned. Consequently, the theory does account for how change takes place over time (see Table 7-3).

Cumulativity. Shaping involves the learning of a new behavior from the starting point of previously learned behaviors. Later behavioral acquisitions are

Table 7-3   Ratings of Operant Conditioning for Characteristics of Development

CHARACTERISTIC	RATING
Temporality	Pass
Cumulativity	Pass
Directionality	?
New mode of organization	Fail
Increased capacity for self-control	Fail

built bit by bit, incrementally upon earlier acquisitions. Even complex behavioral chains are comprised of the sequential addition of new elements to the behavioral string. Thus, the theory passes this characteristic.

Directionality. Directionality implies a certain sense of developmental progress superimposed on the acquisition of new behaviors. In one sense, operant conditioning meets this condition—in the sense that adults' behaviors are somehow different from infants' and children's behaviors, but the most important dimension of difference is quantity: adults simply have acquired more behaviors and more behavior chains (this property was already covered under the cumulativity criterion). It is unclear in what other respects the theory accounts for directionality in behavior change. Moreover, the notion that behaviors that get acquired are *not* necessarily permanent or enduring (they can be extinguished) tends to imply that development so conceived is essentially nondirectional in nature. These considerations lead me to question (without passing or failing) whether or not the theory really accounts for the characteristic of directionality.

New Mode of Organization. This characteristic implies that accounts of development explain changes that result in new organizational rules or processes not previously present in the organism. The unit of organization for operant conditioning is the *association* that is formed between a response and its reinforcing stimulus. An adult's behaviors are organized no differently from the child's, although each one's behaviors may be controlled by different stimuli. Each has learned specific response-stimulus associations that govern their behavior. While new associations are learned, these represent new additions (cumulativity) to the same mode of organizing behavior rather than the acquisition of new modes of organization. Since the association unit is the only unit of behavioral organization recognized in operant conditioning, it fails this criterion.

Increased Capacity for Self-Control. The capacity for self-control is not recognized as a property of human, or for that matter, of animal nature. Skinner (1971) argues that we are all controlled all of the time. Even when we do what we want to do, we have been controlled through prior reinforcement contingencies to learn to want to do certain things more than others. So, while Skinner views self-control and free will as both illusions and bad philosophy, there is one specific sense in which he would admit that individuals can acquire increasing self-control. Individuals can be trained to control their own reinforcement contingencies, as is the case with many institutionalized patients who are taught basic self-maintenance skills. However, self-control of one's own reinforcement contingencies must itself be controlled by other reinforcers. Simply put, operant conditioning recognizes no acquisitions in human nature that diminish the environment's control over our behavior. Consequently, it fails this criterion.

SUMMARY POINTS

1. Pavlovian or classical conditioning *elicits* responses because the controlling stimulus (UCS or CS) precedes the behavioral response. Operant or instrumental conditioning requires an active organism that is instrumental in producing consequences of its action.

2. Thorndike proposed the *law of effect* to explain how some behaviors, because they are reinforced more often than others, increase in their response probability.

3. The theory of operant conditioning presupposes that infants begin their learning with a phylogenetically determined set of reflexes, a *tabula rasa* mind, and a naturally active disposition.

4. Operant conditioning attempts to explain the cause-effect relationship between the class of stimulus variables and the class of response variables. Stimulus variables are uniquely defined as measurable consequences of an individual's behavior. The theory adopts scientific attitudes toward research in its use of cumulative records to assess objective, observable, and measurable characteristics of stimulus and response characteristics.

5. The administration of differential reinforcement produces learning of reinforced behaviors but no effect on nonreinforced behaviors. Reinforcers may be primary or secondary.

6. Discriminative stimuli exert powerful control over behavior because they precede and signal the availability of a reinforcer. They have no reinforcing property of their own.

7. Positive reinforcement is the administration of a consequence that increases behavior. Negative reinforcement, the release from an aversive stimulus, also increases behavior. Punishment is the administration of an aversive stimulus; its effect is to decrease behavior.

8. Reinforcement schedules, each with unique effects, may be continuous, intermittent, random, or extinction.

9. Individual operants may be conditioned to occur in a given sequence called a behavior chain, where the last behavior produces reinforcing consequences.

10. The theory's contributions include a scientific methodology, laws of conditioning, and practical applications. It has been criticized for its reductionism, definitions of behavior and reinforcement, and inability to account for biased relations.

11. Operant conditioning rates very high on criteria of scientific worthiness but relatively low on developmental adequacy.

PROBLEMS AND EXERCISES

1. At the end of the chapter on Freud's theory, you were asked to provide a psychoanalytic explanation for *infantile amnesia,* the well-documented phenomenon in which adults fail to remember any infantile experiences. You probably responded in terms of the developing ego and its mechanism of repression or in terms of primary and secondary thought processes. It is now time to provide an operant conditioning explanation of infantile amnesia.

2. Design a behavior modification program to teach an "old dog" new tricks.

3. Design a controlled experiment to analyze the effects of reinforcement delay on learning.

4. A father institutes a behavior modification program to teach his two-year-old son how to put on his jacket.
   a. Identify the relevant factors, concepts, and principles that must be taken into account.
   b. Assume that some degree of chaining will be required. Specify the order in which you would condition the individual behaviors that comprise the chain.
   c. Describe in observable, measurable terms the final form your behavioral chain would take to get reinforced.
5. Using principles of operant conditioning, design a plan to rid a friend of an unwanted behavior and describe how you would evaluate your success.

SUGGESTED READINGS

More about the Theory

Evans, R. I. (1968). *B. F. Skinner: The man and his ideas.* New York: E. P. Dutton.
Schwartz, B., & Lacey, H. (1982). *Behaviorism, science, and human nature.* New York: Norton.
Skinner, B. F. (1953). *Science and human behavior.* New York: Free Press.
———. (1974). *About behaviorism.* New York: Knopf.

Reviews of Research

Kendler, H. (1959). Learning. *Annual review of psychology, 10,* 43–88.
Kling, J. W., & Riggs, L. A. (Eds.). (1971). *Experimental psychology* (3rd ed.). New York: Holt, Rinehart and Winston. (Note: only chapters 14 through 19 are relevant.)
Stevenson, H. W. (1970). Learning in children. In P. Mussen (Ed.), *Carmichael's manual of child psychology. Vol. 1* (3rd ed.). New York: John Wiley and Sons.

Critical Reviews

Chomsky, N. (1959). Review of *verbal behavior* by B. F. Skinner. *Language, 35,* 26–58.
Mogdil, S., & Mogdil, C. (Eds.). (1987). *B. F. Skinner: Consensus and controversy.* London: Falmer Press.
Wessels, M. G. (1982). A critique of Skinner's views on the obstructive character of cognitive theories. *Behaviorism, 10,* 65–84.

Chapter 8

Bandura's Social Cognitive Theory

Preview Questions

What problem left unsolved by traditional operant conditioning theory is solved
  by social cognitive theory? In what ways does Bandura's theory differ from
  the traditional theory of operant conditioning?
What assumptions are made by Bandura's theory?
What are the theory's problems of study and research methods?
What are social cognitive theory's internal and bridge principles?
What change mechanism does the theory propose to explain development?
What contributions and criticisms are associated with the theory?
How does the theory rate for scientific worthiness and developmental ade-
  quacy?

HISTORICAL SKETCH

Social cognitive theory extends radical behaviorism to the analysis of certain cognitive processes, and it accounts for a particular category of behavioral learning
not addressed by Skinner's theory of operant conditioning. Recall that with
operant conditioning Skinner showed how novel behaviors could be acquired
through reinforcement and shaping, an important problem left unsolved by classical conditioning. However, an important class of behaviors that cannot be accounted for by operant conditioning consists of *behaviors that are learned without
any reinforcement.* Consider an example. After watching a "Mr. Rogers" TV
demonstration on how to make artificial flowers using scissors, tape, and old
hosiery, my daughter proceeded to gather up a butter knife, the Scotch tape from
my office, and some socks from her bureau drawer. She proceeded, without notic-
ing me, to tape her socks together and then to try and cut them with the butter

knife. When I finally asked her what she was doing, she told me, "I'm making some flowers like Mr. Rogers did for Mommy." This sequence of activities had never before occurred, although Megan had used a knife at mealtimes. The novelty of this behavioral chain and the novelty of the final utterance, following as it did watching Mr. Rogers making artificial flowers, cannot be explained by operant conditioning because the behavioral sequence and the accompanying utterance had not been previously conditioned for that situation.

The theoretical problem with Megan's behavior is how to explain behaviors acquired all at once without gradual shaping and without the administration of previous reinforcers. A solution has been provided by the *social learning* theories, a name given because they attribute learning and development to social influences.

In this chapter, Albert Bandura's social cognitive theory, the most prominent among social learning theories, will be described. Bandura's emphasis on the social basis of cognitive processes has prompted him to opt for the name *social cognitive theory* (Bandura, 1986). He argues that individuals learn specific cognitive strategies from observing the behavior of others and that these strategies account for the acquisition of novel behaviors.

Albert Bandura was born in 1925 in Mundare, a small hamlet in northern Alberta, Canada. He studied psychology and graduated from the University of British Columbia in 1949. He attended graduate school at the University of Iowa, where his interest in learning theory was supported by a faculty of vigorous and active researchers, including Robert Sears, who was pioneering an effort to recast psychoanalytic theory in terms of social learning.

Bandura was a bright and able student. He received his PhD in 1952, did a clinical internship at the Wichita Guidance Center, then moved to Stanford to become a psychology instructor. His productivity was rewarded there when in only nine years he rose through the professorial ranks to become a full professor. Following the impetus of Robert Sears, Bandura's early investigations focused on social learning and aggression. In collaboration with his first doctoral student, Richard Walters, he spent several years studying the determinants of observational learning. Much of this work was described in an early formulation of what became known as social learning theory (Bandura & Walters, 1963). Recognizing the inherent limitations of operant conditioning for explaining the acquisition of unreinforced social behaviors, and influenced by the heady resurgence of Piaget's cognitivism, Bandura began to examine how individuals acquire abstract, rule-governed behavior. That work led him to study the function of cognitive processes in mediating observational learning.

Extending Skinner's Legacy

Social learning theorists agree to a large extent with Skinner's analysis of operant learning, and they attempt to build on rather than dismantle his basic theory. Foremost in Bandura's earlier analysis of learning was the role of imitation, which has its conceptual foundation in operant conditioning. In an early publication

(Bandura & Walters, 1959, pp. 253–254), Bandura argued that imitation often leads to the reinforcers children seek. For example, they learn to reproduce parents' behaviors because those behaviors produce reinforcement for the parents, and soon the repetition of similar behaviors becomes self-reinforcing because they are valued by the parents. Imitation of the parents, through repeated association with rewards, gradually becomes rewarding in itself. At the same time, children do not haphazardly imitate everything in sight. Bandura and Walters (1963) contend that behaviors are imitated more often when models are of the same sex, well respected, receive tangible rewards for their actions, and are perceived as similar to the observer. Models are less likely to be imitated when their actions are punished and when the model is perceived as different by an observer.

Carrying the analysis a step further, Bandura and Walters (1963) argued that new behaviors could be acquired by simply *observing* a model; it is not necessary that the observer actually produce an overt behavior or even be reinforced. Rather, the reinforcement obtained by the model is itself sufficient to reinforce the observer. Bandura and Walters termed this process *vicarious reinforcement*. They argued that the concept of vicarious reinforcement explained "no trial learning," a widely recognized phenomena where learning occurs in the absence of shaping. Vicarious reinforcement involves conceptual reasoning, since it requires observers to judge expected outcomes about their own behavior on the basis of outcomes produced by models.

Bandura's analysis of social learning has become an important influence on developmental psychology in the past quarter century, during which time it motivated numerous laboratory studies of altruism, aggression, sex role learning, and empathy. While still adhering to the mechanisms of operant conditioning, Bandura has in recent years moved sharply away from radical behaviorism that attempts to account for learning without appealing to mental processes. His latest work emphasizes the influence of cognitive processes that underlie the acquisition of social behaviors. He is now less concerned with imitation per se as a mechanism of behavioral acquisition than he is with the general use of observational learning to acquire information from others. Bandura has also attempted to differentiate between the acquisition phase in which observed behaviors are actually learned and the later performance phase in which learned behaviors are actually displayed. After all, it is as possible for one to learn a fact that is never used as it is to learn a behavior that is never performed. The description of social cognitive theory in this chapter draws extensively from Bandura's (1986) most recent formulation: *Social Foundations of Thought and Action*.

STRUCTURAL COMPONENTS

Assumptions

Bandura (1986, pp. 18–22) identifies several important capabilities that he believes are endemic to human nature. These capabilities are not necessarily fully functional in the newborn, though their functioning is prerequisite to observational learning.

First, infants are assumed to possess a collection of innately organized reflexes. Biological programming, however, also implies a potential for learning that reflects, on the one hand, a high degree of behavioral plasticity and, on the other hand, physiological constraints that limit the flexibility of human nature.

Second, Bandura assumes that a *symbolizing capacity* gives humans a powerful tool for processing and transforming their experiences into internal models that guide future actions. Symbols are essentially cognitive states and may include both rational judgments and irrational beliefs.

Third, the capacity for *forethought* influences our present actions. Forethought is the ability to anticipate specific actions, consequences, or events that have not yet occurred and that, therefore, cannot have become a part of our personal history. Desirable goals (symbolically represented) often motivate behaviors that are most likely to bring about their actualization.

Fourth, Bandura assumes the capacity for *vicarious learning,* that is, learning by observation. Moreover, he assumes that neonates can imitate certain activities that vary considerably depending on who the models are and how they perform. This is an important assumption because it presumes that people are capable of learning rules that generate and regulate their actions without having to go through a lengthy trial and error process of discovery. Bandura notes with some irony that the power of observational learning is found in the fact that children are not taught to swim or medical students to perform surgery by having them discover through trial and error the personal effects of their efforts.

Fifth, *reflective self-consciousness* enables individuals to think about their own thoughts and attribute meaning to their experiences. The quality of reflection not only improves understanding, but also provides a means for evaluating and altering one's thinking. The capacity for self-reflection influences individuals' self-concepts in terms of verifying beliefs, monitoring ideas, and deciding how much effort to invest in certain activities and whether they are approached anxiously or with confidence.

Problems for Study

Phenomena to Be Explained

Social cognitive theory attempts to explain socialization, including processes whereby individuals acquire their society's norms of thought and action. Like Wilson and sociobiology, Bandura differentiates social learning phenomena into several classes of effects.

Observational Learning Effects.   The theory attempts to explain how individuals acquire the ability to perform any *novel* behavior, including standards of judgment, thinking skills, and rules for generating behavior that have no reinforcement history. Novel performance in this sense includes new behaviors as well as new organizational patterns composed of previously acquired but separate components, as might occur when a child utters a novel sentence containing words previously learned or when a person moves to a new house thereby reorganizing furniture, appliances, and decorations in a unique and distinctive manner.

Inhibitory and Disinhibitory Effects.   Previously learned responses may be strengthened or weakened under certain circumstances, or they may not occur at all. For example, most people decelerate when they pass a police officer, or they eat more slowly than usual at an expensive restaurant. In other instances, behavior may be accelerated, as when children learn to become more talkative as bedtime approaches. Some situations may inhibit behavior altogether. People are far less likely to disobey "no smoking" signs in hospitals and churches than in lavatories or bus stations. One task of the theory is to explain how these inhibitions and disinhibitions are learned.

Response Facilitation Effects.   Whereas disinhibition effects refer to situational variables, response facilitation effects are a function of the behavior of others that may instigate one's behavior when other cues are absent. Response facilitation can occur when models function to activate, direct, or support specific behaviors of other individuals in a particular situation. Response facilitation may be found in peer group pressure or Sunday church, when individuals are likely to behave like others within the specific social context.

Environmental Enhancement Effects.   According to Bandura certain elements of the environment direct attention rather than cue behavior. Behavior that is directed must be explained as much as behavior that is cued. Typically, a model will guide or channel an individual's behavior that has already been cued by environmental signs. For example, children will typically eat more when fed in pairs than when fed alone. Even children who are full will ask for more food if they observe parents snacking.

Methods of Study

The influence of American behaviorism on social learning theory is perhaps most clearly seen in the methods chosen for conducting research. This influence can be found in at least two tendencies. First, social cognitive theorists concentrate their research on observable behavior, and in this way infer the presence of cognitive processes from their analysis of overt, measurable performance. Second, working within the strong empirical tradition established by behaviorism, social learning theorists tend to favor observational and experimental research methods. In particular, studies are often designed to establish a controlled situation in which a single characteristic of a model is isolated and manipulated for the purpose of measuring its influence on a subject's behavior. For example, with situational distractors controlled and all models displaying the same behaviors, one group of children might be asked to observe a real model, another group a video recording of the model, and a third group a televised scenario of the model. The groups may then be compared to determine which group displays the most frequent exhibition of the target behavior.

Internal Principles

Triadic Reciprocality

Bandura proposes only one internal principle that comprises the irreducible explanatory concept of social learning theory: *triadic reciprocal determinism,* or *triadic reciprocality* for short. *Triadic reciprocality* reflects an interactional thesis of human development. According to the concept of *triadic reciprocality,* learning results from the mutual interaction of three causal agents that commingle with one another to codetermine observational learning. These three factors, depicted in Figure 8-1, are behavior, cognition and other personal factors, and the environment. For example, children's responses to their teacher's questions are contingent on their ability to pronounce the words (behavior), on their knowledge of the correct answer (cognition), on how meaningful they perceive the class activity to be (personal factor), and on the conditions of the environment (the type of class, previous responses by other students, teacher's demeanor, etc.).

Bandura (1986) points out how triadic reciprocal causation might occur in our daily lives through the simple act of watching television. Personal preferen-

Figure 8-1 Diagram of triadic reciprocality. The triadic relationship between behavior, cognition and personal factors, and environmental contexts determines social learning. (*Source:* Adapted from Bandura, A. *Social foundations of thought and action: A social cognitive theory.* Englewood Cliffs, NJ: Prentice-Hall, 1986, p. 24 [by permission].)

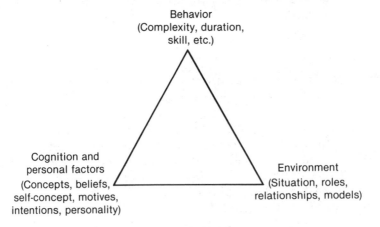

ces (cognition) partially determine which programs we watch at what times from all those available for viewing. Viewing patterns (behavior), in turn, partially determine which programs are available for future viewing. At the same time, advertising and production costs (environment) partially determine what viewers are shown and thus constrain their possible choices.

Bridge Principles

The concept of triadic reciprocality implies the operation of several subordinate factors that constitute the theory's bridge principles. *Differential contributions* consist of the relative influence associated with each of the individual components of reciprocal causation. *Temporal dynamics* of interacting components refer to the timing of behavioral, environmental, and personal events. *Fortuitous determinants*, the role played by chance events, give unexpected opportunities and impose unforeseen constraints on behavior. Each bridge principle is described in turn.

Differential contributions of the triadic factors means that the impact of behavior, environment, and personal factors on social learning varies according to circumstances, individuals, and activities. For example, when environmental conditions are the primary influence, individuals would be expected to behave pretty much the same, much like children eating a meal or teenagers at a rock concert. If environmental constraints are weak, personal factors may dominate a situation, as when students decide what they will do on their first day of summer vacation. Some personal factors like false beliefs, defensive behavior, unusual habits, and unconventional values may be so strong that they partially insulate individuals from corrective environmental influences (Bandura, 1986, p. 24).

With *temporal dynamics* the triadic factors exert their influence over time and often in different amounts (Bandura, 1986). Sometimes, as in attending nursery school and athletic training, the production of an effect occurs gradually and in an irregular fashion because the latency between a cause and its effect may vary according to the behavior, personal factors, and situation. An ardent kiss, for example, produces a more immediate reciprocal effect than does mailing a friendship card, and a steady, conscientious diet produces less immediate but more enduring and beneficial health effects than fasting.

The principle of *fortuitous determinants* refers to the entire class of unforeseen, chance events that alter individuals' life courses in enduring and important ways. Bandura notes that most developmentalists avoid trying to explain how chance events influence learning because their effects are so unsystematic. In contrast, social cognitive theory recognizes that chance plays a more important and enduring role in determining "life paths" than is often recognized. The effects of chance events lie in the kinds of interactive processes they initiate rather than in qualities of the events themselves. For example, an unintended meeting between two children may have little consequence, whereas for two adults, a chance encounter may lead to marriage. Even traffic accidents can inalterably modify one's driving behavior.

Change Mechanism

While the three elements of triadic reciprocality determine what, where, and when observational learning will occur, they do not explain the "how" of behavior acquisition. To explain the mechanisms of observational learning, Bandura differentiates between an *acquisition phase* and a *performance phase.* It is during the *acquisition phase* that new behavior is actually learned. However, once acquired, a behavior may or may not be performed. It is the *performance phase* that determines when a previously acquired behavior will be displayed.

Acquiring new behaviors is controlled by two kinds of processes: attention and retention. *Attentional processes* organize the exploration of the perceptual environment and the perception of activities to be learned. *Retention processes* consist of cognitive operations that transform perceptual sensations into symbolic representations and memories that function as internal models.

A new behavior may be acquired through attention and retention processes, but even so, it may never be displayed. Whether or not a learned behavior is actually performed is a function of two other processes: production and motivation. *Production processes* regulate the manner in which various behavioral skills are combined into new organizations and response patterns. *Motivational processes* determine the conditions under which observationally learned responses will be activated and performed. In this way, behavioral performance depends on prior acquisition, but once behavior has been acquired, its display will depend on various reinforcement contingencies available to individuals. The relationship between acquisition and performance processes is illustrated in Table 8-1.

Bandura emphasizes the cognitive components of learning from models and thus might be expected to be more closely aligned with Piaget's cognitive theory than with behavioral theory. However, Bandura proposes that the elements that comprise cognition are themselves learned and abstracted from models. One does not learn to have cognitive processes through observational learning. Rather, observational learning functions as an important source for knowing what, how, when, and where to activate a specific cognitive representation of a model's behavior. Consequently, Bandura's theory, which locates in external models the source of learning (both cognitive and behavioral), is an example of an exogenous theory even though it utilizes mental constructs like cognitive processes.

Acquisition Phase

Attentional Processes. For observational learning to occur, individuals must do more than be passive sponges to experience. They must pay attention to and accurately perceive the important characteristics of the activity to be learned. *Attentional processes* govern which aspects of a model are ignored, which are attended to, and which are selected from the multitude of possible stimuli for later retention. Bandura argues that model characteristics, such as visibility, discriminability, and complexity of activity can affect attention. For example, teachers and parents both attempt to make observational learning of complex tasks a bit easier by supplementing them with attention-directing aids—decomposing them

Table 8-1   Subprocesses Governing Observational Learning

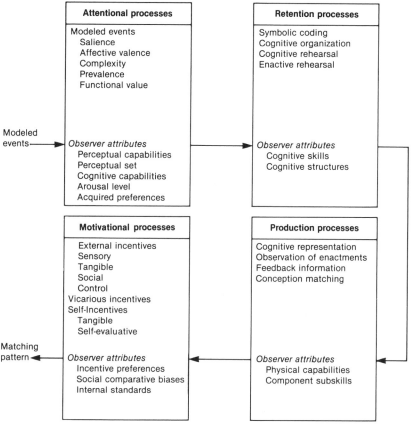

Source: Adapted from Bandura, A. *Social foundations of thought and action: A social cognitive theory.* Englewood Cliffs, NJ: Prentice-Hall, 1986, p. 52 (by permission).

into discernible steps, amplifying them with verbal descriptions, or giving concrete examples. Observer characteristics also play a part in observational learning to the extent that prior learning, familiarity, and training can prepare the perceiver to attend to more subtleties than might otherwise be possible. In addition, models can attract attention by their distinctiveness, prestige, power, and success (Bandura, 1971).

Another component of attention is the functional value or utility of the observed activity. Activities that produce desirable rewards for the model are more likely to be imitated by an observer, and models whose personal attributes are desired by observers (parents, professional athletes, elected officials, or in Megan's case, the girl in her nursery who always wears jewelry) are more likely to be imitated. In short, individuals tend to pay more attention to effective and influential models than to those who are not (Bandura, 1986).

Retention Processes.   Observational learning cannot take place unless people remember the activities they have seen. Memory, in turn, involves the transformation and reorganization of events into mental representations that facilitate retention of these events for later recall. *Retention processes* include symbolic transformations, representational systems, and rehearsal, each of which is described next.

Symbolic transformations enable people to represent observed activities mentally through various representational mediums that reorganize and confer meaning on perceived activities. The two most important representational systems involve *imaginal* and *linguistic constructions.* Sometimes observed activities are abstracted and encoded in terms of symbolic mental images that preserve the personal meaning conferred on them by the observer. It is important to note, however, that Bandura is more concerned with the function served by representational imagery rather than the cognitive and physiological processes whereby such images are produced. The second mode of representation, linguistic symbolization, involves encoding observed activities into language. Verbal representations provide an extremely powerful means of encoding and retaining information. The fact that words often evoke corresponding images implies that the two representational systems function in an integrated rather than mutually exclusive manner.

According to Bandura (1986), symbolic transformations are not simply mental copies. Instead, they are constructive processes in the sense that they confer personal meaning on events while preserving important information that allows later decoding of the symbol into actions. In this respect, *rehearsal* (mental practice) may serve as an important memory aid. By rehearsing or actively practicing observed activities, people are simply less likely to forget. In fact, some behaviors become so highly routinized that they can be performed almost automatically with only minimal representational guidance (e.g., counting, tying shoe laces, throwing a baseball).

Performance Phase

Production Processes.   The second phase of observational learning involves *production processes* that provide the means for using abstract representations of actions and rules of actions to initiate and organize responses according to situation, place, and time. Overall, these processes function to match behavior to one's representation of it by initiating, organizing, guiding, monitoring, and correcting one's behavior. For example, one morning after I forgot to put up my razor, my wife discovered Megan trying to shave her own face. She wasn't very adept at it, and while she didn't cut herself, she did push and pull the razor up and down both sides of her face. This mimicry does not represent a new behavior as much as it does a new organization of component responses, each of which was individually available in Megan's behavioral repertoire (grasping, pushing, pulling). Moreover, the fact that she watched herself "shaving" in front of the bathroom mirror indicates her interest in monitoring her performance.

The extent to which individuals benefit from observing models depends in part on the timing of feedback (consequences), its informational content, and the person who gives it. For example, to enhance student learning, most teachers are trained to display precise behaviors that can be emulated by students, to monitor student performance carefully, and to evaluate feedback as soon as possible and with as much detail as possible.

The ability to reproduce behaviors is also affected by maturation. For example, infants are unable to imitate adult speech, and although toddlers can imitate some speech, they have difficulty imitating a two- or three-step sequence of behaviors. Young children are typically unable to retell the sequence of story events even though they may pay great attention to stories. Maturation may also play a role in determining what has incentive value for individuals. While candy may provide sufficient incentive for children, money is far more likely to be motivating for adults.

Motivational Processes.   Social cognitive theory recognizes that while people may learn new behaviors, some will be performed only rarely and others quite often. *Motivational processes* explain the discrepancy between acquisition and actual performance. Motivation is an important determinant of when, under what circumstances, and how often learned behavior will be displayed. For example, children learn to imitate situation-specific behaviors (e.g., raising their hand to gain recognition in class but not at home or in the car) when they or the model are reinforced only in certain situations but not others. Likewise, motivational incentives may be direct, vicarious, or self-produced. Direct incentives occur when imitated behaviors are followed by external consequences to the observer rather than the model, as when an observer receives a reprimand, a kiss, or a special treat. Vicarious motivation occurs when a model receives reinforcement whether or not the observer is reinforced. For example, my son Matthew watches football with me, not because he gets reinforced but because he recognizes how much I enjoy watching it. Self-produced motivation occurs when individuals reproduce actions that are personally reinforcing in spite of external consequences. In that vein, Megan's first attempts at tying her own shoelaces were warmly praised. Recently, however, she has insisted on tying her own shoes even though she takes so long she misses valuable playtime.

It is important to note at this point that Bandura's concept of vicarious reinforcement contrasts sharply with Skinner's belief that reinforcement operates automatically to condition operant behavior. Bandura maintains that reinforcement operates because it is primarily informative and motivational; that is, the consequences of a model's behavior inform observers of what can reasonably be expected to occur should they perform the same (or a similar) behavior under the same conditions.

EXPLAINING HUMAN DEVELOPMENT: THE RESEARCH

The most supportive research for social cognitive theory is found in the literature on children's socialization. Described here are samples of studies of aggression, altruism, and sex roles.

Aggression

Research on aggression provides one of the most clear-cut examples of children's observational learning. Early studies established the presence of a relationship between parents' and children's behavior. For example, very aggressive children tend to come from families in which parents often fight, commit violent crimes, or exercise severe and erratic punishment (Bandura & Walters, 1959; Glueck & Glueck, 1950; McCord, 1979). Moreover, a steady diet of aggressive cartoons has been shown to be associated with increases in aggressive displays—hitting, kicking, and throwing things—in preschool children (e.g., Friedrich & Stein, 1973; Steuer, Applefield, & Smith, 1971), and these effects seem to be cumulative in that children who consistently prefer violent television are more likely to become aggressive as adults (Eron, Lefkowitz, Huesmann, & Walder, 1972). In one series of typical experiments, institutionalized male delinquents were exposed to either an aggressive or a nonaggressive movie for each of five consecutive nights (Parke, Berkowitz, Leyens, West, & Sebastian, 1977) and were prevented from watching television during the week. Boys in the aggressive condition displayed more restlessness, foot stamping, yelling, and shouting than those exposed to nonaggressive movies. In addition, the boys who watched aggressive movies behaved more violently toward one another following the movies than did the other boys, and this aggressive pattern was most pronounced among the more dominant males.

Certain characteristics of models and situations are associated with the frequency of imitated aggression. For example, children are more likely to model aggression when the model is rewarded or escapes punishment for the aggressive act than when the model is punished (Bandura, 1965; Bandura, Ross, & Ross, 1963). This tendency applies to children even when the aggressive act is fictional rather than real-life, whether it depicts cartoon or real-life characters, and whether presented in live, television, or film format (Meyer, 1972; Stein & Friedrich, 1975). Findings like these suggest that widespread concern over children's viewing of television violence might be justified, although they do not clearly delineate between conditions that promote acquisition versus performance.

However, merely observing aggressive models does not in itself produce imitative aggression. Grusec (1973) and Hicks (1968) have shown, for example, that children's aggressive imitations are reduced when adults express disapproval. On the other hand, merely observing aggressive behavior may also result in: reduced altruism (Drabman & Thomas, 1974; Hapkiewicz & Roden, 1971), reduced emotional sensitivity to violence (Cline, Croft, & Courrier, 1973; Thomas,

Horton, Lippincott, & Drabman, 1977), and a distorted view of social reality (Gross, 1974; Stein & Friedrich, 1975).

Altruism

While children clearly learn aggressive forms of behavior by observing models, they also learn altruism—acts of concern directed at the welfare of others. In a recent review of this research literature, Bryan (1975) concluded that a wide variety of prosocial behaviors—exhibiting sympathy, rewarding others, rescuing, and sharing—can be taught through observational learning. In fact, children learn to behave altruistically even in situations where adults are not present, and they generalize altruistic behavior to situations unrelated to that in which an altruistic model was originally observed (Rice & Grusec, 1975; Rushton, 1975).

The acquisition of altruism through observational learning takes many forms. Nursery-school children whose parents are frequently affectionate exhibit hugging, kissing, and friendly greetings to others (Hoffman & Saltzstein, 1967). Children's television programs such as "Mr. Roger's Neighborhood" and "Sesame Street" often develop themes that demonstrate altruistic relationships between characters, and when entire classrooms of nursery-school children watch either of these programs as part of their daily routines, there is a significant increase in their prosocial behaviors within the classroom environment (Coates, Pusser, & Goodman, 1976; Friedrich-Cofer, Huston-Stein, Kipnis, Susman, & Clewett, 1979). Young children in particular seem to benefit more from watching models than from verbal instructions (Bryan & Walbek, 1971; Grusec, 1972; Grusec & Skubiski, 1970). Finally, models who are warm and attentive toward children (Bryan, 1975; Weissbrod, 1976; Yarrow, Scott, & Waxler, 1973) or are perceived to have power over them (Bryan, 1975; Grusec, 1971) are more likely to be imitated than models lacking these qualities.

In a different vein, the concept of triadic reciprocality posits a crucial role in social learning for situational factors, and a number of studies have examined the manner in which these contextual parameters influence observational learning. For example, the presence of bystanders has been shown to inhibit altruism toward others in distress (Darley & Latane, 1968; Latane & Rodin, 1969), and this inhibiting effect seems to begin in the mid-elementary years (Staub, 1970). Mood may also play an important situational role in observational learning. For example, children asked to think of something that makes them happy are more likely to share money they have been given than children asked to think about other things (Moore, Underwood, & Rosenhan, 1973; Rosenhan, Underwood, & Moore, 1974), and college students who happen (by experimenter design) to experience a positive event (receiving cookies or a gift, finding money) are more willing to help someone with a phone call or by mailing a letter they find (Isen, Clark, & Schwartz, 1976; Levin & Isen, 1975).

Sex Roles

Sex-role development, in terms of behaviors, values, and motivations, has often been associated with observational learning. By the time children are two years old, they already show considerable sex typing in toy and activity preferences (Blakemore, Larue, & Olejnik, 1979; Etaugh, Collins, & Gerson, 1975). Knowledge of sex-role stereotypes comes later, around three years of age (Blakemore, Larue, & Olejnik, 1979; Kuhn, Nash, & Brucken, 1978), by which time preschool and early elementary-school children hold fairly rigid, though concrete, stereotypes. For example, they tend to believe, in spite of parental claims to the contrary, that doctors must be men and nurses must be women. Later in childhood such stereotypes become more relaxed as children realize that many activities are not the exclusive province of one sex, although some behaviors may be more typical of one sex than the other (Garrett, Ein, & Tremaine, 1977; Meyer, 1980). In turn, high-school students hold to more rigid stereotypes than adults (Urberg, 1979).

Sex-role stereotypes consist of mental images of and beliefs about how males and females are "supposed to" behave. These cognitive representations often provide important guides for memory and forethought and may affect the manner in which children attribute meaning to their perceptions. Most people, for example, are prone to ignore or forget information that is incongruent with their beliefs (Martin & Halverson, 1981). Applying this principle to sex-role stereotypes, Koblinsky, Cruse, and Sugawara (1978) read stories to a group of fifth-graders in which male and female characters engaged in both sex-appropriate and sex-inappropriate activities. When asked to retell the stories later on, the children remembered the sex-appropriate activities much better than the sex-inappropriate activities. Even more striking findings were reported by Cordua, McGraw, and Drabman (1979), who showed five- and six-year-old children a short movie about a male nurse and a female doctor. After the film, the children reported that the doctor had been male and the nurse female. Interestingly, children have a harder time remembering a male performing a stereotypical female activity than a female performing a traditional male activity (Cordua, McGraw, & Drabman, 1979; Liben & Signorella, 1980).

Cognitive Regulation

Bandura emphasizes the role cognitive factors play in observational learning because they partly determine which events will be observed, how much attention to invest in various elements of the event, what meaning will be conferred on them, what information will be retained for future retrieval, and what form of representation will be activated for memory. The role of cognitive factors in social learning has been examined in a variety of studies. For example, Krumboltz and Thoresen (1964) report that observers who imitate the problem-solving skills of others experience improved skill at seeking information needed to evaluate possible solutions. Moreover, children who observe models verbalizing their own thought processes in solving problems perform better than children who are simply taught the same rules and strategies through direct instruction (Schunk, 1981).

Cognitive factors influence the perceived effectiveness of models. For example, observational learning is increased when models are perceived to possess high degrees of status (Akamatsu & Farudi, 1978) and social power (Grusec, 1971; Mischel & Liebert, 1967). In addition, people who use self-produced incentives typically achieve more than those who perform the same activities without such incentives or who establish personal goals without rewarding their attainments (Ballard & Glynn, 1975; Bellack, 1976; Martin, 1979; Wall, 1982).

CONTRIBUTIONS AND CRITICISMS OF THE THEORY

Contributions

Observational Learning. Observational learning is an important explanatory concept that accounts for the acquisition of novel behaviors that have not been directly reinforced. This concept is a more direct explanation of how children might imitate something they have seen on television or read in a book than Skinner's account, which posits that novel behaviors must be gradually shaped through reinforcement of successive approximations. The concept of observational learning also has a certain elegant simplicity, a common-sense value, as a theoretical construct that is immensely useful to our understanding of how children learn.

Cognitive Processes. Social cognitive theory presents an account of learning and development that, unlike Skinner, makes a strong appeal to the influence of mental processes in learning. Bandura not only claims that thinking is important, but also attempts to study it to provide an account of the cognitive processes believed to be most influential to social learning. These cognitive processes help us understand how individuals behave not in terms of reality as it actually is, but in terms of how individuals perceive it to be.

Bandura is also different from Skinner in the kind of data deemed to be important to a theory of learning. Where Skinner relied on experiments with animals to derive general laws of learning, Bandura studied children directly. His choice of humans as objects of investigation is more closely connected to the claims he makes about social learning than are generalizations to humans from the results of animal learning experiments. In addition, it may be that the use of human rather than animal subjects is what led Bandura to extend radical behaviorism into cognitive behaviorism. In other words, one is more likely to conclude that cognitive processes play a vital role in behavioral learning if one studies humans than if one studies animals.

Mind and Society. Many contemporary theorists accept the contention that mental development is influenced by social and cultural practices. Bandura's theory attempts to account for this interaction by describing the ways in which mental development is influenced by society in the form of typical adult behaviors to be learned (e.g., (1) patterns of status, power, and authority that make some models more influential than others and (2) culturally valued types of vicarious reinforcement) as well as ways in which the mind influences behaviors to be learned (attentional selectivity, representational capacity, memory). Older children may apply more efficient cognitive processes to understanding a social situation than younger children. Consequently, they typically glean more information, store it more efficiently, and recall it with greater accuracy than younger children. Social cognitive theory describes the interaction between social commerce and mental performance and does it in a way that emphasizes the joining together of mind and society.

Criticisms

Developmental Differences. Bandura emphasizes the role of three factors—environment, behavior, and cognitive processes—in explaining development. However, he gives virtually no attention to developmental differences between infants, children, and adults in terms of the cognitive processes available to them or their ability to profit from models. It seems reasonable to suspect that an infant's social smile in response to a father's face reflects vastly different cognitive processes than those underlying a twelve-year-old's computation of the area of his backyard after reading the school's mathematics book. The unanswered question here is do the processes underlying observational learning change during development and if so how?

Cognitive Processes. In establishing the importance of observational learning, Bandura seems to subscribe to a "copy" theory of knowledge even though he doesn't want to. Recall that he believes symbolic encodings are constructive in the sense that they are not exact copies of a model's behavior. However, his work emphasizes how experience may be represented (and sometimes misrepresented) and stored for later recall. In this way, selective attention, symbolic representations, abstract modeling, and vicarious motivation are all believed to derive from social origins. That is, they derive from external reality and are acquired through observational learning. But social cognitive theory does not explain how symbolic representations of specific events come to organize themselves spontaneously into complex belief structures, personal attitudes and interests, or problem-solving strategies not directly observable in the activities of models.

Possible versus Actual Causes. Bandura's concept of triadic reciprocality identifies a number of possible causes that can influence what, when, and how children acquire social behaviors. Bandura's theory acknowledges the complex interplay of factors believed to underlie children's social learning. At the same time, a theory that attempts to explain social learning should do more than identify and categorize the variety of possible influences that can affect development. It should also specify the manner in which these variables actually do result in social learning, and it should provide precise descriptions of the kinds of acquisitions and performances expected to result when variables interact in specific ways. Such a task is an immense undertaking, and social cognitive theory provides a beginning framework for such an enterprise. While Bandura continues to refine his formulations, some psychologists wonder if it is even possible to predict reciprocal, causal relationships in complex situations.

The situation is not advanced by experimental studies that attempt to isolate possible causes of children's social learning. Such studies, which are often designed to control many variables to study the effects of others, tend to reflect somewhat artificial learning situations. In other words, conclusions derived from experimental studies may not be generalizable to the complex natural ecology of children's lives.

Social Conformity.   Hoffman (1971) argues that social learning theory is limited to explaining how learning leads to similarity between children's behavior and that of adults. Social norms and adult social behavior are implicitly held as targets toward which children should strive, and conformity to such norms is considered a mature state of social learning. The problem Hoffman sees is that unconventional behavior is by implication considered to be "less developed" than conforming behavior. Yet, individuals who display unconventional behavior sometimes lead the way to widespread social reforms in the definition of conventional behavior (e.g., the sexual revolution, the women's movement, the civil rights movement). According to Damon (1983), a theory that assumes that development naturally progresses toward increasing social conformity cannot at the same time explain the development of truly novel forms of behavior that entail new ways of adapting to the world.

EVALUATION OF THE THEORY

Scientific Worthiness

Testability.   There are several reasons social cognitive theory is rated high for its testability (see Table 8-2). As an example of the exogenous paradigm, the theory has much in common with Skinner's operant conditioning. It concentrates on measurements of observable behavior, and the extensive use of experimental situations advances the search for cause-effect relationships. Researchers can clearly test their hypotheses about observational learning because behavioral performance is easily observed. However, while Bandura does differentiate between an acquisition phase and a performance phase in observational learning, the two cannot always be empirically separated. For example, a

Table 8-2   Ratings of Social Cognitive Theory for Scientific Worhiness

CRITERION	HIGH	MODERATE	LOW
Testability	X		
External validity	X		
Predictive validity		X	
Internal consistency	X		
Theoretical economy			X

problem occurs in attempting to disprove observational learning. That is, if an observed behavior is not performed, it is difficult to determine whether its absence is due to a failure of acquisition or performance processes. There is no straightforward, objective means for resolving this problem within the social cognitive framework. Still, the theory's general emphasis on observable behavior, coupled with theoretical relationships that are frequently amenable to experimental study, support the high rating given the theory on this criterion.

External Validity. The theory also gets a high rating for its external validity because of the well-established claim that individuals do acquire new behaviors through observational learning. There exists no compelling evidence that learning cannot occur by observing the activities of models, providing one takes into account the influence of mitigating variables (age of observer, conditions under which observation occurs, motivation, etc.). In fact, the importance of imitation in children's learning is recognized by most psychologists and theorists. For example, Freud invokes a concept like observational learning when he argues that children resolve their Oedipal/Electra complexes by identifying with the same-sexed parent, and Piaget (1962) has devoted considerable attention to the role played by imitation in the development of thought. Even a more demanding analysis indicates that imitation of a model is more likely under some circumstances than others, is influenced by personal values and attitudes, and is mitigated by qualities of the model and characteristics of the behavior that are observed—all of which are elements of triadic reciprocality.

Predictive Validity. Bandura's theory is rated moderate for its predictive validity, primarily because there are so many possible variations within triadic reciprocality that predicting an effect is quite difficult. The theory does not, for example, specify why television violence may be imitated by some individuals but not others or why some people display socially conforming behaviors while others are stridently nonconforming. The inadequate account of the disparity between (1) a general tendency to learn through observation and (2) observational learning in some specific situations but not others is the basis for the moderate rating given on this criterion.

Internal Consistency. The theory garners a high ranking for its internal consistency. Three variables—behavior, environment, and personal cognition—

are consistently used to explain observational learning. Ironically, the failure to acquire new behaviors through observational learning is also attributable to different interactional patterns among the same three kinds of variables. For this reason, social cognitive theory attempts to explain all observational learning as a function of triadic reciprocality. There are virtually no exceptions needed to account for the variety of observational learning effects. Given a specific mixture of interactive causes, only one possible outcome would be expected to occur. Future research will need to be conducted under many different controlled mixtures of these variables and will ultimately determine the internal consistency of the theory. At this time social cognitive theory has not been challenged on grounds of incompatible principles.

Theoretical Economy. The theoretical economy of social cognitive theory is rated moderately low because of two competing considerations. On the one hand, Bandura does attempt to account for an extremely broad array of social behaviors—altruism, creativity, empathy, conformity, aggression, friendship, helplessness, delinquency, and much more. On the other hand, a relatively large number of major assumptions are made about inborn cognitive capacities. Many developmental psychologists would question these assumptions, and some would contend that the cognitive capacities are themselves subject to developmental change rather than being inborn. In addition, one of Bandura's assumptions, that infants are innately predisposed to profit from vicarious reinforcement, is tantamount to saying that a tendency to imitate is an inborn quality. If such a predisposition is an inborn trait, then a theoretical explanation of observational learning, which itself is predicated on vicarious reinforcement, may be little more than a tautology—infants imitate because they are born to imitate. While Bandura's entire theory is not really so simplistic, the various cognitive processes he attributes to birthright play a prominent role in the concept of triadic reciprocality. The problem here is that assuming the presence of certain cognitive processes that later get deployed as explanatory principles of social learning is a fundamental error in theory construction. In sum, Bandura attempts to explain a number of phenomena within a limited developmental domain, and he does it with preliminary assumptions that may be questionable. Moreover, at least one of the assumptions is used as the basis of the social learning argument that many behaviors can be acquired without direct reinforcement. Because of these problems, I have judged the theory to be moderately low in terms of its theoretical economy. The fact that it is not rated at the bottom of the scale on this criterion is due to other considerations, like the broad spectrum of behaviors the theory attempts to explain.

Developmental Adequacy

Temporality. The bridge principle of temporal dynamics is sufficient to pass the theory on this characteristic (see Table 8-3).

Cumulativity. According to the theory, development occurs through the acquisition of new social behaviors. Some behaviors are acquired later in life because they are built upon or added to previously existing behaviors. In this manner certain behaviors (e.g., giving, pushing) may be prerequisite to other behaviors (e.g., altruism, aggression). Adolescents, for example, are generally considered to be "more developed" than children in part because they have more social behaviors and cognitive strategies available to them in any given social situation. Consequently, the theory passes this criterion.

Directionality. Bandura contends that there is a progressive aspect to development, and it can be found in the movement toward increasing socialization. Older children are considered to be more mature because they display more adultlike social behaviors more consistently than do younger children. Although this contention has not been demonstrated experimentally, it is probably true that individuals are more likely to imitate older rather than younger models. For this reason, it is judged to pass this criterion.

New Mode of Organization. Models may be imitated when individuals selectively attend to certain informational cues, encode relevant information for memory, remember the symbolic code, and rehearse the behavior to be modeled. Infants and toddlers are believed to learn new social behaviors in basically the same ways adults do. More mature individuals organize their behaviors around the same principles as youngsters—motivation, selective attention, environmental situation, and model characteristics. At the same time, individuals are believed to modify their memories to correspond to past experiences, and such memories and symbolic encodings of information may be revised and given new meanings in light of new experiences. Modifications of encoded information consist of realigning and correcting one's conceptions in order to bring them into a closer match with actual or expected experiences. However, nothing in this account suggests that individuals evolve new organizational rules or new principles of learning that are not already found in experience. While Bandura attempts to account for learning abstract concepts, such learning is explained in terms of inductive generalizations from specific experiences. The theory does not view development in terms of the kinds of structural reorganizations found in Piaget's and portions

Table 8-3 Ratings of Social Cognitive Theory for Characteristics of Development

CHARACTERISTIC	RATING
Temporality	Pass
Cumulativity	Pass
Directionality	Pass
New mode of organization	Fail
Increased capacity for self-control	Pass

of Freud's theories. Nor does it depict social learning as the result of qualitatively different principles at one age more than at any other age. Consequently, the theory is judged to fail this criterion.

Increased Capacity for Self-Control. Two of the three elements of triadic reciprocality lie outside direct personal control. Still, Bandura argues that forethought and personal motivation are important determinants of observational learning. Through social learning, individuals become more adept at anticipating social situations and matching their behaviors to expected outcomes. This process is not an automatic stamping in of associations between behavior and consequences; it involves judgment about which behaviors displayed by which models under which circumstances will be activated for display at a particular time and for a particular purpose. Consequently, social cognitive theory passes this criterion.

SUMMARY POINTS

1. Social cognitive theory has its roots in American behaviorism, but Bandura extends radical behaviorism to include cognitive factors in his account of social learning. Social cognitive theory attempts to explain how novel behaviors can be acquired in the absence of observable reinforcement.

2. In addition to innate reflexes, Bandura assumes that neonates possess a number of cognitive functions, including capacities of symbol formation, forethought, self-consciousness, and a capacity for vicarious learning.

3. The theory attempts to explain the acquisition of society's norms of thought and action. More specifically, the phenomena to be explained include the effects of observational learning, inhibition and disinhibition, response facilitation, and environmental enhancement. Researchers tend to operate within the American behaviorist tradition in their preference for experimental designs and observational methods.

4. The theory's internal principle is reciprocal triadic determinism. This principle is often called triadic reciprocality, and it refers to the interaction of three kinds of causal influences: behavior, cognitive and personal factors, and situational context.

5. The theory has three bridge principles: the differential contributions of the elements of triadic reciprocality, temporal dynamics, and fortuitous determinants.

6. The mechanism of social learning occurs in two phases—acquisition and performance. The acquisition phase reflects the functioning of attentional and retention processes. The performance phase is governed by production and motivation processes.

7. Bandura's most important theoretical contributions are his account of observational learning (acquisition of novel behaviors in the absence of shaping and observable reinforcement), the influence of cognitive processes on behavioral acquisition and performance, and the interaction of mind and society in individual development.

8. Social cognitive theory has been criticized for its inadequate account of age-related developmental differences, inadequate specificity of cognitive processes, inability to explain clearly the differences between behavioral competence and perfor-

mance, and implications that social conformity is a developmentally mature achievement.

9. The theory was rated moderately high for both its scientific worthiness and its account of characteristics of development.

PROBLEMS AND EXERCISES

1. Perform a simple exercise by comparing children's and adults' capacity to imitate an unusual, complex behavior. Using social cognitive theory, attempt to explain the similarities and differences in their learning.

2. Children and adolescents often sing or hum songs derived from television show themes. Explain the difference in theme songs displayed by these two groups in terms of the theory's internal and bridge principles.

3. Explain the impact "fortuitous determinants" have had on your development by describing a specific chance encounter or event you've experienced. Also describe what you learned and how it affected your life. In your opinion, should a developmental theory account for the role of chance? Why or why not?

4. Many instances of imitation in animals have been published. Do you think Bandura would rely on the same cognitive processes to explain animal imitation as he does human imitation? Why or why not?

SUGGESTED READINGS

More about the Theory

Bandura, A. (1986). *Social foundations of thought and action: A social cognitive theory.* Englewood Cliffs, NJ: Prentice-Hall.

Huston, A. C., Carpenter, C. J., Atwater, J. B., & Johnson, L. M. (1986). Gender, adult structuring of activities, and social behavior in middle childhood. *Child Development, 57,* 1200–1209.

Wishart, J. G. (1986). Siblings as models in early infant learning. *Child Development, 57,* 1232–1240.

Reviews of Research

Akamatsu, T. J., & Thelen, M. H. (1974). A review of the literature on observer characteristics and imitation. *Developmental Psychology, 10,* 38–47.

McCall, R. B., Parke, R. D., & Kavanaugh, R. D. (1977). Imitation of live and televised models by children one to three years of age. *Monographs of the Society for Research in Child Development, 42* (No. 5).

Mischel, W. (1970). A social learning view of sex differences in behavior. In P. H. Mussen (Ed.), *Carmichael's manual of child psychology* (3rd ed., Vol. 2). New York: Wiley.

Critical Reviews

Kuhn, D. (1973). Imitation theory and research from a cognitive perspective. *Human Development, 16,* 157–180.

Chapter 9

Piaget's Cognitive-Developmental Theory

Preview Questions

How did the ideas of Kant and Spencer influence Piaget?

What two assumptions underlie Piaget's theory?

What problem(s) of study does Piaget pose? What phenomena does he study? What methods are employed by Piaget?

What internal principles does Piaget use in his theory?

What bridge principles does Piaget employ to explain child development?

What is the difference between operative and figurative knowledge, and why is that distinction important for Piaget?

What factors influence development, according to Piaget? Among these factors, which is posited as the primary mechanism of development?

What are the major contributions and criticisms of Piaget's theory?

How does the theory rate for its scientific worthiness and developmental adequacy?

HISTORICAL SKETCH

Genetic epistemology is the name Piaget gives to his explanation of the historical, social, biological, and psychological origins of scientific knowledge (Piaget, 1971a). This line of his work tries to answer philosophical questions, but in doing so Piaget often relies on his research in developmental psychology to answer interrelated philosophical and psychological questions. For example, philosophers ask "what is knowledge, and what are its origins?" Developmental psychologists ask "What do people know at different points in their life, and how do they acquire that knowledge?" Piaget asks both questions because he believes that an understanding of what children know and how they come to know can assist philosophers in answering their questions about what constitutes knowledge and how true knowledge is obtained.

Biographical Sketch

Jean Piaget was born in Neuchatel, Switzerland, in 1896, and from his own accounts (Piaget, 1952), he devoted considerable study to biology and philosophy. At the age of ten he published his first scientific paper, a one-page observation of an albino sparrow. When he was an adolescent, his godfather, Samuel Cornut, introduced him to philosophy, thereby sparking a lifelong interest. His mother's psychological ailments and her treatment by a psychoanalyst prompted young Piaget's interest in psychology. Still, his enduring passion for biology dominated, and he continued publishing at a pace that brought him early recognition and an invitation for the position of curator of the mollusk collection at the Museum of Natural History in Geneva. Young Piaget declined the invitation in order to finish high school. By his twenty-first birthday he had published over twenty articles. In college he studied natural science, completing his baccalaureate in 1915 and his doctorate in malacology (the study of mollusks) in 1918.

After receiving his doctorate, Piaget spent several years studying child development; toward that end, he worked in France helping Alfred Binet standardize the Burt reasoning tests for Parisian school children. In that capacity, he became intrigued by the reasons children gave for their *wrong answers*, and he pioneered the use of clinical interviews as a research method.

In 1921 Piaget became director of research at the Jean-Jacques Rousseau Institute in Geneva. He proceeded to launch a series of investigations on the development of children's thought, which made him famous throughout Europe before he was thirty years old. In the ensuing years Piaget held many prestigious positions and wrote extensively about psychology, epistemology, and education before his death in 1980. Piaget, together with Freud and Skinner, is widely considered to be one of the three most important shapers of developmental psychology.

The Stimulus of Kant

Recall from Chapter 3 that Immanual Kant was the architect of the constructivist epistemology. Piaget's (1952) autobiography acknowledges his philosophical indebtedness to Kant, whom he first started reading while an adolescent. While Kant's ideas pervade Piaget's theory, it is the *categories, schemata,* and *interactive constructivism* that are most relevant here. Kant believed that *categories* of experience like space, time, causality, and number were innate structures that filter, shape, and give meaning to all experience. Piaget turned Kant's categories into topics of investigation and showed that they evolve through developmental stages rather than being innate as Kant had claimed. Kant also proposed that knowledge derives from the application of inborn *schemata* to experience. In this view, a scheme is a capacity to form concepts or images that produce meaning when applied to sensations. Piaget borrows the notion of schemata and shows that these infantile action patterns function as the building blocks of knowledge. Finally, Kant's epistemology rejected both rationalist and empiricist explanations of knowledge, a position Piaget (1963, 1971b, 1972) echos in arguing that cognitive development results from a constructive synthesis between organismic structures and environmental stimuli. In the Piagetian sense, knowledge is invented; it can originate neither in innate programming nor in discoveries of things given in reality (von Glasersfeld, 1979, p. 109).

Spencer's Principles of Psychology

Herbert Spencer, Charles Darwin's cousin, believed that evolution was such a powerful natural force that it could be used to explain almost any sort of phenomena. Spencer derived a universal law called the *synthetic principle* from Darwin's theory of evolution, and he argued that this general law was powerful enough to explain biological, psychological, ethical, and even economic development. In Spencer's hands, the synthetic principle had many implications, several of which are direct antecedents of Piagetian concepts.

Theme 1: Ontogeny recapitulates phylogeny. Spencer (1897, vol. 1) believed that there exist important parallels between an individual's development and the evolution of the human race: "Mind rises...in proportion as it manifests the traits characterizing Evolution in general" (p. 189). He argued that the evolution of the brain from simple, autonomic functions to complex symbolic functions was repeated between infancy and adulthood. Piaget's (1971a) genetic epistemology reflects this theme in the view that an individual's cognitive development parallels the development of scientific concepts in the historical advances of science.

Theme 2: Assimilation and Accommodation. Spencer (1902) viewed development as the product of two kinds of tensions—tension between the organism's tendencies to consume the environment it inhabits and antagonistic tensions from environmental pressures that resist consumption (p. 496). Spencer (1897, vol. 1) defined these tensions as accommodation, the adjustment of one's inner structures to external relations (pp. 388–389), and assimilation, the structural complexities that counteract external relations (Spencer, 1902, p. 496). Piaget follows Spencer's lead in claiming that assimilation and accommodation underlie all cognitive development.

Theme 3: Equilibration. Spencer (1902) defined *equilibration* as the ultimate goal of development (p. 495), as a balance between internal functions and external forces. That is, individuals spontaneously regulate their adjustments to the world (accommodation) while simultaneously distorting information (assimilation) to "fit" cognitive apparati. For Piaget, equilibration is a core element of his theory.

Theme 4: Stage Theory of Development. Spencer (1897, vol. 2, p. 513) proposed a theory of mental development composed of hierarchically integrated cognitions that begin with sensations and end with abstract relations—a formulation nearly identical to the stage theory adopted by Piaget. Spencer's first stage, termed *presentation,* consists of sensation and reflexion, which together comprise infants' sole psychological capabilities. *Presentation* is similar in many respects to Piaget's sensorimotor stage. Spencer's second stage, *presentation-representation,* consists psychologically of relations formed between sensations and the environmental stimuli that produced them. These relations comprise simple thoughts and ideas, very much like Piaget's description of symbolic representations typical of the preoperational stage. Spencer's third stage, *representation,* consists of cognitive relations between representations and the objects and events one has experienced. These are relationships of classification and relation, reminiscent of the cognitive activities Piaget describes for the concrete operational stage. Finally, Spencer's fourth stage, *re-representation,* consists of hypothetico-deductive relations that resemble Piaget's description of the formal operational stage. While Piaget's stages are far more specific than Spencer's general account of hierarchically arranged cognitions, Spencer's footprints are clearly evident in cognitive-developmental theory.

The Context of Werner's Organicism

The first English translations of Piaget's research appeared in the 1940s, but they had little influence in America because of the behaviorist orientation that linked the study of observable behavior with a rigorous experimental methodology. Heinz Werner and John Flavell played important roles in popularizing Piaget in the United States.

Heinz Werner drew extensively from anthropology, psychology, and embryology to introduce his *organismic* theory of mental development. His work introduced a new philosophical orientation that established a climate receptive to Piaget's theory. While behaviorism virtually dominated academic psychology between 1930 and 1960, Werner (1948) challenged the inherent reductionism of behavioral theory (see critique of Skinner's theory in Chapter 7). Where behaviorism attempted to reduce complex behavior into simpler, more analyzable units, organicism countered by arguing that behavior could only be understood holistically.

To understand what Werner was getting at, consider a simple example. Hydrogen and oxygen are gases that, when chemically bonded together, produce water. Yet, neither hydrogen nor oxygen is wet. Analyzing water solely in terms of its atomic elements—hydrogen and oxygen—would lead one to erroneously conclude that wetness is not a property of water. Analogously, Werner contended that complex behavior could not be meaningfully understood if analyzed in terms of its discrete, isolated components.

Werner's work challenged the behaviorist agenda during the 1940s and 1950s, and it sensitized American psychologists to the conceptual limitations of behaviorism.

Given the change of climate induced by Werner's organismic theory, one of his students, John Flavell, took up the task of reintroducing Piaget to English readers. In 1963 Flavell published *The Developmental Psychology of Jean Piaget,* an encyclopedic summary of Piaget's methodology, research investigations, developmental theory, and genetic epistemology. In the past quarter century, many of Piaget's books and papers have been translated into English, and his theory has generated a vast amount of research in developmental psychology.

STRUCTURAL COMPONENTS

Assumptions

Piaget makes two important assumptions about the neonate. First, he assumes that we are born with a species-specific set of biological reflexes termed *hereditary organic reactions* (Piaget, 1963, p. 23). These reflexes are preprogrammed maneuvers for engaging the world. Second, Piaget assumes that infants are naturally active; they spontaneously initiate encounters with the environment.

It is important to note here what Piaget does not assume. Where Freud assumed the presence of an irrational mind, the libido, and where Skinner assumed a *tabula rasa* mind ready-made to begin accumulating associations, *Piaget assumes no mind at all.* The irony of this situation should not be overlooked. Piaget's position poses an interesting problem whose solution reflects a degree of philosophical acumen. On the one hand, Piaget knew that by assuming the presence of a mind at birth, he was relieved of the problem of explaining its origin. On the other hand, he recognized that by not assuming its presence at birth he shouldered the responsibility of explaining its ontogenesis. He chose the second route and therein offered an entirely original explanation of mental development.

Problems for Study

The purpose of cognitive-developmental theory is to explain the origin and genesis of knowledge. Like other theories, Piaget's can be viewed in terms of the phenomena it attempts to explain and its primary research methods.

Phenomena to Be Explained

Piaget attempts to explain the ontogenesis of scientific and mathematical knowledge. More specifically, he attempts a formal explanation of how we come to understand space and geometry, movement and speed, time, causality, number, weight, volume, probability, chance, logic, and many other scientific, mathematical, and logical concepts. In addition, he examines the relationship between the development of knowledge and specialized cognitive functions—memory, perception, and language (Piaget, 1970a, pp. 703–731). Finally, he proposes *genetic epistemology* in response to philosophical questions about the nature and origin of knowledge.

Methods of Study

Piaget uses two complementary methods in collecting his developmental data: observations and clinical interviews. When his three children were infants, he recorded copious and detailed observations of their spontaneous activities and their reactions to stimuli he would produce. These notes provided the basis for several books about infant intellectual development.

Based on his early intuitions about children's wrong answers, he later developed a method he called the *clinical interview.* The clinical interview consists of an open-ended collection of questions coupled with a cognitive task or problem. The interview is designed to get children to talk about their strategies, plans, possible solutions, and the meaning of their manipulations. It is worth noting here that from Piaget's point of view, a flexible interview specially attuned to each subject (and therefore not standardized) does not invalidate his data. His aim is to ensure that subjects are given an opportunity to fully divulge their thought capabilities. This "Genevan" notion of standardization is quite different from the American version of test standardization. Where the Genevans emphasize the importance of standardizing the *relationship* between subject and problem, the classical American concept of standardization refers to the sameness of task instructions for each subject.

Internal Principles

Assimilation, Accommodation, and Equilibration

According to Piaget, organic activity is characterized by two opposing tendencies—assimilation and accommodation. *Assimilation* is the tendency toward self-preservation and the incorporation of environmental sensations into the activities and systems already possessed by an individual (Piaget, 1963, p. 6). Every interaction between individual and environment requires some degree of modification to give reality meaning and make it "fit" with previous understanding. For example, the author once borrowed a phrase popularized by an account of national defense—*window of vulnerability*—to describe in a human development class the time span both before and after ovulation when intercourse can lead to pregnancy. That phrase was recorded in one student's notes as "win over ability"—a like-sounding, but different, notion. When the student was later asked what the phrase meant, she indicated that she thought it had something to do with a girl's "win over ability," that is, how readily she could be seduced. This example of assimilation shows how the new concept *window of vulnerability* was distorted, both phonetically and conceptually, to match this student's prior understanding of factors related to getting pregnant.

The purest form of assimilation is play (Piaget, 1962), because it represents a radical distortion of reality in the service of one's own motives and whims. When, for example, toddlers make trains from wooden blocks, "read" stories from Dad's newspaper, and "eat" make-believe cooking from empty pots on the kitchen floor, they are distorting certain qualities of reality by inventing their own meanings. Assimilation is the cognitive function that makes experience meaningful.

Accommodation is the complement to assimilation; it entails adjustments and modifications of the individual to real situations (Piaget, 1966, p. 39). The student in the above example adjusted her previous understanding of pregnancy by apprehending a new technical term—"win over ability." The purest form of accommodation is imitation (Piaget, 1962). When individuals imitate reality, they attempt to copy as precisely as possible (and thus without deliberate distortion) some action in the environment.

All interactions contain some mixture of these complementary tendencies; one action does not assimilate while the next one accommodates reality. Rather, every interaction involves some degree of modification and incorporation of external information and some degree of adjustment to new elements (Piaget, 1963, pp. 6–7).

To illustrate how assimilation and accommodation are interrelated, my son has provided me the following example. During dinner one evening, Megan proclaimed that she'd learned how to count backward, and she proceeded to demonstrate: "Six, five, four, three, two, one." Following the customary parental praise, Matthew announced that he too could count backward, whereupon he turned around on his stool and *with his back to the table* proceeded to count: "One, two, three, six, eleven, three...." Matthew's action, an attempt to imitate his older sister, reflects accommodation in his adjustment to the situation of counting backward. However, assimilation accompanied his imitation when he distorted Megan's meaning to his own—to count backward, one turns backward and counts!

The specific qualities of assimilation and accommodation vary with the context, depending on the individual's prior acquisitions and the specifics of the situation at hand. What is invariant, however, is the fact that they function in every interaction.

Equilibration is one of Piaget's most important concepts. Following Spencer, he viewed equilibration as the process of adaptation whereby assimilation and accommodation are brought into balance. It is the process that regulates all adaptive activities. By adapting to social and physical environments, individuals tend toward *equilibrium* between previously acquired knowledge (assimilation) and new information (accommodation). In another sense, equilibration can be viewed as the process of change in which individuals move from the equilibrium of one stage, through a transition of disequilibrium, to a hierarchically integrated new form of equilibrium at the next stage.

Equilibration is a cognitive extension of organic *auto-* or *self-regulation,* which is always at work coordinating assimilation and accommodation into increasingly flexible cognitive organizations for adapting to novelty and unpredictability in the world (Flavell, 1963, p. 240). More will be said about this concept in the section on change mechanisms.

The Functional Invariants: Organization and Adaptation

Piaget points out that all creatures possess certain invariant processes that function across time and situations to control reproduction, eating, digestion, circulation, and metabolism. Analogously, he believes that intelligence is governed by two invariant functions—*organization* and *adaptation. Organization is a biological and intellectual predisposition to interrelate, order, and arrange individual elements (activities, ideas, functions, etc.) into a systematic whole.* When Matthew demonstrated his prowess at counting backward, he was displaying his own spontaneous arrangement of how "backward" and "counting" were related. Like Matthew, individuals organize their intellectual functioning to confer meaning on their experiences. In contrast, *adaptation is the process of adjusting to the external world.* It consists of an active encounter between the self and external events whereby some adjustment is made that ensures more efficient future encounters. Matthew adapted to Megan's dinner scene by redirecting both parents' attention and claiming for himself the joy of their spontaneous laughter. Adaptation itself has two components: assimilation and accommodation.

Whereas assimilation and accommodation are situation-specific processes, organization and adaptation are long-term, trans-situational tendencies. Assimilation and accommodation help us understand each interaction; organization and adaptation provide transcendent, "big picture" understanding of how specific interactions relate to the larger course of development. Individuals make sense of their world by organizing their experiences. They regulate their activities by relating one experience to another; they differentiate and classify memories; they tune intentions and strategies toward goals that motivate them; and they invent meanings for worldly events. At the same time, one's intellect is constantly adapted to the social and physical environment. Children in every culture, for example, adapt their social behaviors to the cultural requirements for obtaining desired objects and organize these same behaviors in terms of previously successful strategies. Matthew knows how to imitate Megan and thereby receive his share of parental attention. In turn, Megan has an organized "watch this" strategy that has proven adaptive in recapturing parental attention.

The tendency for thought to structure itself while adjusting to and comprehending reality implies that organization and adaptation are complementary, interrelated processes. "It is by adapting to things that thought organizes itself and it is by organizing itself that it structures things" (Piaget, 1963, p. 8).

Bridge Principles

Scheme

A *scheme is an organized, generalizable action pattern.* Experience is always assimilated to an individual's schemes, but at the same time these schemes become elaborated, generalized, and differentiated to accommodate different features of reality. The concept of scheme gives Piaget a way to apply his internal principles directly to the explanation of thought and behavior, since schemes are the means by which reality is structured (through assimilation and accommodation).

It is instructive here to contrast Piaget's concept of *scheme* with Skinner's concept of *operant*. Although the two concepts appear similar, that is only true for the analysis of overt behavior. In fact Piaget's (1963) propensity for labeling schemes according to their predominant behavioral motif—sucking scheme, throwing scheme, scheme of prehension—may have blurred the distinction between operant and scheme. "Operant" signifies a class of similar behaviors whose terminus lies in the capacity for chaining into behavior chains. In contrast, Piaget's "scheme" constitutes the generalizable organization of activity whose ultimate development lies in higher order cognitive structures. Thus, the two concepts—operant and scheme—offer quite different theoretical journeys and yield dramatically different theoretical implications.

Both behavioral and cognitive schemes are constructed throughout life for conferring meaning on experience. They vary widely in their onset, complexity, relationship to one another, and the objects toward which they are directed. For example, children who recognize their mothers in a crowd of picnicking families, teenagers who avoid faddish hair styles solely because of anticipated maternal hassles, and adults who call their mothers long distance every Sunday can all be said to have a "mother" scheme.

Operations

Cognitive operations are reversible mental action patterns. Mental operations originate in the infant's sensorimotor schemes, which, through internalization, give rise to mental representations. Representations later become organized into reversible mental transformations called operations. The significance of operations in Piaget's theory can be found in the names he gives to three developmental stages: *preoperational, concrete operational,* and *formal operational.*

There are many kinds of cognitive operations: addition, subtraction, multiplication, and division; one-to-one and many-to-one correspondences; and symmetrical and asymmetrical relations. These somewhat forboding terms are really quite manageable when one understands the rather ordinary activities to which they apply. For example, a child could perform mental operations to figure out that John is the shortest of his three friends, provided that Samuel is taller than Matt and Matt is taller than John. In reaching that conclusion, the child would simply perform the operation of asymmetrical, transitive inference ($A > B$, $B > C$, therefore $A > C$). A useful rule of thumb is that there corresponds a mental operation for such mathematical symbols as plus, minus, times, equals, less than, greater than, and so forth (Flavell, 1963, p. 166). Some of the mental operations are described more completely in the following section.

Cognitive Structures

The part of Piaget's theory that has received the most widespread attention is the sequence of cognitive-developmental stages. Piagetian stages differ markedly from Freud's and Erikson's, a point to which we now turn.

Piaget's Concept of "Stage."   Piaget's stages have four general properties that differentiate them from the kinds of stages proposed by Freud and Erikson. First, Piagetian stages are stable, cohesive, organized systems of interrelated actions and potential actions called *structured wholes*. Second, stages occur in a universal sequence; they cannot be rearranged or skipped. Third, later stages are transformations of earlier stages. This means that when stage change occurs, one cognitive structure evolves through reorganization and adaptation into a hierarchically inclusive new intellectual structure that preserves previous knowledge within a more differentiated and integrated system of operations. Once the reorganization has occurred, the previous stage no longer exists. Unlike Freud and Erikson, Piaget contends that there can be no developmental regression once earlier stages have been irreversibly transformed into new cognitive structures.

Operative and Figurative Aspects of Knowledge.   Piaget (1970a, pp. 717–719) differentiates between two aspects of cognitive functioning: the *figurative* aspect and the *operative* aspect. Figurative knowing is oriented toward organizing sensory data by grasping reality as it appears without attempting to transform it. This aspect of knowledge derives from perceptual, linguistic, and imitative activities. Much of our early socialization and schooling concentrates extensively on figurative knowledge, especially in terms of learning names—word names, object names, color and shape names, counting and number names, people's first and last names, story and song names, food names, tool and toy names, rule names, game names, state names, and date names.

Operative aspects of knowledge constitute what Piaget calls *logico-mathematical* knowledge, which occupies most of his theoretical attention. Operative knowledge derives from cognitive activities that transform and enrich an object with properties or new relationships of classification, order, composition, and arrangement. For example, number is not a property we derive from an object; it is a property of our counting activity. So, when we count the number of objects in a collection, the number we derive represents operative, or logico-mathematical knowledge.

Piaget's study of the development of figurative knowledge, especially perception, memory, imitation, and language (e.g., Piaget, 1962, 1968, 1969; Piaget & Inhelder, 1969, 1971, 1973) has led him to conclude that it is actually organized by higher order operative knowledge. For example, perception without intelligence to direct it would have no meaning from Piaget's point of view. In this vein, perception, like the other figurative aspects of knowledge, is essentially an activity that is organized, directed, and interpreted by operative knowledge.

The foregoing discussion has prepared us for an examination of Piaget's four cognitive-developmental stages. The *sensorimotor* stage consists of six subperiods during infancy which comprise practical intelligence—action knowledge. The *preoperational* stage marks the beginning of thought and the marvelous prelogical intellectual antics associated with early childhood. The *concrete operational* stage heralds the onset of logico-mathematical operations that empower thinking with a quality of logical cohesion for understanding experience. The *for-*

mal operational stage represents a transcendence of reality in a sense: that is, the individual becomes capable of operating mentally on hypotheses and propositions, some of which may be contrary to fact.

The Sensorimotor Stage.   Recall that Piaget does not assume a neonatal mind. His explanation of how the mind originates can be found in his description of the six subperiods that comprise the sensorimotor stage. This stage marks the development of generalizable action patterns called *schemes* whereby the infant evolves from a biological, proactive organism into a truly psychological being capable of thinking. Sensorimotor knowledge, constructed through assimilation and accommodation of schemes to the external world, is not contemplative; rather, it is a *pragmatic knowledge in action* that consists of increasingly complex and differentiated coordinations of schemes for relating to objects.

Neonates and young infants do not understand objects unless they are acting on them. In this sense we can say that newborns understand only their own activities, their schemes, before they understand the objects of their actions. Later, such knowledge comes to include the properties of objects themselves. Only when the schemes become differentiated according to object characteristics and inter-coordinated with one another does the infant understand that objects continue to exist independent of actions performed on them. This important achievement Piaget calls *object permanence.* By the end of the sensorimotor period, infants become capable of mentally representing objects, a sign that the preoperational stage has begun.

Sensorimotor development entails six subperiods whose *sequence* rather than their timing is Piaget's concern. Thus, the approximate age ranges show that infants may progress at different rates.

1. REFLEXES (BIRTH TO 1 MONTH).   The infant possesses innate *active* reflexes that occur spontaneously as well as in response to stimuli. For example, infants naturally grip their hands quite tightly, suck while sleeping as well as when their cheek is stroked, and flail arms, head, and legs in what seem to be unconnected bursts of activity. Through repetition (assimilation) the reflexes become generalized, and inactive reflexes gradually disappear (e.g., spontaneous sucking, reflexive grasping). At the same time, contact with the environment modifies the reflexes through accommodation. For example, most mothers discover that their newborns may take several days to a week to develop efficient sucking routines where they can search out, find, grasp, and then suck on the nipple with sufficient vigor to produce a satisfactory flow of milk.

2. ACQUIRED ADAPTATIONS AND PRIMARY CIRCULAR REACTIONS (1 TO 4 OR 5 MONTHS).   Assimilation and accommodation are at first essentially undifferentiated. During the second substage, differentiation produces the first acquired adaptations called *primary circular reactions* (Piaget, 1963, p. 66). These primary circular reactions are adjustments created by the infant's own activity and are directed at prolonging novel activities (Piaget, 1963, p. 55). Anticipatory signs first

appear, as when an infant stops crying in anticipation of nursing when it sees its mother unbutton her blouse.

Sensory schemes (perception, prehension, audition) begin to intercoordinate, as when infants move both head and eyes toward a sound in anticipation of seeing what they hear. Piaget calls this intercoordination *reciprocal assimilation,* because the schemes mutually assimilate each other—like "listening to the face while looking at the voice" (Piaget, 1963, p. 87). However, because reciprocal assimilations are guided by directly perceived sensations, they still lack conscious intention (Piaget, 1963, p. 145).

3. SECONDARY CIRCULAR REACTIONS (5 TO 8 MONTHS). *Secondary circular reactions* lead to *rediscovering* (rather than prolonging) gestures that produce interesting events. These reactions begin when infants associate their own activity with some interesting result, but this does not imply that they understand how the event was produced. Secondary circular reactions are aimed at reconstructing or rediscovering the means that produce an interesting result, rather than the event itself (Piaget, 1963, p. 175). The secondary circular reactions are the transitional links between preintelligent schemes and the genuinely intentional activities of the next subperiod.

Piaget believes that infants fail to understand that objects continue to exist independent of actions performed on them. This "out of sight, out of mind" interpretation is supported by two lines of evidence. First, when a toy is taken away from an infant and placed beneath a cloth, the infant acts as if the object no longer exists and makes no attempt to search for the toy or to remove the cloth that covers it. Second, when presented with a variety of different objects (cotton balls, tin foil, toy cars, golf balls, crayons), infants perform the same exploratory schemes on each. They may alternate, for example, between looking, mouthing, shaking, and hitting, but they show no systematic differentiation between objects. Piaget believes that the same explanation accounts for both of these situations. Schemes (the action patterns) are still fused with and undifferentiated from their external ends (the objects and goals on which they operate). The infant's only meaning is the meaning of its own activities—what it can do. So far as the infant is concerned, when its schemes cease operation, objects lose their existence. At this point, there is still no conscious awareness of the self, because infants have not yet discovered their bodies as objects in a world of objects.

4. COORDINATION OF SECONDARY CIRCULAR REACTIONS (8 TO 12 MONTHS). Action intelligence is no longer limited to rediscovering old means for producing interesting events; it is extended to producing events through *new combinations* of schemes. Accommodation consists of adjusting previously constructed schemes to the primary characteristics of objects, and assimilation extends the acquired schemes by combining and recombining them into new combinations.

A very important accomplishment occurs at this substage—the onset of *intentionality.* Piaget defines intention as the differentiation between means and ends, between procedures and objects, and substage 4 marks the first differentiations and coordinations of schemes according to the qualities of objects acted upon

(1963, p. 211). Substage 4 infants behave differently with different objects, and they search out to retrieve a hidden object. These refinements reflect active reorganizations of schemes and lead to the construction of an objective universe of objects whose permanence is independent of the schemes and is thus detached from the self (Piaget, 1963, p. 211). This capability is the first objective evidence of *object permanence* and intentionality.

Contrary to some accounts (e.g., Salkind, 1981, p. 201; Thomas, 1985, p. 273), Piaget believes that infants are incapable of thinking or forming concepts before the end of the sensorimotor stage. He argues (Piaget, 1963, pp. 210–262) that differentiation between means and ends is the *creation of intentionality* (Piaget, 1963, p. 226) only in sensorimotor actions and does not reflect mental activity.

5. TERTIARY CIRCULAR REACTIONS (12 TO 18 MONTHS). *Tertiary circular reactions* consist of "the discovery of new means through active experimentation" (Piaget, 1963, p. 267). Whereas old schemes were combined and applied to new situations in substage 4, this substage produces active groping (Piaget, 1963, p. 264) whereby infants adapt themselves to unfamiliar situations not only by applying schemes already acquired, but also by trying to fashion entirely new schemes in the act of solving problems. Schemes are varied and mutated much like action-experiments conducted in order to see what fluctuations result. These variations, adjusted after the fact according to the results obtained, produce new, more differentiated schemes.

6. THE INVENTION OF NEW MEANS THROUGH MENTAL COMBINATIONS (18 TO 24 MONTHS). This subperiod marks the beginning of thought and the transition from sensorimotor action to mental representation. The two most important advances of this transition are those of *invention* and *representation.* In its interactions, the infant begins to anticipate the results of its schemes, and these anticipations occur mentally rather than empirically. That is, internal coordinations consist of true inventions applied to *mental representations* and occur *before* schemes are actually activated (Piaget, 1963, p. 341). In short, the infant begins to anticipate before acting by *mentally combining* schemes designed to produce certain results.

How infants become capable of mental functioning at this point when no such capacity was assumed at their birth is a matter of some controversy. Piaget (1962, pp. 62–77; 1963, pp. 341–356) contends that the external schemes, by becoming increasingly regular, rapid, and automated, also gradually become *internalized.* Internalization produces mental images of schemes that had previously been carried out only in action, thereby enabling infants to invent mentally and before the fact new relationships between schemes, which had previously been discovered only on the physical plane and only during or after the activity itself. Substage 6 is the beginning of mind. The first mental representations are images of *the infant's own schemata.* Later, as mental capacity becomes more differentiated and efficient, it generates images of objects as distinct from action schemes.

Most people have routine memory lapses that are analogous to the action-to-thought evolution posited by Piaget. For example, we sometimes begin to do something (e.g., fetch a drink from the kitchen) only to be distracted along the way and end up forgetting what we set out to do. When that happens, we typically attempt to retrace our steps by repeating the same activities we were engaged in when we had the original idea. According to Piaget, the reason this strategy works is that our actions are the original source of mental representations. Our natural expectation is that by reproducing the original activities we will reproduce the original ideas.

Piaget's account of sensorimotor intelligence contrasts sharply with endogenous theories that view mental functioning as a product of biological maturation and exogenous theories that posit sensation and perceptual experience as the source of thought. To summarize, Piaget sees individuals as biological creatures that are inherently proactive. Infantile actions incorporate reality (assimilation) while adjusting to it (accommodation). Through repetition, generalization, and differentiation, actions become organized and adapted to reality and give rise to intention when schemes (means) become differentiated from objects (ends). Finally, thinking begins when internalized schemes evoke mental images, and these images gradually become extended to the world of objects.

Preoperational Stage (approximately 2 to 7 years). The end of the sensorimotor stage is also the beginning of the *preoperational* stage. The most important new ability of this stage is the *semiotic function,* which enables the child to perform mental actions (imagination, memory, symbolization, etc.) and mental manipulations of objects that replace the previous stage's physical activities. The most powerful of the semiotic functions is language, which provides the user with both a ready-made system of symbols for relating to objects and for socializing thought through communicative interactions with others.

Operative knowledge in this stage consists of egocentric intuitions and preconcepts (Piaget, 1966) that are nonlogical but semisocialized patterns of thinking. Figurative knowledge in this stage consists of the specific mental images, memories, symbols, and language actually used by the child. However, Piaget (1970a, 1984) contends that language is subordinate to and organized by intellectual development rather than being a medium that shapes it. The most notable characteristics of the preoperational stage are the following.

NARROW FIELD OF ATTENTION. The preoperational child *centers* on only one element of a situation at a time, though many details may be noticed in rapid succession. This cognitive *centration* limits thought to only one idea at a time, a serious constraint that is sometimes the source of misjudgments, as when, for example, a youngster sees a penguin swimming at the zoo and decides it must be a fish or when another notices that the water in one container is higher than in a second and judges the first to have "more water" without taking into account the width of the containers. While ideas may occur in relatively rapid sequence, true comparisons are not possible since a comparison requires simultaneous evaluation of two or more pieces of information. Children's *narrow field of attention* often leads them to notice situational details missed by adults who are more concerned with the "big picture" than the minutiae of details.

IMMACULATE PERCEPTION. In terms of preoperational thought, "seeing is believing." Preoperational children often fail to differentiate between the apparent and the real, and they tend to believe that something is real even if it is only imagined. For example, they may believe that dream monsters and television characters are real. Moreover, they may believe that the moon follows them simply because it looks that way to them. Finally, the attraction of magic shows lies in the fun of watching animals appear and disappear, not in the challenge of figuring out how such contrary-to-fact phenomena are possible (simply because they are not seen to be contrary-to-fact in the child's own mind).

SUBJECTIVE EGOCENTRISM. Preoperational thought is subjectively egocentric, meaning that thinking derives from, is directed by, and aims toward ends determined by the child's own point of view. Thought is socialized to the point that it can be communicated, but it is not yet socialized to the point where one's thinking can take account of others' points of view. Thus, children talking on a phone may simply nod their heads in response to Grandpa's questions, or they may think it perfectly appropriate to get Mommy a new toy or some bubble gum for Mother's Day.

Preoperational egocentrism implies that children believe something simply by the force of thinking it. Moreover, specific patterns of egocentric concepts have been identified by Piaget (1960). *Animism* can be found in the child's tendency to attribute life to inanimate objects, as when children think clouds are alive because they move. *Artificialism* reflects the belief that natural geologic features (e.g., mountains and lakes) were built by people a long time ago for their own purposes (e.g., they wanted some place to camp and fish and swim). *Finalism* is the belief that nothing in nature occurs by chance; everything must have a reason. Finalism may sometimes produce the never-ending stream of "why" questions typical of early childhood.

Finally, the same subjectivity of thought that originates in the child's own motivations recognizes neither the fallibility of logical contradiction or the necessity of logical relationships. Parents often find, for example, that their preoperational children resist the persuasive powers of logical reasoning; the difficulty can be found in the child's inability to recognize the force of reason and logic.

UNIDIRECTIONAL THINKING. Preoperational thought is *unidirectional* in its remarkably durable tendency to extend itself simply through its own activities without evidence of self-correction or awareness of contradiction. A child's recounting of a story or an event, for example, is held together more by the order in which memories are evoked than by the original order in which the events occurred. Thought is one way both in the sense that it lacks the reversibility present at the next stage and in the sense that it reflects the functioning of *transductive* reasoning. Transduction occurs when the child reasons from one particular to the next without maintaining an overall goal or aim. Each reasoning event is connected to the previous one simply by its order in the sequence. An excellent example of transductive reasoning is found in the description of classification abilities later in the chapter.

A final point about this stage is in order. Preoperational thought is *abstract*, precisely because it is thinking. Thinking requires the ability to represent mentally both objects and experiences. Mental representations are symbolic cognitive abstractions of things. For example, images of objects are not the objects themselves, nor are memories of events the events themselves. While levels of abstracting ability develop in concert with the stages of cognitive ontogenesis, the ability to think abstractly is the very hallmark of symbolic thought achieved at the preoperational stage.

Piaget believed that the most important quality of each stage was the structure of reasoning rather than how many facts one knew. Consequently, he developed a number of tasks to elicit reasoning about scientific concepts. Table 9-1

Table 9-1   Selected Piagetian Tasks

CONSERVATION OF NUMBER

Problem: Maintain the relationship of equality across irrelevant changes that perceptually distort the equality.

Initial Presentation: two rows of coins, each containing the same number. Question: Does each row have the same number of coins or does one have more than the other?

Responses: Both preoperational and concrete operational children indicate that each row has the same number.

Change 1: Stretch out coins in the bottom row so that it begins before and ends after the top row. Question: Now does each row have the same number of coins or does one have more than the other? How can you tell?

Responses: Concrete operational children maintain the equality in spite of the appearance of inequality. Preoperational children tend to assert that there are now more elements in the bottom row because "they take up so much more room" (immaculate perception).

Change 2: Compact the bottom row so that it begins after and ends before the top row. Question: Now does each row have the same number of coins or does one have more than the other? How can you tell; how do you know for sure?

Responses: Concrete operational children continue to maintain that each row has the same number of elements, in spite of the appearance. Preoperational children, however, now assert that the top row has more because "it's longer" (narrow field of attention) or "'cause this one (top row) comes to here and this one (bottom row) only comes to here" (immaculate perception).

ANALYSIS OF REASONING

Preoperational children believe that the number of coins is a function of the length of the row, in spite of how many coins the row has and in spite of attempts to count the number of coins. Concrete operational children argue that just changing the length of the row does not alter the quantity of coins. They believe that evaluating the one-to-one correspondence of coins in each row is a more valid means of determining their inequality than is merely looking at the length of the row. Counting is quantitative and numerical.

Table 9-1 (cont)

CLASSIFICATION OF GEOMETRIC SHAPES

Problem: Logically classify an assortment of items that differ in terms of size (large and small), shape (circles and squares), and color (white and green). Subjects are asked to "Put the things that go together over here and things that go together a different way over here." Subjects are asked to explain how the items in one class are the same and different from items in another class.

Preoperational Collections

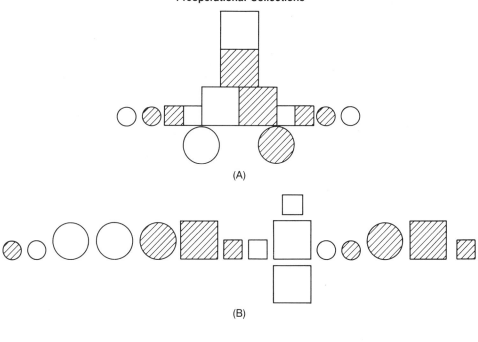

(A)

(B)

Concrete Operational Classifications

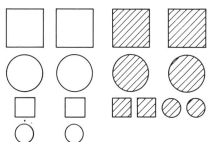

ANALYSIS OF PERFORMANCE

Preoperational children sometimes (top example) form "graphic collections," picturelike arrays of the elements to be sorted. Other times (bottom example) they may reveal transductive reasoning in adding new elements to an array simply because it shares *one or more* properties with the previous item. Their explanations reveal unidirectional thought: "This one is red, and this one is green, and this one is a little one, and this is a big one, etc." Concrete operational children sort objects by their physical qualities and explain their classifications in terms of size, shape, or color.   *(continued)*

Table 9-1 (cont)

CLASS INCLUSION

Problem: Understand that elements can belong simultaneously to both a subordinate and a super-ordinate class. Children are presented with four pictures of daisies and six pictures of tulips. The task is performed only when children answer "yes" to the following two preliminary questions: Are daisies flowers? Are tulips flowers?

Questions: Are there more tulips or more daisies? Are there more daisies than flowers? Are there more tulips or flowers? How come?

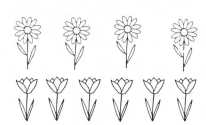

ANALYSIS OF RESPONSES

Preoperational children are able to, based on the perceptual inequivalence, answer that there are more tulips than daisies. However, they believe that there are more tulips than flowers because they can see the tulips and understand that there are more tulips than daisies (immaculate perception). Moreover, they contend that there are more tulips than daisies when asked "are there more tulips or flowers?" Their reasoning reflects the narrow field of attention underlying the cognitive inability to simultaneously operate on both subordinate and superordinate classes.

In contrast, concrete operational children are able to consider both the hierarchical category (flowers) and its inclusive classes (tulips and daisies) simultaneously. Consequently, the class in-clusion questions are answered correctly: there are more flowers than tulips and more tulips than daisies.

summarizes several Piagetian tasks and responses characteristic of the preoperation-al and concrete operational stages. Where appropriate, the underlying cognitive characteristic of thought is also identified.

Concrete Operational Stage (approximately 7 to 14 years, but may last through adulthood). The concrete operational stage signals the beginning of cog-nitive operations on concrete objects. In Piaget's lexicon, *an operation is a reversible mental activity that is part of a holistic mental system of interdependent transformations.* The term *concrete* refers to the child's ability to cognize and operate on elements of physical reality that can be experienced. It is not required that these elements be physically present and manipulable; what is important is that the elements be capable of being physically experienced or imagined. The current rage among many elementary teachers to provide their students with Piaget-inspired concrete "manipulatives" reflects a misreading of Piaget, who contends that concrete operational thought applies itself to physically present objects *and to ideas that derive from physical experience.*

Piaget uses the term *operational* to describe the child's cognitive ability to perform reversible logical and mathematical transformations on concrete entities. In this sense, concrete operational thought is said to be *logico-mathematical* in na-ture (Piaget, 1966, 1970a).

Conservation tasks, because they require logical and mathematical operations for their solutions, are often employed to assess the presence of concrete operational thinking. The task itself is not that important to Piaget. Rather, it is the presence or absence of underlying cognitive operations revealed in children's reasoning about the tasks that makes their use so important in Piaget's theory. In that vein, it is instructive to take a closer look at the premier Piagetian task, conservation of liquid, or in Piaget's (1965a) lexicon, the *conservation of continuous quantity.* Table 9-2 shows the structure of the task, preoperational and concrete operational responses, and an analysis of children's reasoning in terms of underlying cognitive operations.

While preoperational reasoning reflects the cognitive characteristics described earlier for that stage, concrete operations are given logico-mathematical names like *identity, transitivity, inversion-negation,* and *reciprocity.* Piaget (1965a) contends that it is precisely the invention of such operations that marks the difference between preoperational and concrete operational thinking. In other words, the difference between one cognitive stage and another is not a matter of knowing more; it is a difference in cognitive structure that a child applies to making sense of the world.

The important distinction between knowing facts and understanding them can be demonstrated in the liquid conservation problem where both preoperational and concrete operational know the same facts but derive diametrically opposing implications about what they mean. For example, if asked directly, both groups of children will say that no extra liquid has been added or taken away from the original amount, that it is the same liquid they began with, that one container is taller but thinner and the other shorter but wider, and that if the water were poured back into the original container it would be the same amount. Children in both stages possess the *same facts* about the conservation task. Yet, the preoperational fails to conserve while the concrete operational conserves. The reason for such a dramatic difference in judgment lies in the more complex cognitive structure of the concrete operational child.

COGNITIVE REVERSIBILITY. One of the most important achievements of the concrete operational stage is the construction of *reversible cognitive operations.* Reversibility implies a degree of cognitive *decentration,* the ability to think simultaneously about two or more aspects of a situation at the same time, which makes true comparisons possible. For example, in the liquid conservation task, the concrete operational child evaluates the increase in height, compares it with the decrease in width, and concludes that the two physical changes in dimension *compensate* each other.

There are two types of operational reversibility: inversion/negation operates on classes of objects, and reciprocity operates on relationships between objects. Reversible operations return a mental action to its original starting point. In the liquid conservation task, for example, a child who understands that the pouring of the water from one container to another logically implies that it can be unpoured or poured back is demonstrating a reversible mental transformation.

Table 9-2   Conservation of Continuous Quantity

Problem: Understand that liquid quantities are not changed when they reside in differently shaped containers.

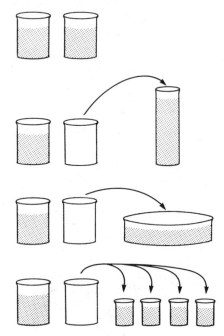

Initial Presentation: Two containers, same size and shape, containing equal amounts of water. Proceed only when subject indicates that each container contains the same amount of liquid.

Change 1: Pour liquid from one container into the taller, narrower container. Question: Now does each glass have the same amount to drink, or does one have more than the other? How can you tell?

Change 2: Return liquid to the original container, ascertain its equivalence, then pour one container into the shorter, wider container. Question: Now does each container have the same amount to drink, or does one have more than the other? Can you tell me how you know that for sure?

Change 3: Return liquid to the original container, ascertain its equivalence, then pour one container into several small cups. Question: Now does this (point to original container) have the same amount to drink as these (point to small cups) or does one have more than the other? How can you tell that they are the same/are different?

ANALYSIS

Preoperational children typically reason that the amount of liquid changes with each transformation and in correspondence to one of the dimensions of the containers. The examples of reasoning below are typical of reasons used to justify nonconserving responses.

Concrete operational children manifest a conserving orientation due to the presence of reversible operations of classification and relation. Examples of their reasoning and the underlying cognitive operations can be found below right.

Preoperational Reasons	*Concrete Operational Reasons*
The water is higher/taller (narrow field of attention).	If I pour it back it will be the same (inversion - negation).
It looks like more (immaculate perception).	It is taller but narrower, so it is the same (reciprocity, compensation).
It is more spread out (immaculate perception).	It started out the same, so it has to stay the same (transitivity).
I can just tell (egocentrism).	It looks like more, but it isn't (identity).
My mother told me (unidirectional thinking).	None was added or taken away, so it is still the same amount (identity).

Reversibility makes the concrete operational child's thinking bidirectional in contrast to the unidirectional thought of the preoperational child. Each of the logico-mathematical operations Piaget attributes to this stage is a particular kind of reversible, mental transformation.

LOGICAL OPERATIONS OF CLASSIFICATION AND RELATION. The operations of classification and relation reflect Piaget's view that the child is a natural scientist, logician, and mathematician. The operations form a tightly knit group of interconnected, mutually implied mental actions that comprise the child's operative knowledge at this stage. While a detailed description of the concrete operations is beyond the scope of this book, a brief look at a few examples may be instructive. Interested readers may wish to examine Flavell's (1963, pp. 172–201) more comprehensive treatment.

Classification entails operations like *inversion/negation, resorption,* and *closure.* The *inversion/negation* operation means that classes can be composed and decomposed through opposing transformations that cancel each other. For example, beginning with the class of sons, we can add the class of daughters to produce the class of children. This transformation can be undone by subtracting the class of daughters from the class of children to arrive at the original class of sons. The operation of *resorption* holds that every class plays an identity element to subordinate classes. For example, if one adds tulips and daisies to the superordinate class of flowers, one obtains the original class of flowers rather than more flowers. The absence of this operation in the preoperational stage explains why young children are unable to solve the class inclusion problem shown in Table 9-1. *Closure* implies that elements of a class can be combined to form new classes, and classes can be combined to form new classes. For example, this operation gives concrete operational children the capacity to understand that the addition of two classes, say dogs and cats, yields a new class—common pets. Moreover, common pets plus uncommon pets produces the class of pets.

Relational operations include *reciprocity, tautology,* and *transitivity. Reciprocity* is similar to inversion/negation: any logical relationship implies an equivalent but opposite relationship. For example, if Susan is older than Jane, then Jane is younger than Susan. *Tautology* holds that every relation plays an identity element with itself. For example, if Sally is taller than Judy, and both girls grow the same amount during the year, then Sally is still taller than Judy. Finally, *transitivity* implies that if A is related to B in the same way that B is related to C, then A is related to C in the same manner. If Judy and Brenda are the same weight, and Brenda and Sharon are the same weight, then Judy and Sharon must also be the same weight.

Concrete operations underlie children's ability to understand the conservations and the characteristics of logical classification and relation. A child does not perform every mental operation each time a problem is presented. However, since these operations are interdependent, children are believed to have the competence to perform all of them if needed. These operations are important because they in large part define what is meant by "rational" thought. Yet rational thought requires one more characteristic, numerical quantification, to become genuinely scientific.

THE CONCEPT OF NUMBER. Piaget (1965a) believes that the child's understanding of number derives from the intersection of operations of classification (cardinal value) and operations of asymmetrical relation (ordinal value). Concrete operational thought reflects the mental ability to "unite parts into a whole, to divide a whole into parts, to co-ordinate equivalences and to multiply relationships" (Piaget, 1965a, p. 240). The number system acts as powerful cognitive "glue" that binds into a single, holistic system the concrete operations of classification and relationship.

Formal Operational Stage (approximately 14 years through adulthood). Formal operations extend thought to propositional logic through the construction of new higher order operations called the *INRC group* (Inhelder & Piaget, 1958). To assess these operations, Piaget has designed tasks to represent complex scientific phenomena.

In one problem, for example, subjects are asked to determine what controls the period of a pendulum. To solve the problem, subjects use a simple pendulum apparatus to measure the effect of the following possible variables: *weight* (several weights differ from light to heavy), pendulum *length* (ranging from short to long), *impetus* or force imparted at the start of the pendulum's swing (ranging from small to large), and *height* at which the pendulum's swing is initiated (ranging from low to high). Subjects are asked to conduct several experiments to assess the influence of the four variables. The problem is to be able to isolate the effects of one variable from the effects of the other three. This task is useful in differentiating concrete operational solutions, involving classification and arranging of variables, from formal operational solutions that reflect testing of all possible combinations of variables (Inhelder & Piaget, 1958, pp. 73–79). Tasks like this one reveal several cognitive qualities not manifested at earlier stages.

HYPOTHETICO-DEDUCTIVE REASONING. Formal operational thought is said to be *hypothetico-deductive* because the mind is capable of formulating hypotheses and deducing their logical implications. Whereas the concrete operational thinker reasons in terms of concrete experiences, the formal operational thinker reasons in terms of possibilities. These possibilities are not arbitrary imaginings or fantasies freed of cognitive constraints or objectivity (Inhelder & Piaget, 1958, p. 255). Rather, such possibilities entail the logical permutation of potential realities and the consideration of "if…then" logical relationships. The advantage of hypotheses over reality states is that hypotheses can be contrary to fact, and yet their logical implications will still be valid (though not necessarily true). Two examples are instructive.

1. Premises: If grapes are larger than oranges, and
                      if oranges are larger than watermelons,

   Valid conclusion: then grapes are larger than watermelons.

2. Premises: If adults are larger than babies, and
                      if children are larger than babies,
   Invalid conclusion: then adults are larger than children.

The first conclusion is logically valid though untrue. It follows by deductive inference from its premises. The second conclusion is true but invalid because it does not follow by deductive inference from its premises.

Hypothetico-deductive thinking elevates childhood understanding from contemplation of action to the science of explanation. For example, scientific phenomena consist of both simple and complex events. Simple, single-cause events are fully comprehensible with concrete operationals. However, whenever variables interact to produce complex events (e.g., weather, corrosion, combustion, ice), then sorting out their individual and interactional effects requires a system that will generate all their possible combinations. The formal operations comprise such a system, which recognizes the operation of univariate as well as multivariate causes.

THE INRC GROUP.   The INRC group is a system of reversible, logical transformations that Piaget (Inhelder & Piaget, 1958) posits as the cognitive structure of formal operational thought. The INRC group—consisting of the operations of *inversion, negation, reciprocity,* and *correlativity*—operates on entire propositions, unlike the concrete operations that operated on single elements of experience. Consequently, the INRC operations work equally well on both contrary-to-fact as well as true-to-fact propositions. Table 9-3 shows how INRC operators function when applied to two propositions: (1) John loves Mary and (2) Mary loves John. Note that the result of each transformation can be reached by applying either a single or a combination of operators. This is what Piaget means when he says that the cognitive structure is a holistic system of mutually implied operations. For example, one achieves the same effect by applying a negation operation as one does by applying first a reciprocity and then a correlativity operation. Thus, within the INRC group of operations, the following equalities exist: I = NRC; N = IRC; R =

Table 9-3   How the INRC Operations Work

	Proposition 1: John loves Mary.	
	Proposition 2: Mary loves John.	

OPERATOR	NAME	TRANSFORMATION
I	Identity	John loves Mary and Mary loves John. (identity = no change)
N	Negation	John *doesn't* love Mary *or* Mary *doesn't* love John. (negation = change propositions and connector)
R	Reciprocity	John *doesn't* love Mary and Mary *doesn't* love John. (reciprocity = change proposition)
C	Correlativity	John loves Mary *or* Mary loves John. (correlativity = change connector)

INC; and C = INR. Verify these equalities by carrying them out on the two propositions in Table 9-3.

THINKING ABOUT THINKING.   Formal operational thought can be turned inward on itself; adolescents can contemplate their own thoughts and take those thoughts as objects of thinking itself. For example, adolescents often exhibit a preoccupation with personal thoughts, chronic self-consciousness, and the attribution to others of motives thought to be highly critical of oneself. Elkind (1974, p. 67) refers to this as the *imaginary audience* because adolescents often seem to imagine themselves performing before an audience of critics who are as interested in teenagers' shortcomings as are the teenagers themselves. Similarly, adolescents often imagine themselves in a *personal fable* where they are somehow immune to natural forces such as aging, death, and disaster (and pregnancy, about which many adolescents say "I didn't think it would happen to me").

Change Mechanism

Piaget (1970a) identifies four factors that work together to produce cognitive development. The first three he terms the "classical factors" because they are widely recognized as influences on development. These include biological maturation, physical experience, and social experience. The fourth factor, *equilibration*, is the most important because it regulates the other three.

Biological Maturation.   Biological maturation, especially the growth of the nervous system, sets the maximum limits of development. It produces new possibilities for cognitive construction but does not predetermine intellectual abilities per se. Consequently, the maturational factor provides a necessary but not sufficient condition for cognitive progress. While cognitive development could not proceed in the absence of maturation, the former cannot be reduced to the latter.

Experience.   Experience contributes a worldly context of sensations within which cognitive constructions become adapted. There are two kinds of experience, analogous to the operative-figurative distinction described earlier. *Physical experience* consists of behavioral or perceptual sensations derived from objects (e.g., color, mass, texture), and these sensations result in figurative knowledge. It is important to note that children do not acquire physical experience by reading off their sensory impressions like a photocopying machine. All actions are accompanied by some degree of assimilation (distortion and meaning making) to prior cognitive structuration. Object permanence, for example, is dependent on the schemes previously constructed by the infant, and lacking a scheme of the permanent object, an infant will be unable to derive "permanence" from its own physical experiences.

In contrast, *logico-mathematical experience* is produced by the coordination of one's actions (whether mental or physical) on objects. This kind of experience gives rise to operative knowledge, which occurs, for example, when a child discovers that the sum of a collection of items is the same in spite of their arrangement or the order in which they are counted. With logico-mathematical experience it is the individual's coordinations of actions rather than the objects themselves that constitute the source of operative knowledge. Piaget believes that it is not the quantity of experience that determines cognitive development—rather, it is the fact of experience. For example, it does not matter whether children have brightly colored toys and laser guns in America or twigs and stones in Argentina. What matters is that they have experience with objects because objects provide opportunities for physical and mental manipulation, which is the source of operative knowledge.

Social Transmission. Society provides the cultural milieu that transmits to individuals the "social facts" of figurative knowledge: the names, expectations, rules, and events whose meaning is logically arbitrary but still necessary for orderly interpersonal conduct. Learning to count to twenty, for example, is a fact of social transmission; learning that twenty cows and twenty minutes are not equivalent amounts is a matter of operative knowledge. Socialization leads to cooperation, and Piaget (1966) is fond of pointing out that social cooperation is a necessary condition for the evolution of cognitive operations. Social transmission, through child rearing, schooling, and especially language learning, arms the child with the social "facts" for getting along with other people. But social transmission is like the other "classical factors" in that it is a necessary but not sufficient condition for cognitive development.

Equilibration. Equilibration regulates the interplay between the three "classical" factors. In fact, Piaget believes that cognitive development is primarily the work of equilibration (1970a, p. 725), which makes it the most important of the four factors.

Equilibration is the process of organic and intellectual self-regulation, which may be either retroactive (feedback derived after the fact from hindsight) or proactive (feedback derived before the fact from anticipation). Following Piaget's lead, Langer (1969, 1974) has noted that *cognitive conflict* may be induced from either intrinsic (intrapsychic) or from extrinsic (interpersonal, self-object) sources. In either case, the cognitive conflict is believed to produce a state of disequilibrium that promotes cognitive change. For example, when an individual has two logically inconsistent ideas or beliefs, self-reflection may result in modification of one, the other, or both ideas into a more parsimonious cognition. Similarly, acts of accommodation to external situations adapt cognitive instruments for later assimilation. Cast in a different light, equilibration can be conceived as a "mini-max" function whose operation both maximizes the information gained in any interactional assimilation while simultaneously minimizing the information lost.

Finally, one cannot divorce the process of equilibration from the states of equilibrium attained through that process. These states are the cognitive structures that characterize the Piagetian stages of cognitive ontogenesis.

EXPLAINING HUMAN DEVELOPMENT: THE RESEARCH

Far too much research on Piaget's theory has been conducted to summarize here. Given the attention Piaget's stages have received, I have chosen to concentrate on various claims Piaget makes about the sensorimotor, concrete, and formal operational stages.

Sensorimotor Stage

There are two predominant types of research studies associated with this stage: studies of the sequentiality of the six substages and object permanence studies.

Sequentiality Studies. Glick's (1975) review of the relevant literature suggests that in spite of cultural differences in child rearing practices, there is little variation in the sequence of sensorimotor substages. At the same time, there exist individual and cultural variations in the speed of sensorimotor development (Bovet, 1976).

Uzgiris and Hunt (1974), using a number of behavioral indices, have performed the most extensive studies of the sensorimotor sequence of substages in such areas as object permanence, schemes, imitation, space, and causality. In another large study of 295 infants, Corman and Escalona (1969) tested the sequentiality of sensorimotor developments related only to object permanence and space. The results of both these studies were supportive of Piaget's description of sensorimotor development. Moreover, Kramer, Hill, and Cohen (1975), in a more narrowly focused study of substages 3 and 4, also confirmed Piaget's depiction of infancy.

Object Permanence. The development of *object permanence* has been studied in human as well as nonhuman (monkey and cat) infants. The picture here is less uniform than the sequentiality research. While there is support for Piaget's claim that object permanence occurs in substage 4 (Gratch, 1972; Gratch & Landers, 1971; Harris, 1973, 1974), infant performance varies as a function of memory requirements (Harris, 1973, 1974), task difficulty (Bower & Wishart, 1972), and performance criteria (Bower, 1974).

Concrete Operational Stage

Research on this stage was quite extensive during the 1960s and 1970s. A number of studies have attempted to replicate Piaget's (1965a) two major claims about conservation: first, that it develops in three phases (absence of conservation, followed by a mixture of conservation and nonconservation reasoning, and finally complete conservation reasoning), and second that conservation of quantity develops before conservation of weight, which develops before conservation of volume.

Brainerd and Brainerd (1972) devised independent tests of each of the three phases and administered these to children aged five to seven years. The

Brainerds reported that not a single subject deviated from the predicted order. Many others have reported substantially the same findings (Brainerd, 1976; Curcio, Kattef, Levine, & Robbins, 1977; Dodwell, 1960, 1961; Elkind, 1961; Lovell & Olgilvie (1960).

Many training studies have been reported in the literature, most of which have assessed the impact of direct instruction of operational rules (e.g., inversion/negation, compensation, identity) on conservation performance. In a widely cited review of this research Murray (1976) concluded that a decade and a half of early training studies produced generally unsuccessful results; that is, training was found to be ineffective in leading to conservation concepts. Many of these training studies were actually tests of children's rule learning (figurative knowledge), which should have no effect on the synthetic construction of concrete operational reasoning. Puzzling, however, is the fact that a few of the later training studies have demonstrated successful instructional strategies in what were essentially replications of earlier, unsuccessful attempts.

Some researchers have reported success at teaching nonconservers how to use the identity operator to improve conservation performance (Hamel, 1971; Hamel & Riksen, 1973; Siegler & Liebert, 1972). Similarly, Goldschmid (1968) and Halford and Fullerton (1970) found that training nonconservers on the use of the compensation rule was an effective means of producing conservation responses in later tests. Other training studies have attempted to elicit conservation performance by directly teaching the inversion/negation operation. Excellent reviews of this literature can be found in Beilin (1971) and Glaser and Resnick (1972), who conclude that this kind of training tends to improve conservation performance, though it does not guarantee it, in originally nonconserving children. It is important to note here, however, that attempts to teach conservation either directly or indirectly through operation training has itself been criticized as a misguided endeavor to speed up rather than understand development (Voyat, 1977).

A second type of training study has examined the use of cognitive disequilibrium to induce disequilibrium. Along this line, some researchers have reasoned that cognitive disequilibrium could be produced either by juxtaposing two contradictory ideas or by juxtaposing interpersonal disagreements about conservation. Disequilibrium produced by cognitive conflict would be predicted to lead nonconservers to an equilibrium state of reasoning that produces conservation responses. Successful training studies of this type have been reported by a number of researchers (Inhelder, Bovet, Sinclair, & Smock, 1966; Inhelder & Sinclair, 1969; Langer, 1969; Murray, 1972; Murray, Ames, & Botvin, 1977).

Formal Operational Stage

Piaget (Inhelder & Piaget, 1958) contends that formal operational thought is characterized by hypothetico-deductive reasoning, and more specifically by the structure of the INRC group of operations. Both Ennis (1975, 1976, 1977) and Parsons (1960) have shown that Piaget's propositional logic (the INRC group) is quite different from the propositional logic used by logicians. Nevertheless, the question of how well it reflects adolescent and adult thinking has been assessed by a number of investigators.

Using one of the largest samples in a study of its kind, Kuhn, Langer, Kohlberg, and Haan (1977) individually tested 256 subjects, aged 10 to 50 years. Subjects were given Piaget's pendulum and correlation tasks. These researchers reported (1) no age differences in cognitive performance on either task, (2) approximately 70 percent exhibited predominantly formal operational reasoning, and (3) only 30 percent exhibited exclusively formal operational reasoning. These findings are consistent with those obtained earlier by Nadel and Schoeppe (1973), Tomlinson-Keasey (1972), and Schwebel (1975). In short, these researchers have found that only about 30 percent of thirteen-year-olds show formal reasoning, whereas about 60 percent of college students exhibit formal reasoning.

Such evidence indicates that most adolescents and adults do not achieve the full stage of formal operations. This underachievement is not really a problem for Piaget's theory. First, his primary concern is with the sequence rather than the terminus of cognitive stages. Second, certain evidence suggests that formal operations may exist in a latent inactive state, untapped by certain kinds of measurements (which would account for the low incidence of fully formal adolescents and adults) until elicited by situations where their use is more readily recognized (Stone & Day, 1978, 1980).

Other Validation Studies

Invariant Sequence. Perhaps the most impressive evidence marshalled to date concerns Piaget's hypothesized universal sequence of stages. Piaget claims that children develop through the same stages in the same order in spite of vast differences in their cultural milieu, educational training, and personal experiences. Focusing primarily on the childhood and adolescent stages, many researchers have used Piagetian tasks to test the sequence of stages. Support for the stage sequence has been found among North Slope Eskimos of Alaska (Feldman, Lee, McLean, Pillemer, & Murray, 1974), Mexicans (Price-Williams, Gordon, & Ramirez, 1969), Costa Ricans and Koreans (Younniss & Dean, 1974), African Woloff (Greenfield, 1966), Rwandese (Pinard & Lavoie, 1974), Aborigines (Dasen, 1972; De Lemos, 1969), French-speaking Canadians (Laurendeau & Pinard, 1962; Pinard & Lavoie, 1974), Iranians (Mosheni, 1966), Norwegians (Hollos, 1975; Hollos & Cowan, 1973), Hungarians (Hollos, 1975), and many other cultures. Although the sequence of stages posited by Piaget has been consistently supported, Kamara and Easley (1977) note that non-Western, nonurban, low socioeconomic status children tend to lag one to several years behind their Western, urban, middle-class peers in the acquisition of concrete operations.

Factor Analyses. A number of investigators have examined the interrelationship between mental operations Piaget claims comprise the cognitive structures. Such relationships have been examined using factor analysis, a statistical technique used to gauge the strength of association between single variables and how well these variables cluster together into identifiable groups or "factors." Using this technique, a number of researchers have shown that the concrete and formal operational structures tend to reflect the kinds of correlations between the mental operations Piaget attributes to those stages (Gray, 1976; Lawson, 1978; Lawson & Nordland, 1976; Rubin, 1973; Stephens, McLaughlin, Miller, & Glass, 1972; Toussaint, 1974).

In spite of its research base, Piagetian theory has often been criticized. Interested readers may wish to examine one or more of the following summaries. Mogdil and Mogdil (1983) present an interdisciplinary analysis of Piaget's contributions to education, philosophy, sociology, psychology, and language development. Sigel, Brodzinsky, and Golinkoff (1981) critique both general concepts and specific implications of Piagetian theory in suggesting how researchers might transcend its limits. Finally, Vuyk (1981) summarizes critiques of the theory as well as the kinds of responses one would expect from a Piagetian point of view.

CONTRIBUTIONS AND CRITICISMS OF THE THEORY

Contributions

Scientist/Philosopher. To Piaget, children are scientist-philosophers whose curiosity naturally motivates them to investigate nature and make sense of their experiences. This belief challenges exogenous views that treat children as recipients of learning (tabula rasa minds to be filled with factual information) and endogenous views that see children as slaves to their own genes. Piaget's portrait reserves for children a primary role in constructing their own knowledge.

Stages. Piaget's cognitive-developmental stages have concentrated psychologists' attention on *how* children understand their experiences rather than on how many facts they know. Moreover, the widespread belief that humans are rational animals finds its most exhalted expression in the logico-mathematical expressions Piaget uses to describe cognitive structures. What makes Piagetian stages different from those of other theorists is that they represent transformations of earlier modes of understanding into qualitatively different organizations of knowledge. These stages have provided educators with many insights into children's readiness for certain kinds of instructional content and have led to innovations (see Chapter 11) in curriculum design.

Methodology. Piaget revolutionized child study. His methods, incorporating scientific tasks and clinical interviews, challenged the assumption that experimental control and quantifiable measurement were the sine qua non of psychology. Moreover his clinical interviews rejected the American notion of test standardization, which required that subjects be tested under the *same conditions.* Piaget's methodology promotes a flexible approach to testing to ensure that subjects are given an opportunity to perform at their maximum capability. The plethora of Piagetian-style research published in the 1960s and 1970s has left in its wake a heightened appreciation among developmental psychologists of the kind of discoveries Piaget's methodology can lead to.

Philosophy-Psychology. Piaget's genetic epistemology represents a unique blend of psychology and philosophy. He uses his copious research to argue that rationalist and empiricist interpretations of knowledge are neither psychologically redeemable nor philosophically tenable. In an age when psychologists tend to forget their historical symbiosis with philosophy, Piaget forged a new awakening between questions of fact (psychology) and questions of meaning (philosophy).

For example, Piaget's distinction between operative and figurative aspects of knowledge corresponds to philosophers' questions about ontology (what is fact) and epistemology (how facts are known), and his theory addresses the development of both aspects. For example, concerning the operative aspect of knowledge, sensorimotor schemes become transformed and reorganized first into preoperational intuitions, then reversible concrete operations, and ultimately into the formal operational INRC group. At the same time figurative knowledge evolves correspondingly from sensations and perceptions of objects to mental images and representations of objects to classifications of and relations between objects and finally to hypotheses and propositions. The development of ontological (figurative) and epistemological (operative) knowledge is interdependent in the same way as the philosopher's questions about the what and the how of factual knowledge.

Criticisms

Operation. One of the most important concepts of Piagetian theory is the operation. But because operations are a mentalist construct, they tend to be difficult to verify empirically. Tests of the mental operations hypothesized for concrete and formal operational stages have reported that some but not all operators are present in a given situation. Such findings call into question Piaget's contention that cognitive stages are holistic structures whereby the presence of one mental operation implies the empirical presence of many others.

Formal Operations. A minor controversy has arisen around the contention that formal operations is the terminus of cognitive development. As noted earlier, some researchers have reported that a significant portion of adolescent and adult population fails to achieve formal reasoning (Elkind, 1961; Kuhn, Langer, Kohlberg & Haan, 1977; Nadel & Schoeppe, 1973; Schwebel, 1975; Tomlinson-Keasey, 1972). In addition, other researchers have argued that cognitive development continues beyond the formal operational stage (Commons, Richards, & Kuhn, 1982; Riegel, 1973, 1975).

Three kinds of responses have been made to these criticisms. First, Piaget (1972) has acknowledged that some people do not achieve the stage of formal operations, and he contends that adolescent aptitudes and interests sometimes lead to vocational choices where formal reasoning is not developmentally adaptive. He also believes that a number of people may reason formally in their chosen professions but still fail to show formal operations on tests of science and logic. Second, the theory emphasizes the sequence of cognitive-developmental stages rather than their terminus. Studies cited earlier lend strong support to the sequentiality claim of Piaget's stages. Third, Piaget does not discount the possibility of postformal stages of reasoning. In fact, the internal principles of organization and adaptation imply the possibility of increasingly more adequate cognitive structures.

The Concept of Stage. Piaget's concept of a cognitive-developmental stage has been severely criticized because it reflects qualitative rather than quantitative distinctions between cognitive structures. For example, Brainerd (1973, 1977, 1978a, 1978b), a well-known critic of Piaget, contends (1) that developmental changes Piaget attributes to equilibration can be explained by simpler principles of learning; (2) that qualitative transformations can be reduced to quantitative accumulations of learning; and (3) that Piaget's own developmental stages can be explained by an endogenous, maturational account of development. While Piagetian theorists allow that the origin of qualitative changes must ultimately reside in the continuity of development, they also disagree with Brainerd in their belief that cognitive development is best conceptualized in stagelike rather than maturational or learning terms.

EVALUATION OF THE THEORY

Scientific Worthiness

Testability. Because Piaget is a mentalist, his theory is rated only moderate for testability (see Table 9-4). Concepts like equilibration, mental operations, and cognitive structures are not directly observable and therefore cannot easily be tested. Nevertheless, other Piagetian concepts like scheme can be more directly tested, and *inferences* drawn from Piaget's concepts can be assessed by both verbal and behavioral data. On balance, Piaget's theory seems to be more testable than Freud's but less testable than Skinner's.

Table 9-4 Ratings of Piaget's Theory for Scientific Worthiness

CRITERION	HIGH	MODERATE	LOW
Testability		X	
External validity	X		
Predictive validity		X	
Internal consistency		X	
Theoretical economy	X		

External Validity. The theory is rated high for its external validity. What is amazing here is that so many of Piaget's discoveries about child development went undiscovered for so long: object permanence, cognitive egocentrism, conservation, the concept of number, hypothetical reasoning. The evidence supporting Piaget's theory is substantial, and the cross-cultural component of the validation research is impressive. Piaget's most important major contentions—the theory of stages, as well as the cognitive capabilities theorized for each stage—accord fairly well with what is known about infant, child, and adolescent development. In fact, a whole new area of research in children's social cognitive development is expanding cognitive-developmental principles to the analysis of children's social knowledge and relationships. Consequently, a high rating is given for this criterion.

Predictive Validity. The theory's predictive validity reflects a large body of empirical research that has attempted to test theoretically derived predictions, many about specific interrelationships between two or more cognitive functions. For example, Piaget's prediction that intellectual functioning in large part determines linguistic development has received considerable empirical support (e.g., Applebee, 1978; Green, 1979, 1985; Templeton & Spivey, 1980). Although exceptions exist, many other attempts to verify theoretical predictions indicate that its predictive validity is moderately high.

Internal Consistency. On the one hand, Piaget maintains a steadfast constructivist interpretation of development that is unswerving in its anti-endogenous and anti-exogenous orientation. It would be difficult to argue that Piaget at any time poses an inconsistent plot in his message that intellectual development is dynamic, organized, adaptive, and constructivist in nature. There is, on the other hand, a major inconsistency in Piaget's theory. Piaget maintains that a cognitive stage is a holistic structure, a general mode of action or operation. If a cognitive stage fits this conception, then one would expect that when one stage is transformed into the next, the new stage becomes operational in a relatively complete way and should therefore permeate the thought of the child. Yet, considerable evidence indicates that what happens is that the new stage, rather than exhibiting a general mode of operation, only gradually gets applied to the field of experience. To account for this gradual elaboration, Piaget invokes a principle he calls *de calage*, or small differences in development. The concept of de calage seems to be a contradiction to the concept of a holistic, structured stage. The importance of this problem for Piaget's stage concept is sufficient to result in only a moderate rating for internal consistency.

Theoretical Economy. Piaget's theory ranks high on theoretical economy for two reasons. First, his theory makes only two assumptions about the nature of the child at birth, fewer than any other theory in the text. Moreover, he does not make the mistake of assuming qualities of mind when he knows that those qualities are the very elements he must explain. Second, his theory attempts to account for the development of a broad range of cognitive phenomena from birth to adulthood.

Developmental Adequacy

Overall, Piaget's theory is rated very high for its developmental adequacy. Individual ratings are shown in Table 9-5.

Temporality. Since Piaget explains development as a gradual process of organization and adaptation that occurs between birth and maturity, his theory passes this criterion.

Cumulativity. Earlier developmental stages function as cognitive preparation for later stages. Moreover, later stages build upon, expand, and transform cognitive capacities acquired in earlier stages. Consequently, his theory passes this criterion.

Directionality. The inherent directionality of Piaget's theory is best captured by his concept of equilibration, which regulates cognitive development toward increasing logical adequacy. Later stages are logically more adequate than earlier stages because individuals can solve all the problems solved at earlier stages while simultaneously solving new kinds of problems not previously solvable. For example, concrete operational children retain the representational capacities of preoperational children, but they are organized into a cognitive structure of reversible operations capable of classification and relation that cannot be performed at the preoperational stage. Piaget's theory passes this criterion because his theory represents human cognitive development as a gradual evolution toward progressively more adequate structures of knowledge.

New Mode of Organization. Piaget's cognitive-developmental stages are transformations of earlier modes of knowing into new, more adequate structures. In all his work, Piaget's depiction of a cognitive structure is as an organized system of mutually implied cognitive abilities that comprise a structured whole. In this sense, each of Piaget's stages is conceived as a new mode of organization vis-à-vis the previous stage. For this reason, the theory passes this criterion.

Table 9-5 Ratings of Piaget's Theory for Characteristics of Development

CHARACTERISTIC	RATING
Temporality	Pass
Cumulativity	Pass
Directionality	Pass
New mode of organization	Pass
Increased capacity for self-control	Pass

Increased Capacity for Self-Control. In contrast to sensorimotor actions, the beginning of mental representation at the onset of the preoperational stage allows children to cognize symbolic realities without actually having objects physically present. In addition, formal operational thought is able to anticipate *possible circumstances* and thereby adjust itself ahead of time. Such "feedforward" is more than being able to anticipate what in fact will be the result of one's actions; it is the ability to cognize possible results and adjust planned activities to maximize certain potential effects while minimizing other possible effects. These examples indicate how thought first transcends objects and eventually transcends reality and even controls it to some extent. Consequently, Piaget's theory does explain how development reflects an increased self-control, so it passes this criterion.

SUMMARY POINTS

1. Piaget's theory draws extensively from ideas first set forth in Kant's epistemology and Spencer's developmental psychology.
2. Werner's organismic psychology established a zeitgeist that made possible the acceptance of Piaget's theory in this country.
3. Piaget makes two assumptions about the newborn: that it has innate, biological reflexes and that it is inherently proactive.
4. The theoretical problem of cognitive-developmental theory is to explain the origin and genesis of scientific and mathematical knowledge. Applied to individual development, this problem amounts to explaining the development of logico-mathematical thought. Piaget's methods include observations for infants and clinical interviews for children and adolescents.
5. The theory's internal principles are assimilation and accommodation, equilibration, and the functional invariants of organization and adaptation.
6. The theory proposes three bridge principles: schemes, the building blocks of knowledge; cognitive operations, reversible mental actions; and cognitive structures, organized systems of interrelated mental activities and cognitive operations. The cognitive structures are associated with four stages of cognitive development: the sensorimotor stage, the preoperational stage, the concrete operational stage, and the formal operational stage.
7. The four mechanisms of development include the three classical factors—biological maturation, physical experience, and social experience—which are regulated by the most important factor, equilibration.
8. Piaget's most important contributions are: a conception of children as inquiring scientist/philosophers, a conception of psychological stages irreducible to maturational timetables, a methodology that combines cognitive problems with clinical interviews, and the application of psychological data to longstanding philosophical questions. The three most prevalent criticisms of his theory concern his concepts of operation and stage and his description of formal operations as the terminus of cognitive development.
9. Piaget's theory is rated moderately high for its scientific worthiness and high for its developmental adequacy.

PROBLEMS AND EXERCISES

1. Most people cannot remember any specific events from their infancy (before about two years of age). This widely acknowledged phenomena is called infantile amnesia. Freud would explain infantile amnesia as due either to the defense mechanism of repression (memories are retained in the unconscious but are repressed by the ego) or to the onset of secondary process thought. Skinner would explain the same phenomena as the result of extinction; infantile behaviors do not continue to be reinforced once we reach childhood, so they are extinguished. How would Piaget explain infantile amnesia?

2. Piaget (1962, p. 63) describes the following observation. One afternoon his daughter (16 months old) observed another youngster throw a temper tantrum. The daughter had never before seen a temper tantrum. The following afternoon she proceeded to scream and stamp her feet several times in succession while in her playpen. The problem here is to explain how Piaget's daughter could have performed such a "deferred imitation." It is important to follow Piaget's lead here. He cannot attribute his daughter's actions to memory, since no mind exists to remember. Another explanation must be sought. Compare your answer with the explanation Piaget gives in *Play, Dreams and Imitation in Childhood* (1962, pp. 67–86).

3. Administer the cognitive task on liquid conservation described in this chapter to three children, each between six and seven years of age. Be sure to ask the children to justify their responses with reasons. Are all three children in the same cognitive stage? Why or why not? How can you tell?

4. Most normal children reach concrete operations between five and eight years of age. Congenitally deaf children who have never heard nor spoken language also reach this stage as do congenitally blind children who have never been able to inspect their environment visually. Both language and perception can be ruled out as sources of knowledge because deaf and blind children become concrete operational without these sensory modalities. Similarly, but for other reasons, maturation can be ruled out as an explanation. Given this situation, provide a Piagetian explanation for the acquisition of concrete operational thinking.

SUGGESTED READINGS

More about the Theory

Duckworth, E. (1972). The having of wonderful ideas. *Harvard Educational Review, 42,* 217–231.

Gallagher, J. M., & Reid, D. K. (1981). *The learning theory of Piaget and Inhelder.* Monterey, CA: Brooks/Cole.

Piaget, J. (1960). *The child's conception of the world.* Totowa, NJ: Littlefield, Adams.

Piaget, J., & Inhelder, B. (1969). *The psychology of the child.* New York: Basic Books.

Reviews of Research

Ashton, P. T. (1975). Cross-cultural Piagetian research: An experimental perspective. *Harvard Educational Review, 45,* 475–506.

Dasen, P. R. (1972). Cross-cultural Piagetian research: A summary. *Journal of Cross-Cultural Psychology, 3*, 23–29.

Gratch, G. (1977). Review of Piagetian infancy research: Object concept development. In W. F. Overton & J. M. Gallagher (Eds.), *Knowledge and development*. New York: Plenum Press.

Mogdil, S., & Mogdil, C. (1976). *Piagetian research: Compilation and commentary.* (Vol. 7). Rochester, UK: NFER Publishing Co.

Critical Reviews

Brainerd, C. J. (1978). The stage question in cognitive-developmental theory. *The Behavioral and Brain Sciences, 1*, 173–213.

Brown, G., & Desforges, C. (1979). *Piaget's theory: A psychological critique.* London: Routledge & Kegan Paul.

Mogdil, S., Mogdil, C., & Brown, G. (Eds.) (1983). *Jean Piaget: An interdisciplinary critique.* London: Routledge & Kegan Paul.

Sigel, L., Brodzinsky, D. M., & Golinkoff, R. M. (Eds.). (1981). *New directions in Piagetian theory and practice.* Hillsdale, NJ: Lawrence Erlbaum.

Vuyk, R. (1981). *Overview and critique of Piaget's genetic epistemology: 1965–1980.* (Vol. 1). London: Academic Press.

Chapter 10

Kohlberg's Theory of Moral Development

Preview Questions

What are the general similarities and differences between Piaget's theory and Kohlberg's theory of moral development?

What problem does Kohlberg address and what methods are used to collect data?

What are Kohlberg's internal and bridge principles? How do these compare with Piaget's?

What change mechanism is proposed by Kohlberg?

What contributions and criticisms are associated with the theory?

How does Kohlberg's theory rate for its scientific worthiness and developmental adequacy?

HISTORICAL SKETCH

Lawrence Kohlberg's affinity for Piaget's genetic epistemology is evident in his philosophically grounded theory of moral development. In fact, in describing children as natural moral philosophers, Kohlberg (Kohlberg & Gilligan, 1971) parallels Piaget's contention that children are natural scientists. In addition, he relies extensively on cognitive-developmental theory to account for moral ontogenesis.

Lawrence Kohlberg, born in 1927, grew up in a suburb of New York City and later attended an elite prep school, Andover Academy. Before going to college, however, he aided the Israeli cause by working on a freighter that ran the British blockade in transporting Jewish refugees from war-torn Europe to Israel. In 1948 he enrolled at the University of Chicago, where his scores on admission tests were so high that a number of courses were waived, allowing him to complete his undergraduate degree in one year. He continued his graduate work there and focused on moral thinking in adolescent males. He had the good fortune to be trained by outstanding academicians—Charles Morris in philosophy, Bruno Bettleheim and Carl Rogers in clinical psychology, and Bernice Neugarten and Robert Havighurst in developmental psychology (Kohlberg, 1984, p. vii).

Following the completion of his dissertation, Kohlberg continued a longitudinal study of the moral development of his dissertation subjects as they grew into adulthood and middle age. In 1968 he moved to Harvard University as a professor of education and social psychology. At Harvard he founded the Center for Moral Education. Together with a number of colleagues, he began to investigate the universality of moral development in different cultures. It was on one of these excursions that Kohlberg contracted an illness that led to a gradual deterioration of his health. During the 1970s, he worked with a group of Cambridge teachers to found the Cluster School, an alternative school based on his philosophy of the "just community." Cluster students were challenged to participate with their teachers in defining their own educational goals. In recent years, Kohlberg refined his theory, working on practical applications for education and penal reform, and taught classes on moral development. He died in 1987.

From Piagetian Roots

Early in his career, Kohlberg developed the conviction that Piaget's account of cognitive development was basically sound, but his own analysis of moral development did not square with Piaget's. To understand Kohlberg's theory, it is important to recognize the limitations he found in Piaget's account of moral development.

First, Piaget (1965b) defines morality as a system of rules and locates the origin of morality in children's respect for rules. But such a definition is non-Piagetian because it is nonconstructivist. That is, rules are socially determined and reflect specific cultural values rather than reflecting universal qualities (like Piaget's cognitive stages). It is ironic that Piaget should propose universal stages of cognitive development but culturally specific learning of moral rules. In short, Kohlberg recognized that Piaget had set forth a learning (exogenous) account rather than a constructivist account of moral development.

Second, Piaget contends that motives underlying moral behavior are derived from respect and other moral feelings. Kohlberg's (1969, 1974) analysis of moral development, however, indicates that moral feelings do not reflect age-related developmental trends. It is again ironic that Piaget accounted for moral development in terms of figurative knowledge (moral feelings, elements of respect, and specific rule learning) when his account of cognitive development concentrates so heavily on rational constructions and reorganizations of operative knowledge.

Beginning with his dissertation three decades ago, Kohlberg (1958) has consistently espoused a formula for moral development that addresses the problems with Piaget's analysis. For example, Kohlberg developed a methodology, the moral dilemma, derived from Piaget's clinical interview technique and focused not on consequences or rules but on reasoning and judgment. Moreover, by rooting his conception of morality in philosophical conceptions of justice and fairness (see Rawls, 1971), he avoided reducing moral thinking to the amount of respect one holds for people and rules. In the end, Kohlberg's theory of moral development is structurally quite similar to Piaget's theory of cognitive development.

As noted in the previous chapter, simply positing a sequence of developmental stages does not in itself classify a theory as constructivist in nature. Stage theories may, after all, embody markedly different notions of what constitutes a "stage" (compare Piaget with Freud, for example). Kohlberg's theory is classified here as constructivist because he contends that moral development stages are characterized by constructive reorganizations of earlier stages, and he believes that moral reasoning derives from resolutions of interpersonal conflicts. Some of his important theoretical statements can be found in *Stage and Sequence* (1969), *From Is to Ought* (1971), *The Philosophy of Moral Development* (1981), and the *Psychology of Moral Development* (1984).

STRUCTURAL COMPONENTS

Assumptions

Psychologists who attempt to explain the ontogeny of personality, behavior, and cognition typically anchor their work in infancy to show how later psychological states include but transcend early states. Kohlberg is decidedly different in this respect, and this difference should not be overlooked by the conscientious reader. Kohlberg makes no attempt to root his theory in the early years of infant development. Instead, he assumes that a certain amount of cognitive development has already occurred, and from that foundation then offers an explanation of the development of moral judgment.

First, Kohlberg takes cognitive development in infancy and early childhood for granted. For example, he assumes that children cognitively differentiate between social and physical objects and that they understand that social objects (people) are energetic and proactive, as opposed to the purely passive responses of physical objects. More specifically, people engage one another in social interactions, and through their interpersonal commerce, they construct patterns of expectations that proscribe and regulate social behavior. Social interactions, rather than learning of social norms and values, are thus viewed as the basis of moral development.

Second, Kohlberg defines morality as *justice* and *fairness*, and he believes that an individual's moral judgments reflect cognitive rather than emotional processes. In this sense, moral development is viewed as the *rational, cognitive construction* of ethical premises, rules, and conclusions that motivate moral judgments. The importance of this assumption is that it leads Kohlberg to seek the roots of moral reasoning in the intellectual constructions of youth rather than in such other processes as reinforcement, modeling, and identification (Kohlberg, 1971, p. 155). His theory provides a framework for understanding how moral reasoning develops from stages of less adequate conceptions of justice toward stages of more adequate conceptions of justice (Levine, Kohlberg, & Hewer, 1985, p. 95). His primary concern is with moral thought, as opposed to moral behavior. Similar to the manner in which Piaget differentiates between figurative and operative knowledge, Kohlberg differentiates between content and structure in moral reasoning. In this way Kohlberg attempts to identify in subjects' reasoning their use of operations of justice involving equality, reciprocity, and equity.

Third, Kohlberg assumes that individuals differentiate between (1) manifest behaviors, (2) the underlying intentions that motivate behavior, and (3) the overt consequences of individuals' actions. This assumption is reflected in his methodology where he elicits from subjects their reasoning about how these three factors interrelate and influence moral judgments.

Problems for Study

Phenomena to Be Explained

Kohlberg attempts to study and explain the cognitive ontogeny of moral reasoning. His theoretical problem is far more limited in scope than that of any other theorist covered in this text. In fact, Kohlberg declines any attempt to explain the entirety of morality, preferring instead to concentrate on the rational foundations of moral judgments. He does not, for example, attempt to explain immorality (sadism, cheating, torture), forms of jurisprudence (court martial, trial by jury), or types of litigation (criminal, civil), nor does he attempt to account for superficial forms of social conformity—obedience, honesty, friendliness, or other social virtues.

Methods of Study

Kohlberg has developed a series of moral dilemmas that place into conflict competing moral claims and personal rights of hypothetical individuals. The subject's task is to resolve the dilemmas and provide an appropriate moral justification. Each subject is told a dilemma, followed by an extensive open-ended interview that probes the subject's resolution and rationalizations. A typical moral dilemma is the following story of Heinz.

> A woman was dying from a rare form of cancer. A local druggist had concocted a cure, but it was very expensive to make. The woman's husband went to the druggist to buy the cure, but the druggist wanted too much money for it. The druggist declined to negotiate a loan or to sell it for a lower price. The husband was desperate, so he decided to steal the drug. (adapted from Kohlberg, 1971, p. 156)

Alternatively, more direct methods have been developed for measuring moral development, the most noteworthy being the Defining Issues Test, a short paper and pencil test developed by James Rest. This test has been shown to have high validity and reliability in terms of yielding results similar to those obtained by Kohlberg (see Rest, 1979).

Internal Principles

Cognitive Conflict and Equilibration

Cognitive conflict is Kohlberg's term for Piaget's concept of equilibration. Cognitive conflict occurs when an individual has two beliefs that may be contradictory (e.g., never lie—don't get in trouble) or when a belief conflicts with external information (e.g., liars are punished—my friends lie and don't get caught). Cognitive conflict leads to the invention of moral principles and beliefs that reflect resolutions of intrapersonal and interpersonal conflicts. The equilibration of cognitive conflict produces increasing differentiation and hierarchic integration of moral concepts. This process occurs in the course of interaction with the social environment (Kohlberg, 1971, p. 183) and leads to increasingly adequate reasoning about justice and fairness. In this vein, later stages of moral reasoning are capable of resolving more moral conflicts and more interpersonal points of view in a more self-consistent way than earlier moral stages. Cognitive conflict is constructive in the sense that individuals invent moral rationalizations to make sense out of and to solve moral problems. These rationalizations, in turn, become increasingly organized and adaptive as more complex moral problems are recognized and solved. The relationship between this and the other two internal principles is shown in Figure 10-1.

Cognitive Development

One of the internal principles of Kohlberg's moral development theory is Piaget's cognitive-developmental stages. This state of affairs is explicitly recognized by Kohlberg (1971, pp. 185–188), who argues that Piaget's cognitive-developmental stages provide the psychological apparatus required for increasingly complex social-moral judgments. In this way moral judgments are believed to be extrapolations of underlying cognitive operations; cognitive stages provide necessary but not sufficient criteria for moral reasoning (Kuhn, Langer, Kohlberg, & Haan, 1977).

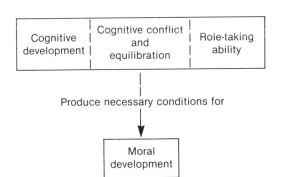

Figure 10-1 Schematic of the relationship between Kohlberg's three internal principles.

Kohlberg contends that moral reasoning is constrained but not solely determined by one's level of cognitive development. This cognitive-moral relationship is described more completely in the section on research findings.

Role-Taking Ability

Being specialized cognitive functions that are adapted to and regulate interpersonal activities, moral judgments require the capacity to assess multiple points of view. Since interpersonal conflicts are comprised of clashes between different points of view and different interests, one's adaptation to these clashes must to some extent rely on role-taking ability. Role taking in Kohlberg's sense represents the ability to take the point of view of another person, to see things from others' points of view, and to understand the values others bring to a particular situation. Opportunities for role taking, for looking at situations from multiple points of view, and for examining the consequences of each viewpoint are prerequisite social experiences for the development of moral reasoning. Individuals capable of role taking and understanding competing points of view have a higher potential for moral development than those whose role-taking abilities are more limited.

Bridge Principles

Kohlberg's stages comprise the most important bridge principle in his theory. These stages reflect the same kinds of qualities as Piaget's cognitive-developmental stages. In fact, Kohlberg's affinity for Piaget's constructivism can be found in his explicit recognition of the following qualities that Piaget only implies.

1. Stages occur in an invariant sequence in spite of varying environmental conditions.
2. Developmental stages are "structured wholes" consisting of psychological organizations that unify superficially different behaviors.
3. Developmental stages reflect qualitative differences in the general mode of reasoning rather than quantitative differences in how much information one knows.
4. Developmental stages represent hierarchical integrations and reconstructions of lower stages.

These qualities are general properties of the specific sequence of moral development stages proposed by Kohlberg.

Moral Stages

Kohlberg's stages of moral development are grouped within three major levels. The *preconventional* level, stages 1 and 2, consists of moral reasoning that is personal and interpersonal but that predates genuinely social considerations. The *conventional* level consists of stages 3 and 4, each of which reflects different conceptions of moral imperatives deriving from social origins. The *postconventional* level, stages 5 and 6, transcends societal interests and turns moral decision making toward universal principles of individual conscience. In short, different moral development stages reflect different organizations and underlying structures of moral reasoning. Behaviors are not necessarily indicative of one's moral stage. In fact, the same behavior can occur at different stages because it is the individual's reasoning that indicates moral stage, not the behavior itself. The description of moral development stages that follows has been adapted from Kohlberg (1984, pp. 174–176).

Level I—Preconventional Morality. At Level I, moral judgments are subordinated to personal interests in terms of what is good for the individual.

STAGE 1: HETERONOMOUS MORALITY—PUNISHMENT AND OBEDIENCE ORIEN-TATION. Regarding something as good or bad depends on whether the act is rewarded or punished. Punished acts are bad, and rewarded acts are good, both regardless of an individual's intentions. The power of authority determines right and wrong. Moral right means not breaking rules to avoid punishment, obeying authorities because of their superior power, and avoiding physical damage to persons and property. This stage is presocial and egocentric because others' points of view are not differentiated from the self's.

STAGE 2: INDIVIDUALISTIC MORALITY—INSTRUMENTAL PURPOSE AND EX-CHANGE. Moral actions and decisions are cast in terms of self's wants and needs, which to be met may also satisfy the needs of others. Justice is not dictated by arrangement or power, because people follow the cosmic law of mutual backscratch: "You help me, and I'll help you." Thus, moral right means acting in ways that meet one's own needs and letting others do the same; right includes living up to interpersonal agreements. The social perspective is concrete and individualistic. Each person has his own perspective and interests. These may sometimes come into conflict, thus making morality relative to the individual.

Level II—Conventional Morality. Justice is determined by society's rules, as cast in the expectations and laws of cultural groups like families, peer groups, churches, clubs, states, and nations.

STAGE 3: MORALITY OF INTERPERSONAL EXPECTATIONS, RELATIONS, AND IN-TERPERSONAL CONFORMITY—GOOD-BOY, GOOD-GIRL INTUITIONS. Justice is determined by one's peer and social group's expectations as well as one's desire to please the important others. One attempts to be helpful in terms of peer group and social group needs. Intentionality becomes more important than the consequences of a well-intended action. Being good is important because it affirms stereotypical virtues (e.g., trust, loyalty, respect, empathy, gratitude). Socially, this perspective involves an understanding of the individual in relation to others, including an awareness of shared feelings, agreements, and expectations that take precedence over personal interests.

STAGE 4: MORALITY OF SOCIAL SYSTEMS AND CONSCIENCE—LAW-AND-ORDER ORIENTATION. Justice is defined as fulfilling one's contractual obligations. Laws are to be upheld because they keep the social system orderly. Moral right means contributing to society and following one's conscience in living up to defined obligations. Doing what is moral means doing one's duty, respecting social authorities, and acting to maintain the established social order simply for the greater benefit of society vis-à-vis the individual, since individuals also benefit from society's order. The social perspective of this stage differentiates society's point of view from the perspective of interpersonal agreements and motives.

Level III—Postconventional Morality.   This level consists of reasoning in terms of principles of justice that are independent of personal authority, social status, or society's rules. Justice is independent of an individual's association with any particular authority, social group, or cultural expectation, which is not to say that morality is egocentric.

STAGE 5: MORALITY OF SOCIAL-CONTRACT, UTILITY, AND INDIVIDUAL RIGHTS. Society's values, rules, and expectations should generally be followed because they comprise an implicit social contract. Some nonrelative values and rights, like *life* and *liberty*, however, must be upheld in any society regardless of majority opinion. One is obliged to obey society's rules to provide the greatest good for the most people. Thus, laws are made for public welfare and to protect all people's rights. The social perspective is defined as *prior-to-society*, which means that concerns for values, rights, and due process underlie the making of social rules. Morality may occasionally conflict with legality.

STAGE 6: MORALITY OF UNIVERSAL ETHICAL PRINCIPLES.   Justice is based on self-chosen but not egocentric ethical principles. Society's laws are to be followed because they usually rest on such principles. When laws violate these principles, one acts in accordance with the moral principle. Moral reasoning appeals to comprehensiveness, reciprocity, universality, and consistency, which are abstractions (like the Golden Rule) rather than concrete moral rules like the Ten Commandments. Such moral concepts consist of principles that all humanity should follow to protect the rights of individuals. Moral right involves the rational validity of moral principles and a sense of personal commitment to them. The social perspective of this stage views the moral point of view as the presumptive foundation from which social arrangements derive.

In recent years Kohlberg has backed off about his conception of stage 6, largely because it is used by virtually no one. In his early work, Kohlberg classified some of his subjects at this stage, but as the theory has been fine-tuned, it appears that there is little empirical evidence for the existence of this stage. Still, Kohlberg may be ahead of Piaget on this point. Where Piaget posits formal operations as the terminus of cognitive development because that is the highest stage empirically demonstrated by his subjects, Kohlberg hypothesizes a stage above that demonstrated by his subjects. If the constructivist thesis is true, then it should be possible to derive a hierarchical organization of moral principles greater than that actually demonstrated by individuals, a criticism of Piagetian theory Kohlberg may have anticipated. In this sense, stage 6 may represent an idealization of moral judgment, a transcendent stage that, like some criticisms of Piaget's theory, may anticipate a level of development toward which development evolves.

The differences between Kohlberg's stages can be seen in Table 10-1, which contains examples of possible reasons both for and against Heinz stealing the drug for his wife. Note that the examples are categorized by the underlying reasoning and not whether they are in favor of or against the husband stealing the drug.

Moral Thought and Moral Action

In recent years, Kohlberg (1984, pp. 252–257) has added to his theory a distinction between *A* and *B* substages. Individuals whose moral reasoning is type *A* tend

Table 10-1 Examples of Moral Reasoning

Stage 1	If you let your wife die, you will get in trouble. You'll be blamed for not spending the money to save her and there will be an investigation of you and the druggist for your wife's death.
	You shouldn't steal the drug so you won't go to jail.
Stage 2	Heinz may not get much of a jail term if he steals the drug, but he'll still have his wife when he gets out.
	If Heinz does not steal the drug, his wife will die, but it isn't his fault his wife has cancer.
Stage 3	No one will think you are bad if you steal the drug, but your wife's relatives will hate you if you don't. If she dies, you'll never be able to face them again.
	Not only the druggist, but also everyone else will think you're a criminal too. You'll bring dishonor on yourself and your family.
Stage 4	If you have any sense of honor, you won't let your wife die just because you're afraid to do the only thing that will save her. You'll always feel guilty that you caused her death if you don't do your duty to her.
	If you steal the drug, you'll have to go to jail. You'll always feel bad that you broke the law, even though you're desperate.
Stage 5	You would lose other people's respect, not gain it, if you don't steal. If you let your wife die, it would be out of fear, not out of reasoning it out. People wouldn't trust you anymore.
	Heinz shouldn't steal the drug, even though his wife will die. She'll understand that you can't just go around stealing, because it would mean people could steal from her too, and she wouldn't want that.
Stage 6	If you don't steal the drug and let your wife die, you'd always condemn yourself afterward. You wouldn't be blamed because you'd have lived up to the law.
	If you do steal the drug, the jury would understand but wonder what to do with everyone else who thought they had a good reason for stealing. They'd put themselves in your place and think that maybe they'd do the same thing, or maybe they wouldn't.

Source: Adapted from Kohlberg, L. Stage and sequence: The cognitive-developmental approach to socialization. In D. A. Goslin (Ed.), *Handbook of socialization theory and research.* Chicago: Rand McNally & Company, 1969, pp. 381–383 (by permission).

toward a moral orientation involving rules and authority. *B*-type individuals orient toward moral concepts of fairness, equality, and reciprocity. Kohlberg argues that this distinction has important implications for understanding the relationship between moral judgment and moral action, a problem that has long perplexed those interested in figuring out why some individuals act on their moral principles and others don't. In his view, individuals at the same stage of moral development use similar moral principles to justify their responses to moral dilemmas. However, *B*-type individuals are far more likely to engage in moral actions than are *A*-type individuals. Moreover, when moral development occurs, movement from type *A* to type *B* is more likely than from *B* to *A*. However, there is also a tendency for *A*-type individuals and for *B*-type individuals to remain the same type within their progression through the moral development stages.

Change Mechanism

Kohlberg believes that moral development is the product of cognitive conflict in the same sense that Piaget's process of equilibration is used to account for cognitive development. Cognitive conflict naturally occurs when individuals interact from different points of view (e.g., I want something; you want something else). Role taking, through opportunities to take the viewpoint of another, provides experiential discrepancies between one's own point of view and that of another person. For example, through role taking one may discover a conflict between one's own wishes and the wishes of others, as occurs when one one group believes in busing to achieve school integration while another group believes in neighborhood schools to achieve educational choice. Role-taking ability applies to moral judgment when one's own reasoning takes into account and adapts to the reasoning of others.

   Cognitive conflict is the "motor" that drives moral development. More specifically, Kohlberg believes that an *optimum mismatch* between the conceptual or moral systems of two individuals who differ by only one stage can produce an ideal level of cognitive conflict for the lower staged individual. Through cognitive conflict, individuals synthesize competing claims, expectations, and principles to construct a principle that resolves or at least minimizes the conflict. Turiel (1966), one of Kohlberg's colleagues, has attempted to apply the concept of cognitive conflict and optimal mismatch to determine if it is effective in promoting moral development. This, as well as Kohlberg's own attempts to induce moral development, is described in the following section.

EXPLAINING HUMAN DEVELOPMENT: THE RESEARCH

A number of Kohlberg's claims about moral development have been tested empirically. Several of the most important claims are examined in this section: universality of the stage sequence, cognitive and role-taking prerequisites for moral development, and attempts to promote development of moral reasoning.

Stage Sequence

Kohlberg claims that his stages are rational constructions of moral principles and not culturally specific learning of social norms and rules. Thus, the development of moral reasoning should follow a universal sequence that is independent of varying cultural experiences.

In the most comprehensive review to date, Snarey (1985, 1987) examined 45 cross-cultural studies that tested Kohlberg's claim for universality. These studies included both cross-aged and twenty-year longitudinal studies ranging from India to Israel and from New Guinea to Taiwan. Some researchers used standard Kohlberg dilemmas; others created completely new dilemmas. In spite of the variety of cultures studied and the differences in methodology used by various researchers, Snarey concluded that the available evidence provides strong support for the universal sequence and presence of Kohlberg's first four stages. At the same time Snarey found little evidence in those studies to support Kohlberg's postconventional stages among non-Western cultures.

The failure of many researchers to find evidence of postconventional moral reasoning has recently been examined by Vasudev and Hummel (1987), who cite Snarey (1985) in arguing that the absence of principled moral reasoning in non-Western cultures may be more attributable to degree of urbanization than to culture per se. Specifically, cross-cultural studies of Kohlberg's theory have tended to use subjects from small tribes and villages. Such subjects typically have not experienced the kinds of complex interpersonal relationships and conceptual issues that are associated with higher education and urban societies. As a test of their reasoning, Vasudev and Hummel (1987) sampled 112 middle- and upper-class residents in an urbanized region of India and reported finding that 11 percent of the adults used principled moral judgments to solve moral dilemmas.

A second line of evidence that bears more directly on the issue of stage sequentiality derives from Kohlberg's own longitudinal study of moral development. This work is based on a sample of 50 males, half middle-class and half working-class, studied every three years for over a decade. Kramer's (1968) analysis of this longitudinal data generally corresponds to Kohlberg's claim for stage ordering, with the exception of six lower-class delinquents who appeared to "regress" in their moral development.

Two other studies bear on the invariant sequence issue. In a ten-year longitudinal study, Snarey, Reimer, and Kohlberg (1985) examined Israeli children and adolescents (both males and females). The results showed that subjects who developed through the first five stages did so in the invariant sequence proposed by Kohlberg. Moreover, no sex differences in moral maturity were reported. In a similar study, Nisan and Kohlberg (1982) conducted a ten-year longitudinal study of moral development in Turkish city and village males. Their results indicated an invariant sequence through stage 4 and the presence of some stage 5 reasoning among city but not village males.

While these findings do not prove Kohlberg's theory, they are consistent with his claim of a universal sequence of stages. The importance of this empirical support should not be overlooked because it is difficult to imagine how other theoretical perspectives might account for the cross-cultural data. For example, endogenous theories that posit age-specific development have difficulty accounting for the age variation associated with each moral stage and the fact that some individuals fail to achieve higher moral stages. At the same time, exogenous theories do not explain how learning of culture-specific norms and rules could result in a universal sequence of stages.

Cognitive and Role-Taking Development

Kohlberg claims that the development of moral reasoning at a particular stage is predicated on the presence of (1) specific underlying cognitive operations and (2) related role-taking abilities. Evidence bearing on each of these claims is examined here.

The most extensive study of the relationship between cognition and moral reasoning was conducted by Kuhn, Langer, Kohlberg, and Haan (1977), who tested 265 individuals from two generations—130 parents averaging about 50 years of age and 135 of their children between the ages of 10 and 30 years. Subjects were individually administered two Piagetian tasks to determine their stage of cognitive development and four of Kohlberg's moral dilemmas to assess their stage of moral reasoning. The results of the study revealed several noteworthy patterns of development. First, regardless of age, 94 subjects who showed no evidence of formal operational reasoning also showed no principled (stages 5 or 6) moral reasoning, whereas 96 percent of those who showed stage 5 or stage 6 moral reasoning also showed evidence of formal operational thinking. Second, 76 percent of subjects who showed formal operational thought were scored at the conventional (stages 3 or 4) level of moral development. Third, the higher a subject's cognitive performance the more likely that subject was to use principled moral reasoning in the Kohlberg dilemmas. In a similar study, Smith (1979) reported that in a sample of 100 children aged 8 to 14 years, concrete operational thinking and the transition to formal operational thought were associated with stages 2 and 3 of moral development, respectively. Such data provide modest correlational support for Kohlberg's claim that specific levels of cognitive development may be necessary but are not themselves sufficient prerequisites to achieving particular moral development stages.

Several studies have examined the claim that role-taking ability underlies the ability to reason at particular moral stages. For example, Selman (1971) found that cognitive perspective taking was significantly correlated with stage of moral reasoning in a sample of 60 children from 8 to 10 years old. In a one-year follow-up of 10 children who had been previously categorized as preconventional moralizers lacking role-taking ability, Selman found that none had achieved conventional morality unless they also displayed role-taking ability. Similarly, Kuhn (1972) examined this relationship in 68 kindergarten through sixth-grade children. She found that her subjects achieved stage 2 of moral reasoning only if they demonstrated the role-taking ability to attribute intention to another person. Finally, Smith (1979) concluded from her study of moral reasoning and role taking in 100 youngsters from 8 to 14 years old that the level of complexity in role-taking ability precedes corresponding levels of moral reasoning.

Although the evidence suggests support for Kohlberg's claims of cognitive and role-taking prerequisites to moral development, it is still not conclusive because most studies have used cross-sectional (different subjects tested at the same time) rather than longitudinal (same subjects tested at different times) research designs. These correlations between cognition, role-taking, and morality are important, but they do not directly test the developmental priority for each person (in what order do the three domains develop?), which can only be addressed with careful longitudinal studies (Kurdek, 1978).

Promoting the Development of Moral Reasoning

Kohlberg believed that moral development can be promoted through opportunities for role taking that induce cognitive conflict. Cognitive conflict occurs when individuals recognize (1) that their moral values provide inadequate solutions to a moral problem or (2) that the moral reasoning of others provides better solutions to moral problems than their own. Cognitive conflict is theoretically important because it is the psychological mechanism that promotes moral development.

Most attempts to induce moral development derive from Turiel's (1966) study that tested the hypothesis that exposure to higher levels of moral reasoning would produce greater stage change than exposure to any other stage of moral reasoning. Turiel reasoned theoretically that if a stage of moral reasoning consists of increasingly complex, hierarchic reorganizations of earlier reasonings, then individuals should prefer moral reasoning one stage higher than their own (moderately more complex organization). To test his hypothesis, Turiel exposed a sample of twelve- to thirteen-year-old boys to one of four conditions: reasoning at one stage above their predominant moral stage (+1), reasoning two stages above their own (+2), and reasoning one stage below their own (−1). A fourth group provided a control sample. A Kohlberg moral dilemma was administered to determine pre- to post-test gains. Turiel found that his subjects virtually always understood levels of moral reasoning lower than their own, almost never understood reasoning at +2 stages above their own, and sometimes understood reasoning at +1 stage above their own. Moreover, only the +1 stage reasoning condition produced significant progress in subjects' moral reasoning. The −1 group regressed slightly, but the regression was much less than the progress of the +1 group. Turiel argues that these results cannot be accounted for by supposing that subjects had simply memorized the moral reasoning presented to them. Alternatively, he concludes that the progress of the +1 group is attributable to *cognitive conflict* brought about by an optimum mismatch between subjects' own level of moral reasoning and the organizational adequacy of the next higher stage.

In a more naturalistic vein, Turiel (1974, 1977) interviewed college students to determine both their moral judgment stage and their reasoning strategies for novel moral problems. Following the same subjects over several years, he found that these adolescents exhibited both the logical contradictions and cognitive confusion during transition from one moral stage to the next that would have been predicted if these subjects were experiencing cognitive disequilibrium.

To assess direct interventions, Blatt and Kohlberg (1975) instituted a program of moral education using ten- and eleven- as well as sixteen-year-olds' school classrooms. They found that class discussions of moral conflicts and moral problems resulted in a significant improvement in moral reasoning. In a replication of the Blatt and Kohlberg study, Hayden and Pickar (1981) engaged seventh-grade girls in ten weeks (covering six and one-half hours) of discussions about moral dilemmas. The program produced an average 10 percent gain in students' moral maturity.

Other studies using Rest's (1975) Defining Issues Test (DIT) as a measure of moral development have sought to induce moral development through various kinds of intervention strategies. Few of these studies have reported significant pre- to post-test gains in moral maturity (see Coder, 1975; Panowitsch, 1975). In a recent review of 55 intervention studies using Rest's DIT, Schaefli, Rest, and Thoma (1985) reported that 45 percent reported significant progress in moral judgment. Interested readers might wish to examine the Schlaefli, Rest, and Thoma study because it reports a number of difficulties reviewers have in piecing together many studies that sample different age groups, use different methods and intervention strategies, and end up with different results. For our understanding of how Kohlberg's theory can be used to promote moral development, the picture seems to suggest that studies that use his moral dilemma interviews, that attempt to promote cognitive conflict, and that use long-term interventions tend to report more favorable results than those that do not.

CONTRIBUTIONS AND CRITICISMS OF THE THEORY

Contributions

Individuals as Moral Philosophers. Analogous to Piaget's model of children as natural scientists, Kohlberg believes that individuals are moral philosophers (Kohlberg, 1968a; Kohlberg & Gilligan, 1971). Kohlberg's claim about people being moral philosophers is interesting because it implies that individuals ask philosophical questions about the nature of morality (e.g., "What does moral mean?" "What is it to be moral?" and "What is the moral thing to do in this situation?") and that they consider relevant evidence and reasons in arriving at answers to these questions. The point Kohlberg wishes to make is that children, adolescents, and adults quite naturally and without benefit of formal philosophical training attempt to solve moral problems by thinking about them.

Morality as Rational Intelligence. One of the most important points Kohlberg makes is that morality is more a matter of intellect than of emotion. This view is considered an important contribution because it is strikingly different from and challenges common-sense notions of moral reasoning. Many people intuitively believe that morality is a matter of one's emotional state. Such concepts of morality have been soundly rocked by Kohlberg's analysis of moral development.

The argument against emotionality and specific instruction has been most succinctly conceptualized by Bailey (1980, p. 120), who notes that morality must invoke a system of rational principles or else there can be no morality at all. The reason is that all appeals to nonrational processes such as one's feelings or emotions lead to indefensible solutions to moral problems. For example, consider the case for morality by *feelings* and morality by *sympathy*. One might argue that we do moral deeds out of feeling because they feel right. In other words, to relate one's feelings to an "appropriate" moral action requires a rational judgment, otherwise the perception of a feeling and its associated need to act would remain unconnected with each other.

In arguing for the priority of rationality over emotion, Kohlberg does not mean to convey the impression that personal feelings are irrelevant to moral problems. Hoffman (1975, 1976, 1977, 1983), for example, has shown that empathy plays a powerful role in the internalization of moral conduct and that empathy is an important influence on altruistic motives. Kohlberg does not dispute Hoffman's claims. Instead, he contends that emotions, like empathy, are in themselves insufficient grounds for making moral judgments. In support of Kohlberg's position on this issue, Bailey (1980) contends that acting out of sympathy for another is simply inadequate to sustain a claim that an act is "moral." That is, one cannot claim to be acting morally when one acts out of sympathy; the real test of morality is determined by how one acts toward those for whom indifferent or hostile feelings are held. In fact, we often judge ourselves high on the moral scale (because there is no other justification for our deeds) precisely when we do act to assist those for whom we have no sympathy at all.

Kohlberg has significantly advanced the psychological understanding of morality by demonstrating its connections to rational reflection. In this way, his theory contributes an explanation of moral development that is not susceptible to the same theoretical and empirical problems as explanations that posit morality as a quality of feeling states.

Cultural Universals. Kohlberg's theory suggests that there is something about social interaction between individuals that produces increasingly adequate thinking about ethical issues, and this in spite of diverse cultural traditions, customs, and values. Up until the 1970s, when Kohlberg's theory began receiving widespread attention among developmental psychologists, it was widely believed that morality was a matter of learning norms and values promulgated by society. By concentrating his analyses on the structures of moral reasoning rather than its content, Kohlberg has argued that individuals in very different cultures develop through the same sequence of moral stages. This universal sequence has focused attention on the similarities of individual and cultural contexts rather than on their differences.

Education for Moral Development. The Center for Moral Education at Harvard has for nearly two decades attempted to devise strategies for using Kohlberg's theory to promote moral development. Unlike Piaget, Kohlberg has actively promoted techniques and ideas directed at improving education. Some of his early publications are related to enhancing cognitive development in general (Kohlberg, 1966, 1968b; Kohlberg & Mayer, 1972), but many of his later publications report educational strategies designed to improve moral reasoning (Kohlberg 1972, 1973, 1974, 1975a, 1975b, 1977, 1980; Kohlberg & Colby, 1975). For Kohlberg, moral education is designed for the purpose of improving students' moral reasoning and thus does not constitute indoctrination or learning socially sanctioned virtues and conventions. What makes this work so important is its radically different, constructivist approach to moral development without invoking more traditional strategies like imitation and factual learning.

Criticisms

Reliability and Validity. Kohlberg's theory has been challenged on a number of grounds for its purported lack of reliability and validity. One problem with empirical validity is Kohlberg's claim that stage 6 completes the hierarchy of moral development stages. The evidence to support that claim is scanty at best. Other than some literary references about the moral reasoning of Socrates, Jesus, and Martin Luther King, there is little evidence that real people actually reach stage 6 (Locke, 1979, 1980).

A second criticism is that because the theory derived from interviews with males, it inherently misrepresents women's moral development. This problem has been noted most eloquently by Gilligan (1977, 1982), who contends that, much like the psychological tradition that spawned it, Kohlberg's theory tends to result in the categorization of males at higher moral development stages than same-aged females. For example, based on her own interviews with women facing real-life moral dilemmas, Gilligan believes that Kohlberg's theory tends to categorize females as stage 3 and is insensitive to some of the most dominant female moral concerns like the power of mercy and the wisdom of interpersonal caring, each of which would be categorized by Kohlberg as emotional rather than rational criteria. Kohlberg denies any sex bias in his methodology, pointing out that same-aged females and males typically average about the same on moral dilemmas. At the same time he believes that Gilligan has usefully enlarged the domain of moral judgment by adding to his justice orientation an orientation toward personal responsibility and care (Levine, Kohlberg, & Hewer, 1985).

Among the most frequently cited criticisms are those outlined by Kurtines and Grief (1974), who have systematically evaluated Kohlberg's work from a psychological measurement (psychometric) point of view. They argue that his methodology has both low reliability (consistency) and low validity (accurately measuring moral thinking). There is nothing, for example, that guarantees that subjects will give honest (as opposed to socially acceptable) answers about their own reasoning. Moreover, Kurtines and Grief also note that two raters who read the same interview material may judge a subject at entirely different moral development stages. They also note that individuals may often behave in ways different from the motivations and justifications they describe in moral reasoning interviews. Finally, Kurtines and Grief believe that Kohlberg's measurement of development insufficiently distinguishes between subjects' moral justifications and their vocabulary. Such criticisms are noteworthy, although Kohlberg believes that interviews provide an extremely rich source of data that should not be overlooked in the quest for psychological understanding. In recent years, Kohlberg and his colleagues have attempted to argue for the validity of their moral measurement techniques while also attempting to improve the precision of scoring moral judgment interviews (see Colby & Kohlberg, 1987).

Why Be Moral? A theory of moral development should answer the most fundamental question of all: Why be moral? Kohlberg would probably attempt to answer the query by stating "Because it's the right thing to do." However, such a retort will not do. The difficulty of the question has been underscored by Hare (1960) and Hyland (1979) who argue that no deductive justification of moral principles is possible. It is not a matter of whether this or that moral principle should hold in a given situation, but rather why hold or apply any moral principles at all...ever? Such questions are bothersome because if morality cannot be derived from a logical justification, as Kohlberg is wont to think, then some other kind of justification not clearly recognized by his theory must be provided.

EVALUATION OF THE THEORY

Scientific Worthiness

Testability. Kohlberg measures moral judgment by presenting moral dilemmas to subjects and inquiring of them both their resolution of the dilemmas and their justification for the resolution. Subjects, in turn, put into words their solutions and the kinds of cognitive concerns they considered in formulating their responses. In this way, Kohlberg is a mentalist (stages, rational judgment, *A*-versus *B*-type moral reasoning, and cognitive conflict). Kohlberg commits himself to the inferential leap required to move from verbal self-reports to claims about the presence of these theoretical constructs. He claims, in support of his inferences, that his theoretical formulations represent patterns in his data that are natural, personal formulations of moral principles. In all fairness to Kohlberg, his theory does seem to reflect reasonable inferences about the data he reports. Still, inferences like Kohlberg's that appeal to mentalist constructs are not based on direct observation. Consequently, Table 10-2 shows my moderate rating for the theory's testability.

Table 10-2 Ratings of Kohlberg's Theory for Scientific Worthiness

CRITERION	HIGH	MODERATE	LOW
Testability		X	
External validity	X		
Predictive validity		X	
Internal consistency	X		
Theoretical economy			X

External Validity. Kohlberg and his colleagues have marshalled a large body of cross-cultural data that they argue supports the theory of a universal sequence of moral development stages. While criticisms of technical difficulties with such data should not be ignored, one cannot easily overlook the general patterns of moral development stages across quite diverse cultures. Moreover, the theory seems to accord well with parents' and teachers' intuitions about children's moral integrity. Young children seem naturally to be more attuned to obedience and authority (stage 1) than to other kinds of moral invocations. In contrast, many adolescents rebel against obedience to authority in order to live up to the expectations of others (stage 3). Finally, if we consider important historical figures who contributed greatly to the advancement of social morality (e.g., Socrates, Jesus, Martin Luther King), we would probably agree that they exemplified what Kohlberg terms principled moral reasoning. For these reasons, Kohlberg's theory is judged moderately high in terms of its external validity.

Predictive Validity. Most of the evidence for the predictive validity of Kohlberg's theory derives from experimental tests of the logical adequacy of later stages vis-à-vis earlier stages and from attempts to induce development of moral reasoning educationally. The Turiel experiment, for example, demonstrated that subjects at a given moral development stage understood earlier but not later stages of moral reasoning. Also, attempts by Kohlberg and his cohorts to induce moral development through educational programs have met with moderate success. Such attempts to draw out and evaluate the implications of Kohlberg's theory reflect a moderately good degree of predictive validity. At the same time, however, these efforts must be balanced against the findings of non-Kohlbergians who have failed to replicate his results. A rating of moderate for Kohlberg's predictive validity represents a conservative estimate of this complex situation.

Internal Consistency. The theory is rated high for its consistency with the constructivist paradigm and with Piaget's cognitive-developmental theory. Nonconstructivist views are consistently rejected. Kohlberg discards both maturationist (endogenous) and learning (exogenous) explanations of moral development in favor of a constructivist interpretation.

Theoretical Economy. Morality is a complex phenomenon. As such its explanation should be comparably complex, and Kohlberg's theory is faithful to that expectation. He attempts to explain only the relatively small portion of human conduct called moral judgment. To accomplish that goal, three major assumptions are made. Consequently, the theory lies somewhere between those that assume less and explain more and those that assume more and explain less. Given the additional consideration that Kohlberg's assumptions are far more complex than most others introduced in this text, it garners a moderately low rating for theoretical economy.

Developmental Adequacy

Temporality. Kohlberg's account of moral development clearly passes this criterion (see Table 10-3). Children's moral judgments reflect time-related construction of increasingly complex moral principles. Moral reasoning evolves through many years of social interaction.

Cumulativity. The theory is cumulative in the sense that later stages of moral reasoning build on and replace moral concepts from early stages. Moreover, Kohlberg argues that stages cannot be skipped but rather occur in a universal sequence. In this way, later moral concepts add important distinctions and principles to moral judgments of earlier stages.

Directionality. Kohlberg believes that moral development evolves from less adequate to more adequate forms of reasoning. More adequate moral reasoning of later stages resolves not only more moral problems but also moral problems of a different kind vis-à-vis earlier stages. In this way Kohlberg's theory holds that moral development is directed toward increasing moral equilibrium, and thus it passes this criterion.

New Mode of Organization. Moral development consists of cognitive reorganizations of earlier stages into new rational structures that involve moral values and principles not present at earlier stages. Structural reorganizations of this type represent precisely what is meant by the concept of a new mode of organization. Later stages entail moral structures applied to solving moral situations that are not manifest at earlier stages. Thus, the theory passes this criterion.

Increased Capacity for Self-Control. Moral development evolves toward a state of increasingly autonomous moral reasoning. Stages 1 and 2 are

Table 10-3 Ratings of Kohlberg's Theory for Characteristics of Development

CHARACTERISTIC	RATING
Temporality	Pass
Cumulativity	Pass
Directionality	Pass
New mode of organization	Pass
Increased capacity for self-control	Pass

defined by concepts of fairness that are personal and situation specific. At stages 3 and 4, reasoning shifts toward more socially defined and thus more stable moral principles. This element of stability reflects an increase in self-regulation to the extent that moral principles have been incorporated into individuals' own reasoning; that is, moral reasoning is used to solve moral problems in increasingly diverse situations. Finally, as argued by Kohlberg, stages 5 and 6 involve moral principles that should be followed by humanity. Presumably, if everyone were developed to stage 6, all moral difficulties and problems would be solvable in ways that were universally acknowledged to be fair. The point here is this: increased capacity for self-control develops hand-in-hand with the development of moral reasoning because increasingly adequate moral principles allow one to generalize robust moral solutions across situations without having to reinvent moral solutions for each situation. Given these considerations, Kohlberg's theory is judged to pass this criterion.

SUMMARY POINTS

1. Kohlberg's theory is basically a cognitive-developmental theory applied to the specific area of moral judgment.
2. The theory assumes that morality is essentially justice and fairness; a matter of rational, constructive thinking that depends on prerequisite cognitive stages and one's ability to differentiate between motives, behaviors, and consequences.
3. Kohlberg attempts to explain the development of moral reasoning by using moral dilemmas coupled with extensive clinical interviews.
4. Internal principles of Kohlberg's theory are equilibration or cognitive conflict, cognitive-structural development, and role-taking ability.
5. The theory's bridge principle is the universal sequence of moral development stages and the relationship between moral stages and moral behavior.
6. The change mechanism in Kohlberg's theory is cognitive conflict, his preferred term for Piaget's concept of equilibration.
7. Kohlberg's most enduring contributions include his image of people as natural moral philosophers, the notion that morality reflects rational rather than emotional considerations, his view of moral development as following a universal sequence of stages, and his work in moral education.
8. Criticisms of Kohlberg's theory often refer to serious questions about its reliability, validity, and philosophical concerns about "why be moral?"
9. The theory gets a moderate rating overall for its scientific worthiness and a high rating for its developmental adequacy.

PROBLEMS AND EXERCISES

1. Reread the moral dilemma described earlier in this chapter, then answer the following questions.
   Should Heinz have stolen the drug to save his wife? Why?

What if he didn't love her? Should he have stolen it anyway? Why?

Should he steal the drug to save another relative? Why?

Should he steal the drug to save a stranger? Why?

If Heinz gets caught and admits he stole the drug, how should the judge sentence him? Why?

Examine your answers to the "Why?" questions (these are your moral rationales) and try to distill the common, underlying moral principles that recur in your reasoning. See if you can determine your stage of moral development for this dilemma.

2. Administer the same dilemma and accompanying questions to a child, a teenager, an adult, and a retired person. Try to figure out their stage of moral reasoning by gleaning the moral principles of their judgments from their responses. Does moral development appear to increase with age in your limited sample? If so, why? If not, why not? In either case, have you evidence that supports or contradicts Kohlberg's theory?

3. Review the series of experiments described by Milgram (1974) to test obedience to authority. Identify the moral issues and problems in these studies. How would Kohlberg analyze Milgram's results?

SUGGESTED READINGS

More about the Theory

Gilligan, C. (1977). In a different voice: Women's conceptions of self and of morality. *Harvard Educational Review, 47,* 481–517.

Kohlberg, L. (1973). Contributions of developmental psychology to education: Examples from moral education. *Educational Psychologist, 10,* 2–14.

Kohlberg, L., & Gilligan, C. (1971). The adolescent as a philosopher: The discovery of self in a postconventional world. *Daedalus, 100,* 1051–1086.

Levine, C., Kohlberg, L., & Hewer, A. (1985). The current formulation of Kohlberg's theory and a response to critics. *Human Development, 28,* 94–100.

Reviews of Research

Schlaefli, A., Rest, J. R., & Thoma, S. J. (1985). Does moral education improve moral judgment? A meta-analysis of intervention studies using the Defining Issues Test. *Review of Educational Research, 55,* 319–352.

Snarey, J. R. (1985). Cross-cultural universality of social-moral development: A critical review of Kohlbergian research. *Psychological Bulletin, 97,* 202–232.

Critical Reviews

Aron, I. E. (1977). Moral philosophy and moral education: A critique of Kohlberg's theory. *School Review, 85,* 197–217.

Boyes, M. C., & Walker, L. J. (1988). Implications of cultural diversity for the universality claims of Kohlberg's theory of moral development. *Human Development, 31,* 44–59.

Kurtines, W., & Grief, E. B. (1974). The development of moral thought: Review and evaluation of Kohlberg's approach. *Psychological Bulletin, 8,* 453–470.

Simpson, E. L. (1974). Moral development research. A case study of scientific cultural bias. *Human Development, 17,* 81–106.

Sullivan, E. V. (1977). *Kohlberg's structuralism: A critical appraisal.* Toronto: Ontario Institute for Studies in Education.

Chapter 11

Educational Applications

Preview Questions

What three educational ideologies are related to theories of development?
What psychological assumptions about the nature of development and the
needs of children underlie each of the educational ideologies?
What do the different ideologies define as appropriate educational goals?
What individuals and teaching strategies are associated with each of the three
educational ideologies?
According to each ideology, what are the most relevant and appropriate kinds of
strategies for evaluating the educational experiences of students?

THEORETICAL PARADIGMS AND EDUCATIONAL IDEOLOGIES

The process of education requires teachers to intervene in children's lives for the
explicit purpose of changing them in important ways. After all, if one assumes that
children are already fine just the way they are and that there is no need to change
anything, then there would be no need for education at all. Educational interventions, then, are predicated on beliefs about what children *should* learn, which in
turn, *should* comprise the goals of an educational program. Educational goals
reflect implicit assumptions about children's basic nature and educational needs,
appropriate methods of teaching, and relevant data for evaluating educational
progress. Virtually every educational act teachers perform is directed by either explicit or implicit choices about these issues.

There is a close relationship between the developmental paradigms introduced in this text and certain educational ideologies. Developmental theories cannot strictly determine educational practice because education requires explicit
choices about what children *should* learn and about what they *ought to* know
(Kohlberg & Mayer, 1972). At the same time, there is no need to downplay the importance of developmental theories for education. After all, implicit assumptions
about children's needs and how they learn are inextricably linked to educational

219

policies. Much of the treatment given here to the relationship between developmental theories and educational practice has been drawn from Kohlberg and Mayer's (1972) analysis of educational goals.

Three Educational Ideologies

An educational ideology is much like a theoretical paradigm. It reflects certain predisposing assumptions that are held by members sharing the ideology. Ideologies differ from one another in terms of the content of these underlying assumptions. The most important assumptions underlying an educational ideology concern the goals of education, the essence of the child, the teacher's role in delivering educational content, appropriate instructional methodology, and methods of evaluation.

Instructional programs can be differentiated with respect to three essential issues related to the definition of educational objectives. These issues require choices in terms of (1) the locus of educational change sought, (2) the time frame within which educational goals should operate, and (3) the level of individualization of educational experience. Each issue can be posed in terms of questions the conscientious educator must answer. First, should educational goals focus on developing children's internal states or their behaviors? Second, assuming some degree of both is important, should the goals of education give priority to *humanitarian* criteria and immediate experience or to *educative* criteria and long-term consequences? Third, should educational progress concentrate on the individual child's needs or on those needs that all children share?

With respect to the first issue, endogenous and exogenous paradigms represent opposite positions, whereas the constructivist position attempts to balance concerns for internal and behavioral changes. On the second issue, both endogenous and exogenous paradigms concentrate on producing short-term changes, while constructivists aim for long-term consequences. Concerning the third issue, the exogenous and constructivist paradigms would aim educational programming toward developmental changes that have both universal, and by implication, individual impact. The endogenous perspective emphasizes individual development and thus places heavy emphasis on instructional content that maximizes children's opportunities for self-expression.

The Romantic Ideology

The *romantic* educational ideology closely parallels the endogenous paradigm of developmental theories. Within this ideology, children are viewed as possessing an innate "inner worth" that demands respect and consideration. Psychoanalysis suggests to educators that there are dynamic, libido-driven forces that unconsciously control all psychological processes, thereby influencing any attempt at academic training. For this reason, and because psychoanalytic therapy was itself an educational endeavor, education and psychoanalysis are fundamentally inseparable. Moreover, educational use of psychoanalytic theory relies implicitly on

Freud's concept of *sublimation*, the displacement of psychic energy away from erotic objects and toward intellectual and socially productive pursuits. Following in Freud's footsteps, some educators have attempted to establish schools that provide an environment of freedom in which children can develop naturally "without the psychic distortions that produce neuroses in adults" (McClellan, 1967, p. 246).

Romantics tend to value childhood because it reflects an inherent and natural plan that leads to the formation of the self. G. Stanley Hall, the founder of child psychology in America, summarizes the romantic's position in his belief that educators and parents should defend children's happiness and rights by keeping out of "nature's way" (1901, p. 24).

If children's inner nature is to be respected as a matter of conviction, then it stands to reason that educational practices should be flexible enough to permit their inner "good" to develop unshackled by the constraints, values, and rigid expectations of teachers. In fact, since children are believed to grow according to an inherent natural plan, romantic educators like A. S. Neill (the Summerhill School) view education as a process of providing opportunities for learning that children themselves say they want. After all, children know best what interests them.

The Traditionalist Ideology

The *traditionalist* ideology corresponds in many respects to the exogenous paradigm. In fact, traditionalist educators make extensive use of concepts derived from operant conditioning and social learning theories. According to this ideology, the task of education is to transmit to each generation a specific body of information that reflects society's values. The teacher's job is clearcut—to transmit to younger generations specific facts, skills, and moral values.

Children are believed to be inherently malleable and are shaped by the consequences of their behaviors. Effective education utilizes the science of learning derived from behavior analysis. Because children's experiences are so important in molding their behavior, teachers play vital roles in establishing effective learning environments.

The Progressive Ideology

The *progressive* ideology reflects a strong interactional-constructivist orientation. This ideology views the goal of education as the development of thinking and reasoning. Unlike the romantics, progressives do not assume that development occurs as the unfolding of some natural plan or that education should foster children's own self-interests. Unlike the traditionalists, progressives view learning in terms of problem-solving ability rather than the learning of specific facts and skills. Progressive educators view the task of education as providing problems and cognitive conflict that stimulate the development of logical and critical thought.

Table 11-1 Elements of Educational Ideologies

	ROMANTICISM	TRADITIONALISM	PROGRESSIVISM
Paradigm	Endogenous	Exogenous	Constructivism
Psychological assumptions about nature of children	Children develop according to a natural plan	Children are malleable and the product of their experiences	Children are scientist-philosophers who adapt to problems and organize their knowledge
Educational goals	Happiness, self-fulfillment, self-knowledge	Specific skills, body of facts, social norms and values	More adequate reasoning and problem solving; development
Teaching strategies	Opportunities for play and freedom	Skill building, practice, direct instruction	Induce cognitive conflict; discovery learning
Educational evaluation	?	Teacher-made and standardized tests	Cognitive tasks and interviews

Table 11–1 summarizes the important elements of educational ideologies, which are described in the following sections. For each ideology, the associated paradigm, psychological assumptions about the nature of children, educational goals, typical teaching strategies, and methods of evaluation are identified.

THE ENDOGENOUS PARADIGM AND ROMANTIC EDUCATION

Psychological Assumptions

Underlying the three educational ideologies are implicit psychological assumptions about children's needs and about how children learn and develop. The romantic's vision of education reflects the underlying belief that endogenous forces propel child development. The environment, including the educational programming, may speed up, frustrate, or retard development without changing its biological course. Moreover, in the romantic's vision, while children may profit and learn from many activities, the value of experience lies in maturational "readiness." Some experiences have greater impact than others on children's learning, but this impact is a function of the particular interests, abilities, and self-concepts that have already matured. Finally, the unfolding of the maturational plan is seen as the source of individual differences.

The romantic ideology derives in part from a phenomenologist epistemology; that is, it holds that knowledge and reality emanate from the individual's inner experience of the world. Knowledge, in this view, reflects the truth of self-awareness and self-knowledge and may draw from emotional as well as intellectual intuitions. Educational objectives reflect concern for children's inner states.

The romantic stresses the importance of providing educational experiences that further children's mental health, happiness, satisfaction, self-fulfillment, curiosity, and creativity.

Educational Goals

In attempting to assure children's self-fulfillment, the romantic would let children take the lead in determining their own educational interests and activities. Such an attitude marks the child-centered philosophy of A. S. Neill, founder of the Summerhill School. Neill believes that children's happiness requires a hands-off pedagogy and the abolition of school authority. In fact, he argues that educators should let children be themselves and not force them to do anything they don't want to do (Neill, 1960, p. 297).

The romantic educator is dedicated to humanitarian values and concentrates on short-term educational goals that are believed to lead to a happier, better adjusted childhood. Romantics stress an *open, child-centered* set of educational values wherein students are tended with kindness, indulgence, flexibility, and understanding. Children are valued because they have feelings and ideas. The teacher's job is to provide experiences that are personally satisfying for children. Education may include the development of skills and academic material not because they are worthwhile in themselves but because they heighten personal awareness and thus facilitate self-expression.

Finally, the romantic ideology insists on the need for individualized educational objectives, and teachers attempt to provide experiences determined appropriate on a child-by-child basis. Schools are for children, so education should be humanistic; children should achieve self-knowledge, happiness, and self-fulfillment.

Teaching Strategies

Theories of development have their most identifiable impact on educational methodology. Typically, educators draw from a theory's change mechanism to plan lessons that produce effective learning. Yet, the romantic ideology makes that kind of application untenable. After all, endogenous interpretations of human nature (Freud, Erikson, Wilson), which rely on hereditary and maturational forces rather than environmental influences, leave little room for teachers to influence their students' predetermined developmental pathways. Consequently, teachers following the romantic inclination must acknowledge the powerful influence of innate programming while still offering some contribution to children's development

A. S. Neill founded the Summerhill School in England in 1921 and is widely recognized as one of the founders of open education. His ideas reflect a purely romantic, endogenous orientation to schooling and thus provide a good example of how educational romantics approach educational practices. His ideas are examined next. Interested students may also wish to examine two of Anna Freud's

(1952, 1979) writings about educational implications of psychoanalytic theory. Her ideas are not examined here because they are more prescriptive generalizations than educational practices.

A. S. Neill

A. S. Neill's beliefs reflect a psychoanalytic approach to educational experience. He was not particularly interested in pedagogy. Rather, he contended that children in a free environment would learn what, when, and as they needed to learn.

Neill (1960) believes that children learn quite well on their own accord. Artificial inducements and required lessons are simply unnecessary. He argues that since children learn what they want to learn, books, paperwork, examinations, and other vestiges of traditional schooling are profoundly unimportant (p. 25). Most book learning, for example, is considered useless because it teaches information that is unimportant to practical living and because it does not deal with freedom, love, self-determination, or personal character. Moreover, homework should be condemned simply because children hate it (p. 378). What children need is "tools and clay and sports and theater and paint and freedom" (p. 25).

Neill does not dispute the importance of learning. However, he believes learning should be subordinated to play (p. 62); fantasy play is good for young children because it builds imagination and self-confidence. For older children, cooperative games develop social understanding and empathy, while competitive games promote motor coordination and cognitive strategies. Learning should always be child-centered, flexible, noncoercive, and relevant to children's lives. Neill's endogenous position is clear when he argues that the importance of learning traditional academic subjects pales against the importance of "life's natural fulfillment—of man's inner happiness" (p. 24). Finally, children don't need to be taught discipline or how to behave, since they learn right from wrong on their own, even without teacher pressure (Neill, 1960, p. 254).

Educational Evaluation

The romantic ideology evaluates educational experiences in terms of idealized, global concepts like personal happiness, mental health, and self-fulfillment. These constructs are believed to be the products of virtuous behavior and expressions of desirable personality traits. For example, mentally unhealthy persons are believed to exhibit such undesirable traits as selfishness, paranoia, depression, stubbornness, pessimism, or immaturity. In contrast, happy and mentally healthy individuals exhibit altruism, friendliness, integrity, creativity, self-confidence, industry, and optimism.

The use of tests is anathema to the romantic ideology, which aims to develop the person rather than directly teach specific knowledge. In fact, the issue of educational evaluation is a bit disconcerting to the romantic, who may ask "evaluate what?" Since development is deemed to be a spontaneous unfolding of individual biological programming, what is the sense of evaluating such an unfolding in terms of test norms or society's expectations? Such a practice would be tantamount to passing judgment on the individual's own personal tendencies by presupposing what course personal development ought to take. It makes no sense to establish evaluation guidelines or norms from the romantic point of view because growth and development are highly individual; individuals are not necessarily expected to behave according to social norms.

THE EXOGENOUS PARADIGM AND TRADITIONALIST EDUCATION

Psychological Assumptions

The traditionalist ideology views children's learning and development as the product of the accumulated experiences and environmental forces acting on them during their lifetime. School environments provide reinforcing or punishing consequences, and children are expected to learn from their successes and mistakes, thereby altering their behavior. Learning is seen as an accumulation of associations built up and stored from environmental encounters. The educational environment constitutes forces that guide learning and development wherein teachers and parents mold children by giving them facts, building their skills, and providing sufficient opportunities for practice.

This ideology derives from an empiricist epistemology wherein knowledge is believed to derive from experience, or more specifically, external reality determines the sensations that we experience. These sensations are the ultimate source of knowledge, which is objective in the dual sense that its content and source both lie outside the realm of inner experience. Education, then, is predicated on the need to establish learning environments that correspond with real world knowledge. Educational goals stress the need for behavioral conformity to cultural standards such as good citizenship and industry. Children study the classical subjects (reading, writing, and arithmetic) because learning specific behaviors associated with them is believed to produce moral, productive adults who live harmoniously within the context of a productive society. In this context, learning specific desirable behaviors and facts becomes the goal of education. Implied here is the notion that children can and ought to be shaped by practicing correct responses and by associating the consequences with their responses (Kohlberg & Mayer, 1972, p. 456).

Educational Goals

Like romantics, traditionalist educators also concentrate on short-term goals that typically include learning specific *skills* (reading and word attack skills, math computation skill and accuracy, writing habits, and accuracy of factual knowledge). Teachers encourage children to learn correct answers and to conform to rules of classroom conduct. Group training in specific academic and social behaviors is the order of the day. Long-term success and a productive life are ultimately expected to accrue to students whose behavior is judged by teachers to conform most closely to the class's and the school's rules of conduct.

The time frame for educational goal setting is long-term performance and maintenance of behavioral acquisitions, although this implicit goal is sometimes masked by educators who believe that simple conformity to specific classroom rules is more important than the long-term benefit for the student. For example, while students may be expected to learn and display behavioral skills in accord with each teacher's expectations, such skills and abilities are, for the most part, defined by society's concept of good, productive citizenship. Correct answers to specific factual questions may be memorized, rehearsed, and repeated until they are learned. Still, such factual learning is taught for the specific purpose of equipping individuals with information deemed educationally desirable for informed citizenship. Teachers model desirable behaviors and reinforce them in children because these are believed to reap the most favorable consequences in the long run.

The traditionalist ideology takes a middle ground on the issue of individual versus universal educational goals. Because it reflects concerns for what is socially good and desirable, it places social conformity in high esteem and defines educational goals in terms of objectives that should be applied to and learned by all children of a given culture. The traditionalist educational agenda can be defended as being in society's best interest, since it functions to preserve the values, knowledge, and behavioral norms of the culture.

The traditionalist ideology requires that children be taught specific facts and skills in the traditional subjects because they incorporate society's values and norms. In this vein, our society expects its youth to learn basic reading and mathematical skills as well as factual information about science, social studies, and personal health. Moreover, socially desirable values like honesty, industry, dedication, allegiance, a sense of the common good, frugality, responsibility, conservation, and a balance between rugged individualism and interpersonal cooperation are anticipated outcomes of both public and private education. It is important to note that learning these facts and social values is important, not for any inherent good or for reasons related to better thinking and reasoning, but because it is believed to produce good citizenship, which benefits society as a whole.

Teaching Strategies

The exogenous paradigm, specifically Skinner's operant conditioning, has furnished educators with many directly relevant and useful concepts for implementing effective educational programs. We examine here some of Skinner's ideas about applying behavior analysis to educational problems.

B. F. Skinner

Skinner (1961, 1965, 1968; Skinner & Krakower, 1968) has devoted considerable thought and energy to designing specific teaching applications of his behavior analysis. *The Technology of Teaching* contains Skinner's teaching agenda, cast as might be expected, in behavioral terms. In his view, learning takes place under the control of three variables: the situation or learning context, the measurable qualities of behavior itself, and the behavioral consequences or contingencies of reinforcement. By carefully controlling the first and third variables, teachers produce the conditions under which the second, specific behaviors, are learned.

One of Skinner's earliest contributions was the *teaching machine,* a semi-mechanized, student-controlled learning center. In a very real sense, the Skinner box was the earliest teaching machine; it provided reinforcement to laboratory animals for performing specific behaviors. The earliest educational model of Skinner's teaching machine consisted of a wooden box with hand crank and a window through which a written question could be read by the student. The student would select an answer and turn the crank. If the answer was correct, the crank would turn a paper spool to the next question. Incorrect selections locked the crank and prevented it from turning. The teaching machine underwent many improvements and eventually became quite sophisticated. It became the forerunner of programmed, self-paced instruction. Today, modern computers driven by their software programs and controlled by student learners comprise the latest version of teaching machine technology.

According to Skinner (1968), teaching can be radically improved by taking advantage of technological improvements in behavior analysis. To accomplish this, teachers must give up the idea that teaching is an art and that some individuals are "born" to be teachers. On the contrary, effective teachers are trained to be effective by carefully controlling the conditions under which learning is maximized. The following examples from *The Technology of Teaching* illustrate how teachers can utilize behavioral technology to improve educational programming.

Programmed instruction is quite effective in transmitting factual knowledge, simple skills, and complex material that has been "decomposed" into individual components. Complex topics should be "decomposed" into their individual components. For example, science experiments can be broken down into a sequence of individual tasks. Students work on each task until it is mastered, only then moving on to the next in the sequence.

Programmed instruction can also be used to teach students to attend to relevant material selectively and to learn how to learn. When teachers arrange the classroom environment and various learning tasks so that differential reinforcement is contingent on students' selective attention, their students learn to pay attention to more educationally relevant stimuli and to ignore educationally irrelevant stimuli. There are various effective strategies to teach children how to learn. *Rote* memorizing is a time-consuming but effective means for learning specific material. Memorizing involves *verbal rehearsal* or verbal practice and has an advantageous side effect; specific terms or phrases may serve as prompts for other related material. Other "learning how to learn" skills are also effective. For example, learning how to use symbolic devices to encode verbal or pictorial material from memory is a powerful strategy for improving memory.

Programmed instruction is also effective in motivating students to learn. Because instructional lessons are composed of many units, each of which functions as a prompt for a response, programmed instruction is designed to make weak reinforcers or small amounts of strong reinforcers effective. When teachers test for material with a weekly quiz, they are unwittingly working against effective learning. They are delaying reinforcement rather than administering it immediately. It is no wonder students learn to "cram" the night before exams; learning material during the week goes unreinforced until Fridays. Programmed instruction maximizes the effect of reinforcers because instructional steps are small; consequently, reinforcement is immediate and frequent.

Students don't always learn new material or new skills when first presented; opportunities for review and practice are often necessary. New skills become somewhat automatic when they are *overlearned* or drilled through continued practice. Practice is important for more than just learning new material and skills; it is an important means for establishing *transfer* of learning. Transfer occurs when a response is generalized to new conditions, like when a student figures out that adding two- or three-digit numbers is much like adding single-digit numbers.

Show-and-tell activities, teacher demonstrations, and audio-visual programs are often used in elementary classrooms to stimulate learning. Such activities may be only coincidentally related to learning. These activities fail not because children are inattentive, but because there is no plan for the systematic application of positive reinforcement (Skinner, 1968, pp. 104–106). Young children need to be taught how to look, listen, and learn. Colorful and comfortable classroom settings may establish a reinforcing environment and a positive attitude toward learning. Yet, no matter how attractive, interesting, and stimulating educational material may be, it may often go unlearned. For learning to occur, students must do something active that can be reinforced.

Skinner believes that schools have regularly failed to produce students with genuine creativity, and this failure is due in part to the misguided belief that creativity is an innate and untrainable quality. However, he contends that creativity can be shaped by arranging educational environments to reinforce originality. By designing reinforcement contingencies for unusual responses, teachers can rapidly shape their students to produce creative behaviors. Artists, dancers, and writers train their skills, and by reinforcing selected choices they learn how to recognize and produce novel qualities. For creativity to occur, it is important to arrange a situation that evokes a high quantity of behavior. In brainstorming sessions, for example, responses are reinforced simply for being emitted, no matter how ridiculous, absurd, or bizarre they may be.

Finally, Skinner's prescription for effective teaching suggests that teachers be able to design and implement effective behavior modification programs that are individualized for students and instructional content. To be effective, teachers should know how to identify a reinforcer on the basis of its effects, how to establish an effective learning environment that minimizes undesirable and maximizes desirable behaviors, and how to control the administration of reinforcers.

Skinner acknowledges that designing instructional programs is a complex undertaking. Yet, complex learning can be decomposed into its constituent elements, and behaviors can be shaped and maintained through judicious use of discriminative stimuli and differential reinforcement.

Educational Evaluation

Because it reflects so strongly an exogenous orientation, with a corresponding emphasis on objective measurement, traditional education has often employed "objective" measures of student learning. Such "objective" measures generally fall into two categories: teacher-made tests and standardized tests. Teacher-made tests are probably the most widely used of all evaluation strategies, and they comprise the backbone of such other "objective" measures of learning as course grades, class rank, and grade point average. Standardized achievement tests (e.g., California Achievement Test, Scholastic Aptitude Test) are widely used by educational systems to evaluate student learning.

Traditionalists view educational goals in terms of benefits to society. Test scores are used to evaluate learning because they are generally believed to have relatively good *predictive validity.* That is, test scores derived at one time are believed to be relatively accurate predictors of success later on. Success in education, in turn, serves society's interest in the sense that better educated individuals are expected to be among society's most productive and best citizens.

THE CONSTRUCTIVIST PARADIGM AND PROGRESSIVE EDUCATION

Psychological Assumptions

The progressive ideology views learning as a dialectical synthesis formed in children's interactions with the social and physical environment. Children are viewed as curious scientist-philosophers seeking to make sense out of the world and their experiences. Progressives maintain that logical reasoning and problem-solving abilities evolve through complex, interactional processes rather than didactic instruction. The progressive view parallels Piaget's psychological constructivism, which maintains that a moderate or optimal degree of discrepancy between a child's expectations and actual events constitutes the most effective environment for developmental change.

The progressive ideology attempts to integrate the romantic's concern about internal states with the cultural transmission concern for social relevance. It derives from a dialectical-constructivist epistemology, and it emphasizes a concern for cognitive competence but in a functional-adaptive sense rather than in the phenomenological sense of the romantics or the empiricist sense of the traditionalists.

Progressives rely on constructivist interpretations of childhood. They believe that important developmental changes should be sought not within the child or the environment, but in the quality of the child's adaptive interactions.

This position maintains that environments are not fixed contexts, but rather that environments change children just as children change their environments. The progressive ideology seeks changes that are interactional and adaptive (not conforming) in nature.

Educational Goals

Progressive educators look toward long-term educational consequences. They believe that learning is desirable when it produces improved cognitive competence for solving complex problems and for adapting to complex interpersonal situations. Education is valued in terms of its lifelong effect on the development of thinking and reasoning, a vastly different agenda than the romantic's concern with self-fulfillment or the traditional concern with specific facts and behavioral conformity. The progressive program seeks to produce individuals who know how to question society's values, because questioning is viewed as an impetus to better, more adequate reasoning. Progressives strive for educational programs that seek not to fulfill youthful interest and curiosity, but that invoke intellectual curiosity toward new meanings and stretch personal interests toward new interactions.

Finally, the progressive ideology seeks educational goals that are universally valid, regardless of the specific cultural milieu in which a child resides. Such a stance is in clear opposition to the romantics, who view educational goals as personal and individualistic, and it stands in sharp contrast to the traditionalist's program, which requires that educational goals be culturally specific.

Teaching Strategies

Progressive education is geared toward producing individuals who are problem solvers and who are capable of resolving difficulties through logical, well-reasoned strategies. While John Dewey's educational philosophy is closely associated with the progressive agenda, the development of educational methodology derives from the work of others. In this respect, both Piaget and Kohlberg have directly influenced educational practice with their ideas.

Piaget

Piaget (1971c) has attempted to provide new insights and directions for educators, although his writings have tended to be more general than specific. He suggests, for example, that any attempt to revise educational practices in line with experimental findings from child development must include systematic changes in teacher preparation. In this vein, Piaget (1971c, pp. 129–133) argues in favor of extensive training in child psychology for elementary school teachers and in adolescent psychology for secondary teachers. Only with an understanding of the intellectual functioning of children and adolescents can teachers expect to design effective and psychologically relevant lessons.

Piaget anchors his suggestions for educational practice in his own research. He suggests, for example, that the purpose of education is primarily to *adapt* the child to an adult's world (1971c, p. 137). Thus, teaching should engage children actively rather than passively in the solution of problems (p. 137). One way to do this is to provide sufficient play (pp. 155–157) for exercising the intellectual functions of cooperation, strategy, and symbolism. For older children and adolescents, teachers should utilize imaginative and symbolic games (e.g., chess, checkers) that exercise intellectual operations rather than factual recall. Learning facts should always be subjugated to reasoning about them.

Educators who attempt to apply Piaget's theory to children's learning often rely on his principle of construction. They sometimes interpret construction to mean that children must act on their environment by physically manipulating concrete objects. Such a contention is only partly correct. Physical manipulation itself, the act of handling objects, is far less important than the kind of feedback children derive from their manipulations. What is important about physical manipulation for young children is the kind of intellectual activity it engages. The vital connection between intelligence and activity is glossed over in textbook treatments of Piaget's theory (Hess & Croft, 1975). Cognitive activity requires that children be attentive, alert, engaged, and anticipatory in their intellectual strategies. Consequently, educational programs that require children to manipulate objects may be short-sighted and incomplete unless intellectual activity accompanies physical manipulations (Inhelder, Sinclair, & Bovet, 1974).

Teachers can help students construct knowledge by giving direct feedback about their actions on objects and their reasoning about objects (Kamii, 1972, p. 117). For older children and adolescents, teachers should concentrate on assigning problems that require students to contemplate possible solutions and test them intellectually before verifying the solutions in practice. Almy (1979, p. 181) suggests that teachers should be knowledgeable about their students' level of cognitive development. In that way they will be able to answer questions when appropriate, pose new problems to engage students' inquiring activities, or refrain from answering in situations where a student's approach seems guided toward an appropriate solution.

Lovell (1979) has emphasized the need to match instructional content to students' stages of development. When a mismatch occurs between the assimilative capacities of a student's cognitive stage and the academic content of lessons, learning difficulties may occur in science, mathematics, geography, language arts, and other areas of the curriculum. Concerning geography, for example, Lovell (1979) notes that preoperational children understand simple map symbols that resemble the item they represent (e.g., miniature buildings and trees). Concrete operational students understand more abstract map symbols (direction, contour, relative location), but they are unable to comprehend more complex concepts of map scale or topography. Formal operational students, in turn, can understand such symbolism as well as complex geographical relationships between culture, subsistence patterns, and environment (Lovell, 1979, p. 201–202).

Karplus (1974) and his colleagues (Karplus, Lawson, Wollman, Appel, Bernoff, Howe, Rusch, & Sullivan, 1977) have relied extensively on cognitive-developmental theory in designing the Science Curriculum Improvement Study (SCIS), a set of materials and methods used by many science teachers throughout the country. SCIS is designed to provoke cognitive disequilibrium through a teaching/learning cycle that incorporates four phases: *exploration, explanation, extension,* and *evaluation.* During the *exploration* phase, teachers use concrete materials to engage students with science situations, activities, demonstrations, and questions that will motivate inquiry with minimal teacher interference. During the *explanation* phase, teachers give direct instruction (using lectures, films, diagrams, charts, and pictures) in how to organize the exploratory activities. This phase is designed to reduce and organize any disequilibrium that occurred during the first phase by teaching students new concepts that can explain their exploratory experiences. The *extension* phase is aptly named, since it is designed to extend the exploratory experiences and explained concepts to new material and thereby consolidate general rules and concepts invented in the earlier phases. *Evaluation,* the fourth phase, is used to measure student learning and can assist teachers in designing future learning cycles that prevent certain difficulties.

Kohlberg

Like Piaget, Lawrence Kohlberg (1966) has written about general educational issues and the need for educational reform (Kohlberg & Mayer, 1972). Unlike Piaget, however, Kohlberg (1968b, 1970, 1973) has commented extensively on particular educational practices and has developed specific curriculum innovations, implemented them, and evaluated their effectiveness (Blatt & Kohlberg, 1975; Kohlberg, 1972, 1973, 1974, 1975a, 1975b, 1977, 1980; Kohlberg & Turiel, 1971).

Over the past fifteen years, a number of educational programs have attempted to use Kohlberg's theory to promote developmental change in students' moral judgments. Reviews of such programs (Enright, Lapsley, & Levy, 1983; Lawrence, 1980; Lemming, 1981) suggest that approximately half have been effective in promoting moral development, and the greatest success occurs when programs last at least several months and when students participate in group discussions of moral dilemmas and ethical controversies (Schlaefli, Rest, & Thoma, 1985).

The most important pedagogical considerations of Kohlberg's theory are as follows. First, students should be grouped heterogeneously so that individuals vary in their moral development stage. This variation is vital because cognitive conflict is unlikely to occur if each individual is at the same moral development stage. Second, groups should be assigned the task of resolving moral dilemmas and ethical controversies. It is important that they understand that group resolutions should evolve from the give and take of discussion between group members. The importance of these discussions should not be overlooked or cut short, because they are believed to provide the kind of interpersonal cognitive conflicts that influence the development of moral judgment. Third, teachers play an important but nondirective role in guiding moral discussion groups (see below). Fourth, these discussions should be, to the extent possible, integrated within the normal school curriculum. They tend to be most effective when discussions of moral issues are made an integral part of other courses (e.g., social studies), as opposed to having teachers schedule discussion groups in an isolated and ad hoc manner that artificially segregates them from students' other academic concerns. Fourth, exposure to moral dilemma discussions should be at least ten to twelve weeks in duration. Shorter exposures to moral discussion groups tend to produce little developmental effect; longer exposures produce about the same as that found with ten to twelve weeks' exposure (Schlaefli, Rest, & Thoma, 1985).

Teachers are most effective when they pose questions about and problems with students' solutions and when they motivate groups to improve and revise their solutions to moral dilemmas. Consequently, teachers neither direct students to arrive at a particular solution nor hint at correct or appropriate solutions. Educators should query students about the implications of their moral solutions and request them to evaluate the effects of their resolutions by giving new information or by posing "what if..." hypothetical situations.

Suppose, for example, that during a civics lesson on individual rights a teacher wanted to stress the moral tension between personal liberty and freedom on the one hand and civic responsibility on the other. The teacher might begin by asking groups of students to resolve the standard Heinz dilemma (see Chapter 10). The groups might then be asked to compare their solutions and justifications and revise their positions in light of opposing considerations offered by other groups. Finally, groups might request to test the adequacy of their revised solutions (regardless of whether or not they believe that Heinz should steal the drug) by addressing each of the following considerations posed in Kohlberg's original interview format:

> Should Heinz steal the drug if he doesn't love his wife? What role does love play in determining a husband's duty to his wife? Does the husband have a duty to steal the drug for his wife? Does the wife have a right to expect her husband to steal to save her life?

> If it's not Heinz's wife but a cousin instead who is dying of cancer, should Heinz steal the drug anyway? What if the dying person was a close personal friend of Heinz's? What if it were a complete stranger? What role does one's kinship play in determining the moral thing to do in this case?

> What rights does the druggist have in this case? What obligation does Heinz have to respect the personal property of the druggist? Is there any difference between Heinz stealing the drug to save his wife and a poor person stealing money to feed his family? If by stealing the drug Heinz deprives other dying people of being saved, does he have the right to do that?

> If Heinz steals the drug and is caught, does society have a duty to see that Heinz is prosecuted? What obligation does Heinz have to society? How does one determine a moral and just resolution to conflicts that occur between well-intentioned individuals or between individuals and society?

The teacher's primary goal in raising these issues is to produce cognitive conflict in students so that the natural process of moral equilibration can occur. Specific recommendations for teachers can be found in Galbraith and Jones (1976), who provide suggestions for setting up group discussions and selecting dilemmas for class discussion. They also give recommendations for teachers on how to function as discussion leaders.

The role of interpersonal conflict in producing educational progress has been examined by Johnson and Johnson (1985), who compared two kinds of structured academic conflict: controversy versus debate. They found that teaching methods that emphasized controversial material were far more effective than classroom debates in promoting active searches for more information about the assigned topic, more reflective reevaluation of one's position, more attitudinal change, more liking for the subject matter and the instructional material, and higher levels of self-esteem.

Educational Evaluation

The evaluation strategy of progressive educators is *developmental-philosophic* (Kohlberg & Mayer, 1972, p. 477); that is, educational experience is valued if its aims are philosophically justifiable and if it contributes to psychological development. Although the philosophical justification is beyond the scope of this text, the developmental component is extremely relevant. Education, claim the progressives, should be evaluated in terms of the extent to which it produces increasingly adequate psychological structures and rational cognitive strategies. Consequently, evaluation methods may include clinical interviews (with cognitive tasks or moral dilemmas), certain kinds of behavioral assessment, and naturalistic observations.

To assess the psychological impact of his moral education programs, Kohlberg compares pre- and post-test interviews of moral judgment. He believes that educational programs are effective if they lead to qualitative changes in one's developmental stage.

Many educators who attempt to work within the constructivist paradigm share Kohlberg's belief that educating for development implies an evaluation strategy of looking for stage changes in cognitive or moral development. However, an equally valid form of evaluation, though it is not often employed, would consist of examining educational effectiveness in terms of how well programs improve stage consolidation—the extent to which cognitive structures have become elaborated to new areas.

SUMMARY POINTS

1. The *romantic* educational ideology is associated with the endogenous paradigm of developmental theories. The *traditionalist* ideology emphasizes educational processes that reflect concepts derived from exogenous developmental theories.

The *progressive* educational ideology incorporates a constructivist view of educational experience.

2. The *romantic* ideology stresses the inherent freedom, spontaneity, and self-determination of children. It emphasizes personal happiness, creativity, and self-fulfillment. Romantic teachers provide opportunities for learning in response to children's expressed interests. Children develop and learn best when teachers facilitate their natural interests.

3. The *traditionalist* ideology emphasizes children's need to learn the knowledge, skills, and values of the predominant social order. It emphasizes direct teaching, programmed instruction, and practice of specific facts and skills deemed necessary for productive citizenship. Children learn best when teachers reinforce specific learning about factual material, the acquisition of new skills, and the maintenance of appropriate behavioral conduct.

4. The *progressive* ideology is concerned with the development of rational analysis and judgment. Educational experiences should stimulate the intellect into more adequate reasoning strategies and better solutions to problems. Progressive teachers make education inquiry oriented; they engage children's spontaneous curiosity about how things work with questions and materials that require investigation, in both the social and physical world. Group problem solving and discussions are employed to promote cognitive conflict and intellectual development.

5. Concerning educational goals, the romantic ideology looks for educational programs that emphasize internal, short-term, and individual goals. The traditionalist ideology seeks learning that is common to children within a culture and that produces long-term, external changes. The progressive ideology maintains that education should pursue goals that are universal, long-term, and interactional (a synthesis of internal and external) in nature.

6. A. S. Neill approaches education from the romantic position. He concentrates on establishing an open education environment that maximizes students' freedom to pursue their own interests.

7. B. F. Skinner views education from the traditionalist point of view. He believes teachers should use programmed instruction and arrange their classroom environments so as to maximize instructional effectiveness of behavior modification.

8. Jean Piaget and Lawrence Kohlberg approach education from a progressive orientation. Piaget argues that teachers can improve their effectiveness by being well trained in developmental psychology and by applying their psychological training to children's education. He also believes that teachers could have a greater impact on their students' intellectual development by carefully designing lessons to induce cognitive disequilibrium. Kohlberg views the role of the teacher in much the same manner. He argues that teachers best facilitate cognitive conflict, and hence moral development, when they engage students in group discussions of controversial issues and moral dilemmas.

SUGGESTED READINGS

Freud, A. (1979). *Psychoanalysis for teachers and parents.* New York: Norton.

Freud, A. (1952). The role of the teacher. *Harvard Educational Review, 22,* 229–234.

Galbraith, R. E., & Jones, T. M. (1976). *Moral reasoning: A teaching handbook for adapting Kohlberg to the classroom.* Minneapolis: Greenhaven Press.

Karplus, R. (1974). *Science curriculum improvement study: Teachers handbook.* Berkeley, CA: University of California, Lawrence Hall of Science.

Kohlberg, L., & Turiel, E. (1971). Moral development and moral education. In G. Lesser (Ed.), *Psychology and educational practice.* Chicago: Scott Foresman.

Lemming, J. S. (1981). Curricular effectiveness in moral/values education: A review of research. *Journal of Moral Education, 10,* 147–164.

Neill, A. S. (1960). *Summerhill.* New York: Holt Publishing Co.

Skinner, B. F. (1968). *The technology of teaching.* New York: Prentice-Hall.

Chapter 12

Counseling Applications

Preview Questions

What counseling therapies are associated with the endogenous, exogenous, and constructivist paradigms?

Of the counseling therapies described, what assumptions about human nature are made by each?

How do these therapies view the needs of clients?

What goals are associated with each therapy, and how do these goals reflect theoretical paradigms?

What techniques are used by the therapies described here?

THEORETICAL PARADIGMS AND COUNSELING STRATEGIES

Developmental theorists, as we saw in the previous chapter, may not necessarily take an interest in translating their work into intervention strategies. In fact, of the theorists described in this book, only Freud wrote extensively about psychotherapy, although Skinner and Bandura have had their own influence. What often happens is that others take up the work of an important theorist and work out its applications. Sometimes counselors will work not from a specific theory, but from a certain framework or point of view they believe represents tenable assumptions about client needs and therapeutic outcomes. Other times, elements of different theories will be combined to yield a novel therapeutic technique.

While there is no one-to-one correspondence between developmental theories and counseling therapies, the previous chapters have provided a sound foundation for examining the counseling implications of developmental theories. The approach taken in this chapter will be to outline one counseling example reflecting each of the major theoretical paradigms. These counseling approaches will be examined in terms of (1) the assumptions made about human nature, (2) the needs imputed to individuals who seek counseling, (3) the aims of counseling, and (4) the techniques utilized by counselors. This plan should enable readers to understand some of the intraparadigmatic similarities among and interparadigmatic differences between counseling approaches.

Counseling therapies associated with the endogenous paradigm tend to focus on altering internal psychological states like thoughts and feelings in part because of their predisposing assumption that the course of individual growth is governed by either internal deterministic forces or by self-reflective choices. The salient point is that human nature is thought to reflect the functioning of processes resident within the individual. Endogenous-oriented counselors believe that individuals need the kind of guidance and counseling that will liberate them from debilitating feelings, enhance their self-awareness and self-esteem, and increase their control over their lives. Counseling goals generally include enhanced confidence, increased personal freedom, and enlightened self-interest. While many counseling techniques are used, all are designed to improve *intra*personal psychological functioning as a means to more satisfying interpersonal relations rather than vice versa. An example of this approach is play therapy, which has its theoretical roots in psychoanalytical theory.

Counselors who practice within the exogenous paradigm generally use techniques derived from behavioral theory. It is assumed that behavior is the most important dimension of personal functioning and that behavior is controlled by environmental consequences. Exogenous-oriented counselors generally aim to reduce maladaptive behavior. Behavioral therapies employ techniques derived from classical (Pavlovian) conditioning, operant conditioning, and social learning theory. Behavior modification is the primary tool used in behavioral therapy.

Relatively few counselors have attempted to develop therapeutic programs within the constructivist paradigm. Natural therapy builds on the spontaneous structuring and organizing tendencies of the psyche and attempts to promote personal development by providing a therapeutic context in which clients can construct new meanings for themselves.

THE ENDOGENOUS PARADIGM AND PLAY THERAPY

Play is one of the most pervasive activities of childhood. In psychoanalytic theory, it is viewed as a libidinal instinct; activities engaged in by infants and children in pursuit of the pleasure principle (Walder, 1979). Play may also be performed simply for the functional pleasure of the activity itself, without any significance being attached to its object or outcome. Amster (1982) sees play as an integral part of children's world; it is the way they communicate, their media of give and take in social interaction, their means of testing reality, and the activity in which they both incorporate and master reality (p. 33).

The use of play therapy to treat disturbed children began with Melanie Klein (1932) and Anna Freud (1946), who formulated their own psychoanalytic approaches to working with children. Klein, for example, set up a playroom supplied with toys to encourage the spontaneous play of her child clients. She substituted the interpretation of children's play for her adult clients' free association. In her view, play therapy has led to a greater understanding of early psychosexual stage development, especially in terms of young children's fantasies, anxieties, and defenses (Klein, 1982).

Play therapy was an important advancement from a psychoanalytic point of view because of the many problems associated with treating children's developmental problems. For example, traditional psychoanalysis with children is often difficult because they are less articulate than adults and less motivated to talk about their memories. Consequently, the method of free association proved inappropriate for children. Moreover, they are often brought in for therapy against their will, whereas adults typically undergo voluntary treatment (Lebo, 1982).

Assumptions

As a manifestation of the pleasure principle, children's play is assumed to reflect both conscious and unconscious material. Conscious material is played out through reenactments of the child's recent experiences. These reenactments often involve youthful distortions in factual information as these serve the libido's purposes. More important, however, is the role of unconscious material in children's play, which is a complex, distorted assortment of the child's repressed memories, anxieties, and unfulfilled wishes (Amster, 1982, p. 42). This assumption is important because it directs the primary purpose of play therapy: providing an opportunity for children to release inner turmoil.

Needs

Children need play, and they routinely engage in it under normal circumstances. Still, some psychoanalysts maintain that some children need play therapy to modify their defense mechanisms, overcome debilitating anxieties, or release pent-up emotional turmoil. These children include those who experience disturbing events, who are recipients of unusual social expectations, or who fear personal bodily harm. Children need play therapy when normal outlets of unconscious expression are blocked or effectively repressed by the ego. Such children might include those who have experienced parental divorce, the birth of a sibling, or prolonged dependence. An especially poignant example of such a need occurs with children who must be hospitalized.

Children who are hospitalized experience a radical shift in their lives; they are separated from people and contexts that provide security and stability—parents, siblings, peers, home, school. Children's natural fears of loss may be double edged. On the one hand, they are threatened with the fear of being separated from their loved ones; on the other hand, they often fear losing some part of themselves in surgery at the hands of strangers (Adams, 1982, p. 301).

The needs of hospitalized children are partly a function of maturational factors. Infants tend to be most concerned with elements of maternal proximity and physical comfort. Preschoolers often fear mutilation and loss of autonomy accompanied by guilt and shame. Finally, elementary school children tend to be concerned with losing their sense of competence and mastery and with being separated from school and playmates (Adams, 1982, p. 301).

When fear and anxiety inhibit a child's natural social interactions, when they inhibit or distort children's behavior, then there exists a profound need to provide opportunities for venting tension. This is the primary need addressed by play therapy.

Goals

Amster (1982) has identified several goals of play therapy. First, therapists use play to achieve a *diagnostic understanding* of children's wishes, self-perceptions, inhibitions, social relations, preoccupations, and fears. Second, play therapy is useful for establishing a personal rapport in a safe and secure environment. Establishing a trustworthy social relationship is especially important for young children who may be unable to articulate their concerns and for older youth who may show resistance to a stranger's interest. Third, play materials provide opportunities that, together with the therapist's encouragement, help children recognize distortions in their normal play activities and thereby break through their defenses against anxiety. Fourth, play therapy is used to promote catharsis. The cathartic use of play helps children release unconscious tensions on symbolic play material rather than in potentially anxiety-provoking real-life situations. Fifth, play therapy is designed to strengthen the ego by providing opportunities to learn how to play. Developing ego strength in this manner is an important goal for children because their capacity to play effectively is correlated in later life with work capacity (Amster, 1982). In this sense, play provides children with a source of gratification for libidinal desires that, through improved self-concept, is believed to enhance their capacity for future accomplishments.

Techniques

According to Amster (1982), there are many techniques for engaging in play therapy, but all have both diagnostic and therapeutic uses. Among the different techniques used are storytelling (Gardner, 1982), finger painting (Arlow & Kadis, 1976), and costume play (Marcus, 1982).

One of the most successful means of helping young children in play therapy is through the use of puppets to work symbolically through problems with certain interpersonal relationships (Hawkey, 1982). For example, a therapist could suggest a game involving several puppets, one each to represent the child, his siblings, and his parents (Yura & Galassi, 1982). In a make-believe situation, a child can act as he wishes toward the other family members. If even this situation is too threatening, a "family" of animal puppets can be employed for the same purpose. In either situation the therapist plays a number of roles and sets up different situations to see how the child reacts. It is sometimes helpful to have a child play through a typical day at home, in which case the therapist might begin with "Here's Jennifer just getting out of bed in the morning. What happens next?"

Children confined to hospitals can benefit directly and immediately from well-structured play therapy. In a particularly noteworthy case, one hospital uses group play designed to emphasize ego-oriented activities that get children to reenact, fantasize, and master anxiety associated with their hospitalization (Adams, 1982). Natural hospital materials—syringes and needles (with ends blunted), intravenous tubes, suture sets, tongue depressors, stethoscopes, and bandages—are used in conjunction with a miniature hospital and play dolls and puppets. Children act out the roles of the hospital staff on doll patients, performing make-believe surgery, bandaging wounds, and giving injections. Often verbal descriptions accompany the playing out of unconscious wishes and fears. It is particularly important, since hospitalized children tend to feel isolated from families and peers, to have play therapy run in group sessions.

Play therapy is *not* designed to have children sit around and play by themselves while an observing therapist watches with disinterested objectivity. On the contrary, the therapist's job is to elicit play activities by actively participating in the play experience, by setting up safe but anxiety-provoking situations, and by providing support for children who are coming in contact with their unconscious fears.

Setting limits is another important quality of play therapy. Limits help the ego direct catharsis by channeling and promoting the release of unconscious desire. By establishing limits for play, the therapist encourages children to choose symbolic objects of gratification for erotic interests (Ginott, 1982). By experiencing successes with toy objects, children learn socially acceptable channels for playing, and these in turn become useful models for channeling psychic energy in everyday interactions.

Ginott (1982) maintains that limits help children strengthen their ego control. They are set in ways that preserve children's self-respect and are not punitive or arbitrary. Moreover, without negative consequences, children's natural resentment to limits and their wish to break them are recognized and incorporated into the play therapy by providing "acting out" channels for expressing these feelings. Ginott suggests a four-step sequence for establishing limits in play therapy: (1) recognize children's feelings and promote their expression, (2) state clear limits for specific acts, (3) point out alternative channels of expression, and (4) help children express their feelings of resentment about the limits.

THE EXOGENOUS PARADIGM AND BEHAVIORAL THERAPY

The exogenous paradigm views human nature as a reflection of the physical and social environment individuals occupy. Behavioral therapy represents an exogenous approach to counseling. It assumes that inappropriate behaviors have been acquired under reinforcing circumstances and that new behaviors can be learned through the systematic application of well-designed behavior modification programs. In addition, it is assumed that people can be conditioned to control their own reinforcers effectively, an important element of therapy if individuals are to function within normal social interactions. Therapeutic needs are highly individualized since maladaptive behaviors are specific to the person and often to a particular situation. Goals of behavior therapy are straightforward: extinguish inappropriate behaviors while simultaneously teaching appropriate ones. Counseling techniques are based on specific applications of principles derived from behavior analysis. While there is variation in counseling specifics, most behavioral therapies have a common origin in the behavior modification principles described in Chapter 7.

It should come as no surprise that B. F. Skinner's influence on behavioral therapy is extensive. Like Freud, Skinner is a strict determinist; he believes that behavior is shaped and maintained by its reinforcing consequences. Unlike endogenous theorists, however, he believes that psychologists and counselors should focus on behavior rather than some internal psychological states.

Assumptions

Behavioral therapists assume that overt, maladaptive behavior is the most important psychological symptom to be treated. They also believe that current conditions that maintain behavior are therapeutically more important than early experiences or the conditions under which behaviors were acquired. Psychological problems are assumed to be behavioral problems; individuals are troubled because their behavior is associated with troublesome consequences. Thus, disentangling troublesome consequences from the reinforcers that maintain behavior is an important preliminary step in effective counseling.

There are two other elements in the treatment of behavioral disorders. First, counseling practices are constantly monitored. Objective measurements provide the data for determining therapeutic effectiveness, and programs are revised whenever appropriate. If a particular plan is not effective, it is replaced with another, which in turn is also evaluated for possible revision. Second, therapy is always individualized. Specific people have specific problems in specific circumstances due to specific causes.

Needs

Behavior disorders typically imply two distinct needs. First, because inappropriate behaviors are assumed to be maintained by some reinforcement schedule, therapists need to identify these reinforcers and either delete them or prevent the context in which they occur from happening. For example, if one knows that a friend always gets drunk at parties, then it would be important to find nonparty activities to engage the friend's time. Second, individuals need to learn new behaviors to replace their maladaptive ones. The need for new behaviors in old contexts suggests either that novel behaviors be learned for the first time or else that previously acquired behaviors be adapted to and practiced in situations where they had previously been absent.

Goals

Establishing specific, precise, measurable goals is the bedrock of behavioral therapy. These goals, usually established by clients but sometimes suggested by therapists, define the desired outcomes.

Although specific goals differ from client to client, the constant problem across all therapeutic programs is to establish effective conditions for learning. The solution may or may not involve the active participation of the client. In institutionalized settings, for example, individual goals may be established for patients even without their consent. Institutional goals might include, for example, returning psychotic patients to society, providing self-maintenance skills to mental retardates, and teaching sign language or lip reading to the deaf.

Therapists sometimes request that their clients sign written contracts that specify agreements about goals, methods, and rules of treatment. Gottman and Leiblum (1974) believe that such a procedure has the following advantages: it increases the chances of clients acting on their therapist's recommendations, it emphasizes active client participation in achieving the therapeutic goals, and it connects the treatment procedures with the goals of counseling.

Techniques

Unlike endogenous-oriented counselors, behavioral counselors function as program directors in charge of diagnosing specific behavior problems and as experts in designing programs that improve behavioral functioning. Behavior modification is the basic fabric from which many specific applications have been woven. Described here are the behavioral techniques of relaxation, token economies, assertion training, and self-management.

Relaxation Therapy. Relaxation therapy has grown in importance since the 1960s when the benefits of biofeedback were widely publicized. It may be used to alleviate both psychological and medical conditions, and it is helpful in alleviating stress, anxiety, and insomnia as well as high blood pressure, migraine headaches, and asthma. The primary purpose of relaxation therapy is to teach clients how to control their own muscular relaxation. Learning how to relax takes time, training, and consistent daily practice.

Relaxation training consists of conditioning individuals through shaping to learn progressive states of muscular rest. Clients typically work through a programmed set of directions that may begin with one part of the body and move toward sequential relaxation of the entire body. Deep, regular breathing is often included in relaxation exercises, and some clients are instructed to think about pleasant thoughts or experiences to assist their relaxation. Finally, some individuals find it helpful to work on identifying muscle tension. Then, by comparing tense with relaxed conditions, they become increasingly adept at localizing and relieving it.

Token Economies.   Token economies derive from operant conditioning principles. Within the framework of a well-designed behavioral modification program, tokens, which can later be exchanged for desired prizes or privileges, are used as reinforcers. Tokens may be physical objects (coins, chips) or they may be abstract symbols (checkmarks, stars, ranks). Typically, token economies are used in group rather than individual counseling. It is usually desirable, however, to have available a variety of other reinforcers to supplement the use of tokens. It is also possible for one to use punishment by taking away tokens for inappropriate behavior.

Whether or not one uses tokens for reinforcement or takes them away for punishment, there are several other elements that can greatly influence the effectiveness of token economies. For example, it is important that individuals be told what behaviors lead to specific amounts of punishment or reinforcement. Token economies should gradually be phased out and replaced by social reinforcers to increase intrinsic motivation if a new behavior is to be maintained outside the clinical setting. Token economies that are prolonged and not replaced with more intrinsic reinforcers may well be serving the management needs of staff for client dependency and conformity instead of preparing clients for the outside world (Corey, 1986, p. 186).

Ayllon and Azrin (1968) pioneered the modern version of a token economy with an institutionalized group of psychotic patients who were unable to perform even basic personal hygiene. The counselors used tokens as reinforcers for the patients when simple tasks like making their beds or combing their hair were completed. More tokens were awarded for more complex tasks like cleaning the ward. Patients could exchange their tokens for certain items, commodities, or privileges. Over time, nearly all patients learned self-maintenance skills, and some even worked at jobs usually performed by staff members. Ayllon and Azrin note that as their patients became less dependent and more responsible, their self-esteem improved.

Self-Management.   One of the most important things a therapist can accomplish for a client is to transfer the power of behavioral principles to the client. This is what is involved in teaching individuals how to use behavior management to control their own behavior. As a first step, clients must be decisive and specific about the behaviors they want to control. Once these have been identified with sufficient definition, the client and therapist agree on a reinforcer that is both effective and under the client's control. The final step requires accurate and specific monitoring of one's progress. A behavioral diary (a cumulative record kept by the client) must be kept to assess one's progress in terms of the original goals and of the administration of self-controlled reinforcers. One problem with self-management therapy is that it relies exclusively on the ability to control oneself. Specifically, an individual must be able to administer reinforcement at the proper time and for the appropriate behavior. The irony here is that if the individual had been capable of self-management in the first place, then presumably the problem behavior would not have occurred. At the very least, individuals capable of self-management are by definition capable of controlling their behavior. Thus, it is reasonable to ask, why do such individuals need self-management therapy? Presumably the answer is that through therapy an individual can become increasingly aware of the environmental conditions that function as discriminative stimuli that cue problem behavior.

THE CONSTRUCTIVIST PARADIGM AND NATURAL THERAPY

The constructivist paradigm has several properties that distinguish it from the endogenous and exogenous perspectives. First, it views individuals in terms of organized action patterns or structures. These structures represent holistic, interrelated actions rather than discrete components. Second, development is interactional; it is not the product of maturation or of specific learning. Third, individuals develop from less adaptive ways of knowing to more adaptive ways of knowing. Knowledge is not simply subjective meaning; it is personal meaning that has been constructed and adapted to one's experiences. Understanding is not given in maturation or learning; it is the product of invention.

The constructivist paradigm, primarily influenced by Piaget, has spawned a therapeutic approach that is substantially different from those already outlined. Constructivist-oriented counselors reject behavioral treatments that reduce therapy to the extinction of undesirable behavior and the concomitant acquisition of desirable behavior. They equally reject endogenous therapies that concentrate on establishing self-knowledge, personal freedom, and emotional satisfaction. Robert Kegan, for example, suggests *natural therapy* as an approach that concentrates on how the *self* is transformed over time through personal activities that confer meaning on experience. In one sense, Kegan proposes a unique approach to ego psychology with a Piagetian twist.

Natural Therapy

Robert Kegan (1982) proposes what he calls *natural therapy,* an approach that even with its emphasis on ego development is a decidedly non-Freudian and non-Eriksonian interpretation of the evolving self. Kegan describes ego development in terms of qualitative stages and structural principles of organization, adaptation, and reorganization. In one sense, natural therapy is both a developmental theory and a therapy.

As a basis for his therapeutic approach, Kegan posits five stages in the development of the *self,* each stage reflecting a new sense in which individuals are *held* throughout their lives. Being held means a psychological state of embeddedness. As infants we are embedded in our parents; as adults we are embedded in society and social roles. The psychological support we receive from others and from social institutions is more than an influence on the development of self; it *is* the self (Kegan, 1982, p. 257). Accordingly, Kegan's stages—incorporative, impulsive, imperial, interpersonal, and institutional—reflect qualitatively distinct organizations of embeddedness and support. Movement from one stage to the next includes a radical transformation and reorganization of the previous self into a hierarchically inclusive and structurally more comprehensive self-definition. In addition, stage change includes phases of both growth (consolidation and elaboration) and loss (transformation of the old into the new).

Natural therapy begins with the development of self. What Kegan proposes is that therapists concern themselves with assessing the adequacy of the various supportive contexts that ultimately define an individual's self. In other words, just as the uterus sustains the development of the prenate, natural environments also nourish the development of the individual. Kegan sees the life cycle as a sequence of naturally therapeutic contexts: the mothering one; family, school, and peer groups; reciprocal one-to-one relationships; identity-confirming situations that publicly recognize personal performance; and intimate adult relationships (Kegan, 1982, p. 257).

If the self is organized around the supports available to it from others or from social units, then the evaluation of those support systems, in terms of their sequence, form, and function, would provide a therapist with information about the adequacy of an individual's self. It is the therapist's task to determine how well the individual's culture of embeddedness is performing its various functions of continuity, confirmation, and contradiction (Kegan, 1982, p. 258).

Assumptions

Kegan accepts the basic constructivist principles of Piaget's cognitive-developmental theory and Kohlberg's theory of moral development. The self is a constructed meaning; it is organized; interpersonal conflict promotes hierarchic integration of one self into a more adaptive self. Moreover, natural therapy assumes that the basic processes of development are "naturally" therapeutic in the sense that development itself is the normal state of affairs. As long as individuals develop normally, there should be no problem that requires therapeutic intervention. However, when the cultures of embeddedness fail to provide a supportive context, an individual may experience certain deficiencies. Finally, while knowledge of developmental theory is invaluable for effective counseling, there is more involved than simply memorizing the stages of development. Kegan believes that the most fundamental knowledge of development is found in the assumptive conviction that individuals are continually evolving persons—change is natural; stagnation is not. Thus, even successful therapy does not "fix" people, it prepares them to continue the journey of the evolving self.

Needs

Individuals need a developmentally appropriate culture of embeddedness. Both cognitive and affective needs require careful attention to the quality, form, and substance of cultural caring. Individuals need cultural support in a variety of ways. A good culture of embeddedness secures the integrity of the wider community while assisting the active role of the individual. Cultures of embeddedness also assist the individual in "letting go," thereby promoting growth and development rather than the status quo. When larger cultures of embeddedness include vital elements and are consistent with earlier ones, they promote continuity and coherence in the individual's development (Kegan, 1982, p. 260).

Goals

The primary goal of natural therapy is to facilitate personal development of the self by establishing in the therapeutic context an individualized culture of embeddedness specially matched to the client's developmental needs. In this vein, psychotherapy should be directed toward the development of psychic equilibration (Kegan, 1982, p. 273), which is achieved when cognitive and emotional structures operate in functional harmony. This occurs when one's culture of embeddedness supports and promotes one's evolving self.

While the therapy very much reflects a concern for development as the goal of therapy, Kegan takes some issue with Kohlberg and Mayer (1972), who argue that education should aim to induce individuals from one developmental stage to the next. Kegan believes that such a goal misses the point for most counseling situations. After all, people are not their stages, and strategies that address stages rather than people may overlook the tremendous importance of the personal experience.

Establishing developmental goals for therapy is not easy. Clients may resist counseling directed at long-term developmental goals because they feel hard-pressed to cope with their immediate situation. Even "reasonably normal" people might resist a program of valuable learning experiences if they cannot be assured of some immediate and tangible benefits. Yet, the therapist must protect against the client's understandable rush for immediate solutions.

Techniques

Natural therapy is relatively new, but according to Kegan it is more a matter of approach and attitude than specific techniques. Natural therapy counselors view their clients' problems as opportunities for growth that are disguised as problems. Accordingly, the therapist attempts to work with the client's experience of having a problem rather than trying to solve the problem or trying to make the problem less painful. As Kegan (1982) puts it, therapists have a loyalty to their clients' evolution of *meaning-making* activities. Consequently, counselors attempt to join their clients in the evolution of meaning-making rather than solving problems produced by the meanings clients make of their experiences. In fact, Kegan (p. 274) thinks the therapist should prize the "person-as-meaning-maker," even during painful experiences. In this way, therapists should try to join their clients in the experience of their painful feelings (rather than working to relieve the pain) because those feelings are part of clients' self-definitions.

Natural therapists become involved in their clients' equilibrative activities. This is done by responding to problems in terms of having or being in the problem with the client. While empathy is important, there is more. Counselors become companions to their clients' experience of knowing (meaning-making) and compatriots in the re-cognition whose time is due (Kegan, 1982, p. 276). The point of such an alliance is to provide the client with a psychologically supportive culture of embeddedness in which development can naturally occur.

Natural therapy requires a delicate balance between being too empathic (one must, after all, understand what the client is experiencing) and being too directive in making sure that a supportive interpersonal culture is established. In this regard, Kegan suggests that a client-centered orientation may provide a powerful way to communicate such a context to a client, but that is only the first step that consists of the "meaning that is made" of a client's situation. The second step is to recognize the interpretation of the meaning that is made. This is the step taken by many endogenous therapies that strive to make clients aware of their own functioning. The third step, absent in other counseling approaches, is the joint experience of the situation (the experience of meaning making), which transcends the client's own subjective experience. It is this experience that the therapist shares with the client, and it is the camaraderie of sharing that provides the cultural context of support needed for development.

Kegan believes that natural therapy provides a framework and a guide for applying psychological knowledge to counseling practice (p. 288). He suggests that counselors can do much more than they are currently trained to do in giving "preventive" practice and psychological support for client development.

SUMMARY POINTS

1. Counseling therapies can be classified according to their paradigmatic orientation. Play therapy, originating from psychoanalytic principles, is an example of the endogenous approach to counseling. Behavioral therapy is the predominant counseling approach of the exogenous paradigm. Natural therapy represents a constructivist approach to counseling.

2. Play therapy, following Freud's lead, assumes that children are motivated by unconscious and sometimes conscious material that produces distortions in their interactions. Consequently, children are presumed to need some form of tension venting to release inner turmoil. The goals of play therapy are to achieve diagnostic understanding, establish a secure relationship, break down defenses against anxiety, promote catharsis, and strengthen the ego. Finally, play therapy techniques include individual and group play with toys, puppets, painting, costumes, and storytelling. In addition, setting limits on play serves a therapeutic function.

3. Behavior therapy assumes that behavior is controlled by its consequences, and conditions that control current behavior are assumed to be more important than early childhood experiences. Individuals need to learn appropriate social behaviors, and they need to delete from their day-to-day lives reinforcers that maintain maladaptive behaviors. The most fundamental goal of behavior therapy is to establish conditions for learning. The specifics of such a goal are highly individualized, since they depend on the specific needs of individuals. Examples of behavioral therapy include the specialized application of behavior modification techniques called relaxation therapy, token economies, and self-management.

4. Natural therapy (Robert Kegan) proposes a counseling orientation derived from developmental principles of organization and construction. The therapy is based on a theory of stages in the development of "self." The theory holds that normal development is itself a natural therapy, since worldly problems are solved in adaptive and normative ways. Problems occur when cultures (personal, parental, interindividual, societal) restrict the support available for personal development. This approach assumes that development is naturally therapeutic and that change is the normal state of personal existence. Clients are in need of supportive intrapersonal and interpersonal cultures, each of which promotes self-definition. Goals of therapy include providing a culture of embeddedness, which increases psychological equilibrium. Techniques reflect attitudes toward counseling rather than specific methods. These include establishing a supportive context, direct experience of client problems, engaging the client's meaning-making activities, and the camaraderie of sharing personal problems.

SUGGESTED READINGS

Kazdin, A. E. (1980). *Behavior modification in applied settings.* Homewood, IL: Dorsey Press.

Kegan, R. (1982). *The evolving self.* Cambridge, MA: Harvard University Press.

Landreth, G. L. (Ed.) (1982). *Play therapy: Dynamics of the process of counseling with children.* Springfield, IL: Charles C. Thomas.

Chapter 13

Are Theories Compatible?

Preview Questions

What does it mean to be a theoretical eclectic?
What does a theoretical purist contend?
What is the eclectic-purist controversy?
What pragmatic arguments can be marshalled to resolve the controversy?
What logical arguments can be marshalled to resolve the controversy?
What implications does this resolution have for the professional?

Within the field of applied psychology, professionals like counselors and educators make many decisions that affect the individuals they serve. These decisions often require the selection, application, and evaluation of theoretical principles.

The purpose of this chapter is to examine one of the most pervasive and perplexing issues in the field of applied psychology—the controversy that exists between theoretical eclectics and theoretical purists. The controversy centers on the issue of which of two mutually exclusive positions are in the best interests of the students and clients professionals serve. On the one hand, theoretical eclectics argue that using a variety of theories makes them more flexible in meeting individual needs. On the other hand, theoretical purists contend that individuals are best served by adhering to the interpretations and principles of a single perspective.

All professionals take a position on the eclectic-purist controversy, whether they know it or not. Most often, their position is not consciously decided but is implicit in the kinds of professional decisions they make. In this chapter many of the implicit assumptions of the eclectic and purist positions are explicitly examined.

THE CASE FOR THEORY COMPATIBILITY:
THEORETICAL ECLECTICISM

Some professionals pride themselves in being *eclectic,* by which they mean that they pick and choose elements from different theories to suit their needs. Eclectics may reject some theories in their entirety, reject others in part, and accept still others in their entirety. This decision is typically made on the basis of personal intuition, needs, or sense of value.

A number of arguments support the eclectic's position. These are outlined in Table 13-1 and described in more detail in the following paragraphs.

Eclectics see human nature as extremely complex, and they recognize that no single theory can account for all this complexity. Since individual theories attempt to account for only a portion of human nature (see Chapter 1), eclectics argue that theories are like pieces of a complex puzzle. When correctly fitted together into a complex mosaic, the various pieces can produce a more complete picture than any single piece (or single theory).

The puzzle analogy makes a powerful appeal to common sense. But the analogy can be extended another step. People are not just complex; they also display tremendous variation. The eclectic believes that since people differ so much from one another, different theories are needed to account for different kinds of people. If one theory isn't appropriate for a particular person or a particular kind of problem, then another theory might do a better job. In addition to selecting from among possible theories, eclectics may also select from among one or more principles that derive from very different theories. These principles may be employed singly or in combination with one another.

Regardless of the profession involved, eclectics tend to subscribe to a *matching* strategy wherein the professional relies on matching up a theory with the kind of person or problem to be treated. If one can identify the proper match between person/problem and theory, then the treatment plan should be straightforward. For example, if a student displays a behavior problem, then principles of operant conditioning and behavior modification would be indicated. If the same or another student shows signs of cognitive misunderstanding, then some plan for cognitive conflict might be devised. Accordingly, eclectics could argue that excellent professionals earn their reputation because they do a careful job of *matching* and thus produce a high number of educational or therapeutic successes.

Table 13-1   Basic Tenets of Theoretical Eclecticism

Matching theory to specific humans and needs allows for individualization.
Benefits to students and clients are maximized.
Assumption free means one can view reality as it really is.
Dogma free means no distortion by making people fit a single theory.
Greater efficiency and less error produce no distortion.
Theories are basically compatible.

Eclectics make a strong appeal to common sense considerations. Teachers and counselors who are eclectic in orientation believe themselves to be in a position to address the needs of their students or clients because they allow themselves the freedom to select from all theories the one that is most appropriate for a particular problem. Teachers, for example, can select from many educational methods only those they believe most useful in teaching different material, and counselors can adopt whatever concepts or theories they believe can most adequately help resolve their clients' particular problems.

Eclectic teachers may use principles of operant conditioning to set up skill and drill exercises where memorization of factual material is important, but they can also utilize Piagetian concepts in their mathematics and science lessons, where conceptual understanding is more important than memorization. They may even call on their understanding of psychoanalysis to select therapeutic reading materials for students experiencing parental divorce or exhibiting certain phobias (see, for example, Bettleheim, 1976). Psychologists may involve a similar collection of theories to treat their clients' varied problems. The point here is that eclectics believe they can best individualize and specialize their work by using whatever theory or concepts are most relevant to an individual's needs.

It would be unfair to characterize an eclectic as a proverbial "jack of all trades, master of none." Eclectic teachers and counselors take their professional work seriously, and they understand the difficult responsibility of having to learn many different theories to understand the kinds of choices these theories enable them to make. To be effective eclectics, practitioners have to become experts or near experts in each theory so that appropriate matches between theory and situation can be made. There is nothing, however, in being an eclectic that guarantees that a teacher or counselor will actually learn each theory well, or, once learned, will actually use it in a manner consistent with its original design.

In essence, the arguments that favor eclecticism rest primarily on *pragmatic* grounds. Using concepts derived from many theories is believed to be maximally beneficial because programs can be individualized to a particular person and specialized to a specific need. Eclecticism offers a common-sense approach to the many varied problems encountered by human service professionals, and teachers and counselors are more often than not trained in an eclectic approach. However, when eclecticism is carefully examined, a number of hidden difficulties become apparent.

Because they are free of the dogma of any single theory, eclectics believe that their position allows them to view human nature pretty much as it really is. Underlying this belief is the assumption that problems can somehow define themselves and that it is theories that distort rather than clarify our understanding of human nature. Ultimately, the eclectic wants to argue that by making no predisposing assumptions, new situations are viewed more clearly, information is gathered more objectively, and decisions about the nature of the problem and the solution required are made with more efficiency and less error than would be possible with non-eclectics. The trouble with this argument is that problems are never self-evident; they do not spontaneously identify themselves to teachers or therapists. Professionals, like scientists, cannot simply read off a body of data and thereby know what it means. Often the most difficult professional task is figuring out how to organize data and thus arrive at an interpretation of what "the problem" is. If it is true that theories give facts meaning (see Chapter 1), then by implication both educational and clinical problems are observer-defined rather than reality-defined.

Consider an example. Two eclectic counselors have an individual suffering from anorexia nervosa, an eating disorder that leads to rapid, sustained weight loss and sometimes death. The first counselor may decide that the anorexic is suffering from a weak ego and unconscious fear of sexual maturity; consequently, psychoanalytic treatment is in order. The second counselor may decide that the disorder is due to eating habits that have somehow been reinforced by members of the client's family. Thus, radical behavior modification is indicated. The ultimate problem for us is to determine which therapist is right. Is it simply a matter of each one being entitled to an opinion? If so, then there is no reasonable way to hold professionals accountable for their work. If not, then something must intervene to help us decide the proper identification of a problem. That "something" usually comes in the form of predisposing assumptions that guide the interpretation of data. These assumptions, in turn, are found in theory. But if an eclectic makes the decision to begin with a theory instead of a problem, then how is one to decide which theory to start with? No obvious answer comes to mind.

The analogy that theories are like pieces of a puzzle, and that by fitting them together one gets a more complete view of human nature than would be possible with a single theory, is powerful. Perhaps the reader, like me, can almost picture the pieces falling into place: get enough theories, put them together, and you're bound to get a better picture of human nature than any single theory can give.

In this vein, one of the strongest cases for theoretical eclecticism can be found in attempts to synthesize the concepts of one theory with those of another because this kind of work produces new knowledge. Eclectic syntheses like this generally take one of two forms. In the first form, the job of synthesizing two concepts is accomplished by assimilating the meaning of one to the meaning of another, often attempted by showing that one concept actually contains the other as a special case. For example, Bereiter and Englemann (1966) have designed a preschool educational program derived from learning theory that emphasizes daily drills on concepts and definitions. They believe that didactic instruction is an effective means for directly training kindergarten children to perform Piagetian formal operational tasks. More specifically, they attempt to incorporate Piaget's theory of cognitive development into learning theory: Piaget's formal operations are assimilated to a specific case of learning.

One of the most comprehensive efforts at synthetic assimilation was undertaken by Sears (Sears, Whiting, Nowlis, & Sears, 1953; Sears, Maccoby, & Levin, 1957; Sears, Rau, & Alpert, 1965), who spent many years attempting to incorporate psychoanalytic concepts into a systematic analysis of behavior. In the main, Sears has been concerned with understanding childhood dependency and aggression.

For example, where dependency for Freud was seen as the manifestation of maturation and psychosexual conflict, it became in Sears's analysis simply the manifestation of secondary reinforcement processes that arise because the parent is instrumental to the reduction of primary drives in the child.

Interested readers may find it helpful here to examine some other attempts at synthetic assimilation. Attempts have been made to assimilate some of Piaget's concepts into Skinnerian principles of operant conditioning (Berlyne, 1960, 1965; Gholson & Beilin, 1979) and to assimilate certain Freudian concepts into Piaget's (Decarie, 1965; Wolff, 1960).

In the second form of synthesis, concepts from two or more different theories are incorporated into a new, hierarchically inclusive concept not specific to the original theories. For example, Brainerd (1981) has proposed a synthesis of Piagetian and learning theory accounts of how children acquire probability concepts. He argues that what develops is not cognitive stages or specific learning, but rather a working-system memory containing three kinds of storage operations and three types of processing operations.

Both forms of eclectic synthesis have in common the assumption that theory concepts are compatible either with each other or with some hierarchical unifying concept. However, one problem encountered in these and other theoretical integrations is that they often encompass only a synthesis of theoretical parts isolated from the context of the whole theory. Such isolation tends to strip important theoretical principles of much of their meaning. Moreover, all too often, authors of such syntheses do not attempt to demonstrate that the approaches they have synthesized are in fact compatible (Kendler, 1986; Vuyk, 1981).

THE CASE FOR THEORY INCOMPATIBILITY:
THEORETICAL PURITY

Theories within the same paradigm tend to describe similar though not identical assumptions, problems of study, internal and bridge principles, and change mechanisms. Consequently, their structural components tend to reflect *intra*paradigm consistency.

A theoretical purist contends that because theories in different paradigms are inconsistent, only a single theory or paradigm should be used in one's professional practice. It is not necessary that one actually believe a preferred theory to be "true," but for matters of consistency it is important to adopt one theory or one paradigm to interpret data, diagnose problems, and formulate educational plans or therapeutic strategies.

Underlying the purist's position is the belief that many theories rely on mutually exclusive assumptions, thus rendering the theories themselves logically incompatible. Logical incompatibility occurs when two theories assert claims about human nature that cannot both be true. Conversely, two theories are logically compatible if both can be right about a claim. It is possible for all theories to be wrong as a matter of empirical evidence in their claims about human nature.

The issue here, however, is a logical one; if two or more theories make mutually exclusive claims, it is possible for only one at most to be right.

Purists believe that theoretical paradigms are mutually exclusive perspectives that frame mutually exclusive theories. In his analysis of the history of science, Kuhn (1970, pp. 103–109) argues this point in the following manner. Paradigmatic differences are both necessary and irreconcilable. Paradigms determine the important problems to be solved, the methods of investigations to be employed, and the standards of solution accepted by a community of scientists. For example, problems in one paradigm may be thought to be irrelevant, trivial, or even nonproblems within a second paradigm. Competing paradigms disagree about what constitutes a problem, what is proper methodology, and what constitutes a solution. Moreover, because one paradigm will satisfy the criteria it sets for itself while failing criteria dictated by another paradigm, paradigms are destined to debate endlessly about their respective merits and talk past each other without connecting.

Hultsch and Hickey (1978) have also attacked the eclectic's position in their analysis of psychological theories and paradigms. Specifically, they argue that different paradigms employ mutually exclusive definitions of external validity; theories in one paradigm actually define reality differently than theories in another paradigm. Paradigms see different psychological realities even when they appear to be looking at the same phenomena. For example, both Freud and Piaget emphasized the fact that infants tend to suck a variety of objects (apparently the same realities). However, recall that Freud viewed sucking as the channeling of psychic energy with the unconscious aim of reducing tension. For him, that was the psychological reality of sucking. Piaget, on the other hand, views sucking as a generalizable, organized action pattern—a scheme—for relating to objects. In this view, sucking is seen as an intellectual event. This point is much more important than simply claiming that different theorists collect only the data that interest them. Where one paradigm pursues data that will lead to causal explanations of human nature, another may seek data that promote formal explanations. Competing paradigms may well view each other's information as invalid, irrelevant, or scientifically impermissible.

The importance of Hultsch and Hickey's point is that paradigms are paradigms precisely because they have different, mutually exclusive world views. Endogenous, exogenous, and constructivist paradigms (and their constituent theories) hold different assumptions about human nature and they define it in terms of mutually exclusive qualities. To come full circle, the purist believes that the eclectic's puzzle analogy is a false analogy. Theories are not like pieces of a single puzzle; at best they are like pieces from radically different kinds of puzzles.

Following the puzzle analogy a bit further, what sometimes happens when one attempts to merge pieces from different puzzles is that the pieces get bent and no longer resemble their original shape. Something like this is what happened, according to Kendler (1986), with Lerner and Kauffman's (1985) recent attempt to synthesize both the organismic and contextualist world views. Despite their intended aim, Kendler shows that what Lerner and Kauffman ended up with was a revised concept that, rather than being synthetic and hierarchical, is a distortion of its origins. Furthermore, to arrive at a hierarchically inclusive concept of development, Lerner and Kauffman distorted the meaning of the two original conceptions of development they were trying to synthesize. The consequence of this distortion is that Lerner and Kauffman end up with a concept of development that is not clearly related to or inclusive of either the organismic or contextualist world view (Kendler, 1986, p. 94).

Unlike eclectics who stress complementarity, theoretical purists tend to concentrate on the logical inconsistencies that exist between families of theories. Table 13-2 shows an outline of some of the major paradigmatic claims whose logical inconsistencies underscore the purist's arguments. The most important of these claims are concerned with (1) assumptions made about the nature of the newborn human infant, (2) the contribution of the environment to the organism's development, (3) the relation between organism and environment, and (4) the location of the change mechanism.

The table also shows that the three major paradigms begin with contradictory assumptions. For example, consider the infant's mind. Endogenous theories assume that human infants have a mind in both form and content. Wilson assumes an evolved, species-specific mental capacity containing preprogrammed strategies for learning social rules. Freud assumes an unconscious mind, the id, which contains the psychic energy that motivates all goal-directed behavior. Skinner, an exogenous theorist, assumes a *tabula rasa* mind in form but without content. Piaget the constructivist posits no mind at all—neither form nor content. Accordingly, the primary theories in each of the three major paradigms make logically contradictory assumptions about the neonate's mental capabilities. The implication is that these theories view humans in *fundamentally different and irreconcilable ways*.

Table 13-2 Outline of Theoretical Arguments

ISSUE	PARADIGM		
	Endogenous	*Exogenous*	*Constructivist*
Nature of organism	Inborn mind, irrational id	Empty mind, tabula rasa	No mind
Role of environment	Minor	Major	Major
Organism-environment interaction	Major emphasis on organism	Major emphasis on environment	Major emphasis on both
Change mechanism	Maturation, internal	Consequences, external	Equilibration, interactionnal
Locus of change mechanism	Organismic, internal	Environmental, external	Interactional
Locus of significant problems	Within organism	Outside of organism	Adaptive interaction
Type of change needed	Organism	Environment	Interaction

The three major paradigms also take contradictory positions with respect to the influence of the environment and the relationship between the organism and environment. For example, the endogenous perspective holds that environment plays a supportive but noncausal role in the scope and sequence of developmental acquisitions. The environment is important, but only as a source of sustenance and variation for the maintenance of genetically programmed changes that unfold in a relatively fixed and rigid manner. Exogenous theories take the opposite position. The causes of human learning are believed to be environmental events that shape and mold innately flexible individuals. Finally, constructivist theories view the environment as important, but not in a causal, deterministic sense. Without environment, a synthetic construction between sensations and organismic structures is not possible. Exogenous and endogenous theories take logically opposing positions with regard to the environment. The constructivist position is logically compatible with the exogenous position in terms of the importance of the environment but not in viewing environmental events as causes of developmental change. Rather, the environment is instrumental in development, not because it supplies reinforcement, but because its resistance to individual activity poses problems in need of adaptive solutions and because environmental objects can be organized and manipulated, thereby providing informational feedback. At the same time, constructivist theories are logically incompatible with endogenous theories.

Endogenous and exogenous theories reflect contradictory positions with regard to the nature of organismic-environmental interaction and the nature and locus of change mechanisms that produce development. Moreover, endogenous theories locate developmental problems within the individual and specify developmental needs in terms of organismic variables. In contrast, exogenous theories define problems in terms of environmental events that shaped maladaptive behavior and specify developmental needs in terms of designing effective environments to control individual behavior. The constructivist position holds that both developmental problems and individual needs are functions of adaptive interactions between organism and environment.

In summary, the purist believes that while theories within a paradigm may be compatible with one another, theories from different paradigms hold logically contradictory positions about human nature. Endogenous and exogenous interpretations of human development cannot both be true. Constructivist theories cannot be true if either endogenous or exogenous interpretations are also true.

RESOLVING THE ECLECTIC–PURIST DEBATE

The eclectic's strongest arguments derive from *pragmatic* considerations. Eclectics believe that different theories represent complementary visions and explanations of human nature that can be called upon to solve human problems in meaningful ways. This position has a common-sense appeal to it that cannot easily be ignored. After all, theories are necessarily limited in scope and explanatory power (Chapter 1), and therein no theory by itself can provide a complete account of human development. By increasing the number of theories at one's disposal, the eclectic reasons, one can thereby vastly increase the range of problems one can deal with effectively.

The purist's arguments concentrate on issues of *logical adequacy and consistency.* Purists, by definition, subscribe to a single theory or single paradigm. It is not important for our analysis which theory or paradigm a purist might adopt; what is important is that the purist maintains a theoretical alliance within rather than across paradigms. Nothing prevents the purist from changing alliances from time to time, so long as the change is treated as a stable, enduring commitment when it is made.

The arguments described above reflect the respective strengths of each position: the logical adequacy of the purist's position versus the pragmatic superiority of the eclectic's. Each position has its weak points: the purist position is pragmatically inadequate, the eclectic logically inconsistent.

How Can the Eclectic–Purist Controversy Be Resolved?

The debate between theoretical eclectics and theoretical purists is a controversy because good reasons exist for each position. Certain fields like physics, chemistry, and biology adhere to one predominant paradigm that unifies scientists in the questions they ask, the methods they use, and the interpretations they give to data. These fields do not exhibit the eclectic-purist controversy to nearly the extent that it occurs in psychology, largely because members of the scientific community agree about the "rules of the game." Unfortunately, the field of developmental psychology has no unifying paradigm. Instead, psychologists face an amazing array of choices among theories. The issues raised by Kuhn (1970) earlier in this chapter indicate how difficult it is to get scientists to agree on the essential elements of human nature when they begin with different questions (world views), speak different languages (theoretical jargon), study different realities (phenomena), and maintain different rules of evidence for interpreting reality (internal and bridge principles). In the absence of agreements about what should be studied, the range of permissible assumptions, the methodology for collecting data, and the rules for interpreting data, psychology will remain unable to resolve the debate. Consequently, no definitive resolution to the controversy is possible at this time.

If the Controversy Cannot Be Resolved, then How Does One Go about Deciding Whether to Be an Eclectic or a Purist?

Professionals, by their practice, invariably take a position on the debate. Even for those who attempt to bypass self-reflection and conscious choice, one position or the other is implied in their work. Working through the following steps may help the reader arrive at a personal decision about the eclectic-purist controversy. Keep a tally of your responses to each step, and when you have finished, weigh your evidence carefully. You should be able to arrive at a decision that is personally meaningful for you.

Step 1. Identify and list the characteristics of human nature that you believe to be most important. A short list is better than a long one. Compare your list with the assumptions about human nature made by endogenous, exogenous, and constructivist theories. Do you find that your list matches closely the assumptions of only one paradigm or that they are scattered across the paradigms? A good match is one piece of evidence that you might be more closely aligned with theoretical purists than eclectics. In contrast, finding your assumptions scattered among the three paradigms is evidence that you might feel more comfortable with an eclectic position.

Step 2. Carefully examine the kinds of problems addressed by theories in each paradigm and determine how relevant those problems are for your work. You might rank a theory's problems for study "high," "moderate," or "low" for relevance. Next, examine your set of rankings. If you find that one paradigm tends to garner "high" rankings and the others "low" rankings, then you have a second piece of evidence that suggests a purist position. However, you may find that no single paradigm can be readily identified as "high" in relevance for the problems it studies. In that case, you may have evidence suggesting an eclectic position.

Step 3. Examine the methods used by theories in each paradigm to collect data. Do the methodologies used within a single paradigm seem to make better sense to you than methods used in the other paradigms? If so, then you have further evidence supporting a purist's position. If, however, methods used by different paradigms seem to make equally good sense to you, then this constitutes further evidence of an eclectic's stance.

Step 4. Given the scope and limits of your profession, carefully review each theory's claims about the change mechanism(s) of human development. Do the change mechanisms in each paradigm seem to be equally relevant to your professional mission and make good sense as described and documented by the theorist? Affirmative answers indicate an eclectic orientation; negative answers are more closely associated with theoretical purity.

Step 5. Finally, review the strongest arguments that support each side of the eclectic-purist controversy. Recall that the eclectic's position reflects a strong orientation toward pragmatic values, the purist's toward logical adequacy and consistency. Which set of arguments do you think makes the strongest case? Which set is the most personally compelling? Which position would you rather defend if challenged by an informed other? Your answer to these questions constitutes the final piece of evidence needed to decide your own position on the debate.

Step 6. Tally the responses in your analysis. Your response to step 5 should probably be weighed more heavily than any other. If your responses tend to orient toward the purist's position, then there are probably personal assumptions, values, and beliefs that make that position more personally and professionally meaningful for you. In contrast, if your responses tend to be aligned with the eclectic's position, it is likely that your intuitions and attitudes are more attuned to theoretical eclecticism.

Final Comment

From my point of view, the problems inherent in eclecticism together with the logical inadequacy of that stance persuade me that the purists occupy a more defensible position. At the same time, eclecticism seems to offer an appeal to real-world problems and solutions.

The ultimate goal of human service professionals is to be able to provide effective solutions to educational and clinical problems. Effectiveness is far more likely to follow understanding than to precede it. In this vein, understanding the issues in the eclectic-purist controversy provides stepping stones (rather than stumbling blocks) that lead to better understanding of the human condition. Learning about theories of development and the issues that accompany their study will, I believe, ultimately lead to better solutions to educational and clinical problems than are currently available.

SUMMARY POINTS

1. Eclectics believe that their program is more pragmatic and applicable to a variety of problems than the purist program.
2. Purists believe that theories from different paradigms are mutually exclusive and logically contradictory.
3. Psychological paradigms claim mutually exclusive positions with regard to assumptions about the neonate, the role of the environment, the locus of the change mechanism, and the nature of human problems needing correction.
4. There is probably no way to resolve the eclectic-purist controversy given the multiplicity of theories and paradigms currently vying for the main stage in psychology.

PROBLEMS AND EXERCISES

1. Six-year-old Andrew, whose father divorced his mother when he was an infant, seems well adjusted. His mother uses psychological withdrawal rather than corporal punishment to control him when he misbehaves. Andrew recently spent an afternoon watching a TV program in which a frog was dissected to reveal its internal organs. After listening to the narrator's explanation of the goings-on, Andrew went out to play baseball with a few of his buddies. An hour later, he was discovered sneaking out of the family's garage. Inside was the mutilated body of

the family cat. After questioning, Andrew admitted to having taken a kitchen knife in order to "see inside the cat." Andrew's upset mother wants you, with your knowledge of developmental theories, to explain to her why Andrew killed the family cat.

Each student should prepare an explanation for the mother, making sure to identify which theory provides the most adequate explanation of Andrew's behavior. Students should compare explanations and decide among themselves which explanation is "right."

2. Infants throughout the world display two universal characteristics that are acquired between eight and twelve months. On the one hand, they begin to display *stranger anxiety*, a new fear of strangers where previously no fear was shown. On the other hand, they also begin to show *separation anxiety*, displays of distress when separated from their mothers in novel situations. Each student should prepare an explanation of the origins of stranger and separation anxieties, making sure to explain which developmental theory makes the most sense and why. Students should compare their explanations and reach a concensus decision about which theory best fits the facts of separation and stranger anxiety.

3. Write an essay defending theoretical eclecticism. Write a second essay defending theoretical purity.

SUGGESTED READINGS

Hultsch, D. F., & Hickey, T. (1978). External validity in the study of human development: Theoretical and methodological issues. *Human Development, 21,* 76–91.

Kendler, T. S. (1986). World views and the concept of development: A reply to Lerner and Kauffman. *Developmental Review, 6,* 80–95.

Kuhn, T. S. (1970). *The structure of scientific revolutions.* (2nd ed.). Chicago: University of Chicago Press.

Lerner, R. M., & Kauffman, M. B. (1985). The concept of development in contextualism. *Developmental Review, 5,* 309–333.

Overton, W. F., & Reese, H. W. (1973). Models of development: Methodological implications. In J. R. Nesselroade & H. W. Reese (Eds.), *Life-span developmental psychology: Methodological issues.* Minneapolis: University of Minnesota Press.

Sears, R. R., Whiting, J.W.M., Nowlis, V., & Sears, P. S. (1953). Some child-rearing antecedents of aggression and dependency in young children. *Genetic Psychology Monographs, 47,* 135–234.

References

Abraham, K. (1927). The influence of oral erotism on character formation. *Selected papers.* London: Hogarth.

Adams, G. R., & Fitch, S. A. (1982). Ego stage and identity status development: A cross-sequential analysis. *Journal of Personality and Social Psychology, 43,* 574–583.

Adams, G. R., & Montemayor, R. (1983). Identity formation during early adolescence. *Journal of Early Adolescence, 3,* 193–202.

Adams, G. R., Shea, J. A., & Fitch, S. A. (1979). The relationship between identity status, locus of control, and ego development. *Journal of Youth and Adolescence, 8,* 81–89.

Adams, M. A. (1982). A hospital play program: Helping children with serious illness. In G. L. Landreth (Ed.), *Play therapy: Dynamics of the process of counseling in children.* Springfield, IL: Charles C. Thomas.

Ainsworth, M. D. (1967). *Infancy in Uganda: Infant care and the growth of love.* Baltimore: Johns Hopkins University Press.

Ainsworth, M.D.S., Bell, S. M., & Stayton, D. J. (1972). Individual differences in the development of some attachment behaviors. *Merrill-Palmer Quarterly, 18,* 123–143.

Akamatsu, T. J., & Farudi, P. A. (1978). Effects of model status and juvenile offender type on the imitation of self-reward criteria. *Journal of Consulting and Clinical Psychology, 46,* 187–188.

Alexander, J. F. (1973). Defensive and supportive communications in family systems. *Journal of Marriage and the Family, 35,* 613–617.

Allen, E., Beckwith, B., Beckwith, J., Chorover, S., Culver, D., Duncan, M., Gould, S., Hubbard, R., Inouye, H., Leeds, A., Lewontin, R., Madansky, C., Miller, L., Pyeritz, R., Rosenthal, M., & Shreier, H. (1978). Against "sociobiology." In A. L. Caplan (Ed.), *The sociobiology debate: Readings on the ethical and scientific issues concerning sociobiology.* New York: Harper and Row.

Almy, M. (1979). The impact of Piaget on early childhood education. In F. B. Murray (Ed.), *The impact of Piagetian theory on education, philosophy, psychiatry, and psychology.* Baltimore: University Park Press.

Alper, J., Beckwith, J., Chorover, S., Hunt, J., Inouye, H., Judd, T., Lange, R., & Sternberg, P. (1978). The implications of sociobiology. In A. L. Caplan (Ed.), *The sociobiology debate: Readings on the ethical and scientific issues concerning sociobiology.* New York: Harper and Row.

Amster, F. (1982). Differential uses of play in treatment of young children. In G. L. Landreth (Ed.), *Play therapy: Dynamics of the process of counseling in children.* Springfield, IL: Charles C. Thomas.

Anderson, J. E. (1957). Dynamics of development: System in process. In D. B. Harris (Ed.), *The concept of development.* Minneapolis: University of Minnesota Press.

Applebee, A. N. (1978). *The child's concept of story: Ages two to seventeen.* Chicago: University of Chicago Press.

Archer, S. L. (1982). The lower age boundaries of identity development. *Child Development, 53,* 1551–1556.

Arlow, J., & Kadis, A. (1976). Finger painting with children. In C. Schaefer (Ed.), *The therapeutic use of child's play.* New York: Jason Aronson.

Ayllon, T., & Azrin, N. (1968). *The token economy: A motivation system for therapy and rehabilitation.* New York: Appleton-Century-Crofts.

Azrin, N., & Lindsley, D. (1956). The reinforcement of cooperation between children. *Journal of Abnormal and Social Psychology, 2,* 100–102.

Bailey, C. (1980). Morality, reason and feeling. *Journal of Moral Education, 9,* 114–121.

Baldwin, A. L. (1967). *Theories of child development.* New York: Wiley.

Ballard, K. D., & Glynn, T. (1975). Behavioral self-management in story writing with elementary school children. *Journal of Applied Behavior Analysis, 8,* 387–398.

Bandura, A. (1965). Influence of model's reinforcement contingencies on the acquisition of imitative responses. *Journal of Personality and Social Psychology, 1,* 589–595.

––––––. (1971). Analysis of modeling processes. In A. Bandura (Ed.), *Psychological modeling.* Chicago: Atherton, Aldine.

––––––. (1986). *Social foundations of thought and action: A social cognitive theory.* Englewood Cliffs, NJ: Prentice-Hall.

Bandura, A., Ross, D., & Ross, S. A. (1963). Imitation of film-mediated aggressive models. *Journal of Abnormal and Social Psychology, 66,* 3–11.

Bandura, A., & Walters, R. (1959). *Adolescent aggression.* New York: Ronald Press.

––––––. (1963). *Social learning and personality development.* New York: Holt, Rinehart and Winston.

Barash, D. P. (1977). *Sociobiology and behavior.* New York: Elsevier.

Barkow, J. H. (1982). Return to nepotism: The collapse of a Nigerian gerontocracy. *International Political Science Review, 3,* 33–49.

Barlow, G. W. (1980). The development of sociobiology: A biologist's perspective. In G. W. Barlow & J. Silverberg (Eds.), *Sociobiology: Beyond nature/nurture?* Boulder, CO: Westview Press.

Barnes, C. A. (1952). A statistical study of the Freudian theory of levels of psychosexual development. *Genetic Psychology Monographs, 45,* 105–175.

Bates, J. E., Maslin, C. A., & Frankel, K. A. (1985). Attachment security, mother-child interaction, and temperament as predictors of behavior-problem ratings at age three years. In I. Bretherton & E. Waters (Eds.), Growing points of attachment theory and research. *Monographs of the Society for Research in Child Development, 50* (No. 209), 167–193.

Becker, W. C., Madsen, C. J., Jr., Arnold, R., & Thomas, D. R. (1967). *Journal of Special Education, 1,* 287–307.

Beckner, M. O. (1972a). Mechanism in biology. In P. Edwards (Ed.), *The encyclopedia of philosophy* (Vols. 5–6). New York: Macmillan and Free Press.

––––––. (1972b). Vitalism. In P. Edwards (Ed.), *The encyclopedia of philosophy* (Vols. 7–8). New York: Macmillan and Free Press.

Beilin, H. (1971). The training and acquisition of logical operations. In M. F. Rosskopf, L. P. Steffe, & S. Tagack (Eds.), *Piagetian cognitive-developmental research in mathematics education.* Washington, DC: National Council of Teachers of Mathematics.

Bellack, A. S. (1976). A comparison of self-reinforcement and self-monitoring in a weight reduction program. *Behavior Therapy, 7,* 68–75.

Beloff, H. (1957). The structure and origin of the anal character. *Genetic Psychology Monographs, 55,* 141–172.

Bereiter, C., & Englemann, S. (1966). *Teaching disadvantaged children in preschool.* Englewood Cliffs, NJ: Prentice-Hall.

Berlyne, D. E. (1960). *Conflict, arousal, and curiosity.* New York: McGraw-Hill.

————. (1965). Curiosity and education. In J. D. Krumboltz (Ed.), *Learning and the educational process.* Chicago: Rand-McNally.

Bertrand, S., & Masling, J. (1969). Oral imagery and alcoholism. *Journal of Abnormal Psychology, 74,* 50–53.

Bettleheim, B. (1976). *The uses of enchantment: The meaning and importance of fairy tales.* New York: Knopf.

Bickard, M. H. (1978). The nature of developmental stages. *Human Development, 21,* 217–233.

Bijou, S. W. (1970). What psychology has to offer education—now. *Journal of Applied Behavior Analysis, 3,* 65–71.

Blakemore, J. E., Larue, A. A., & Olejnik, A. B. (1979). Sex-appropriate toy preferences and the ability to conceptualize toys as sex-role related. *Developmental Psychology, 15,* 339–340.

Blatt, M., & Kohlberg, L. (1975). The effects of classroom moral discussion upon children's moral judgment. *Journal of Moral Education, 4,* 129–161.

Blum, G. S. (1949). A study of the psychoanalytic theory of psychosexual development. *Genetic Psychology Monographs, 39,* 3–99.

Bolgar, H. (1954). Consistency of affect and symbolic expression: A comparison between dreams and Rorschach responses. *American Journal of Orthopsychiatry, 24,* 538–545.

Boring, E. G. (1957). *A history of experimental psychology* (2nd ed.). New York: Appleton-Century-Crofts.

Bovet, M. (1976). Piaget's theory of cognitive development and individual differences. In B. Inhelder & H. E. Chipman (Eds.), *Piaget and his school.* New York: Springer-Verlag.

Bower, T.G.R. (1974). *Development in infancy.* San Francisco: W. H. Freeman.

————. (1977). *A primer of infant development.* San Francisco: W. H. Freeman.

Bower, T.G.R., & Wishart, J. G. (1972). The effects of motor skill on object permanence. *Cognition, 1,* 165–172.

Bowlby, J. (1958). The nature of the child's tie to his mother. *International Journal of Psychoanalysis, 39,* 350–373.

————. (1969). *Attachment and loss.* (Vol. 1, Attachment). New York: Basic Books.

————. (1973). *Attachment and loss.* (Vol. 2, Separation). London: Hogarth.

————. (1980). *Attachment and loss.* (Vol. 3, Loss). New York: Basic Books.

Boyd, R., & Koskela, R. N. (1970). A test of Erikson's theory of ego-stage development by means of a self-report instrument. *Journal of Experimental Education, 38,* 1–14.

Brainerd, C. J. (1973). Neo-Piagetian training experiments revisited: Is there any support for the cognitive-development stage hypothesis? *Cognition, 2,* 349–370.

————. (1976). Does prior knowledge of the compensation rule increase susceptibility to conservation training? *Developmental Psychology, 12,* 1–5.

————. (1977). Cognitive development and concept learning: An interpretative review. *Psychological Bulletin, 84,* 919–939.

————. (1978a). Learning research and Piagetian theory. In L. S. Siegel & C. J. Brainerd (Eds.), *Alternatives to Piaget: Critical essays on the theory.* New York: Academic Press.

————. (1978b). The stage question in cognitive-developmental theory. *The Behavioral and Brain Sciences, 1,* 173–213.

————. (1981). Working memory and the developmental analysis of probability judgments. *Psychological Review, 88,* 463–502.

Brainerd, C. J., & Brainerd, S. H. (1972). Order of acquisition of number and liquid quantity conservation. *Child Development, 43,* 1401–1405.

Brender, W. J., & Kramer, E. (1967). A comparative need analysis of immediately-recalled dreams and TAT responses. *Journal of Projective Techniques and Personality Assessment, 31,* 74–77.

Brenman-Gibson, M. (1984). Erik Erikson and the "ethics of survival." *Harvard Magazine, 87* (3), 58–64.

Broden, M., Bruce, C., Mitchell, M. A., Carter, V., & Hall, R. V. (1970). Effects of teacher attention on attending behavior of two boys at adjacent tables. *Journal of Applied Behavior Analysis, 3*, 199–203.

Brooks, J. (1969). The insecure personality: A factor analytic study. *British Journal of Medical Psychology, 42*, 395–403.

Bryan, J. H. (1975). Children's cooperation and helping behaviors. In E. M. Hetherington (Ed.), *Review of child development research* (Vol. 5). Chicago: University of Chicago Press.

Bryan, J. H., & Walbek, N. H. (1971). Preaching and practicing generosity: Children's actions and reactions. *Child Development, 41*, 329–353.

Butterworth, G., & Castillo, M. (1976). Coordination of auditory and visual space in newborn human infants. *Perception, 5*, 155–160.

Caplan, A. L. (1978). Introduction. In A. L. Caplan (Ed.), *The sociobiology debate: Readings on the ethical and scientific issues concerning sociobiology.* New York: Harper and Row.

Cartwright, R. D. (1966). Dream and drug-induced fantasy behavior. *Archives of General Psychiatry, 15*, 7–15.

Cassirer, E. (1960). *The logic of the humanities.* New Haven, CT: Yale University Press.

Chagnon, N. A. (1979). Mate competition, favoring close kin, and village fissioning among the Yanomamo Indians. In N. Chagnon & W. Irons (Eds.), *Evolutionary biology and human social behavior: An anthropological perspective.* North Scituate, MA: Duxbury Press.

———. (1981). Terminological kinship, genealogical relatedness and village fissioning among the Yanomamo Indians. In R. Alexander & D. Tinkle (Eds.), *Natural selection and social behvior: Recent research and new theory.* New York: Chiron Press.

———. (1982). Sociodemographic attributes of nepotism in tribal populations: Man the rule-breaker. In King's College Sociobiology Group (Ed.), *Current problems in sociobiology.* Cambridge: Cambridge University Press.

Chapman, M. (1988). Contextuality and directionality of cognitive development. *Human Development, 21*, 92–106.

Chomsky, N. (1957). *Syntactic structures.* The Hague: Mouton.

———. (1959). A review of *verbal behavior* by B. F. Skinner. *Language, 35*, 26–58.

———. (1965). *Aspects of a theory of syntax.* Cambridge, MA: Massachusetts Institute of Technology.

———. (1976). *Reflections on language.* New York: Pantheon.

Ciaccio, N. V. (1971). A test of Erikson's theory of ego epigenesis. *Developmental Psychology, 4*, 306–311.

Clignet, R., & Sween, J. (1974). Urbanization, plural marriage, and family size in two African cities. *American Ethnologist, 1*, 221–242.

Cline, V. B., Croft, R. G., & Courrier, S. (1973). Desensitization of children to television violence. *Journal of Personality and Social Psychology, 27*, 360–365.

Coates, B., Pusser, H. E., & Goodman, I. (1976). The influence of "Sesame Street" and "Mister Rogers' Neighborhood" on children's social behavior in the preschool. *Child Development, 47*, 138–344.

Coder, R. (1975). Moral judgment in adults. Unpublished doctoral dissertation, University of Minnesota.

Colby, A., & Kohlberg, L. (1987). *The measurement of moral judgment.* (2 vols.). New York: Cambridge University Press.

Coles, R. (1970). *Erik H. Erikson: The growth of his work.* Boston: Little, Brown.

Commons, M. L., Richards, F. A., & Kuhn, D. (1982). Systematic and metasystematic reasoning: A case for levels of reasoning beyond Piaget's stage of formal operations. *Child Development, 53*, 1058–1069.

Comrey, A. L. (1965). Scales for measuring compulsion, hostility, neuroticism and shyness. *Psychological Reports, 16*, 697–700.

———. (1966). Comparison of personality and attitude variables. *Educational and Psychological Measurement, 26*, 853–860.

Constantinople, A. (1969). An Eriksonian measure of personality development in college students. *Developmental Psychology, 1,* 357–372.

Cordus, G. D., McGraw, K. O., & Drabman, R. S. (1979). Doctor or nurse: Children's perception of sex typed occupations. *Child Development, 50,* 590–593.

Corey, G. (1986). *Theory and practice of counseling and psychotherapy* (3rd ed.). Monterey, CA: Brooks/Cole.

Corey, J. R., & Shamow, J. (1972). The effects of fading on the acquisition and retention of oral reading. *Journal of Applied Behavior Analysis, 5,* 311–315.

Corman, H. H., & Escalona, S. K. (1969). Stages of sensorimotor development: A replication study. *Merrill-Palmer Quarterly, 15,* 351–361.

Cossairt, A., Hall, R. V., & Hopkins, B. L. (1973). The effects of experimenter's instructions, feedback, and praise on teacher praise and student attending behavior. *Journal of Applied Behavior Analysis, 6,* 89–100.

Curcio, F., Kattef, E., Levine, D., & Robbins, O. (1977). Compensation and susceptibility to compensation training. *Developmental Psychology, 7,* 259–265.

Daly, M., & Wilson, M. I. (1981). Abuse and neglect of children in evolutionary perspective. In R. Alexander & D. Tinkle. *Natural selection and social behavior: Recent research and new theory.* New York: Chiron Press.

Damon, W. (1983). *Social and personality development.* New York: Norton.

Darley, J. M., Latane, B. (1968). Bystander intervention in emergencies: Diffusion of responsibility. *Journal of Personality and Social Psychology, 8,* 377–383.

Dasen, P. R. (1972). The development of conservation in aboriginal children: A replication study. *International Journal of Psychology, 7,* 75–85.

Decarie, T. G. (1965). *Intelligence and affectivity in early childhood.* New York: International Universities Press.

De Lemos, M. M. (1969). The development of conservation in aboriginal children. *International Journal of Psychology, 4,* 255–269.

Dement, W. C. (1960). The effect of dream deprivation. *Science, 131.* 1705–1707.

Dement, W. C., & Fisher, C. (1963). Experimental interference with the sleep cycle. *Canadian Psychiatric Association Journal, 8,* 400–405.

Dodwell, P. C. (1960). Children's understanding of number and related concepts. *Canadian Journal of Psychology, 14,* 191–205.

———. (1961). Children's understanding of number concepts: Characteristics of an individual and of a group test. *Canadian Journal of Psychology, 15,* 29–36.

Doland, D. J., & Adelberg, K. (1967). The learning of sharing behavior. *Child Development, 38,* 695–700.

Dorjahn, V. R. (1958). Fertility, polygyny and their interrelations in Tenne society. *American Anthropologist, 60,* 838–860.

Douvan, E., & Adelson, J. (1966). *The adolescent experience.* New York: Wiley.

Drabman, R. S., & Thomas, M. H. (1974). Does media violence increase children's tolerance of real-life aggression? *Developmental Psychology, 10,* 418–421.

Dreisch, H. (1914). *The history and theory of vitalism.* London: Macmillan.

Eiduson, B. T. (1959). Structural analysis of dreams: Clues to perceptual style. *Journal of Abnormal and Social Psychology, 58,* 335–339.

Elkind, D. (1961). Children's discovery of the conservation of mass, weight, and volume: Piaget replication study II. *Journal of Genetic Psychology, 98,* 219–227.

———. (1974). *Children and adolescents.* New York: Oxford University Press.

Ennis, R. H. (1975). Children's ability to handle Piaget's propositional logic: A conceptual critique. *Review of Educational Research, 45,* 1–41.

———. (1976). An alternative to Piaget's conceptualization of logical competence. *Child Development, 47,* 903–919.

———. (1977). Conceptualization of children's logical competence: Piaget's propositional logic and alternative proposals. In L. S. Siegel & C. J. Brainerd (Eds.), *Alternatives to Piaget: Critical essays on the theory.* New York: Academic Press.

Enright, R., Lapsley, M., & Levy, M. (1983). Moral education strategies. In M. Pressley & I. Lewin (Eds.), *Cognitive strategy research: Educational applications.* New York: Springer-Verlag.

Erikson, E. H. (1959). Identity and the life cycle. *Psychological Issues* (Monograph 1). New York: International Universities Press.

―――. (1963). *Childhood and society* (2nd ed.). New York: Norton.

―――. (1964). *Insight and responsibility.* New York: Norton.

―――. (1968). *Identity: Youth and crisis.* New York: Norton.

―――. (1972). Autobiographical notes on the identity crisis. In G. Holton (Ed.), *The twentieth century sciences: Studies in the biography of ideas.* New York: Norton.

―――. (1980). *Identity and the life cycle.* New York: Norton.

Eron, L. D., Lefkowitz, M. M., Huesmann, L. R., & Walder, L. O. (1972). Does television violence cause aggression? *American Psychologist, 27,* 253–263.

Essock-Vitale, S., & McGuire, M. T. (1980). Predictions derived from the theories of kin selection and reciprocation assessed by anthropological data. *Ethology and Sociobiology, 1,* 233–243.

Etaugh, C., Collins, G., & Gerson, A. (1975). Reinforcement of sex-typical behaviors of two-year-old children in a nursery school setting. *Developmental Psychology, 11,* 255.

Etzel, B. C., & Gewirtz, J. L. (1967). Experimental modification of caretaker-maintained high-rate operant crying in a 6- and 20-week old infant (Infans tyrannotearus): Extinction of crying with reinforcement of eye contact and smiling. *Journal of Experimental Child Psychology, 5,* 303–317.

Evans, R. I. (1968). *B. F. Skinner: The man and his ideas.* New York: E. P. Dutton.

Fancher, R. E. (1979). *Pioneers of psychology.* New York: Norton.

Feldman, C. F., Lee, B., McLean, J. D., Pillemer, D. B., & Murray, J. R. (1974). *The development of adaptive intelligence.* San Francisco: Jossey-Bass.

Ferster, C. B., & Skinner, B. F. (1957). *Schedules of Reinforcement.* New York: Appleton.

Finney, J. C. (1961a). The MMPI as a measure of character structure as revealed by factor analysis. *Journal of Consulting Psychology, 25,* 327–336.

―――. (1961b). Some maternal influences on children's personality and character. *Genetic Psychology Monographs, 63,* 199–278.

―――. (1963). Maternal influences on anal or compulsive character in children. *Journal of Genetic Psychology, 103,* 351–367.

Fischer, J. L. (1981). Transitions in relationship style from adolescence to adulthood. *Journal of Youth and Adolescence, 10,* 11–24.

Fischer, W. F. (1963). Sharing in preschool children as a function of amount and type of reinforcement. *Psychology Monographs, 68,* 215–245.

Fisher, C. (1965a). Psychoanalytic implications of recent research on sleep and dreaming. Part I: Empirical findings. *Journal of American Psychoanalytic Association, 13,* 197–270.

―――. (1965b). Psychoanalytic implications of recent research on sleep and dreaming. Part II: Implications for psychoanalytic theory. *Journal of American Psychoanalytic Association, 13,* 271–303.

Fisher, S. (1970). *Body experience in fantasy and behavior.* New York: Appleton-Century-Crofts.

―――. (1973). *The female orgasm.* New York: Basic Books.

Fisher, S., & Greenberg, R. P. (1985). *The scientific credibility of Freud's theories and therapy.* New York: Columbia University Press.

Fiss, H., Klein, G. S., & Bokert, E. (1966). Waking fantasies following interruption of two types of sleep. *Archives of General Psychiatry, 14,* 543–551.

Flavell, J. H. (1963). *The developmental theory of Jean Piaget.* New York: D. Van Nostrand.

Foulkes, D. (1969). Drug research and the meaning of dreams. *Experimental Medicine and Surgery, 27,* 39–52.

Foulkes, D., & Rechtschaffen, A. (1964). Presleep determinants of dream content: Effects of two films. *Perceptual and Motor Skills, 19,* 983–1005.

Freedman, D. G. (1979). *Human sociobiology: A holistic approach.* New York: The Free Press.

Freud, A. (1946). *The ego and the mechanisms of defense.* New York: International Universities Press.

———. (1952). The role of the teacher. *Harvard Educational Review, 22,* 229–234.

———. (1979). *Psychoanalysis for teachers and parents.* New York: Norton.

*Freud, S. (1900). *The interpretation of dreams.* Vols. 4 and 5.

———. (1908). *Character and anal eroticism.* Vol. 9.

———. (1909). *Analysis of a phobia in a five-year-old boy.* Vol. 10.

———. (1913). *Totem and taboo.* Vol. 13.

———. (1914). *The Moses of Michelangelo.* Vol. 13.

———. (1917). *On transformations of instinct as exemplified in anal eroticism.* Vol. 17.

———. (1920). *Beyond the pleasure principle.* Vol. 18.

———. (1923). *The ego and the id.* Vol. 19.

———. (1927). *The future of an illusion.* Vol. 21.

———. (1928). *Dostoevsky and parricide.* Vol. 21.

———. (1930). *Civilization and its discontents.* Vol. 21.

———. (1933a). *New introductory lectures on psycho-analysis.* Vol. 22.

———. (1933b). *Why war?* Vol. 22.

———. (1940). *An outline of psychoanalysis.* Vol. 23.

Freud, S. (1963). *A general introduction to psychoanalysis.* New York: Simon & Schuster.

Friedrich, L. K., & Stein, A. H. (1973). Aggressive and prosocial television programs and the natural behavior of preschool children. *Monographs of the Society for Research in Child Development, 39* (Whole No. 151).

Friedrich-Cofer, L. K., Huston-Stein, A., Kipnis, D. M., Susman, E. J., & Clewett, A. S. (1979). Environmental enhancement of prosocial television content: Effects on interpersonal behavior, imaginative play, and self-regulation in a natural setting. *Developmental Psychology, 15,* 637–646.

Frommer, E., & O'Shea, G. (1973). The importance of childhood experience in relation to problems of marriage and family building. *British Journal of Psychiatry, 123,* 161–167.

Galbraith, R. E., & Jones, T. M. (1976). *Moral reasoning: A teaching handbook for adapting Kohlberg to the classroom.* Minneapolis: Greenhaven Press.

Gardner, R. A. (1982). Mutual storytelling technique. In C. Schaefer (Ed.), *The therapeutic use of child's play.* New York: Jason Aronson.

Garrett, C. S., Ein, P. L., & Tremaine, L. (1977). The development of gender stereotyping of adult occupations in elementary school children. *Child Development, 48,* 507–512.

Gelfand, D. M., Hartmann, D. P., Cromer, C. C., Smith, C. L., & Page, B. C. (1975). The effects of instructional prompts and praise on children's donation rules. *Child Development, 46,* 980–983.

Gesell, A., & Ilg, F. L. (1949). *Child development.* New York: Harper and Row.

Gholson, B., & Beilin, H. (1979). A developmental model of human learning. In H. W. Reese & P. Lipsitt (Eds.), *Advances in child development and behavior.* (Vol. 13). New York: Academic.

Gilligan, C. (1977). In a different voice: Women's conceptions of self and of morality. *Harvard Educational Review, 47,* 481–517.

———. (1982). *In a different voice: Psychological theory and women's development.* Cambridge, MA: Harvard University Press.

Ginott, H. G. (1982). Therapeutic intervention in child treatment. In G. L. Landreth (Ed.), *Play therapy: Dynamics of the process of counseling in children.* Springfield, IL: Charles C. Thomas.

*Unless otherwise noted, Sigmund Freud references are from: J. Strachey, ed. and trans., *The standard edition of the complete psychological works of Sigmund Freud.* 24 vols. London: The Hogarth Press and the Institute of Psychoanalysis, 1953–1962.

Glaser, R., & Resnick, L. B. (1972). Instructional psychology. In P. H. Mussen & M. Rosenweig (Eds.), *Annual review of psychology.* Palo Alto, CA: Annual Reviews.

Glick, J. (1975). Cognitive development in cross-cultural perspective. In F. D. Horowitz (Ed.), *Review of child development research* (Vol. 4). Chicago: University of Chicago Press.

Glueck, S., & Glueck, E. T. (1950). *Unraveling juvenile delinquency.* Cambridge, MA: Harvard University Press.

Goldman, F. (1948). Breastfeeding and character formation. *Journal of Personality, 17,* 83–103.

———. (1950–51). Breastfeeding and character formation. II. The etiology of the oral character in psychoanalytic theory. *Journal of Personality, 19,* 189–196.

Goldman-Eisler, F. (1951). The problem of "orality" and of its origin in early childhood. *Journal of Mental Science, 97,* 765–782.

Goldschmid, M. L. (1968). Role of experience in the acquisition of conservation. *Proceedings of the American Psychological Association, 76,* 361–362.

Gottheil, E., & Stone, G. C. (1968). Factor analytic study of orality and anality. *Journal of Nervous and Mental Disease, 146,* 1–17.

Gottman, J. M., & Leiblum, S. (1974). *How to do psychotherapy and how to evaluate it.* New York: Holt, Rinehart & Winston.

Gottschalk, L. A., Gleser, G. C., & Springer, K. J. (1963). Three hostility scales applicable to verbal samples. *Archives of General Psychiatry, 9,* 254–279.

Gould, S. J. (1977). *Ever since Darwin: Reflections in natural history.* New York: Norton.

———. (1980). Sociobiology and the theory of natural selection. In G. W. Barlow & J. Silverberg (Eds.), *Sociobiology: Beyond nature/nurture?* Boulder, CO: Westview Press.

Gratch, G. A. (1972). A study of the relative dominance of vision and touch in six-month-old infants. *Child Development, 43,* 615–623.

Gratch, G., & Landers, W. F. (1971). Stage IV of Piaget's theory of infants' object concepts: A longitudinal study. *Child Development, 42,* 359–372.

Gray, J. P. (1984). *A guide to primate sociobiological theory and research.* New Haven, CT: HRAF Press.

Gray, W. M. (1976). The factor structure of concrete and formal operations: A confirmation of Piaget. In S. Mogdil & C. Mogdil (Eds.), *Piagetian research: Compilation and commentary* (Vol. 4). Austin, TX: Slough.

Green, M. G. (1979). The developmental relation between cognitive stage and the comprehension of speaker uncertainty. *Child Development, 51,* 666–674.

———. (1985). Talk and doubletalk: The development of metacommunication knowledge. *Research in the Teaching of English, 19,* 9–24.

Greenberg, R., Pearlman, C., Fingar, R., Kantrowitz, J., & Kawliche, S. (1970). The effects of dream deprivation: Implications for a theory of the psychological function of dreaming. *British Journal of Medical Psychology, 43,* 1–11.

Greenfield, P. M. (1966). On culture and conservation. In J. S. Bruner, R. Olver, & P. M. Greenfield (Eds.), *Studies in cognitive growth.* New York: Wiley.

Gross, L. (1974). The real world of television. *Today's Education, 63,* 86–92.

Grossmann, K., Grossmann, K. E., Spangler, G., Suess, G., & Unzner, L. (1985). Maternal sensitivity and newborns' orientation responses as related to quality of attachment in northern Germany. In I. Bretherton & E. Waters (Eds.), Growing points of attachment theory and research. *Monographs of the Society for Research in Child Development, 50* (No. 209), 167–193.

Grotevant, H. D. (1983). The contribution of the family to the facilitation of identity formation in early adolescence. *Journal of Early Adolescence, 3,* 225–237.

Gruen, W. (1964). Adult personality: An empirical study of Erikson's theory of ego development. In B. Neugarten (Ed.), *Personality in middle and late life.* New York: Atherton Press.

Grusec, J. E. (1971). Power and the internalization of self-denial. *Child Development, 42,* 93–105.

————. (1972). Demand characteristics of the modeling experiment: Altruism as a function of age and aggression. *Journal of Personality and Social Psychology, 22,* 139–148.

————. (1973). Effects of co-observer evaluations on imitation: A developmental study. *Developmental Psychology, 8,* 141.

Grusec, J. E., & Skubiski, S. L. (1970). Model nurturance, demand characteristics of the modeling experiment, and altruism. *Journal of Personality and Social Psychology, 14,* 352–359.

Halford, G. S., & Fullerton, J. J. (1970). A discrimination task which induces conservation of number. *Child Development, 41,* 205–213.

Hall, C. S., & Van de Castle, R. L. (1965). An empirical investigation of the castration complex in dreams. *Journal of Personality, 33,* 20–29.

Hall, F., & Pawlby, S. (1981). Continuity and discontinuity in the behavior of British working-class mothers and their first born children. *International Journal of Behavioral Development, 4,* 13–36.

Hall, G. S. (1901). The ideal school based on child study. *The Forum, 32,* 24–39.

Hall, R. V., Lund, D., & Jackson, D. (1968). Effects of teacher attention on study behavior. *Journal of Applied Behavior Analysis, 1,* 1–12.

Hamburger, V. (1957). The concept of "development" in biology. In D. B. Harris (Ed.), *The concept of development.* Minneapolis: University of Minnesota Press.

Hamel, B. R. (1971). On the conservation of liquids. *Child Development, 14,* 39–46.

Hamel, B. R., & Riksen, B.O.M. (1973). Identity, reversibility, rule instruction, and conservation. *Developmental Psychology, 9,* 66–72.

Hames, R. B. (1979). Relatedness and interaction among the Ye'kwana: A preliminary analysis. In N. Chagnon & W. Irons (Eds.), *Evolutionary biology and human social behavior: An anthropological perspective.* North Scituate, MA: Duxbury Press.

Hamilton, W. D. (1964). The genetical theory of social behavior, I, II. *Journal of Theoretical Biology, 7,* 1–52.

Hapkiewicz, W. G., & Roden, A. H. (1971). The effect of aggressive cartoons on children's interpersonal play. *Child Development, 42,* 1583–1585.

Hanson, N. R. (1958). *Patterns of discovery.* Cambridge, England: Cambridge University Press.

Hare, R. M. (1960). *The language of morals.* Oxford: Oxford University Press.

Harris, D. B. (1957). Problems in formulating a scientific concept of development. In D. B. Harris (Ed.), *The concept of development.* Minneapolis: University of Minnesota Press.

Harris, F. R., Johnston, M. K., Kelley, C. W., & Wolf, M. M. (1964). Effects of positive social reinforcement on regressed crawling of a nursery school child. *Journal of Educational Psychology, 55,* 35–41.

Harris, P. L. (1973). Perseverative errors in search by young children. *Child Development, 44,* 28–33.

————. (1974). Perseverative search at a visibly empty place by young children. *Journal of Experimental Child Psychology, 18,* 535–542.

Hart, B. M., Allen, K. E., Buell, J. S., Harris, F. R., & Wolf, M. M. (1964). *Journal of Experimental Child Psychology, 1,* 145–153.

Hawkey, L. (1982). Puppets in child psychotherapy. In C. Schaefer (Ed.), *The therapeutic use of child's play.* New York: Jason Aronson.

Hayden, B., & Pickar, D. (1981). The impact of moral discussions on children's level of moral reasoning. *Journal of Moral Education, 10,* 131–134.

Heinstein, M. I. (1963). Behavioral correlates of breast-bottle regimes under varying parent-infant relationships. *Monographs of the Society for Research in Child Development, 28,* Whole No. 88.

Hempel, C. G. (1966). *The philosophy of natural science.* Englewood Cliffs, NJ: Prentice-Hall.

Hess, R., & Croft, D. (1975). *Teachers of young children.* Boston: Houghton-Mifflin.

Hetherington, E. M., & Brackbill, Y. (1963). Etiology and covariation of obstinacy, orderliness, and parsimony in young children. *Child Development, 34,* 919–943.

Hicks, D. J. (1968). Effects of co-observer's sanctions and adult presence on imitative aggression. *Child Development, 39,* 303–309.

Hill, J. P. (1980). The family. In M. Johnson (Ed.), *Toward adolescence: The middle school years. The seventy-ninth yearbook of the National Society for the Study of Education.* Chicago: University of Chicago Press.

Hively, W. (1962). Programming stimuli in matching to sample. *Journal of the Experimental Analysis of Behavior, 5,* 279–298.

Hodgson, J. W., & Fischer, J. L. (1979). Sex differences in identity and intimacy development in college youth. *Journal of Youth and Adolescence, 8,* 37–50.

Hoffman, M. (1971). Identification and conscience development. *Child Development, 42,* 1071–1082.

———. (1975). Developmental synthesis of affect and cognition and its implications for altruistic motivation. *Developmental Psychology, 11,* 607–622.

———. (1976). Empathy, role-taking, guilt, and development of altruistic motives. In T. Lickona (Ed.), *Moral development and behavior.* New York: Holt, Rinehart & Winston.

———. (1977). Moral internalization: Current theory and research. In L. Berkowitz (Ed.), *Advances in experimental social psychology* (Vol. 10). New York: Academic Press.

———. (1983). Affective and cognitive processes in moral internalization. In E. T. Higgins, D. N. Ruble, & W. W. Hartup (Eds.), *Social cognition and social behavior: Developmental perspectives.* New York: Cambridge University Press.

Hoffman, M. L., & Saltzstein, H. D. (1967). Parent discipline and the child's moral development. *Journal of Personality and Social Psychology, 5,* 45–47.

Holland, J. G. (1961). New directions in teaching machine research. In J. E. Coulson (Ed.), *Programming learning and computer-based instruction.* New York: Wiley.

Hollos, M. (1975). Logical operations and role-taking abilities in two cultures: Hungary and Norway. *Child Development, 46,* 638–649.

Hollos, M., & Cowen, P. A. (1973). Social isolation and cognitive development: Logical operations and role-taking abilities in three Norwegian social settings. *Child Development, 44,* 630–641.

Horney, K. (1967). *Feminine psychology.* New York: Norton.

Hultsch, D. F., & Hickey, T. (1978). External validity in the study of human development: Theoretical and methodological issues. *Human Development, 21,* 76–91.

Hurley, P. J. (1982). *A concise introduction to logic.* Belmont, CA: Wadsworth.

Hyland, E. (1979). Towards a radical critique of morality and moral education. *Journal of Moral Education, 8,* 156–167.

Inhelder, B., Bovet, M., Sinclair, H., & Smock, C. D. (1966). On cognitive development. *American Psychologist, 21,* 160–164.

Inhelder, B., & Piaget, J. (1958). *The growth of logical thinking from childhood to adolescence.* New York: Basic Books.

Inhelder, B., & Sinclair, H. (1969). Learning cognitive structures. In P. H. Mussen, J. Langer, & M. Covington (Eds.), *Trends and issues in developmental psychology.* New York: Holt, Rinehart & Winston.

Inhelder, B., Sinclair, H., & Bovet, M. (1974). *Learning and the development of cognition.* Cambridge, MA: Harvard University Press.

Isaac, B. L., & Feinberg, W. E. (1982). Marital form and infant survival among the Mende of rural upper Bambara chiefdom, Sierra Leone. *Human Biology, 54,* 627–634.

Isen, A. M., Clark, M., & Schwartz, M. F. (1976). Duration of the effect of good mood on helping: "Foodprints in the sands of time." *Journal of Personality and Social Psychology, 34,* 385–393.

Jacob, T. (1974). Patterns of family conflict and dominance as a function of child age and social class. *Developmental Psychology, 10*, 1–12.

Jacobs, M. A., Knapp, P. H., Anderson, L. S., Karush, N., Meissner, R., & Richman, S. J. (1965). Relationship of oral frustration factors with heavy cigarette smoking in males. *Journal of Nervous and Mental Disease, 141*, 161–171.

Jacobs, M. A., & Spilken, A. Z. (1971). Personality patterns associated with heavy cigarette smoking in male college students. *Journal of Consulting and Clinical Psychology, 37*, 428–432.

Jeffrey, W. E. (1958). Variables in early discrimination learning I. Motor responses in the training of a left-right discrimination. *Child Development, 29*, 269–275.

Johnson, D. W., & Johnson, R. (1985). Classroom conflict: Controversy versus debate in learning groups. *American Educational Research Journal, 22*, 237–256.

Josselson, R. L. (1973). Psychodynamic aspects of identity formation in college women. *Journal of Youth and Adolescence, 2*, 3–52.

Josselson, R., Greenberger, E., & McConochie, D. (1977). Phenomenological aspects of psychosocial maturity in adolescence. Part II. Girls. *Journal of Youth and Adolescence, 6*, 145–167.

Jung, C. G. (1921). *The psychology of the unconscious.* London: Kegan Paul.

———. (1923) *Psychological types.* New York: Harcourt, Brace.

——— (1953). *Collected Works.* New York: Pantheon.

Kacerguis, M. A., & Adams, G. R. (1980). Erikson stage resolution: The relationship between identity and intimacy. *Journal of Youth and Adolescence, 9*, 117–126.

Kamara, A., & Easley, J. A. (1977). Is the rate of cognitive development uniform across cultures? A methodological critique with new evidence from Themne children. In P. R. Dasen (Ed.), *Piagetian psychology: Cross-cultural contributions.* New York: Gardner.

Kamii, C. (1972). An application of Piaget's theory to the conceptualization of a preschool curriculum. In R. Parker (Ed.), *The preschool in action.* Boston: Allyn & Bacon.

Karplus, R. (1974). *Science curriculum improvement study: Teachers handbook.* Berkeley, CA: University of California, Lawrence Hall of Science.

Karplus, R., Lawson, A., Wollman, W., Appel, J., Bernoff, R., Howe, A., Rusch, J., & Sullivan, R. (1977). *Science teaching and the development of reasoning: General science.* Berkeley, CA: University of California, Lawrence Hall of Science.

Kegan, R. (1982). *The evolving self.* Cambridge, MA: Harvard University Press.

Kendler, T. S. (1986). World views and the concept of development: A reply to Lerner and Kauffman. *Developmental Review, 6*, 80–95.

Kennedy, H. (1986). Trauma in childhood: Signs and sequelae as seen in the analysis of an adolescent. *The Psychoanalytic Study of the Child, 41*, 209–219.

Kimeldorf, C., Geiwitz, P. J. (1966). Smoking and the Blacky orality factors. *Journal of Projective Techniques and Personality Assessment, 30*, 167–168.

Klein, M. (1932). *The psychoanalysis of children.* London: Hogarth Press.

———. (1982). The psychoanalytic play technique. In G. L. Landreth (Ed.), *Play therapy: Dynamics of the process of counseling in children.* Springfield, IL: Charles C. Thomas.

Kline, P. (1969). The anal character: A cross-cultural study in Ghana. *British Journal of Social and Clinical Psychology, 8*, 201–210.

Kling, J. W. (1971). Learning: Introductory survey. In J. W. Kling & L. A. Riggs (Eds.), *Experimental psychology* (3rd ed.). New York: Holt, Rinehart & Winston.

Kling, J. W., & Schrier, A. M. (1971). Positive reinforcement. In J. W. Kling & L. A. Riggs (Eds.), *Experimental psychology* (3rd ed.). New York: Holt, Rinehart & Winston.

Koblinsky, S. G., Cruse, D. F., & Sugawara, A. I. (1978). Sex role stereotypes and children's memory for story content. *Child Development, 49*, 452–458.

Kohlberg, L. (1958). The development of modes of moral thinking and choice in the years 10 to 16. Unpublished doctoral dissertation, University of Chicago.

———. (1966). Cognitive stages and preschool education. *Human Development, 9*, 5–17.

———. (1968a). The child as a moral philosopher. *Philosophy Today, 7*, 25–30.

————. (1968b). Early education: A cognitive-developmental view. *Child Development, 39,* 1013–1062.

————. (1969). Stage and sequence: The cognitive-developmental approach to socialization. In D. A. Goslin (Ed.), *Handbook of socialization theory and research.* Chicago: Rand McNally.

————. (1970). Reply to Bereiter's statement on Kohlberg's cognitive-developmental view. *Interchange, 1,* 40–48.

————. (1971). From is to ought: How to commit the naturalistic fallacy and get away with it in the study of moral development. In T. Mischel (Ed.), *Cognitive development and epistemology.* New York: Academic.

————. (1972). The cognitive-developmental approach to moral education. *Humanist, 32,* 13–16.

————. (1973). Contributions of developmental psychology to education: Examples from moral education. *Educational Psychologist, 10,* 2–14.

————. (1974). Education, moral development and faith. *Journal of Moral Education, 4,* 5–16.

————. (1975a). The cognitive-development approach to moral education. *Phi Delta Kappan, 61,* 670–677.

————. (1975b). Moral education for a society in moral transition. *Educational Leadership, 33,* 46–54.

————. (1977). The implications of moral stages for adult education. *Religious Education, 72,* 183–201.

————. (1980). High school democracy and educating for a just society. In R. Mosher (Ed.), *Moral education: A first generation of research.* New York: Praeger.

————. (1984). *Essays on moral development* (Vol. II, The psychology of moral development). San Francisco: Harper and Row.

Kohlberg, L., & Colby, A. (1975). Moral development and moral education. In G. Steiner (Ed.), *Psychology and the twentieth century.* Zurich: Kindler Verlag.

Kohlberg, L., & Gilligan, C. (1971). The adolescent as a philosopher: The discovery of self in a postconventional world. *Daedalus, 100,* 1051–1086.

Kohlberg, L., & Mayer, R. (1972). Development as the aim of education. *Harvard Educational Review, 42,* 449–496.

Kohlberg, L., & Turiel, E. (1971). Moral development and moral education. In G. Lesser (Ed.), *Psychology and educational practice.* Chicago: Scott Foresman.

Kramer, R. B. (1968). Changes in moral judgment response pattern during late adolescence and young adulthood: Retrogression in a developmental sequence. Unpublished doctoral dissertation: University of Chicago.

Kramer, J. A. Hill, J. T., & Cohen, L. B. (1975). Infants' development of object permanence: A refined methodology and new evidence for Piaget's hypothesized ordinality. *Child Development, 46,* 149–155.

Krumboltz, J. D., & Thoresen, C. E. (1964). The effect of behavioral counseling in group and individual settings on information-seeking behavior. *Journal of Counseling Psychology, 11,* 324–333.

Kuhn, D. (1972). Role-taking abilities underlying the development of moral judgment. Unpublished manuscript, Columbia University.

Kuhn, D., Langer, J., Kohlberg, L., & Haan, N. S. (1977). The development of formal operations in logical and moral judgment. *Genetic Psychology Monographs, 95,* 97–188.

Kuhn, D., Nash, S. C., & Brucken, L. (1978). Sex role concepts of two- and three-year-olds. *Child Development, 49,* 445–451.

Kuhn, T. S. (1970). *The structure of scientific revolutions* (2nd ed.). Chicago: University of Chicago Press.

Kurdek, L. A. (1978). Perspective taking as the cognitive basis of children's moral development: A review of the literature. *Merrill-Palmer Quarterly, 24,* 3–28.

Kurtines, W., & Grief, E. B. (1974). The development of moral thought: Review and evaluation of Kohlberg's approach. *Psychological Bulletin, 81,* 453–470.

Lana, R. E. (1976). *The foundations of psychological theory.* Hillsdale, NJ: Lawrence Erlbaum.

Langer, J. (1969). Disequilibrium as a source of development. In P. H. Mussen, J. Langer, & M. Covington (Eds.), *Trends and issues in developmental psychology*. New York: Holt, Rinehart & Winston.

———. (1974). Interactional aspects of cognitive organization. *Cognition, 3,* 9–28.

Latane, B., & Rodin, J. (1969). A lady in distress: Inhibiting effects of friends and strangers on bystander intervention. *Journal of Experimental Social Psychology, 5,* 189–203.

Laurendeau, M., & Pinard, A. (1962). *Causal thinking in the child.* New York: International Universities Press.

La Voie, J. C. (1976). Ego identity formation in middle adolescence. *Journal of Youth and Adolescence, 5,* 371–385.

Lawrence, J. A. (1980). Moral judgment intervention studies using the Defining Issues Test. *Journal of Moral Education, 9,* 178–191.

Lawson, A. E. (1978). The development and validation of a classroom test of formal reasoning. *Journal of Research in Science Teaching, 15,* 11–24.

Lawson, A. E., & Nordland, F. H. (1976). The factor structure of some Piagetian tasks. *Journal of Research in Science Teaching, 13,* 461–466.

Lazare, A., Klerman, G. L., & Armor, D. J. (1966). Oral, obsessive, and hysterical personality patterns. *Archives of General Psychiatry, 14,* 624–630.

Leacock, E. (1980). Social behavior, biology, and the double standard. In G. W. Barlow & J. Silverberg (Eds.), *Sociobiology: Beyond nature/nurture?* Boulder, CO: Westview Press.

Lebo, D. (1982). The development of play as a form of therapy: From Rousseau to Rogers. In G. L. Landreth (Ed.), *Play therapy: Dynamics of the process of counseling in children.* Springfield, IL: Charles C. Thomas.

Lemming, J. S. (1981). Curricular effectiveness in moral/values education: A review of research. *Journal of Moral Education, 10,* 147–164.

Lenington, S. (1981). Child abuse: The limits of sociobiology. *Ethology and Sociobiology, 2,* 17–29.

Lennenberg, E. H. (1967). *Biological foundations of language.* New York: Wiley.

Lerner, R. M., & Kauffman, M. B. (1985). The concept of development in contextualism. *Developmental Review, 5,* 309–333.

Levin, P. F., & Isen, A. M. (1975). Further studies on the effect of feeling good on helping. *Sociometry, 38,* 1141–1147.

Levine, C., Kohlberg, L., & Hewer, A. (1985). The current formulation of Kohlberg's theory and a response to critics. *Human Development, 28,* 94–100.

Liben, L. S., & Signorella, M. L. (1980). Gender-related schemata and constructive memory in children. *Child Development, 51,* 11–18.

Lightcap, J. L., Kurland, J. A., & Burgess, R. L. (1982). Child abuse: A test of some predictions from evolutionary theory. *Ethology and Sociobiology, 3,* 61–67.

Lincourt, J. L. (1986). Personal communication. Charlotte, NC.

Livingstone, F. B. (1980). Cultural causes of genetic change. In G. W. Barlow & J. Silverberg (Eds.), *Sociobiology: Beyond nature/nurture?* Boulder, CO: Westview Press.

Lockard, J. S., & Adams, R. M. (1981). Human serial polygyny: Demographic, reproductive, marital, and divorce data. *Ethology and Sociobiology, 2,* 177–186.

Locke, D., (1979). Cognitive stages or developmental phases? A critique of Kohlberg's stage-structural theory of moral reasoning. *Journal of Moral Education, 8,* 168–181.

———. (1980). The illusion of stage six. *Journal of Moral Education, 9,* 103–109.

Lorenz, K. T. (1963). *On aggression.* New York: Harcourt, Brace, & World.

Lovell, K. (1979). Intellectual growth and the school curriculum. In F. B. Murray (Ed.), *The impact of Piagetian theory on education, philosophy, psychiatry, and psychology.* Baltimore: University Park Press.

Lovell, K., & Olgilvie, E. (1960). A study of the concept of conservation of substance in the junior school child. *British Journal of Educational Psychology, 30,* 109–118.

Low, B. S. (1979). Sexual selection and human ornamentation. In N. Chagnon & W. Irons (Eds.), *Evolutionary biology and human social behavior: An anthropological perspective*. North Scituate, MA: Duxbury Press.

Macht, J. (1971). Operant measurement of subjective visual acuity in nonverbal children. *Journal of Applied Behavior Analysis, 4*, 23–36.

Madsen, C., Jr., Becker, W., & Thomas, D. (1968). Rules, praise, and ignoring: Elements of elementary classroom control. *Journal of Applied Behavior Analysis, 1*, 139–150.

Maier, S. F. (1970). Failure to escape traumatic shock: Incompatible skeletal motor responses or learned helplessness? *Learning and Motivation, 1*, 157–170.

Maier, S. F., & Seligman, M.E.P. (1976). Learned helplessness: Theory and evidence. *Journal of Experimental Psychology, 105*, 3–46.

Marcia, J. (1966). Development and validation of ego-identity status. *Journal of Personality and Social Psychology, 3*, 551–558.

Marcus, I. (1982). Costume play therapy. In C. Schaefer (Ed.). *The therapeutic use of child's play*. New York: Jason Aronson.

Marr, M. J. (1979). Second-order schedules and the generation of unitary response sequences. In M. D. Zeiler & P. Harzem (Eds.), *Reinforcement and the organization of behavior*. New York: Wiley.

Martin, C. L., & Halverson, C. F. (1981). A schematic processing model of sex typing and stereotyping in children. *Child Development, 52*, 1119–1134.

Martin, J. (1979). Laboratory studies of self-reinforcement (SR) phenomena. *The Journal of General Psychology, 101*, 103–150.

Masling, J., Rabie, L., & Blondheim, S. H. (1967). Obesity, level of aspiration, and Rorschach and TAT measures of oral dependence. *Journal of Consulting Psychology, 31*, 233–239.

Mattheson, D. R. (1974). Adolescent self-esteem, family communication, and marital satisfaction. *Journal of Psychology, 86*, 35–47.

McAdams, D. P., Ruetzel, K., & Foley, J. M. (1986). Complexity and generativity at mid-life: Relations among social motives, ego development, and adults' plans for the future. *Journal of Personality and Social Psychology, 50*, 800–807.

McClellan, J. E., Jr. (1967). Philosophy of education, influence of modern psychology on. In P. Edwards (Ed.), *The encyclopedia of philosophy*. (Vol. 5–6). New York: Macmillan Publishing Co. and The Free Press.

McCord, J. (1979). Some childrearing antecedents of criminal behavior in adult men. *Journal of Personality and Social Psychology, 37*, 1477–1486.

McCully, R. S., Glucksman, M. L., & Hirsch, J. (1968). Nutrition imagery in the Rorschach materials of food-deprived, obese patients. *Journal of Projective Techniques and Personality Assessment, 32*, 375–382.

McNeill, D. (1970). *The acquisition of language*. New York: Wiley.

McReynolds, P., Landes, J., & Acker, M. (1966). Dream content as a function of personality incongruency and unsettledness. *Journal of General Psychology, 74*, 313–317.

Meer, S. J. (1955). Authoritarian attitudes and dreams. *Journal of Abnormal and Social Psychology, 51*, 74–78.

Meilman, P. W. (1979). Cross-sectional age changes in ego identity status during adolescence. *Child Development, 15*, 230–231.

Meredith, H. V. (1957). A descriptive concept of physical development. In D. B. Harris (Ed.), *The concept of development*. Minneapolis: University of Minnesota Press.

Meyer, B. (1980). The development of girls' sex-role attitudes. *Child Development, 51*, 508–514.

Meyer, T. P. (1972). Effects of viewing justified and unjustified real film violence on aggressive behavior. *Journal of Personality and Social Psychology, 23*, 21–29.

Milgram, S. (1974). *Obedience to authority*. New York: Harper and Row.

Miller, D. R., & Swanson, G. E. (1966). *Inner conflict and defense*. New York: Schocken.

Mischel, T. (1976). Psychological explanations and their vicissitudes. In J. K. Cole (Ed.), *Nebraska Symposium on Motivation, 1975: Conceptual foundations of psychology.* (Vol. 23). Lincoln, NE: University of Nebraska Press.

Mischel, W., & Liebert, R. M. (1967). The role of power in the adoption of self-reward patterns. *Child Development, 38,* 673–683.

Mithaug, E. D., & Burgess, R. L. (1968). The effects of different reinforcement contingencies in the development of social cooperation. *Journal of Experimental Child Psychology, 6,* 402–426.

Miyake, K., Chen, S., & Campos, J. J. (1985). Infant temperament, mother's mode of interaction, and attachment in Japan: An interim report. In I. Bretherton & E. Waters (Eds.), Growing points of attachment theory and research. *Monographs of the Society for Research in Child Development, 50* (No. 209), 276–297.

Mogdil, S., Mogdil, C., & Brown, G. (Eds.). (1983). *Jean Piaget: An interdisciplinary critique.* London: Routledge & Kegan Paul.

Moore, B. S., Underwood, B., & Rosenhan, D. L. (1973). Affect and altruism. *Developmental Psychology, 8,* 99–104.

Mosheni, C. (1966). Piagetian concepts in Iran. In H. Burton & D. Burton (Eds.), *Vistas.* Berkeley, CA: Buena Vista Press.

Mullings, L. (1976). Women and economic change in Africa. In N. J. Hafkin & E. G. Bay (Eds.), *Women in Africa: Studies in social and economic change.* Stanford, CA: Stanford University Press.

Murray, F. B. (1972). The acquisition of conservation through social interaction. *Developmental Psychology, 6,* 1–6.

———. (1976). Conservation deductions and ecological validity. Cited in Mogdil, S., & Mogdil, C., (1976). *Piagetian research.* (Vol. 7). Kent, Great Britain: NFER Publishing Co.

Murray, F. B., Ames, G. J., & Botvin, G. J. (1977). Acquisition of conservation through cognitive dissonance. *Journal of Educational Psychology, 69,* 519–527.

Musham, H. V. (1956). Fertility of Polygynous marriages. *Population Studies, 10,* 3–16.

Nadel, C., & Schoeppe, A. (1973). Conservation of mass, weight and volume as evidenced by adolescent girls in eighth grade. *Journal of Genetic Psychology, 122,* 309–313.

Nagel, E. (1957). Determinism and development. In D. B. Harris (Ed.). *The concept of development.* Minneapolis: University of Minnesota Press.

Nehrke, M. F., Bellucci, G., & Gabriel, S. J. (1977–78). Death anxiety, locus of control and life satisfaction in the elderly: Toward a definition of ego integrity. *Omega, 8,* 359–368.

Neill, A. S. (1960). *Summerhill.* New York: Hart Publishing Co.

Nisan, J., & Kohlberg, L. (1982). Universality and variation in moral judgment: A longitudinal and cross-sectional study in Turkey. *Child Development, 53,* 865–876.

Nowlis, G. H., & Kessen, W. (1976). Human newborns differentiate differing concentrations of sucrose and glucose. *Science, 191,* 865–866.

O'Connor, D. J. (1957). *An introduction to the philosophy of education.* New York: Philosophical Library.

Onkjo, K. (1976). The dual-sex political system in operation: Igho women and community politics in midwestern Nigeria. In N. J. Hafkin & E. G. Bay (Eds.), *Women in Africa: Studies in social and economic change.* Stanford, CA: Stanford University Press.

Orlofsky, J. (1976). Intimacy status: Relationship to interpersonal perception. *Journal of Youth and Adolescence, 5,* 73–88.

Orlofsky, J., Marcia, J., & Lesser, I. (1973). Ego identity status and the intimacy vs. isolation crisis of young adulthood. *Journal of Personality and Social Psychology, 27,* 211–219.

Panowitsch, H. R. (1975). Change and stability in the Defining Issues Test. Unpublished doctoral dissertation, University of Minnesota.

Paranjpe, A. C. (1976). *In search of identity.* New York: Wiley.

Parke, R. D., Berkowitz., L., Leyens, J. P., West, S. G., & Sebastian, R. J. (1977). Some effects of violent and nonviolent movies on the behavior of juvenile delinquents. In L. Berkowitz (Ed.), *Advances in experimental social psychology* (Vol. 10). New York: Academic Press.

Parsons, C. (1960). Inhelder's and Piaget's *The growth of logical thinking*, II: A logician's view. *British Journal of Psychology, 51*, 75–84.

Paterson, C. E., & Pettijohn, T. F. (1982). Age and human mate selection. *Psychological Reports, 51*, 70.

Pawlby, S., & Hall, F. (1980). Early and later language development of children who come from disrupted families of origin. In T. Field, S. Goldberg, D. Stern, & A. Sostek (Eds.), *High risk infants and children: Adult and peer interaction*. New York: Academic Press.

Pepper, S. C. (1942). *World hypotheses*. Berkeley, CA: University of California Press.

Piaget, J. (1952). Autobiography. In E. G. Boring et al (Eds.). *History of psychology in autobiography* (Vol. 4). Worcester, MA: Clark University Press.

———. (1960). *The child's conception of the world*. Totowa, NJ: Littlefield, Adams.

———. (1962). *Play, dreams and imitation in childhood*. New York: Norton.

———. (1963). *The origins of intelligence in children* (2nd ed.). New York: Norton.

———. (1965a). *The child's conception of number*. New York: Norton.

———. (1965b). *The moral judgment of the child*. New York: Free Press.

———. (1966). *Psychology of intelligence*. Totowa, NJ: Littlefield, Adams.

———. (1968). *On the development of memory and identity*. Barre, MA: Clark University Press.

———. (1969). *The mechanisms of perception*. London: Routledge & Kegan Paul.

———. (1970a). Piaget's theory. In P. H. Mussen (Ed.), *Handbook of child psychology* (3rd ed.), Vol. 1. New York: Wiley.

———. (1970b). *Structuralism*. New York: Basic Books.

———. (1971a). *Genetic epistemology*. New York: Norton.

———. (1971b). *Insights and illusions of philosophy*. New York: World Publishing Co.

———. (1971c). *Science of education and the psychology of the child*. New York: Viking.

———. (1972). Intellectual evolution from adolescence to adulthood. *Human Development, 15*, 1–12.

———. (1984). Schemes of action and language learning. In M. Piattelli-Palmarini (Ed.), *Language and learning: The debate between Jean Piaget and Noam Chomsky*. Cambridge, MA: Harvard University Press.

Piaget, J., & Inhelder, B. (1969). Mental images. In P. Fraisse & J. Piaget (Eds.), *Experimental psychology: Its scope and method*. Vol. VII: Intelligence. London: Routledge & Kegan Paul.

———. (1971). *Mental imagery in the child: A study of the development of imaginal representation*. New York: Basic Books.

———. (1973). *Memory and intelligence*. New York: Basic Books.

Piliavin, I. M., Rodin, J., & Piliavin, J. A. (1969). Good samaritanism: An underground phenomenon? *Journal of Personality and Social Psychology, 13*, 289–299.

Pinard, A., & Laurendeau, M. (1969). "Stage" in Piaget's cognitive-developmental theory: Exegesis of a concept. In D. Elkind & J. H. Flavell (Eds.), *Studies in cognitive development: Essays in honor of Jean Piaget*. New York: Oxford University Press.

Pinard, A., & Lavoie, G. (1974). Perception and conservation of length: Comparative study of Rwandese and French-Canadian children. *Perceptual and Motor Skills, 39*, 363–368.

Pitcher, E. G., & Prelinger, E. (1963). *Children tell stories: An analysis of fantasy*. New York: International Universities Press.

Price-Williams, D. A., Gordon, W., & Ramirez, M. (1969). Skill and conservation: A study of pottery-making children. *Developmental Psychology 1*, 769.

Proctor, J. T., & Briggs, A. G. (1964). The utility of dreams in the diagnostic interview with children. In E. Harms (Ed.), *Problems of sleep and dream in children*. New York: Macmillan.

Quine, W. V., & Ullian, J. S. (1978). *The web of belief*. New York: Random House.

Rao, P.S.S., & Inharaj, S. G. (1977). Inbreeding effects on human reproduction in Tamil Nadu of South India. *Annals of Human Genetics, 41*, 87–97.

Rawls, J. (1971). *A theory of justice*. Cambridge, MA: Harvard University Press.

Reese, E. P., Howard, J. S., & Rosenberger, P. B. (1977). Behavioral procedures for assessing visual capacities in nonverbal subjects. In B. C. Etzel, J. M. Leblanc, & D. M. Baer (Eds.),

New developments in behavioral research: Theory, method, and application. Hillsdale, NJ: Lawrence Erlbaum.

Rest, J. R. (1975). Longitudinal study of the Defining Issues Test: A strategy for analyzing developmental change. *Developmental Psychology, 11,* 738–748.

———. (1979). *Development in judging moral issues.* Minneapolis: University of Minnesota Press.

Rice, M. E., & Grusec, J. E. (1975). Saying and Doing: Effects on observer perfomance. *Journal of Personality and Social Psychology, 32,* 584–593.

Riegel, K. F. (1973). Dialectic operations: The final period of cognitive development. *Human Development, 16,* 346–370.

———. (1975). Toward a dialectical theory of development. *Human Development, 18,* 50–64.

Rieser, J., Yonas, A., & Wikner, K. (1976). Rodent localization of odors by human newborns. *Child Development, 47,* 856–859.

Rosenhan, D. L., Underwood, B., & Moore, B. (1974). Affect mediates self-gratification and altruism. *Journal of Personality and Social Psychology, 30,* 546–552.

Royce, J. R. (1976). Psychology is multi-: methodological, variate, epistemic, world view, systematic, paradigmatic, theoretic, and disciplinary. In J. K. Cole (Ed.), *Nebraska Symposium on Motivation, 1975: Conceptual foundations of psychology* (Vol. 23). Lincoln, NE: University of Nebraska Press.

Rubin, K. H. (1973). Egocentrism in childhood: A unitary construct? *Child Development, 44,* 102–110.

Ruse, M. (1979). *Sociobiology: Sense or nonsense?* Boston: D. Reidel.

Rushton, J. P. (1975). Generosity in children: Immediate and long-term effects of modeling, preaching, and moral judgment. *Journal of Personality and Social Psychology, 31,* 459–466.

Russell, E. S. (1945). *The directiveness of organic activities.* Cambridge, England: Cambridge University Press.

Rutter, M., Quinton, D., & Liddle, C. (1983). Parenting in two generations: Looking backwards and looking forwards. In N. Madge (Ed.), *Families at risk.* London: Heinemann.

Rychlak, J. F., & Brams, J. M. (1963). Personality dimensions in recalled dream content. *Journal of Projective Techniques, 27,* 226–234.

Ryff, C. D. (1982). Successful aging: A developmental approach. *The Gerontologist, 22,* 209–214.

Sagi, A., Lamb, M. E., Lewkowicz, K. S., Shoham, R., Dvir, R. & Estes, D. (1985). Security of infant-mother, -father, and -metapelet attachments among kibbutz-reared Israeli children. In I. Bretherton & E. Waters (Eds.), Growing points of attachment theory and research. *Monographs of the Society for Research in Child Development, 50* (No. 209), 257–275.

Salkind, N. J. (1981). *Theories of human development.* New York: D. Van Nostrand.

Sanghvi, L. D. (1966). Inbreeding in India. *Eugenics Quarterly, 13,* 291–301.

Sarles, R. M. (1975). Incest. *Pediatrics Clinics of North America, 22,* 633–641.

Saul, S., Sheppard, E., Selby, D., Lhamon, W., Sachs, D., & Master, R. (1954). The quantification of hostility in dreams with reference to essential hypertension. *Science, 119,* 382–383.

Schaffer, H. R., & Emerson, P. R. (1964). The development of social attachments in infancy. *Child Development Monographs, 29* (No. 2).

Schlaefli, A., Rest, J. R., & Thoma, S. J. (1985). Does moral education improve moral judgment? A meta-analysis of intervention studies using the Defining Issues Test. *Review of Educational Research, 55,* 319–352.

Schultz, D. P. (1975). *A history of modern psychology* (2nd ed.). New York: Academic Press.

Schunk, D. H. (1981). Modeling and attributional effects on children's achievement: A self-efficacy analysis. *Journal of Educational Psychology, 73,* 93–105.

Schwartz, B. J. (1956). An empirical test of two Freudian hypotheses concerning castration anxiety. *Journal of Personality, 24,* 318–327.

Schwartz, B., & Lacey, H. (1982). *Behaviorism, science, and human nature.* New York: Norton.

Schwebel, M. (1975). Formal operations in first year college students. *Journal of Psychology, 91,* 133–141.

Sears, R. R., Maccoby, E. E., & Levin, H. (1957). *Patterns of child rearing.* Evanston, IL: Row, Peterson.

Sears, R. R., Rau, L., & Alpert, R. (1965). *Identification and child rearing.* Stanford, CA: Stanford University Press.

Sears, R. R., Whiting, J.W.M., Nowlis, V., & Sears, P. S. (1953). Some child-rearing antecedents of aggression and dependency in young children. *Genetic Psychology Monographs, 47,* 135–234.

Seligman, M.E.P. (1975). *Helplessness.* San Francisco: W. H. Freeman.

Selman, R. L. (1971). The relation of role-taking to the development of moral judgment in children. *Child Development, 42,* 79–91.

Sheppard, E., & Karon, B. (1964). Systematic studies of dreams: Relationship between the manifest dream and associations to the dream elements. *Comprehensive Psychiatry, 5,* 335–344.

Sidman, M., & Stoddard, L. T. (1967). The effectiveness of fading in programming a simultaneous form discrimination for retarded children. *Journal of the Experimental Analysis of Behavior, 10,* 3–15.

Siegler, R. S., & Liebert, R. M. (1972). Effects of presenting relevant rules and complete feedback on the conservation of liquid quantity task. *Developmental Psychology, 7,* 133–138.

Sigel, L., Brodzinsky, D. M., & Golinkoff, R. M. (Eds.). (1981). *New directions in Piagetian theory and practice.* Hillsdale, NJ: Lawrence Erlbaum.

Silk, J. B. (1980). Adoption and kinship in Oceania. *American Anthropologist, 82,* 799–820.

Simon, R. J., & Alstein, R. J. (1977). *Trans-racial adoption.* New York: Wiley.

Skinner, B. F. (1938). *The behavior of organisms.* Englewood Cliffs, NJ: Prentice-Hall.

———. (1950). Are theories of learning necessary? *Psychological Review, 57,* 193–216.

———. (1953). *Science and human behavior.* New York: Free Press.

———. (1961). Why we need teaching machines. *Harvard Educational Review, 31,* 377–398.

———. (1965). Why teachers fail. *Saturday Review,* (October 16), 80–81, 98–102.

———. (1968). *The technology of teaching.* New York: Prentice-Hall.

———. (1971). *Beyond freedom and dignity.* New York: Bantam.

———. (1976). *Particulars of my life.* New York: Alfred A. Knopf.

Skinner, B. F., & Krakower, S. A. (1968). *Handwriting with write and see.* Chicago: Lyons and Carnahan.

Smith, M. E. (1979). Moral reasoning: Its relation to logical thinking and role-taking. *Journal of Moral Education, 8,* 41–49.

Snarey, J. R. (1985). Cross-cultural universality of socio-moral development: A critical review of Kohlbergian research. *Psychological Bulletin, 97,* 202–232.

———. (1987). A question of morality. *Psychology Today, 21,* 6–8.

Snarey, J., Reimer, J., & Kohlberg, L. (1985). The kibbutz as a model for moral education: A longitudinal cross-cultural study. *Journal of Applied Developmental Psychology, 6,* 161–172.

Spencer, H. (1897). *The principles of psychology* (Vols. 1 & 2). New York: D. Appleton.

———. (1902). *First principles* (4th ed.). New York: P. F. Collier & Son.

Spitz, R. (1965). *The first year of life.* New York: International Universities Press.

Stafford-Clark, D. (1965). *What Freud really said.* New York: Schocken.

Staub, E. (1970). A child in distress: The influence of age and number of witnesses on children's attempts to help. *Journal of Personality and Social Psychology, 14,* 130–141.

Stein, A. H., & Friedrich, L. K. (1975). Impact of television on children and youth. In E. M. Hetherington (Ed.), *Review of child development research* (Vol. 5). Chicago: University of Chicago Press.

Steinberg, L. D. (1981). Transformation in family relations at puberty. *Developmental Psychology, 17,* 833–840.

Stephens, B., McLaughlin, J. A., Miller, C., & Glass, G. V. (1972). Factorial structure of selected psychoeducational measures and Piagetian reasoning assessments. *Developmental Psychology, 6*, 343–348.

Steuer, F. B., Applefield, J. M., & Smith, R. (1971). Televised aggression and the interpersonal aggression of preschool children. *Journal of Experimental Child Psychology, 11*, 442–447.

Stone, C. A., & Day, M. C. (1978). Levels of availability of a formal operational strategy. *Child Development, 49*, 1054–1065.

———. (1980). Competence and performance models and the characterization of formal operational skills. *Human Development, 23*, 323–353.

Story, R. I. (1968). Effects on thinking of relationships between conflict arousal and oral fixation. *Journal of Abnormal Psychology, 73*, 440–448.

Sudarska, N. (1976). Female employment and family organization in West Africa. In D. G. McGuigan (Ed.), *New research on women and sex roles.* Ann Arbor, MI: University of Michigan Center for Continuing Education of Women.

Suppes, P., & Ginsberg, R. (1962). Experimental studies of mathematical concept formation in young children. *Science Education, 46*, 230–240.

Templeton, S., & Spivey, E. M. (1980). The concept of word in young children as a function of level of cognitive development. *Research in the Teaching of English, 14*, 265–278.

Terrace, H. S. (1963). Discrimination learning with and without "errors." *Journal of the Experimantal Analysis of Behavior, 6*, 1–27.

Tesch, S. A. (1985). Psychosocial development and subjective well-being in an age cross-section of adults. *The International Journal of Aging and Human Development, 21*, 109–120.

Thomas, M. H., Horton, R. W., Lippincott, E. L., & Drabman, R. S. (1977). Desensitization to portrayals of real-life aggression as a function of exposure to television violence. *Journal of Personality and Social Psychology, 35*, 430–458.

Thomas, R. M. (1985). *Comparing theories of child development.* Belmont, CA: Wadsworth.

Thompson, C. (1950). Cultural pressures in the psychology of women. In P. Mullahy (Ed.), *A study of interpersonal relations.* New York: Hermitage Press.

Thompson, P. R. (1980). "And who is my neighbor?" An answer from evolutionary genetics. *Social Science Information, 19*, 341–384.

Thorbecke, W., & Grotevant, H. D. (1982). Gender differences in adolescent interpersonal identity formation. *Journal of Youth and Adolescence, 11*, 479–492.

Thorndike, E. L. (1933). A proof of the law of effect. *Science, 77*, 173–175.

Tochette, P. E. (1968). The effects of graduated stimulus change on the acquisition of a simple discrimination in severely retarded boys. *Journal of the Experimental Analysis of Behavior, 11*, 39–48.

Toder, N. L., & Marcia, J. E. (1973). Ego identity status and response to conformity pressure in college women. *Journal of Personality and Social Psychology, 26*, 287–294.

Tomlinson-Keasey, C. (1972). Formal operations in females from eleven to fifty-four years of age. *Developmental Psychology, 6*, 364.

Toulmin, S. E. (1961). *Foresight and understanding.* Bloomington, IN: Indiana University Press.

Toussaint, N. (1974). An analysis of synchrony between concrete-operational tasks in terms of structural and performance demands. *Child Development, 45*, 992–1001.

Triseliotis, J. P. (1973). *In search of origins.* London: Kegan Paul.

Trivers, R. L. (1971). The evolution of reciprocal altruism. *The Quarterly Review of Biology, 46*, 35–57.

Turiel, E. (1966). An experimental test of the sequentiality of developmental stages in the child's moral judgment. *Journal of Personality and Social Psychology, 3*, 611–618.

———. (1974). Conflict and transition in adolescent moral development. *Child Development, 45*, 14–29.

———. (1977). Conflict and transition in adolescent moral development. II. The resolution of disequilibrium through structural reorganization. *Child Development, 48*, 634–637.

Twardosz, S., & Sajwaj, T. E. (1972). Multiple effects of a procedure to increase sitting in a hyperactive, retarded boy. *Journal of Applied Behavior Analysis, 5,* 73–78.

Urberg, K. A. (1979). Sex role conceptualizations in adolescents and adults. *Developmental Psychology, 15,* 90–92.

Uzgiris, I. C., & Hunt, J. McV. (1974). *Toward ordinal scales of psychological development in infancy.* Urbana, IL: University of Illinois Press.

van Geert, P. (1988). Graph-theoretical representation of the structure of developmental models. *Human Development, 31,* 107–135.

Vasudev, J., & Hummel, R. C. (1987). Moral stage sequence and principled reasoning in an Indian sample. *Human Development, 30,* 105–118.

Veldman, D. J., & Bown, O. H. (1969). Personality and performance characteristics associated with cigarette smoking among college freshmen. *Journal of Consulting and Clinical Psychology, 33,* 109–119.

Vogler, R. E., Masters, W. M., & Merrill, G. S. (1970). Shaping cooperative behavior in young children. *Journal of Psychology, 74,* 181–186.

———. (1971). Extinction of cooperative behavior as a function of acquisition by shaping or instruction. *Journal of Genetic Psychology, 119,* 233–240.

von Glasersfeld, E. (1979). Radical constructivism and Piaget's conception of knowledge. In F. B. Murray (Ed.), *The impact of Piagetian theory on education, philosophy, psychiatry, and psychology.* Baltimore: University Park Press.

von Uexkull, J. (1957). A stroll through the worlds of animals and men. In C. H. Schiller (Ed.), *Instinctive Behavior.* New York: International Universities Press.

Voyat, G. (1977). In tribute to Piaget: A look at his scientific impact in the United States. In R. W. Rieber & K. Salzinger (Eds.), The roots of American psychology: Historical influences and implications for the future. *Annals of the New York Academy of Sciences, 291,* 342–349.

Vuyk, R. (1981). *Overview and critique of Piaget's genetic epistemology: 1965–1980.* (Vol. 1). London: Academic Press.

Walaskay, M., Whitbourne, S. K., & Nehrke, M. F. (1983–84). Construction and validation of an ego integrity status interview. *International Journal of Aging and Human Development, 81,* 61–72.

Walder, R. (1979). Psychoanalytic theory of play. In C. Schaefer (Ed.), *The therapeutic use of child's play.* New York: Jason Aronson.

Wall, S. M. (1982). Effects of systematic self-monitoring and self-reinforcement in children's management of test performances. *The Journal of Psychology, 111,* 129–136.

Ward, M. H., & Baker, B. L. (1968). Reinforcement therapy in the classroom. *Journal of Applied Behavior Analysis, 1,* 323–328.

Waterman, A. S., & Goldman, J. A. (1976). A longitudinal study of ego development at a liberal arts college. *Journal of Youth and Adolescence, 5,* 361–375.

Waterman, A. S., & Waterman, C. K. (1971). A longitudinal study of changes in ego identity status during the freshman year of college. *Developmental Psychology, 5,* 167–173.

Watson, J. B. (1919). *Psychology from the standpoint of a behaviorist.* Philadelphia: Lippincott.

———. (1924). *Behaviorism.* New York: Norton.

Watson, J. B., & Raynor, R. (1920). Conditioned emotional reactions. *Journal of Experimental Psychology, 3,* 1–14.

Weiner, G. (1956). Neurotic depressives and alcoholics. Oral Rorschach percepts. *Journal of Projective Techniques, 20,* 435–455.

Weiss, L., & Masling, J. (1970). Further validation of a Rorschach measure of oral imagery: A study of six clinical groups. *Journal of Abnormal Psychology, 76,* 83–87.

Weissbrod, C. S. (1976). Noncontingent warmth induction, cognitive style, and children's imitative donation and rescue effort behaviors. *Journal of Personality and Social Psychology, 34,* 274–281.

Werner, H. (1948). *Comparative psychology of mental development.* New York: International Universities Press.

———. (1957). The concept of development from a comparative and organismic point of view. In D. B. Harris (Ed.), *The concept of development*. Minneapolis: University of Minnesota Press.

Wertheimer, M. (1961). Psychomotor coordination of auditory and visual space at birth. *Science, 134,* 1692.

Whitbourne, S. K., & Waterman, A. S. (1979). Psychosocial development during the adult years: Age and cohort comparisons. *Developmental Psychology, 15,* 373–378.

White, R. W. (1960). Competence and the psychosexual stages of development. In M. R. Jones (Ed.), *Nebraska Symposium on Motivation*. (Vol. 8). Lincoln, NE: University of Nebraska Press.

White, S. H. (1976). The active organism in theoretical behaviorism. *Human Development, 19,* 99–107.

Whyte, M. K. (1978). Cross-cultural codes dealing with the relative status of women. *Ethnology, 17,* 211–237.

Wilson, E. O. (1975). *Sociobiology: The new synthesis*. Cambridge, MA: The Belknap Press of Harvard University Press.

———. (1978a). Academic vigilantism and the political significance of sociobiology. In A. L. Caplan (Ed.), *The sociobiology debate: Readings on the ethical and scientific issues concerning sociobiology*. New York: Harper and Row.

———. (1978b). *On human nature*. Cambridge, MA: Harvard University Press.

Winestine, M. C. (1985). Weeping during the analysis of a latency-age girl. *The Psychoanalytic Study of the Child, 40,* 297–318.

Wohlwill, J. F. (1966). Comments in discussion on the developmental approach of Jean Piaget. *American Journal of Mental Deficiency, Monograph Supplements, 70,* 84–105.

Wolff, P. H. (1960). The developmental psychologies of Jean Piaget and psychoanalysis. *Psychological Issues, 2,* Monograph 5.

Wolkind, S., Hall, F., & Pawlby, S. (1977). Individual differences in mothering behavior: A combined epidemiological and observational approach. In P. J. Graham (Ed.), *Epidemiological approaches in child psychiatry*. London: Academic Press.

Wolman, B. (1981). *Contemporary theories and systems in psychology* (2nd ed.). New York: Plenum.

Yarrow, M. R., Scott, P. M., & Waxler, C. Z. (1973). Learning concern for others. *Developmental Psychology, 8,* 240–260.

Younniss, J. (1980). *Parents and peers in social development: A Sullivan-Piaget perspective*. Chicago: University of Chicago Press.

Younniss, J., & Dean, A. (1974). Judgment and imagining aspects of operations: A Piagetian study with Korean and Costa Rican children. *Child Development, 45,* 1020–1031.

Yura, M. T., & Galassi, M. D. (1982). Adlerian usage of children's play. In G. L. Landreth (Ed.), *Play therapy: Dynamics of the process of counseling in children*. Springfield, IL: Charles C. Thomas.

Zais, R. S. (1976). *Curriculum: Principles and foundations*. New York: Harper and Row.

Zeiler, M. D. (1979). Output dynamics. In M. D. Zeiler & P. Harzem (Eds.), *Reinforcement and the organization of behavior*. New York: Wiley.

Author Index

Abraham, K., 52
Acker, M., 55
Adams, G. R., 79, 81, 82
Adams, M. A., 239, 240, 241
Adams, R. M., 105
Adelberg, K., 128
Adelson, J., 82
Ainsworth, M. D., 54, 103
Akamatsu, T. J., 153
Alexander, J. F., 81
Allen, E., 107
Allen, K. E., 128
Almy, M., 231
Alper, J., 107
Alpert, R., 54, 253
Alstein, R. J., 103
Ames, G. J., 187
Amster, F., 238, 239, 240
Anderson, J. E., 16, 17
Anderson, L. S., 53
Appel, J., 232
Applebee, A. N., 192
Applefield, J. M., 150
Archer, S. L., 79
Arlow, J., 240
Armor, D. J., 53, 54
Arnold, R., 128
Ayllon, T., 244
Azrin, N., 128, 244

Bailey, C., 211
Baker, B. L., 128
Baldwin, A. L., 21
Ballard, K. D., 153
Bandura, A., 140, 141, 144, 145, 148, 150
Barash, D. P., 99, 102
Barkow, J. H., 103
Barlow, G. W., 107
Barnes, C. A., 53
Bates, J. E., 78
Becker, W., 128
Beckner, M. O., 13
Beckwith, B., 107
Beckwith, J., 107
Beilin, H., 187, 254
Bell, S. M., 54
Bellack, A. S., 153
Bellucci, G., 83
Beloff, H., 54
Bereiter, C., 253
Berkowitz, L., 150
Berlyne, D. E., 254
Bernoff, R., 232
Bertrand, S., 53
Bettleheim, B., 252
Bickard, M. H., 3
Bijou, S. W., 127
Blakemore, J. E., 152
Blatt, M., 210, 232

Subject Index

Comparative Evaluations of Developmental Theories

ENDOGENOUS PARADIGM

Scientific Worthiness	Freud			Erikson			Wilson		
	Hi	Mod	Lo	Hi	Mod	Lo	Hi	Mod	Lo
Testability			X			X		X	
External validity		X			X		X		
Predictive validity		X			X			X	
Internal consistency		X			X		X		
Theoretical economy		X			X		X		
	(pp. 58–60)			(pp. 85–86)			(pp. 110–111)		

Developmental Adequacy	Freud		Erikson	Wilson
	Sequential System	Structural System		
Temporality	Pass	Pass	Pass	Pass
Cumulativity	Pass	Pass	Pass	Pass
Directionality	Pass	Pass	Pass	Pass
New mode of organization	Fail	Pass	Fail	Pass
Increased capacity for self-control	Fail	Pass	?	Pass
	(pp. 60–61)		(pp. 86–88)	(pp. 112–113)